# Fantastic histories

Manchester University Press

MANCHESTER MEDIEVAL LITERATURE AND CULTURE

*Series editors*: Anke Bernau and David Matthews and James Paz

*Series founded by*: J. J. Anderson and Gail Ashton

*Advisory board*: Ruth Evans, Patricia C. Ingham, Andrew James Johnston, Chris Jones, Catherine Karkov, Nicola McDonald, Haruko Momma, Susan Phillips, Sarah Salih, Larry Scanlon, Stephanie Trigg and Matthew Vernon

*Manchester Medieval Literature and Culture* publishes monographs and essay collections comprising new research informed by current critical methodologies on the literary cultures of the global Middle Ages. We are interested in all periods, from the early Middle Ages through to the late, and we include post-medieval engagements with and representations of the medieval period (or 'medievalism'). 'Literature' is taken in a broad sense, to include the many different medieval genres: imaginative, historical, political, scientific and religious.

This is book 55 in the series. To buy or to find out more about the titles currently available in this series, please go to: https://manchesteruniversitypress.co.uk/series/manchester-medieval-literature-and-culture/

# Fantastic histories

## Medieval fairy narratives and the limits of wonder

Victoria Flood

MANCHESTER UNIVERSITY PRESS

Copyright © Victoria Flood 2024

The right of Victoria Flood to be identified as the author of this work has been asserted in accordance with the Copyright, Designs and Patents Act 1988.

Published by Manchester University Press
Oxford Road, Manchester M13 9PL

www.manchesteruniversitypress.co.uk

British Library Cataloguing-in-Publication Data
A catalogue record for this book is available from the British Library

ISBN 978 1 5261 6414 8 hardback
ISBN 978 1 5261 9585 2 paperback

First published 2024
Paperback published 2026

The publisher has no responsibility for the persistence or accuracy of URLs for any external or third-party internet websites referred to in this book, and does not guarantee that any content on such websites is, or will remain, accurate or appropriate.

EU authorised representative for GPSR:
Easy Access System Europe – Mustamäe tee 50,
10621 Tallinn, Estonia
gpsr.requests@easproject.com

Typeset
by Cheshire Typesetting Ltd, Cuddington, Cheshire

For Sam

# Contents

| | |
|---|---|
| Acknowledgements | *page* viii |
| Preface | xi |
| Introduction: fairies in history | 1 |
| 1 'Historia fabulosa': writing fairies in England and Wales | 45 |
| 2 'Relatum ueridica': wonderful history from Gervase of Tilbury to Philippe Mousket | 96 |
| 3 'Le Noble hystoire': romance and history in Jean d'Arras's *Mélusine* | 145 |
| 4 'En rime l'istoire': vanishing history in Couldrette's *Mélusine* and *Richard Coer de Lyon* | 195 |
| Conclusion: between history and romance | 249 |
| Bibliography | 257 |
| Index | 281 |

# Acknowledgements

This book is the product of the advice, guidance, and generosity of multiple networks of friends and colleagues, over eight years of research, four cities, and three countries. It is a course of research which goes back even further still, to the questions which first challenged and enthused me as an undergraduate over a decade and a half ago. Most immediately, I am grateful for the encouraging and constructive advice of my readers at various stages of the development of this manuscript: Aisling Byrne, Megan Leitch, and the anonymous reviewers for Manchester University Press, as well as the insightful advice of my editor, Meredith Carroll, the hard work of Katie Evans and Laura Swift, the patience and exceptional copyediting skills of Fiona Little, and the invaluable support of Jo Bellis on a particularly tricky piece of Old French. Any mistakes that remain are my own. Thanks also must go to Corinne Saunders and the editors and reviewers of *Medium Ævum*, in which my early research on *Mélusine* was published, and which forms the basis of my discussion of the Galfridian affinities of the text in Chapter 3. This project began in the context of a Leverhulme Early Career Fellowship, 'The Politics of the Marvellous: The Fairy Hunt in Insular Culture', originally held at the University of Durham (2014–16), and was completed at the University of Birmingham during a lectureship and associate professorship. The project was associated with an exhibition co-designed with Máire Aspden, Corinne Saunders, Neil Cartlidge, and Palace Green Exhibition Centre, a positive and formative experience in my understanding of the significance of fairy belief. Thanks must also go to the Leverhulme Trust; to colleagues at Birmingham, in particular

## Acknowledgements

Megan Cavell and Gregory Salter, with whom it has been a joy to navigate our first permanent positions; and to Gillian Wright, Rebecca Mitchell, and Andrzej Gasiorek, to whose professional mentorship I have been greatly indebted; to Durham's medievalists, alongside my Leverhulme host Corinne Saunders, Elizabeth Archibald, and Neil Cartlidge; and to Helen Cooper, to whom I owe my first introduction to the fairies of medieval romance.

Great thanks are due to Helen Fulton and colleagues in the Bristol Borders and Borderlands network who listened to, and advised on, an early version of the Welsh material discussed in Chapter 1, and to Helen for her continued support and intellectual generosity. Insights were also welcome from colleagues at the University of Reading Graduate Centre for Medieval Studies, Cardiff University's Medieval and Early Modern Reading Group, and Dale Kedwards and the University of Southern Denmark, where I first explored the question of supernatural belief and scepticism in the company of my kind and clever friend. I would like to express my gratitude also to colleagues at the University of Western Australia, where I was privileged to complete my work on this book in the context of a fellowship from the Institute of Advanced Studies, supported also by Birmingham's International Engagement Fund. With thanks to Andrew Lynch, Marina Gerzic, and Jane Héloïse-Nancarrow for generously hosting me during this period. Thank you also to colleagues at the Centre for the Study of the Middle Ages at Birmingham, in particular Kate Sykes, William Purkis, Elizabeth Lestrange, and Chris Callow, and on the Invisible Worlds project, Catherine A. M. Clarke and Andrew B. R. Elliott, who remind me of the ways in which the pleasure of interdisciplinary collaboration sustains our intellectual lives; and to Elena Parina, Erich Poppe, and my colleagues in the Crossing Borders project, who continually enrich my perspectives. Thanks also to those friends and colleagues who over the past fifteen years have patiently listened to my experiments with fairies and history: Aisling Byrne, Joanna Bellis, Venetia Bridges, Megan Leitch, Jessica Lockhart, and Emily Wingfield; and to Humma Mouzam, Sadegh Attari, Charlotte Palmer, James Galvin, Kelsey Shearman, Bethany Seaman, and Eyan Birt, who are setting out on experiments of their own.

Final acknowledgement, with love, must go to my family and friends, especially my parents, Kookie and Steve, whose continued enthusiasm and excitement for my work does my heart good, and to my husband, Sam, who makes all things possible.

# Preface

Et croy que les merveilles qui sont par universel terre et monde sont le plus vrayes, comme les choses dictes faees

(And I believe the marvels which occur on earth and throughout all creation are eminently true, including those which are said to be the work of fairies)[1]

Some of this [modern] interest in storytelling is to do with doubts about the classic novel, with its interest in the construction of the Self, and the relation of that Self to the culture, social and political, surrounding it.[2]

This book was written during a period of global and local crisis, when critical observations concerning the solace of medieval fantasies seemed to appear everywhere in my reading. I encountered them in my classroom too, where a journey into the world of medieval marvels offered a respite, however temporary, from the pressures of the present. There is something about the quality of the medieval fantastic that lends itself to this: a glimpse of a world no less terrifying than the present but enchanted still. A. S. Byatt, one of the most famous modern remediators of the medieval Mélusine legend, from which this book takes its cue, observes in a series of lectures given in the late 1990s (in the long shadow of the nuclear age) that in medieval 'story forms' we find a de-centring of the concerns of the individual and individual psychologies characteristic of the modern classic novel, and an engagement with 'truths [which] are not connected immediately to contemporary circumstances'.[3] Referencing Chaucer, Boccaccio, and *One Thousand and One Nights*, Byatt proposes that we might find in these models a different understanding of the relationship between the self and the world, beyond the modern age of disenchantment. This is a widespread perception, seemingly independently reached by other critics concerned with literary realism and its contrast with medieval 'forms'. We might note, for example, Amitav Ghosh's writings on modern realist fiction, and its limited reflection thus far of the seemingly incredible consequences of climate change. Ghosh suggests that these reflective capabilities, of the impossible yet true, are found in more obviously fantastic forms with their precedents in the tales of the Middle Ages. He names the same medieval tale collections as Byatt, including the *Decameron* and *One Thousand and One Nights*, which are situated by both writers, tellingly, in relation to fairy tales.[4]

Similarly intuitive to modern literary critics, and undeniably related to this sense of what we might term medieval glamour (in its fullest sense, a synonym for enchantment), is the perception that the medieval historiographical combining of historical fact with improbable marvels was marked by invention; while historical fiction as we recognise it today, generally in relation to the realist novel, had no obvious medieval counterpart. There is an understanding, implicit within this position, that medieval fiction is in some way less obviously subject to historical concerns, while its history is understood to be open to fictionalisation. The present study is intended to scrutinise, and indeed to break open, this set of deep-rooted assumptions, exploring medieval conceptualisations of history and fiction as we find them in the most marvellous of medieval narratives: accounts of fairies. In the following pages I suggest that medieval belief was constructed, whether sincere, cynical, or through a knowing engagement with the fictive, in ways which are by no means distinct from our own relationship to fact and story – acting in the service of what authors, or their readers, needed to believe at any given time. In fact, as my reflections above imply, the story in which we, as modern literary critics, appear to have needed to believe, so much so that we have largely understood it to be intuitive (and indeed, the story I often needed to believe in my classroom during those difficult years), is of medieval literature itself as a space of enchantment. Yet while we must appreciate what is distinctive about the medieval fantastic, we must also resist the desire to de-politicise it. Medieval narratives of the marvellous were as determined by political and ideological investments as the literary and cultural productions of any age. Belief is rarely undiscerning – it is contingent, and informed by historical events, then as now.

## Notes

1 Jean d'Arras, *Mélusine ou la noble histoire du Lusignan*, ed. Jean-Jacques Vincensini (Paris: Librairie Générale Française, 2003), p. 112; Jean d'Arras, *Melusine; or the Noble History of Lusignan*, ed. and trans. Donald Maddox and Sara Sturm-Maddox (University Park, PA: Pennsylvania State University Press, 2012), pp. 19–20.
2 A. S. Byatt, *On Histories and Stories: Selected Essays* (London: Vintage, 2001), p. 124.
3 Byatt, *On Histories and Stories*, p. 124.
4 Amitav Ghosh, *The Great Derangement: Climate Change and the Unthinkable* (Chicago: University of Chicago Press, 2016), pp. 16–17.

# Introduction: fairies in history

> Si dixerimus non esse credendum, scripta illa miraculorum infirmabimus; si autem credendum esse concesserimus, firmabimus numina paganorum.
>
> (If we say that the story should not be accepted, we shall weaken the force of recorded miracles, while if we grant that it should be accepted, we shall give support to the gods of the pagans.)[1]

In the late 1180s Walter Map, a cleric from the Welsh March working at the court of Henry II of England, presented to his royal and aristocratic audience a series of *nugae*, trifles or frivolities: accounts which were, by turns, historical and fabulous. Among these stories we find the earliest written fairy narratives of England and Wales. They appear in a context where at first glance the stakes of the fairy's historical reality appear to be low. In the guise of entertainment, the true might travel with the false, and what better forum for early experiments in fairy fiction than this? Yet, Map assures his readers, all was not necessarily fiction. He wonders at the attested reality of the children of fairies such as the Herefordshire holy man Alnoth, whose origins Map revisits in two variant narratives across *De nugis*, and asks his readers what they might make of such occasions when seemingly impossible, ephemeral occurrences leave a material, genealogical trace:

> Et quid de his fantasticis dicendum casibus, qui manent et bona se successione perpetuant, ut hic Alnodi ...?
>
> (But what shall we say of these fantastic cases, which endure and perpetuate themselves in good succession, as of this Alnoth ...?)[2]

Map's categorical confusion is in many respects a precursor to that of the modern critic, and scholarship on medieval marvels (*mirabilia*) conventionally has been concerned with their ambiguity, and the difficulty of categorisation beyond specific, genre-defined functions.[3] In fact, the very wonder that the medieval marvel inspires would seem to be rooted in its category blurring qualities – its irreducibility. A site of multiple and uncertain meanings, the fairy was by no means universally accepted as a proper subject of historical deliberation. Map elsewhere in his work juxtaposes the open possibilities of Alnoth's marvellous mother with false fairy marvels from Wales, a locus of English paranoia which Map appears to have shared. I suggest that this exercise in differentiation, even and especially in application to a marvel which, by definition, remained in many respects unclosed, is the key to understanding the political functions of the medieval historiographical acceptance or denial of supernatural truth claims.

In the medieval fairy we see not necessarily a sign of fictionality but an engagement with the boundaries of history, and the matter of exactly who gets to tell it. This book approaches the historical and pseudo-historical position of the fairy through the lens of a single case study, to which the tale of Alnoth belongs: the fairy lover or mother as she was integrated within ostensibly historical contexts. From the writings of Map and his contemporaries Gerald of Wales and Gervase of Tilbury to the romances associated with the serpentine fairy Mélusine, the founder and dynastic mother of the house of Lusignan (texts responsive to these earlier Latin *mirabilia*), it explores the principles of historical discernment applied to these narratives and their relative historical positioning.[4] My authors employ a distinctive set of historiographical conventions to distinguish between true and false marvels. The true fairy marvel is conventionally an event within near-history, in the general locality of the author; is attested by credible witnesses (generally male and ecclesiastical or noble) belonging to the dominant community of the historian and his patrons; affirmed by written precedents or accepted commonplace assumptions; and contrasted with less credible, false, often demonic, marvels, generated by groups and persons understood to be suspect, dangerous, and gullible. We see here a construction of credible belief navigated through a rejected counter-position, the dominant trend which, I suggest, characterises medieval historical fairy narratives.

## Fantasy, history, romance

For many public and scholarly readers, medieval narratives of the supernatural are near-synonymous with fantasy. This association may even have prompted some to pick up this book, guided by its title. Yet this is not the type of fantasy which I will discuss – at least, not quite. As critics have recently observed, modern fantasy, with its set of medievalist investments, is too often the lens through which medieval literature is read, to the detriment of our recognition of the nuanced referentiality of medieval literary invention and its extra-textual engagements.[5] While it is true that medieval fairy narratives integrate episodes that today we might regard as fantastic fictions, to their authors and original readers fictionality was not necessarily an automatic assumption. Neither, however, was facticity. While the medieval term commonly applied to fairy encounters, *phantasma* (meaning variously an illusion, a demonic apparition, or a product of the imagination alone; source of the Middle French *fantosme* and Middle English *fantom*), sometimes appears alongside *fingere* (to counterfeit, make up), the term does not consistently or exclusively denote fiction, for *phantasmata* might, under certain conditions, and in the narratives of certain communities, possess a reality status. While the material engagements and effects of fairy *phantasma* are uncertain, it is that very uncertainty which renders it wonderful and so a necessary inclusion in the pages of history.

But what, then, of romance, in which the fairy has customarily been read as an overt marker of the genre's fictionality, a genre which (as I discuss in Chapter 1) shares some of its interests with Map's narrative of Alnoth's conception? Even if we accept the fairy as a naturalised component of medieval history-writing, we must acknowledge that the fairy also appears in medieval romance, in frameworks which are overtly fictive. Yet here too, I suggest, a concern with the historical may be found, although this appears to varying degrees across the romances I discuss. Fredric Jameson famously observed that romance, in its trans-historical forms, must not be understood as an entirely abstracted genre, and that rather its magic is contingent on, and reflective of, the socio-economic conditions of each specific period, which romance makes visible (its fundamental 'worldness').[6] While certainly romance is not the only medieval context in which we find inventions in fiction with this type of recognition value, it does provide examples of this with particular clarity – strikingly so, however initially counterintuitive this might seem, in fairy romance.[7] Aranye Fradenburg suggests in her critique and extension of Jameson that in the marvels of medieval romance we are 'able to locate archaism in capitalism and put the "worn world of realism" next door to "fayerye"'.[8] I propose that the medieval socio-economic and the supernatural worlds are not simply adjacent but interconnected, and the medieval fairy operates in relation to explicitly worldly interests.[9]

If not precisely of a type with this understanding of romance but certainly congruent with it is Jacques Le Goff and Emmanuel Le Roy Ladurie's influential analysis of Mélusine, her clearing of forests and her building of castles and towns, as 'the fairy of economic growth', a very particular, historically specific mode of fantastic wish fulfilment.[10] The acquisition of wealth is perhaps the most powerful form of wish fulfilment present in fairy romance, beyond even the customary role of the fairy in sexual fantasy, which, as Aisling Byrne has observed, is not necessarily the narrative *telos* of fairy romance so much as a nodal point for a series of interconnected interests, in which we must include the protagonist's enrichment, social ascent, and descent.[11] The familiar association of the fairy lover's good graces with good fortune – generally the acquisition of lands and the birth of heirs – speaks to the material values of sex and marriage. We might note the association that Helen Cooper has observed between the figure of the 'fairy mistress' and fantasies of the wealthy heiress that similarly populate romance: a patron who enriches a hero down on his luck and through whom he might even inherit a kingdom, although in the case of the fairy this may come at a cost.[12] I am not suggesting that these works are purely economic or social allegories; rather, gains and losses of this type, as they relate to historical dynasties, are a fundamental part of the logic of these texts. While medieval fairy narratives can be utopian – particularly where the fairy Otherworld is concerned – this is less obviously the case with those fairy mother narratives which find their setting in recognisable histories and geographies, or at least a version of them.[13] Their interests are material in the fullest sense – tied to historical people, places, and genealogies – and in relation to these the fairy's historicity necessarily must be entertained, whether cynically or not.

Attempts to draw clear distinctions between history and romance on a generic basis are frustrated by medieval source material, and the line between the two is invariably porous.[14] Following the lead of both recent and longstanding scholarly approaches to the question of medieval genre, rather than searching for pure romance or history I explore the interpenetration of the two, asking where a particular discourse might dominate, and determine the horizon of reader expectations.[15] Of course, works may be multi-discursive (as are most of my examples), or even unresolved in their attitudes towards fairies – after all, medieval readers do appear to have been capable of nuanced engagement with marvels of an uncertain reality status. As Michelle Karnes has noted, an ability to dwell in ambiguity is a common component of medieval philosophical writings on marvels, even as an aesthetic principle.[16] Such a response is often precisely the grounds of the fairy's appeal as we encounter her in both history and romance, where she embodies a complex paradox which the reader must embrace, at once impossible and real. Yet medieval readers also appear to have read fairies differently across different textual contexts – sometimes historical, sometimes pure fiction. While this instability or contingency might be understood as a modern scholarly 'conundrum',[17] it is also an intellectual, and on occasion a moral and spiritual, exercise conventional within medieval historiographical writing, which encourages its readers to determine the true from the false, and to accept the complexities of marvellous history or knowingly enjoy fiction, as directed by the text's discursive cues.

## Historicising the supernatural

The social, religious, and scientific logics of medieval miracles and marvels have attracted considerable attention – however ambiguous the latter, fairies included, might be in their preternatural causality.[18] More broadly, medieval writings on magic and demonology have been understood to possess their own 'specific rationality', in the context of contemporary understandings of the boundaries of reality.[19] Of course, we cannot assume that supernatural narratives from the Middle Ages necessarily speak to beliefs monolithically held, and as Monika Otter has observed, the marvels of medieval history-writing often read as exercises in rhetoric.[20] We would be making a grave error if we presupposed the complete absence of medieval recognition of fictionality – a kind of supernatural literalism; and indeed, this was the very charge that medieval authors levelled at those groups whose fairy beliefs were understood to be suspect or seditious. Nonetheless, as previous critics have observed, some aspect of historical plausibility remains fundamental within these diverse uses.[21] To borrow a phrase from Stuart Clark's work on the later period of the European witch trials, we might consider how medieval authors were 'thinking with' fairies – that is, the fairy was employed as a vehicle for the expression of cultural meanings, values, and anxieties, not on account of their fictionality but because of their plausibility. My use of Clark is no simple methodological convenience, for my authors share with their early modern counterparts (a similarly clerical class of men) a concern with the limits of creation and of history as revealed by preternatural occurrences.[22] This marvellous material is not just testament to the literariness of history. It belongs to an intellectual framework in which supernatural occurrences were plausible, although on occasion debatable, and the fantastic could be both a predicate of a history's usability and the grounds of its rejection.

The ideological contestation of fairy belief has seen recent attention from Richard Firth Green, who has posited that the demonic fairies of the medieval Latin clerical tradition (the subject of my first two chapters) represent a response to the threat to Christian orthodoxy posed by popular belief.[23] This might be understood in relation to the process that Laurence Harf-Lancner has observed from the late twelfth century onwards: the 'satanisation' of the fairy: that is, the association of phenomena situated outside familiar religious frameworks with the demonic.[24] We might also note the gendered alterity of the particular fairies

I discuss, often aligned with distinctly misogynistic representations and anxieties, associated also on occasion with signifiers of cultural, religious, and racial alterity.[25] Whatever its origins (which seem to be various), for my purposes the demonic associations of the fairy are fundamental to the understanding of a double process of discernment – both spiritual and historical – which is a feature of the early Latin tradition and forms the basis of discernment as a fundamentally political act. In these works, looking through the demonism of the fairy, we see a process of discernment by which some fairy marvels were understood to be genuinely historical, the object of ennobling or spiritually enriching belief; while others were understood to be demonically inspired fictions, testament only to the credulity of the tellers and the illegitimacy of a particular understanding of history.

To circumscribe historical belief is to impugn the credibility, and even maturity, of culture. This association is by no means unique to the Middle Ages, and similar claims define the very foundation of concepts of modernity positioned in opposition to the medieval. In his attempt at a grand narrative of the history of emotions, Johan Huizinga wrote of the violence and simplicity of medieval emotions, responding to cues that might be understood as of 'magic signification', which carried particular force when the world 'was half a thousand years younger'.[26] This is a salient reminder of the fine line that any modern analysis of the pre-modern supernatural must tread – to not automatically assume a supernaturalism entirely at odds with the 'rationality' of the modern age, while acknowledging the historical contexts of wonder responses that in many respects are alien to our own. How might we, then, approach the question of medieval fairy belief? As Byrne has argued in her study of medieval constructions of the Otherworld, we must be alert to the presence of literary tropes and a medieval understanding of history characterised not necessarily by supernatural belief systems but by an extended imaginative engagement that spans the production of both history and fiction.[27] Yet it matters that some, if importantly not all, fairy content was understood to be historical, although its precise significance and causation may have remained obscure. Indeed, this obscurity seems to have been precisely why fairy narratives were of note to medieval historians: they were remarkable in the limits they posed to familiar or quotidian experience. I am concerned, then, not necessarily with the precise nature of what medieval people may have (sometimes) believed about fairies, but the conditions under which fairies could be understood to be historically meaningful.

## History and the wonder response

Although the marvellous aspects of medieval historiography have been conventionally held in tension with historicising impulses, the treatment of *mirabilia* (the fairy included) offers an insight into the medieval historian's sense of his craft.[28] *Mirabilia* signify in a particular relationship to what Gabrielle Spiegel has termed the 'mimetic' function of medieval history-writing: the duty of the historian to report events, no matter how implausible or obscure in their causation, not least as such remarkable events might provide the grounds of political exegesis.[29] Yet even more significantly than this, the communication and assessment of marvellous phenomena models a practice of critical discernment, for the most part positioned in response to narratives in oral circulation recounting events from the recent past.[30] Within this context, the historian assumes the role of an investigator determining what belongs in the history books, the store of received wisdom and of lessons learned, and what does not. Fairy narratives provide a particularly germane example of the types of assessments generally required here, for the fairy is among those marvels that are, by turns, most enthusiastically integrated within, and rejected from, the medieval historical record.

The writing of historical *mirabilia* corresponds to Augustine of Hippo's model of the universe as a web of signs and symbols which might be read exegetically, regarding those marvellous occurrences which appear to resist interpretation as testament to the limitations of human reason, inspiring awe at the mysterious workings of God.[31] This is a framework in which often there was no distinction between *mirabilia* and *miracula*, and while such a distinction did start to emerge in the early thirteenth century, in the context of historical and courtly literatures the division between the two remained a porous one.[32] The testing of the limits of Augustinian wonder and the study of causation are a feature of historical writings from the twelfth century onwards, a period in which we see an increased interest in patterns in nature and a corresponding drive to present, and to rationalise, the marvellous.[33] It has been suggested that contemporary scrutiny of marvels may have fuelled their collection; and *mirabilia* have been understood as an ally to medieval churchmen in the presentation of a world in which disbelief might still be suspended.[34] I understand this invocation of wonder (the Latin *admiratio*) to have possessed a particular utility in the writing of medieval history and the later *merveilles* of dynastic (historical) romance also.[35] I approach this in relation to the construction of wonder that Caroline Walker Bynum notes is particular to medieval 'literature of entertainment'.[36] Within this I include secular historiography drawing on classical and antique concepts of portents and omens, as found in ancient conventions of paradoxography (deliberations on seemingly impossible yet potentially true naturally occurring phenomena – the most famous example of which is perhaps the Plinian peoples).[37] This is distinct from the conventions of wonder-writing invoked in natural philosophy and in devotional writings, although the literature of entertainment on occasion makes use of both religious affect and philosophical deliberation.[38] It is also in contrast to early modern conceptualisations of wonder, which, as Walker Bynum suggests, tend to rest on the 'startle' response or belong to the very specific appropriative wonders of the 'New World' or the *Kunstkammer*, although the commodification of wonder, and the relationship between wonder and commodity, in particular its invocation in narratives of travel, is an association I explore in relation to my later texts in Chapter 4.[39]

The Augustinian conception of wonder presented medieval historical authors with a model for writing the marvels of recent history, not least for the assessment of the credibility of witness testimony. In *De civitate Dei* Augustine cites remarkable recent or current occurrences within the material world by way of proof of a seeming impossibility: the material suffering of the souls of the guilty after death. The eternal fires of hell and purgatory are demonstrated by Augustine via analogy with the mountains of Sicily (an important site in medieval fairy topographies, explored in Chapter 2):

quidam notissimi Siciliae montes, qui tanta temporis diuturnitate ac vetustate usque nunc ac deinceps flammis aestuant atque integri perseverant, satis idonei testes sunt non omne quod ardet absumi, et anima indicat non omne quod dolere potest posse etiam mori.

(certain well-known mountains in Sicily, in spite of their age and their antiquity, still seethe with flames and remain intact, and thus are satisfactory witnesses that not all that burns is consumed. The case of the soul shows that not all that is subject to suffering is subject also to death.)[40]

To this, Augustine adds the incorruptibility of the flesh of the peacock, with which he himself was served in Carthage.[41] The Augustinian suspension of disbelief possesses a clear cognitive-religious function: to think on the volcano and on the peacock is to think on the fires of hell, and to marvel at, and perhaps also to contemplate in terror, the wonder of creation in its fullest sense. This contemplative function is tied directly to the perspectival quality of marvels. In an example which was exceptionally influential on subsequent medieval authors, Augustine notes that the burning of lime is not remarkable from a European perspective, yet if similar properties were attributed to stones found in India, they might inspire wonder in the European beholder.[42]

Wonder contemplates occurrences beyond the quotidian experience of the observer, reporter, or author, and beyond the normative assumptions of the community for whom he writes or reports, and whose horizon of experience he shares. Wonder is an affective mode, which like the emotions more broadly might be understood (at least to some degree) as culturally and historically constructed. I understand this in relation to Barbara H. Rosenwein's model of 'emotional communities'.[43] On occasion, I approach this concept as adjacent to the 'imagined community' of the nation, as proposed by Benedict Anderson, an idea with which medievalists in recent years have productively engaged.[44] However, the 'emotional community' is a far more elastic category, although it is similarly a matter of verbal (textual) representation, appropriate to the study of literary scholars. The 'emotional community' is tellingly approached by Rosenwein in relation to the emotion words (for Rosenwein a 'word hoard') shared by different linguistic as well as social, geographical, and even familial groups.⁴⁵ This is a precedent to which I will return throughout this study, although, as is well noted, we must necessarily respond to the ways in which wonder is staged and the wonder response provoked beyond the notice of common terminology alone.⁴⁶

Emotional communities are rooted in a common understanding of appropriate emotional expression, and wonder and its limits are similarly socially constructed, in relation to both the expression of wonder and its object – the two inextricably connected in the context of medieval history-writing.⁴⁷ This is precisely why the credibility of the wonder response, and the background traditions in relation to which it is understood to operate, are often the primary interests in the cases of authorial discernment I discuss. We find this where authors with Anglo-centric sympathies attempt to read the fairy *mirabilia* of post-conquest Wales; and where western European Christian authors contemplate Islam, Judaism, and heresy. The history of wonder is a history of constructions of difference and perceptual gaps, even as from these texts emerge wonders which we might read most clearly as hybrid cultural formations, from French re-imaginings of Welsh prophecy to Arabic automata in Middle English romance.

## The limits of wonder

In the Augustinian tradition the limits of wonder are as much a cultural construction as wonder itself. Augustine holds that not all apparent marvels correctly inspire wonder. His position is rooted in the credibility of the witnesses and the systems of belief through which marvels are perceived, interpreted, and communicated. Augustine writes of the danger of unknowingly entertaining wonder where the phenomena under discussion are products of demonic illusion, such as those attributed to the intervention of the classical pantheon. As Walker Bynum notes, one of the most important components of medieval wonder in the Augustinian tradition is its 'facticity': one cannot wonder at a thing that does not exist, for within the Augustinian framework wonder is synonymous with belief.⁴⁸ Augustine poses that his opponents might respond to the marvels that he has invoked as analogues to the eternal flames of purgatory and hell with recourse to the charge of historical fabrication. For if one is to believe Augustine's marvels, then one must also believe stories of the marvellous ever-burning lamps of the shrine of Venus, which Augustine suggests are not inexplicable wonders, testament to the glory of God, but the result either of demonic illusion, gulling credulous minds, or human experiments with asbestos, designed to do the same. Augustine acknowledges that the parity between the two phenomena (the false and the true marvel) is a dilemma:

> quia si dixerimus non esse credendum, scripta illa miraculorum infirmabimus; si autem credendum esse concesserimus, firmabimus numina paganorum.
>
> (For if we say that the story should not be accepted, we shall weaken the force of recorded miracles, while if we grant that it should be accepted, we shall give support to the gods of the pagans.)[49]

Augustine's solution lies in the verifiable claims of near-historical reportage. Regarding the marvels of pagan histories, he writes, 'illa sufficiant quae nos quoque possumus experiri, et eorum testes idoneos non difficile est invenire' ('let those [passages] suffice which we ourselves can verify, and of which we can easily find competent witnesses').[50] For Augustine, this evidence necessarily lies beyond the textual. His stated source for Venus's lamps is Pliny the Elder's *Natural History*, pre-Christian textual evidence that Augustine for the most part rejects in his accounts of credible marvels. This forms the basis of another significant precedent for my medieval authors: the historical text, where it is generated outside a familiar framework of values and belief, is a meaningful record only insofar as it can be corroborated by trustworthy extra-textual reportage.

Yet within the Augustinian framework not all demonic effects are necessarily illusory, and demons might work true wonders, with the ultimate aim of leading humanity away from the divine. The incubus – a figure that by the late twelfth century was understood by secular clerics to be synonymous with the fairy – presents an illuminating precedent for medieval writings on fairies.[51] In Book XV of *De civitate Dei* Augustine weighs the arguments for the angelic identification of the sons of God who couple with the daughters of men and engender the antediluvian giants in Genesis 6.2. Although angelic embodiment is, Augustine notes, attested elsewhere in scripture, in a break with previous patristic readings Genesis 6.2 cannot be understood as a narrative of angelic pro-creation: the 'filii Dei' are, he concludes, human, and if such encounters did occur, it was with those who fell with Satan and who are now demonic. Exploring the latter possibility, he adds a further, extra-scriptural, precedent for demonic embodied sexuality:

> Et quoniam creberrima fama est, multique se expertos vel ab eis qui experti essent, de quorum fide dubitandum non esset, audisse confirmant, Silvanos et Panes, quos vulgo incubos vocant, inprobos saepe extitisse mulieribus et earum appetisse ac peregisse concubitum, et quosdam daemones, quos Dusios Galli nuncupant, adsidue hanc inmunditiam et temptare et efficere plures talesque adseverant ut hoc negare inpudentiae videatur, non hinc aliquid audeo definire, utrum aliqui spiritus elemento aerio corporati (nam hoc elementum, etiam cum agitatur flabello, sensu corporis tactuque sentitur) possint hanc etiam pati libidinem ut, quo modo possunt, sentientibus feminis misceantur.

> (Moreover, there is a very widespread report, corroborated by many people either through their own experience or through accounts of others of indubitably good faith who have had the experience, that Silvans and Pans, who are commonly called incubi, often misbehaved towards women and succeeded in accomplishing their lustful desire to have intercourse with them. And the tradition that certain demons, termed Dusii by the Gauls, constantly attempt and perpetrate this foulness is so widely and so well attested that it would seem impudent to deny it. Hence I dare not make any definite statement on the question whether some spirits endowed with bodies consisting of the element air – an element that, even when merely stirred by a fan, is felt by the body with its sense of touch – are also able to experience such lust and so have intercourse in such a way as they can with women who feel the sensation of it.)[52]

This very brief account is generally considered the 'clerical origin statement' of the incubus and its female counterpart, the succubus – both later synonyms for fairies.[53] Augustine's discussion of the Dusii was reworked in Isidore of Seville's *Etymologies*, in the context of Isidore's rejection of pagan beliefs, where he gives as alternative designations for the Dusii *panae* (pans; as in Augustine) and *pilosi* (satyrs), figures which we similarly encounter in twelfth and thirteenth-century *mirabilia* as terms for fairy.[54] Augustine, and the wider tradition which followed from this passage, deny the demon's divinity, although the phenomenon itself is plausible enough.[55] Demonic pro-generation is a possibility that must be credited, although Augustine cannot definitively state the truth of it, and indeed he can understand it only via analogy – the spirit's body operates like air from a fan. It is not an indisputable wonder, but there is no harm in wondering at it. Augustine's studied uncertainty effectively opens up a space of optional belief. Augustine comments elsewhere, in his account of marvels, that while we ought to reject the marvels of pagan antiquity that directly contradict the Bible, 'Sed ea, si volumus, credimus, quae non adversantur libris quibus non dubitamus oportere nos credere' ('We do believe, if we like, such items as do not contradict the books that we have no doubt we are bound to believe'), and indeed the Dusii would appear to cohere with some aspects of scriptural truth.[56]

While the excuse for the account of incubi is exegetical, Augustine's source material is not biblical but rooted in witness testimony, and in this he shares the methodological necessities of later medieval authors engaged with demonic wonders. As Nancy Partner observes:

> ... the Bible and the Fathers only gave assurance that supernatural events could happen, they offered no clear patterns of other criteria according to which the credibility of any particular example could be judged. ... To complicate matters further for a medieval scholar, the immaterial or subtle substance and shifting forms of heavenly agents would have made the search for objectively verifiable evidence pointless even if he has attempted that kind of investigation.[57]

Within this framework, Partner concludes, the primary form of evidence, and credibility check, was 'the testimony of the people who claimed to be witnesses or had spoken with them'.[58] As C. S. Watkins notes, the truth status of a historical event depended not simply on the perceived credibility of eyewitness reporters but on the subsequent 'chain of testators' that communicated this material to the historian, and his sense of their perceived agenda or intellectual ability.[59] I suggest that we might read this in relation to the specific communities in which the wonderful testimony was first generated. Testimony, however, proves unresolved as to the precise mechanics of the marvellous – that is, it can tell us what but not how. This uncertainty was fundamental to the double utility of the incubus, succubus, or fairy in the construction of history and the rejection of fiction. Even after Thomas Aquinas's fuller causal elaboration of demonic pro-generation in the thirteenth century – which denied demons bodies but held them capable of manipulation of human sexuality – the materiality of the experience remained questionable.[60] After all, how might one know the difference between demonic illusion and demonically worked material effects?

In the context of fairy accounts, modelled on Augustinian deliberations on wonder, medieval authors exploited the uncertain reality status of the demonic historical event and its wider meaning, using it to question and probe the limits of testimony, memory, and sense experience, and, above all, the importance of witness credibility, read in relation to the community within which witnesses might be situated. I return to the anecdote with which I began: Walter Map's account of Alnoth, the son of the eleventh-century English lord Eadric Wild and a fairy. Map does not simply offer a statement of the uncertainty that surrounds any understanding of marvellous phenomena, but attempts to derive some general principles from such encounters:

> A fantasia, quod est aparicio transiens, dicitur fantasma; ille enim aparencie quas aliquibus interdum demones per se faciunt a Deo prius accepta licencia ... Et quid de his fantasticis dicendum casibus, qui manent et bona se successione perpetuant, ut hic Alnodi ...?
>
> (From *fantasia*, that is: a passing apparition, *fantasma* is derived. For instance, those appearances that sometimes demons make to some by their own power, first receiving license from God ... But what shall we say of these *fantasticis* cases, which endure and perpetuate themselves in good succession, as of this Alnoth ...?)[61]

A brief comment is needed here on Map's vocabulary. While in medieval Latin *fantasia* can function as a synonym for the bodily organ of *imaginatione*, here it is presented as a synonym for *aparicio*, a mental image termed, where demonic causation is in evidence, *fantasma*.[62] Beyond Map's specific usage, *fantasma* might also be applied to those images conjured by the imagination at a divorce from immediate external stimulus, although Map clearly has in mind a demonic production with, he concludes, material properties. In Augustinian fashion, Map essentially asks whether we see a demonic manipulation of matter (a true wonder) or pure illusion with a false impression of material engagement (a false wonder). In response to this rhetorical questioning, Map identifies the fairy as a point of ephemeral but nonetheless pro-generative engagement – the case is 'fantasticis', meaning not, as it is often translated, imaginary (this would seem to run counter to Map's understanding of the phenomenon) but curiously apparitional. He does not draw on a developed theory of the imagination concerning the component elements of the mind by which sense impressions are processed and/or manufactured (he pre-dates the most influential debates on this in the medieval west), although, as I discuss in Chapter 1, his terminology does appear to draw on early Latin Aristotelian understandings of embodied cognition, understood specifically in relation to maternity.[63] An element of indeterminacy as regards imaginative processes and sensory perception would appear to be precisely Map's point: all we can say is that this particular demonic *fantasma* works material effects, specifically in the sphere of sex and pro-generation. While the precise workings of demonic pro-generation remain uncertain for Map, as they did for Augustine, the event is a verifiable wonder, cemented in the materiality of Alnoth. Alnoth is a figure, pseudo-historical or not, who is presented as credibly real to Map's audience within England, and who appears to be historically contained within the boundaries of the same community for which, and within which, Map wrote. The marvel is thus ostensibly a true one.

Part of the utility of medieval narratives of this type is their position on the very boundary between belief and disbelief. As Steven Justice notes of writing miracles in medieval historiography and hagiography, authors must 'open to inspection the constraints they work on themselves to maintain credit in what seems scarcely credible'.[64] That is to say, to write a miracle one must necessarily entertain scepticism and a sense of the customary limits of the possible – of what seems implausible and yet is true. The treatment of the fairy narratives with which this book is concerned is characteristic of a broader historiographical discourse of belief and doubt that we find in the construction of *miracula* also (if indeed we maintain the distinction between *miracula* and *mirabilia*, which my medieval authors often do not). Further, what Justice writes of the uses of analogy and hypothesis in the construction of *miracula* similarly holds good for *mirabilia*: 'shifting, partial, and unregularizable in its cognitive components; reliant on hypothesis and metaphor; sustained by imaginative habits and improvisations, bracing itself against the mind's revanche but also provoking it'.[65] Across this study, we will have occasion to note the analogical relationship of wonderful accounts of fairies to the mysterious operations of history and of religious faith, rooted in ontologies at once true and obscure. Yet unlike miracles fairy *mirabilia* are not a matter of religious faith (however the analogy might be entertained by medieval authors), and the question of discernment remains open-ended: there is no end point, for example, as we might see with the canonisation of a saint. In this respect, this material lends itself to cynical belief in the modern critical sense of the term: an investment in a remarkable narrative for a very specific political purpose. Nonetheless, the fairy was not necessarily beyond the reach of genuine belief. Medieval fairy narratives often emphasise the value of faith in the seemingly impossible, particularly in relation to the largely unexplained marvels of romance. Similarly, where we encounter disbelief, this is often distinctly cynical: disavowals which rest not on the nature of the phenomenon but its perceived localised cultural and political applications.

## Historia and fabula

In the context of medieval Latin historiography, with which my study begins, the concept of wonder operates in relation to two poles: *historia* (history), in which wonder might be rightly provoked, and *fabula* (fable), an object of wonder only for the gullible.[66] However, the two concepts are not consistently held in opposition to one another in Latin writings of the twelfth century. Walter Map, for example, writes of the 'intellectu mistico' ('mystical meanings') of 'historia' (by which he means biblical history), which he understands in its moral operation to be of a type with 'fabula' (classical myth).[67] Map writes that *fabula* (synonymous with fiction, *ficta*) in its moral or admonitory meanings may be as exemplary as *historia*:

> Nam historia, que ueritate nititur, et fabula, que ficta contexit, et bonos fine florenti beant, ut ametur benignitas, et fedo malos dampnant interitu, uolentes inuisam reddere maliciam; sibique succedunt inuicem in scripturis tum aduersitas prosperitati, tum e conuerso mutacione frequenti, quatinus utraque semper habita pre oculis neutri fiat propter alteram obliuio, sed se medico temperamento moderentur, ne unquam modum superet eleuacio uel fractura, scilicet ut contemplacione futurorum nec sit a spe uacua meditacio, nec a metu libera.
>
> (For *historia*, which is founded on truth, and *fabula*, which weaves together fiction, both of them make the good happy by a flourishing end, that goodness may be loved, and condemn the wicked to a dismal death, wishing to make malice hateful. And in the records there is a constant alternation, now of adversity upon prosperity, now the converse, in frequent change, that so both being ever before our eyes, neither may be forgotten for the other, but men may regulate themselves by a medicinal mixture, that neither rise nor ruin may predominate overmuch, that our thoughts, when we look at the future, may be neither bare of hope nor free from apprehension.)[68]

*Historia* and *fabula* are both here understood to trace the same Boethian movement between good fortune and bad to which Map returns throughout *De nugis*.[69] The two concepts, while distinct, are not obviously antithetical. Both are attested by 'scriptura', translated by James, Brooke, and Mynors as 'the records', which neatly encompasses the textual dimension the term implies. Indeed, as we shall see in Chapter 1, *fabula* appears to be a fraught designation in *De nugis* only when it is applied to oral accounts of the insular past as opposed to classical texts – that is, as Map for the most part understands it, legendary history in the Welsh fashion.

*Fabula* functions as a designation of that which cannot be true, not necessarily because the event itself is implausibly marvellous but because the belief system underpinning the narrative is understood to be incompatible with medieval worldviews, as we find with classical myth and its gods. This categorisation, however, was applied not simply to mythic structures but, by the late twelfth century, to legendary ones understood to be politically problematic. This association begins with the late twelfth- and early thirteenth-century reception of Geoffrey of Monmouth's legendary history of the kings of Britain, his *Historia regum Britanniae* (c. 1138).[70] As D. H. Green notes, the navigation of fiction and history in the *Historia* rests on a fundamental complicity between the author and his earliest Norman audience.[71] Indeed, as Siân Echard has suggested, Geoffrey might be understood as pre-empting the late twelfth-century interest in the distinction between *fabula* and *historia*, 'in the degree to which he builds the *auctoritas* of his version with reference to the *liber vetustissimus*; a parodic joke for the circle of like-minded courtier-historians' for which he wrote.[72] If we can understand the *Historia*, and its source claim (a fortuitously discovered old book in the British tongue), as an example of parody, the joke does not appear to have been understood outside Geoffrey's immediate 'circle'. Geoffrey's work, especially its Arthurian and Merlinian sections, met with scepticism from subsequent Latin historians, even as elements of it were enthusiastically mined.[73] One of the earliest charges to which Geoffrey's material was subject was the misrepresentation of *fabula* as *historia*, and indeed, it is here that in twelfth- and thirteenth-century historiography we find the most pronounced applications of the distinction between the two. High medieval debates around the historicity of Geoffrey's work are doubly relevant to the historiographical position of the fairy in their engagement with two significant related precedents for medieval fairy content: the incubus who is named as the father of the prophet Merlin in Book VI of the *Historia*, and the legend of Arthur's sojourn in Avalon with Morgan le Fay which finds its most extensive treatment in Geoffrey's later *Vita Merlini* (c. 1155), an account of Merlin's adventures in the Caledonian Forest.

In *Historia* VI, Merlin's abilities are speculatively associated by the magi of the British king Vortigern with the demonic knowledge of his father, an incubus, who visits his mother, a princess of the kingdom of Demetia in south Wales, in her convent cell. This is presented as the possible source of Merlin's prophetic knowledge, subsequently displayed in his reading of a historical omen in the first sequence of Book VII, the *Prophetiae Merlini*. Merlin glosses two dragons beneath Vortigern's fortress at Snowdon as signifying the red dragon of the Britons and the white dragon of the Saxons. This figure of territorial contestation is based on an omen that first appears in the ninth-century Cambro-Latin *Historia Brittonum*, although it was probably drawn from a Welsh vernacular background tradition and recurs in subsequent Welsh, English, and French history and prophecy.[74] Merlin's simultaneous association with history and the demonic was endorsed by the end of the twelfth century in Robert de Boron's *Merlin*, the source of the *Merlin* component of the *Lancelot-Grail* cycle, where Merlin appears as a proto-Antichrist saved by the prayers of his mother.[75] In the context of Geoffrey's work, prophecy is a particular class of marvel, held in conjunction with demonic *mirabilia*, and indeed, Geoffrey's earliest detractors appear to have read both the demon and prophecy together as improper objects of wonder. For the late twelfth-century English historian William of Newburgh, Merlin's incubus father provided one of the principal grounds for the rejection of Geoffrey's *Historia*, which William understood as rooted in a falsely historical Welsh background tradition. William writes that demonic prophecy is a deception, which fools the unwary and the naive:

> Denique in suis quamvis subtilioribus conjecturis saepe falluntur et fallunt, cum tamen per divinationum praestigias apud imperitos, quam utique non habent, praescientiam sibi arrogent futurorum.
>
> (In short, they [demons] are often deceived and deceive by their guesses, though these are quite sophisticated, but by means of trickery in their predictions they lay claim amongst naïve people to a foreknowledge of the future which they do not at all possess.)[76]

We might interpret this in relation to the vein of scepticism that Karen Sullivan has associated with high medieval clerical rejections of the 'marvels of Merlin': a moral panic that can be traced in a straight line from the demonic concerns of William and his contemporaries to the rejection of Merlinian prophecy at the Council of Trent nearly four hundred years later.[77] Yet for William, the marvel and its contested status are also historiographical questions, and most significant about William's rejection of Merlin's prophecies is not simply their uncertain religious significance but the ways in which their demonic aspect invalidates their historical status. The lie of Merlin's prophecies is borne out in the erroneous nature of the *Prophetiae*, which for William speak to a Britain that never was and never will be. Anyone possessed of knowledge of 'veterum historiarum' ('ancient histories') recognises the implausibility with which Geoffrey shamelessly calls his work 'Britonum historiam' ('a British history').[78] This is a tradition that goes all the way back to Augustine's rejection of the lamps of Venus, unsubstantiated by credible reportage and the product of demonic illusion.

William suggests that Geoffrey's *Historia* is more fully aligned with fiction than with history, of which Geoffrey's account of Arthur's journey to Avalon in *Historia* XI provides a particularly egregious example (William does not appear to have known Geoffrey's later account of this in the *Vita Merlini*). While, as I have written elsewhere, the return legend in the form that we (and William) know it appears to have been Geoffrey's innovation (a combining of Welsh non-Arthurian prophecy with the Breton hope), the framework was clearly understood by William, like Galfridian prophecy more broadly, to be indicative of Welsh or Breton historical structures relating false marvels and rooted in false belief.[79] He notes Arthur's removal to Avalon, 'Britannicae fingunt fabulae' ('invented in British fables'), from where the Britons (or Bretons) believe he will return.[80] For William this is the icing on the cake of Geoffrey's fabulous invention: the dimensions of Arthur's empire in *Historia* X are as fanciful as his return from a mysterious otherworld. Indeed, for William, Geoffrey's entire history is an otherworldly fiction. Writing of Geoffrey's account of Arthur's far-flung conquests, William asks, 'An alium orbem somniat infinita regna habentem?' ('Is he dreaming of another world containing kingdoms without number?').[81] This has been taken as a precocious recognition of Galfridian fictionality,[82] but what matters most for William here is not the operation of fiction but of English history, as the standard by which Geoffrey's (understood as implicitly Welsh) text is to be measured. William concludes that Geoffrey's text contains none of the rigour that characterises the properly historical endeavours of the English Bede.

By the end of the twelfth century the rejection of Galfridian material as fabulous rather than historical operated for some authors in explicit relation to its fairy content, as we find it in its most developed form in the *Vita Merlini*. A verse work in hexameter (the metre of Greek and Latin epic), presented by the author as undertaken in 'musa iocosa' ('a jocular spirit'; line 1), the *Vita* contains the earliest full allusion to Avalon, rooted in Isidore's description of the Fortunate Isles (as Avalon is also called), and Morgan and her eight sisters, drawn after the classical muses. In a passage that recalls the magic of the classical sorceress Circe, we read of Morgan's expertise in herbs and healing, and the art by which she shapeshifts. The prophet Thelgesin (a re-imagining of the Welsh prophet Taliesin) recalls of Morgan:

> Et resecare nouis quasi dedalus aera pennis
> Cum uult est bristi, carnoti, siue papie
> Cum uult in uestris es aere labitur horis.
>
> (to cleave the air on new wings like Daedalus;
> when she wishes she is at Brest, Chartres, or Pavia,
> and when she will she slips down from the air onto your shores.)
> (lines 923–25)[83]

Morgan's 'mutare figuram' ('changing of form'; line 922), of which we read in the lines immediately preceding, may even be understood as a play on the capabilities of Geoffrey's pseudo-classical poetry – a magical manipulation of poetic *figurae*. Certainly, writings on magic provided an opportunity to deploy literary and rhetorical skills, a practice which appears to have emerged with particular force in the twelfth century.[84] Although, as Harf-Lancner notes, in Morgan and Mélusine we find two distinct representations of the female fairy (the one characterised by an otherworldly journey, the other by the interdiction), I would suggest that in this early representation of Morgan we may well find the seeds of the Mélusinian fairy – shapeshifting and in flight, rooted in the conventions of classical *fabulae*.[85]

Geoffrey's *Vita* appears to have been read, presumably as intended, as a fable, but was mobilised by subsequent authors as a comment on the illegitimacy and instability of Welsh political frameworks of understanding. Notably, the Morgan narrative of the *Vita* contains no obviously Welsh element, and medieval Welsh

## Introduction: fairies in history

literature shows no sizeable influence of Latin, and later French and English, conventions of imagining the *fata*, *fée*, or fairy (although this does not mean that there were not concepts of supernatural lovers and mothers in Wales; these are discussed in Chapter 1). There is no cognate for 'fairy' in Welsh, and the closest Welsh-language counterpart, the *tylwyth teg* ('fair company') does not appear until the fifteenth century, and then it is used ironically.[86] Yet the figure of the fairy came to be associated with Welsh political fantasies. In a reworking of material from the *Vita*, Gerald of Wales writes of the refusal of the Britons to accept Arthur's death at Camlann and his burial by a noblewoman called 'Morganis': 'Propter hoc enim fabulosi Britones et eorum cantores fingere solebant, quod dea quaedam phantastica, scilicet et Morganis dicta, corpus Arthuri in insulam detulit Avalloniam ad ejus vulnera sanandum' ('As a result the credulous Britons and their bards invented the legend that a fantastic goddess called Morgan had removed Arthur's body to the Isle of Avalon so that she might cure his wounds there').[87] Gerald appears to understand his Arthurian sources as oral, and we might situate this in relation to a twelfth-century shift regarding the instability of oral historical memory as regards events of the distant past. Certainly, the Latin authors of my first chapter remark on the instability of distant histories conveyed orally; although we might note that elsewhere in Gerald's work, the veracity of Welsh marvels, and indeed Welsh prophecy, both oral and written, is paramount.[88] During this period, we see a developed association of antiquated British marvels, or pseudo-marvels, with an oral rather than literary historical culture, a feature that Echard has suggested we may similarly find in William of Newburgh's treatment of Welsh content.[89]

Gerald, as we might expect, associates Galfridian or Welsh fables with false or antiquated belief: the ambiguous designation of Morgan, as goddess or sorceress, is presumably intended to recall her classical counterparts such as Circe (as Geoffrey invites). Gerald engages with (or even constructs) a sphere of British (mis) belief understood, as by William of Newburgh, in connection with a Welsh legendary history with supernatural elements. Gerald is also particularly perturbed by the poetic contexts of the legend, which he reads in relation to the narrative's supernaturalism. This association may have been encouraged by the poetic form of the *Vita Merlini*, although this appears to be a feature of rejections of (perceived) Welsh prophetic-historical content from as early as the 1120s.[90] Moral concern regarding the dangers of poetry goes back to Augustine's use of the fabulous content of classical poetry to explain the dangers of undiscerning imaginations, entertaining false wonders. In his seventh letter Augustine writes of the power of imagination to combine images, which allows one to imagine while reading, for example, Medea and her winged dragons, as well as all manner of other fabulous impossibilities:

> To this class belong also those things which have been brought forward as true, either by wise men wrapping up some truth in the folds of such inventions, or by foolish men building up various kinds of superstition: for example, the Phlegethon of Tartarus, and the five caves of the nation of darkness, and the North Pole supporting the heavens, and a thousand other prodigies of poets and of heretics.[91]

The undiscerning imagination is a place of prodigious superstition and heresy. Indeed, Gerald tellingly understands British belief in the return of Arthur from Avalon in relation to religious error: 'sicut Judaei Messiam suum, majori etiam fatuitate et infelicitate, simul ac infidelitate decepti' ('just as the Jews, led astray by even greater stupidity, misfortune, and misplaced faith, really expect their messiah to return').[92] Numerous examples of this type of treatment of Avalon appear throughout the twelfth and thirteenth centuries, and further instances are discussed in Chapters 1 and 2, but suffice it to say here that in medieval rejections of the Avalon legend we find particularly pronounced examples of, to borrow a phrase from Julie Orlemanski, the 'splitting [of] audiences between the gullible and the sophisticated, which is to say, between those who didn't understand fiction properly and those who did'.[93]

Beyond the Merlinian and the prophetic, even before the end of the twelfth century British *fabulae* appear to have been understood as the antithesis of true history. We might recall Wace's disavowal of the marvels of the forest of Brocéliande in his *Roman de Rou* (*c.* 1160s–1170s). Writing of the marvels of this region, including fairies and a wonderful fountain, of which the Bretons tell, he records that he saw only the forest itself:

> La alai jo merveilles querre,
> vi la forest e vi la terre,
> merveilles quis, mais nes trovai,
> fol m'en revinc, fol i alai;
> fol i alai, fol m'en revinc,
> folie quis, por fol me tinc.

(I went there in search of marvels; I saw the forest and the land and looked for marvels, but found none. I came back as a fool and went as a fool. I went as a fool and came back as a fool. I sought foolishness and considered myself a fool.) (lines 6393–98)[94]

In an apparent disavowal of the historical reality status of British marvels with which Wace was engaged in his earlier translation of Geoffrey's *Historia*, the *Roman de Brut* (c. 1155), Wace here unmistakably (distinct from the *Brut*) conflates British wonder with baseless fairy superstition. The author berates himself for making the mistake of believing in apparently unreliable testimony, in terms very similar to the response to Galfridiana, and its perceived Welshness, that we have seen in closely contemporary English historiography. Notably, the term Wace applies to himself, 'fole', is applied elsewhere to British credulity: it is used by the author of the *Lancelot-Grail* to refer to the beliefs of those foolish (or mad, raving) Britons in the time of Arthur who falsely believed Morgan to be divine.[95] To believe erroneously is not simply to lack sophistication but to lack your wits, and the Britons/Bretons were held especially guilty of this.

Less pointedly, although on a continuum, the near-contemporary romances of Chrétien de Troyes and Marie de France are framed as accounts of British marvels that signify in relation not to historical truth but rather to the truth value of abstract concepts like love or chivalry. We might note the type of symbolic reading Marie applies to the marvels of her lais, a 'surplus de sen' which finds courtly truths in otherwise inexplicable fables. The emergence of romance more broadly might be understood, as Douglas Kelly observes, in relation to precisely this kind of untethering of the marvel from history, and the celebration of its abstract or allegorical implications.[96] In this context, the romance *merveille* is not a component in a chain of historical events, which finds it significance in history, but rather an impetus for the *aventure* which forms the very core of romance and is itself part of a closed hermeneutic loop (the *merveille* is the *telos* of the romance; it authorises itself). This association is the legacy of an earlier historiographical understanding of the impossibility of (for the most part reconstructed, often misconstrued, and sometimes entirely fabricated) British fables. The abstraction of the British marvel, and the emergence of the marvellous fictions of romance, is, I suggest, one component of the long historical reception of British *fabulae*, in part as an overt de-politicisation and neutralisation of the perceived political applications of Welsh frameworks of wonder.

## Thinking postcolonially

Implicit in my approach to the cross-cultural and cross-linguistic history of the fairy mother tradition is a vein of postcolonial thought that has catalysed a great deal of significant medieval scholarship over the last three decades, not least in regard to the politics of cross-border reception and influence.[97] Like previous critics, I draw on the work of Homi K. Bhabha, following Bruce Holsinger's charge not simply that postcolonial formulations might be illuminatingly adapted and applied to certain medieval contexts, but that they possess a fundamental integrity in regard to the medieval historian's ethical imperative to explore previously marginalised histories, an interest that has long been the basis of cross-disciplinary dialogue between the study of the medieval and the modern subaltern.[98] Holsinger's observations met a sophisticated response over two decades ago in Ananya Jahanara Kabir and Deanne Williams's discussion of the relationship between medieval orientalism and modern perceptions of the Middle Ages' alterity, both of which induce a wonder response that might be productively resituated by the literary historian who takes a reformed wonder as their tool.[99] I propose a return to the subject of wonder, situated explicitly in relation to Bhabha's positioning of wonder as the grounds of both postcolonial control and critique, mobilised in the nineteenth and twentieth centuries with strategies distinctly in common with the twelfth.

Bhabha explores the discriminatory role of wonder in his 1985 article 'Signs Taken for Wonders'. He begins with a motif that repeats across the nineteenth- and twentieth-century colonial scene: 'the discovery of a book ... wondrous to the extent to which it is repeated, translated, misread, displaced'.[100] Bhabha takes as his first example a colonial account of a discovery just outside Delhi of a printed Bible translated from English into Hindi, which the people of the region identify as their own holy text gifted to them by an angel. They accept the various tenets of Christianity excepting baptism and Holy Communion, the latter on the basis that it is understood to be cannibalistic. Upon discussion with the colonial missionaries, the readers agree to follow all Christian practices if the rest of their countrymen will do the same, a response which simultaneously answers the terms of colonial address and encodes subaltern evasion. For Bhabha, the discovered book is a 'signifier of colonial desire and discipline', which functions as a vehicle for the articulation of difference even as its multiple or contested use entails a necessary level of ambiguity within colonial discourse. It is also the beginning of history: 'the discovery of the book installs the sign of appropriate representation ..., creates the conditions for a beginning, a practice of history and narrative'.[101] This is to say, wonderful misreading is the very foundation of history, fabulous or otherwise – and indeed, this discursive indeterminacy is often precisely the point. My study finds its own originary book not in the translated Bible but in Geoffrey of Monmouth's *Historia*, a narrative with a complex and foundational relationship to insular and continental fairy writings. As we have already seen, the *Historia* was used – like Bhabha's book – to define and circumscribe the religious and political beliefs of communities; but more than this, Bhabha's central designator of unsophisticated wonder, a lack of eucharistic comprehension, is one which, we shall see, recurs across my medieval texts in association with the figure of the succubus and the histories she represents.

The fairy mother tradition reads in relation to the management, and the utility, of wonder as an object of cultural encounters both real and imagined, as a site of both paranoid perception and hybrid cultural emergence. The initial site of historical-literary context my study traces has long been held to be demonstrative of the productive dialogue between postcolonial theory and the medieval past: post-conquest Wales. In contrast to familiar medievalist postcolonial approaches to Wales as a space of English colonial projection, I approach my Welsh-set materials with a mind to what Helen Fulton has identified as an element of Welsh 'co-creation' in English and French understandings of the legendary and supernatural contexts of 'romantic Wales', in the period between the Norman conquests of the 1080s and the fall of the Welsh princes in the reign of Edward I.[102] Importantly, however, discussions of Welsh content in this study are not intended to point to the existence of a 'Celtic' source for the fairies of medieval romance (a caveat I share with Fulton). This claim is a notable feature of a great deal of previous research on *Mélusine* – a particular manifestation of a broader scholarly commonplace in which supernatural but obscure motifs in English and French romance are problematically regarded as 'Celtic' (a term often employed homogenously in this sense to both Welsh and Irish contents).[103] To assume the origins of pan-European fairy legends in Wales is to replicate the marginalising strategies of twelfth- and thirteenth-century Latin chroniclers invested in the supernaturalism of the Welsh. Yet equally we cannot assume that Wales did not participate in currents that appear to have arisen elsewhere in medieval Europe. This was an engagement which – however distorted its reception – shaped English relationships with Welsh historiography, and in turn, informed French and English literary production and history-writing more widely, and perceptions of new peripheries, whether understood in terms of geography or belief.

My interest is in the hybrid cultural formations of cross-border literary history revealed through historicist analysis of the fairy tradition, viewed from the multiple perspectives of insular and continental literary production. I am not, perhaps as one might expect, interested in the body of the fairy mother as a metaphor for medieval cultural hybridity. While the analogy has proved meaningful and productive for a number of critics, as Ana Pairet has cautioned, when approaching the phenomenon of hybridity in its medieval context (a question fundamental to the mimetic or proposed reality status of the fairy in my texts) we must necessarily attend to the fairy's bodily forms within their own historicised intellectual contexts and discursive conventions.[104] I propose, then, to think both medievally and postcolonially, engaging not with the hybrid body of the fairy as metaphor but rather with the cultural debts and affiliations of the communities who told her story, and through which it moved. By extension, therefore, I acknowledge the discursive hybridity of the medieval texts which positioned her within the conventions of both history and romance.

## Chapter overview

My interest in textual influences should not be understood in relation to any claims regarding a definitive textual origin for the fairy mother legend. This study allows for the possibility of spontaneously arising legendary content dispersed across time and space, although we do appear to find levels of interaction between independent cultural background concepts, synthesised by medieval authors. This is the foundation of my analysis in Chapter 1. In *De nugis* the same phenomenon (the fairy mother) appears as the subject of a sustained narrative in both English and Welsh contexts. The English fairy is presented as a historical event (although the material uncertainty of the demon herself is acknowledged), while the Welsh is more straightforwardly fabulous. Map's rejection of Welsh *mirabilia* reads in relation to the prophetic elements he identifies in his Welsh-set fairy narrative, elements which appear to be held in a close relationship to an Anglo-Latin historiographical concern with the British lie of Arthur's return from Avalon, and the (related) representation of Welsh-set fairy *mirabilia* as improper objects of wonder. With all the inconsistency of ideology, in this material the Welsh appear both as credulous *and* as liars, a feature that we find elsewhere in *De nugis* and in Gerald of Wales's Welsh writings also, including his account of the succubus encounter of the false prophet Meilerius (Meilyr). Finally, the chapter explores analogous accounts of English fairies by William of Newburgh, which are possessed of a marvellous historicity that could be situated by English authors only within an English geographical and cultural context. While for late twelfth-century authors in England, English fairy narratives might have a place in the historiographical record, their Welsh counterparts could not.

Into the thirteenth century we see a continuing interest in the historical fairy *mirabile* in the works of historical authors writing in a continental context. Chapter 2 explores the fairy narratives of Gervase of Tilbury, another high medieval collector of *mirabilia*, working under the patronage of the half-English Holy Roman Emperor Otto IV. While Gervase has often been understood as a significant figure in the incipient development of a medieval scientific method analogous to modern understandings of empiricism, he is overtly engaged with the historical status of fairy narratives. Gervase's texts suggest a particular association of the fairy with a figure associated with wonder, and its abuses, elsewhere in medieval history writing: the heretic, a figure inflected in this period by both antisemitic and misogynistic discourses. Given its potent capabilities as a mode of community demarcation, it is perhaps no surprise that the heretical fairy mother also first appears in highly partisan revisionist histories written during this period. Gervase's fairy content corresponds closely with that of Gerald of Wales's near-contemporary *De principis instructione*, directed to the French king, Louis VIII, where we find the first recorded application of the fairy mother to an unnamed countess of Anjou, an ancestor of the Plantagenet kings of England. This was reworked in Philippe Mousket's *Chronique rimée* (composed between 1242 and 1273), which imagines the exclusion from the political community of another (perceived) overmighty woman, an ancestor of Eleanor of Aquitaine who functions as a cipher for Eleanor herself.

The legacy of these politically directed readings is felt in the late medieval French *Mélusine* romances. Chapter 3 traces the debt of Jean d'Arras's adaptative translation and extension of Gervase's fairy narratives, written in the service of Jean, Duke of Berry, who is presented by Jean d'Arras as heir to the house of Lusignan. This is the only single text to which I dedicate an entire chapter, for it represents the fullest, and arguably the most influential, medieval development of the political fairy mother legend. *Mélusine* is presented as a true history that matters not despite but because of the fairy's uncertain reality status, and explicitly holds belief in the marvellous to be the quality of a noble heart. In his construction of this position, Jean utilises the conventions of high medieval fairy *mirabilia*. Like Gervase's, Jean's fairy account is framed as dynastic history, and Jean draws on historiographical strategies derived from Galfridian historiography (both Geoffrey's *Historia* and related traditions). Written in the context of the Hundred Years War, the political investments of Jean's text are very close to its surface, and the romance functions in a new, reformulated, relationship to British marvels of the twelfth century, which here do not discredit but endorse the historicity and reality of marvellous phenomena, held in opposition to English territorial interests in France. The narrative concludes with a revisionist re-imagining of the departure of the English from the fortress of Lusignan, augured by an apparition of Mélusine witnessed by none other than the Welsh rebel, and subject of Welsh political prophecy, Owain Lawgoch. The fairy is a marvel which the English are incapable of fully apprehending, but whose meaning is apparent to the French and the Welsh.

The focus of my fourth and final chapter is the verse reworking of Jean d'Arras's romance in Couldrette's early fifteenth-century Parisian text, written for Guillaume l'Archevêque, the Lord of Parthenay. The balance between history and romance is a point of tension in Couldrette's text, which capitalises on the imagined worlds of Arthurian romance in its expanded treatment of the knight's quest, as a component of historical fiction which derives its political function from its moral exemplarity rather than its absolute historicity. This was in large part, I argue, a response driven by necessity, for unlike Jean d'Arras, Couldrette wrote for a patron at a remove from the fortress of Lusignan itself, without access to contemporary witnesses (fabricated or otherwise) of the fairy's near-historical appearances. However, this discursive re-focusing is similarly a feature of the roughly contemporary *a*-text of *Richard Coer de Lyon*, the earliest Middle English text that we might align with the *Mélusine* tradition, produced a century earlier than the English translations of Jean d'Arras's and Couldrette's texts.[105] Richard's mother, identified not as Eleanor of Aquitaine but as a fairy of Antioch, provokes a wonder response in a historical context that is unashamedly revisionist to the point of being ahistorical. Yet the text nonetheless juxtaposes its credible fictions with the incredible beliefs of Islam and Judaism, occasioned by the romance's geographical interest in Palestine and its surrounding areas. While the events recounted are clearly fictionalised, the religious beliefs entertained are understood to be extra-textually relevant; and the fairy mother, by this period long associated with questions of discernment, presents a convenient vehicle for drawing such distinctions.

## Conclusion

Across the texts surveyed in this book there is a discursive shift, from historical accounts with romance elements to dynastic romances with a greater or a lesser degree of historical referentiality. This does not, however, reveal an inevitable movement towards the full fictionalisation of the fairy, an emptying-out of historical content over time, so much as a highly contingent process by which historical meaning is generated by a given author based on his understanding of the horizon of expectations of his community of readers or audience – a community of wonder. It is on this basis that a fairy narrative might be presented as true or false, and so worthy of belief or not. The trajectory towards fiction in some ways, then, is incidental, a facet of the point at which my study concludes – for certainly, early modern narratives are not without their defences of the realities of fairies. Rather, then, the following chapters chart the medieval construction and contestation of a very particular type of wonderful history, tracing the shifting boundaries of the plausible and the implausible as a site of political value. My authors are interested not in the fairy alone but in the world of contested historical narrative to which she belongs, and the possible futures these envisage. The supernatural is in this respect also the political.

## Notes

1 Augustine, *City of God: Volume VII*, trans. William M. Green, Loeb Classical Library 417 (Cambridge, MA: Harvard University Press, 1963), pp. 34–35.
2 Walter Map, *De nugis curialium: Courtiers' Trifles*, ed. and trans. M. R. James, revised by C. N. L. Brooke and R. A. B. Mynors (Oxford: Clarendon Press, 1983), pp. 160–61.

3  Daniel Poirion, *Le Merveilleux dans la littérature française du Moyen Âge* (Paris: Presses Universitaires de France, 1982); Jacques Le Goff, *The Medieval Imagination*, trans. Arthur Goldhammer (Chicago: University of Chicago Press, 1992), pp. 27–30; Caroline Walker Bynum, 'Wonder', *American Historical Review* 102.1 (1997): 1–26, reprinted in *Metamorphosis and Identity* (New York: Zone Books, 2005), chapter 1; James F. Knapp and Peggy A. Knapp, *Medieval Romance: The Aesthetics of Possibility* (Toronto: University of Toronto Press, 2017). I am concerned with that class of *mirabilia* or marvels that we might understand on the level of event or occurrence that elicits a wonder response, rather than the marvellous plant, animal, or object. For discussion of the latter in its medieval literary context, see Michelle Karnes, 'Wonder, Marvels, and Metaphor in the "Squire's Tale"', *English Literary History* 82.2 (2015): 461–90. While the fantastic and the marvellous are appropriate terms for the material with which I am concerned (which stages both the operation of fantasy and marvels), I do not propose a chronological contestation of our dating of a 'marvellous' or 'fantastic' aesthetic, as proposed for later literature by Tzvetan Todorov – the term carries a different meaning within a medievalist context than within the analysis of later periods. See further Le Goff, *The Medieval Imagination*, pp. 27–30; Walker Bynum, 'Wonder', p. 2.

4  For the most comprehensive previous discussion of the relationship between the *Mélusine* romances and twelfth and thirteenth-century Latin analogues and sources, see Laurence Harf-Lancner, *Les Fées au Moyen Âge: Morgane et Mélusine – la naissance des fées* (Paris: Honoré Champion, 1984), pp. 83–178. Continuity in, and persistence of, historiographical strategies associated with fact, fiction, and referentiality, however, has not previously been an object of study. For detailed discussion of the French romances and their later reception see Lydia Zeldenrust, *The Mélusine Romance in Medieval Europe: Translation, Circulation, and Material Contexts* (Cambridge: D. S. Brewer, 2020).

5  I refer to recent studies of medieval fictionality, which make a claim (in certain contexts) for its real-world referentiality. See *New Literary History: A Journal of Theory and Interpretation* 51.1, 'Medieval Fictionalities' (2020). This special issue is a medievalist response to Catherine Gallagher's brief definition of pre-modern fiction in 'The Rise of Fictionality', in *The Novel*, I: *History, Geography, and Culture*, ed. Franco Moretti (Princeton, NJ: Princeton University Press, 2006), pp. 337–39, which argues that the referentiality that

underlies the birth of the novel is specifically post-medieval and regards medieval literature as a space of pure fantasy. For an association of medieval literature with the mythic (as opposed to historical or realist) truths, see Kathryn Hume, *Fantasy and Mimesis: Responses to Reality in Western Literature* (New York: Methuen, 1984), pp. 30–31.

6 Fredric Jameson, *The Political Unconscious: Narrative as a Socially Symbolic Act* (London: Routledge, 1983), pp. 99–100. See further Fredric Jameson, 'Magical Narratives: Romance as Genre', *New Literary History* 7.1 (1975): 135–63. For an important statement on the historical contingencies that inform the re-use of romance motifs, see Helen Cooper, *The English Romance in Time: Transforming Motifs from Geoffrey of Monmouth to the Death of Shakespeare* (Oxford: Oxford University Press, 2004), esp. pp. 1–6. The mimetic qualities of medieval romance are most famously a point of critical interest in Erich Auerbach, *Mimesis: The Representation of Reality in Western Literature*, trans. Willard R. Trask (Princeton, NJ: Princeton University Press, 2003), pp. 123–42.

7 For a contestation of romance's privileged position see Michelle Karnes, 'The Possibilities of Medieval Fiction', *New Literary History* 51.1 (2020): 209–28 (pp. 210–12).

8 L. O. Aranye Fradenburg, 'Simply Marvelous', *Studies in the Age of Chaucer* 26 (2004): 1–27 (p. 11).

9 We might note similarly 'the colonising uses of imagination and fantasy' that Patricia Clare Ingham has understood to be in operation in romance, as a component of early English imperialism. *Sovereign Fantasies: Arthurian Literature and the Making of Britain* (Philadelphia: University of Pennsylvania Press, 2001), pp. 1–2.

10 Jacques Le Goff, *Time, Work, and Culture in the Middle Ages*, trans. Arthur Goldhammer (Chicago: University of Chicago Press, 1982), pp. 205–24, trans. from Jacques Le Goff and Emmanuel Le Roy Ladurie, *Mélusine maternelle et défricheuse* (Paris: Armand Colin, 1971).

11 Aisling Byrne, 'Fairy Lovers: Sexuality, Order and Narrative in Medieval Romance', in *Sexual Culture in the Literature of Late Medieval Britain*, ed. Amanda Hopkins, Robert Allen Rouse, and Cory James Rushton (Cambridge: D. S. Brewer, 2014), pp. 99–110.

12 Cooper, *English Romance in Time*, p. 225. In relation to this, we must note the uncertainty, uncanniness, and often the violence of fairy encounters in medieval romance and, similarly, be aware of the potentially subversive quality of the tests posed by otherworldly authorities, a counter to the genre's apparent conservatism. See further Corinne

Saunders, *Magic and the Supernatural in Medieval English Romance* (Cambridge: D. S. Brewer, 2010), pp. 206, 232; James Wade, *Fairies in Medieval Romance* (New York: Palgrave Macmillan, 2011), pp. 77–83; Aisling Byrne, *Otherworlds: Fantasy and History in Medieval Literature* (Oxford: Oxford University Press, 2015), pp. 107–40.

13  For a discussion of the fairy Otherworld (particularly when associated with the islands of the western Atlantic) as a space of potentially utopian possibilities, see Byrne, *Otherworlds*, p. 154; Cooper, *English Romance in Time*, p. 75; Helen Fulton, 'Space: Place, Non-Place, and Identity in the Medieval Fairy World', in *A Cultural History of Fairy Tales in the Middle Ages*, ed. Susan Aronstein (London: Bloomsbury, 2021), pp. 135–55.

14  For discussion of the developmental relationship between history and romance, in both insular and continental contexts, see Gabrielle M. Spiegel, *Romancing the Past: The Rise of Vernacular Prose Historiography in Thirteenth-Century France* (Berkeley, CA: University of California Press, 1995); Laura Ashe, *History and Fiction in England, 1066–1200* (Cambridge: Cambridge University Press, 2007).

15  See, for example, Laura Ashe, 'Killing the King: Romance and the Politicization of History', in *Thinking Medieval Romance*, ed. Katherine C. Little and Nicola McDonald (Oxford: Oxford University Press, 2018), pp. 55–67. For an influential early discussion of the problem of medieval genre classifications, see Paul Zumthor, *Towards a Medieval Poetics*, trans. Philip Bennett (Minneapolis, MN: University of Minnesota Press, 1992), pp. 118–36.

16  Karnes, 'The Possibilities of Medieval Fiction', p. 212. This position is extended in Karnes's recent monograph *Medieval Marvels and Fictions in the Latin and Islamic World* (Chicago: University of Chicago Press, 2022), which, however, because of its publication date was not available to me during the period of writing this book (completed in late 2022).

17  Karnes, 'The Possibilities of Medieval Fiction', p. 212.

18  See, for example, C. S. Watkins, *History and the Supernatural in Medieval England* (Cambridge: Cambridge University Press, 2007); Robert Bartlett, *The Natural and the Supernatural in the Middle Ages* (Oxford: Oxford University Press, 2008). For discussion of the ambiguity of fairies, see Wade, *Fairies in Medieval Romance*, p. 74.

19  Richard Kieckhefer, 'The Specific Rationality of Medieval Magic', *American Historical Review* 99.3 (1994): 813–36.

20  Monika Otter, *Inventiones: Fiction and Referentiality in Twelfth-Century English Historical Writing* (Chapel Hill, NC: University of North Carolina Press, 1999), p. 9.

21 Laurie A. Finke and Martin B. Shichtman, *King Arthur and the Myth of History* (Gainesville, FL: University of Florida Press, 2004), pp. 17–18.
22 Stuart Clark, *Thinking with Demons: The Idea of Witchcraft in Early Modern Europe* (Oxford: Oxford University Press, 1997). We might note that in this later period fairies similarly emerge within the historical record, that is, in witch testimonies. See further Diane Purkiss, *Troublesome Things: A History of Fairies and Fairy Stories* (London: Penguin, 2001); Lizanne Henderson and Edward J. Cowan, *Scottish Fairy Belief: A History* (Edinburgh: John Donald, 2007).
23 Richard Firth Green, *Elf Queens and Holy Friars: Fairy Beliefs and the Medieval Church* (Philadelphia: University of Pennsylvania Press, 2016). The direct use of *mirabilia* in the critique of religious orthodoxy was earlier noted by Jacques Le Goff, who suggested that the marvellous might present a form of resistance to the 'official ideology of Christianity', although he by no means held this to be its primary function. Le Goff, *The Medieval Imagination*, p. 32.
24 Harf-Lancner, *Les Fées au Moyen Âge*, pp. 390–409.
25 I omit study of the swan knight, the male counterpart to the historical or quasi-historical fairy mothers I discuss, as a distinct tradition. The swan knight legend was associated from the thirteenth century onwards with one of the leaders of the First Crusade, Godfrey of Bouillon, in which form it appears to have acquired some of the features of the early Mélusine legend. See Harf-Lancner, *Les Fées au Moyen Âge*, pp. 179–98; Simon John, 'Godfrey of Bouillon and the Swan Knight', in *Crusading and Warfare in the Middle Ages: Realities and Representations: Essays in Honour of John France*, ed. Simon John and Nicholas Morton (London: Routledge, 2016), pp. 129–42. For further comment on the acceptance, and rejection, of the swan knight legend by chroniclers of the First Crusade, see Simon John, 'Historical Truth and the Miraculous Past: The Use of Oral Evidence in Twelfth-Century Latin Historical Writing on the First Crusade', *English Historical Review* 130.543 (2015): 263–301 (p. 277).
26 Johan Huizinga, *The Waning of the Middle Ages: A Study of the Forms of Life, Thought and Art in France and the Netherlands in the XIVth and XVth Centuries*, trans. Frederik J. Hopman (New York: St Martin's Press, 1924); the quotation is from p. 9 on 'the violent tenor of life'; the discussion of violence of emotion and magical signification is on p. 50, in relation to birth, marriage, and funeral practices. Huizinga's place in the history of emotions is discussed by Barbara H. Rosenwein, 'Worrying about Emotions in History', *American Historical Review* 107 (2002): 821–45 (p. 823).

27 Byrne, *Otherworlds*, esp. pp. 1–24.
28 For a paradigmatic statement of the tension between the marvellous and the historical see Le Goff, *The Medieval Imagination*, p. 34.
29 Gabrielle M. Spiegel, 'Political Utility in Medieval Historiography: A Sketch', *History and Theory* 14.3 (1975): 314–25.
30 G. T. Shepherd, 'The Emancipation of the Story in the Twelfth Century', in *Medieval Narrative: A Symposium*, ed. Hans Bekker-Nielsen, Peter Foote, Andreas Haarder, and Preben Meulengracht Sorensen (Odense: University of Odense Press, 1979), pp. 44–57, which suggests that we might locate interests in oral sources among Anglo-Latin historians of the twelfth century in relation to a broader cultural shift from orality to literacy. For discussion of the nature of this shift in England during the twelfth century, see Brian Stock, *The Implications of Literacy: Written Language and Models of Interpretation in the Eleventh and Twelfth Centuries* (Princeton, NJ: Princeton University Press, 1983); Michael Clanchy, *From Memory to Written Record: England, 1066–1307* (Oxford: Wiley-Blackwell, 2012).
31 For a succinct discussion of this position, see C. S. Watkins, 'Memories of the Marvellous in the Anglo-Norman Realm', in *Medieval Memories: Men, Women and the Past, 700–1300*, ed. Elisabeth van Houts (London: Pearson Education, 2001), pp. 92–112 (pp. 93–94).
32 For the articulation of this distinction in high medieval theological and philosophical literature, see Walker Bynum, 'Wonder', pp. 4–5.
33 Nancy F. Partner, *Serious Entertainments: The Writing of History in Twelfth-Century England* (Chicago: University of Chicago Press, 1977); Watkins, *History and the Supernatural*, pp. 23–67.
34 Watkins, *History and the Supernatural*, pp. 219–20.
35 For a reading of the historiographical marvel in relation to those of late medieval romance, see John Finlayson, 'The Marvellous in Middle English Romance', *Chaucer Review* 33.4 (1999): 363–408. However, as discussed in Chapter 4, Finlayson's understanding of the role of genre in relation to the referentiality of the romance *merveille*/marvel is not the same as my own.
36 Walker Bynum, 'Wonder', p. 12.
37 Walker Bynum, 'Wonder', pp. 12, 23. See further Lorraine Daston and Katharine Park, *Wonders and the Order of Nature 1150–1750* (New York: Zone Books, 1998), pp. 39–44. For an influential discussion of monsters, see Jeffrey Jerome Cohen, ed., *Monster Theory: Reading Culture* (Minneapolis, MN: University of Minnesota Press, 1996), esp. Cohen, 'Monster Culture (Seven Theses)', pp. 3–25.

38 Walker Bynum, 'Wonder', p. 7 *passim*.
39 Walker Bynum, 'Wonder', pp. 4–5. See further Daston and Park, *Wonders and the Order of Nature*, p. 215 *passim*; Stephen Greenblatt, 'Resonance and Wonder', *Bulletin of the American Academy of Arts and Sciences* 43.4 (1990): 11–34; Stephen Greenblatt, *Marvelous Possessions: The Wonder of the New World* (Chicago: University of Chicago Press, 1991), esp. pp. 72–85; Mary Baine Campbell, *Wonder and Science: Imagining Worlds in Early Modern Europe* (Ithaca, NY: Cornell University Press, 1999).
40 Augustine, *City of God*, VII, pp. 14–15. For discussion of Augustine's role in the development of medieval concepts of purgatory, see Jacques Le Goff, *The Birth of Purgatory*, trans. Arthur Goldhammer (Chicago: University of Chicago Press, 1984), pp. 98–99.
41 Augustine, *City of God*, VII, pp. 14–17.
42 Augustine, *City of God*, VII, pp. 20–21. The 'perspectival' component of Augustinian and medieval wonder is similarly noted by Walker Bynum, 'Wonder', p. 3 *passim*; Daston and Park, *Wonders and the Order of Nature*, p. 62; Keegan Brewer, *Wonder and Skepticism in the Middle Ages* (London: Routledge, 2016), p. 32.
43 For two important early statements on the application of the study of the history of emotions to medieval history and literature, see Rosenwein, 'Worrying about Emotions in History'; Carolyne Larrington, 'The Psychology of Emotion and Study of the Medieval Period', *Early Medieval Europe* 10 (2001): 251–56. Note that we see a distinction between the constructionist approach to the emotions, in which all emotions are a product of socio-historical contexts, and the cognitivist approach, in which emotions operate in relation to common physiological responses and thus have a certain level of trans-historical continuity.
44 Benedict Anderson, *Imagined Communities: Reflections on the Origins and Spread of Nationalism* (London: Verso Books, 2006). For discussion of the application of Anderson to medieval literature and its necessary caveats, see Victoria Flood, *Prophecy, Politics, and Place in Medieval England: From Geoffrey of Monmouth to Thomas of Erceldoune* (Cambridge: D. S. Brewer, 2016), pp. 9–10.
45 Barbara H. Rosenwein, *Generations of Feeling: A History of Emotions, 600–1700* (Cambridge: Cambridge University Press, 2015). See further Barbara H. Rosenwein, *Emotional Communities in the Early Middle Ages* (Ithaca, NY: Cornell University Press, 2006); Damien Boquet and Piroska Nagy, *Medieval Sensibilities: A History of Emotions in the Middle Ages*, trans. Robert Shaw (Cambridge:

Polity Press, 2018), esp. pp. 215–47; Sif Rikhardsdottir, *Emotion in Old Norse Literature: Translations, Voices, Contexts* (Cambridge: D. S. Brewer, 2017). For a succinct overview of relevant scholarship on 'emotional communities', see Barbara H. Rosenwein and Riccardo Cristiani, *What is the History of Emotions?* (Cambridge: Polity Press, 2018), pp. 39–45.
46 Walker Bynum, 'Wonder', p. 15.
47 For a recent situation of wonder in the context of the history of emotions, see Thomas A. Prendergast and Stephanie Trigg, *Affective Medievalism: Love, Abjection and Discontent* (Manchester: Manchester University Press, 2018), pp. 50–69.
48 Walker Bynum, 'Wonder', p. 13.
49 Augustine, *City of God*, VII, pp. 34–35.
50 Augustine, *City of God*, VII, pp. 34–35.
51 This is distinct from medical definitions of the incubus, although medical meanings of the phenomenon, as an alternative point of explanation, are discussed in relation to Gervase of Tilbury's assessment of fairy *mirabilia* in Chapter 2.
52 Augustine, *City of God: Volume IV*, trans. Philip Levine, Loeb Classical Library 414 (Cambridge, MA: Harvard University Press, 1966), pp. 548–51.
53 Nicholas Kiessling, *The Incubus in English Literature: Provenance and Progeny* (Pullman, WA: Washington State University Press, 1977).
54 Isidore of Seville, *The Etymologies of Isidore of Seville*, ed. and trans. Stephen A. Barney, W. J. Lewis, J. A. Beach, and Oliver Berghof (Cambridge: Cambridge University Press, 2006), p. 190.
55 Augustine's rejection of the divinity of incubi is found in Augustine, *City of God: Volume III*, Loeb Classical Library 413, trans. David S. Wiesen (Cambridge, MA: Harvard University Press, 1968), pp. 152–55.
56 Augustine, *City of God*, VII, pp. 34–34.
57 Partner, *Serious Entertainments*, p. 116.
58 Partner, *Serious Entertainments*, p. 116.
59 Watkins, 'Memories of the Marvellous in the Anglo-Norman Realm', pp. 96–97.
60 Dyan Elliott, *Fallen Bodies: Pollution, Sexuality and Demonology in the Middle Ages* (Philadelphia: University of Pennsylvania Press, 1999), pp. 52–60, 127–56; Walter Stephens, *Demon Lovers: Witchcraft, Sex, and the Crisis of Belief* (Chicago: University of Chicago Press, 2003); Norman Cohn, *Europe's Inner Demons: The Demonization of*

*Christians in Medieval Christendom* (London: Pimlico, 2005), p. 34. See further Anke Bernau, 'Bodies and the Supernatural: Humans, Demons, and Angels', in *A Cultural History of the Human Body in the Medieval Age*, ed. Linda Kalof (Oxford: Berg Publishers, 2010), pp. 99–120, 239–44.

61 Walter Map, *De nugis*, pp. 160–61. My translation, modified from the edition for clarity, although the sense intended by the original translators is retained. Unlike the translators, I retain Latin terminology in the English translation where this is a point of ambiguity, discussed in the analysis which follows.

62 For example, Augustine uses *fantasia* in his discussion of confession to mean inner vision, but this is not obviously the sense meant in Map. Augustine, *City of God: Volume V*, trans. Eva M. Sanford and William M. Green, Loeb Classical Library 415 (Cambridge, MA: Harvard University Press, 1965), pp. 486–87.

63 For discussion of medieval theories of the imagination in relation to literary and philosophical marvels, approaches distinct from Map's, see Michelle Karnes, 'Marvels in the Medieval Imagination', *Speculum* 90.2 (2015): 327–65. Map's approach is also distinct from later authors like Geoffrey Chaucer, who appear to have engaged directly with medical theorisations of the imagination. Jacqueline Tasioulas, 'Dying of Imagination in the First Fragment of the *Canterbury Tales*', *Medium Ævum* 82.2 (2013): 213–35. For the most part the authors with whom I am concerned across this book do not articulate a developed psychological or medical understanding of the imagination and its faculties; their primary concern is history and thus the relationship between fairy *phantasmata* (of uncertain reality status) and what Karnes usefully terms the 'extramental world'. Karnes, 'Marvels in the Medieval Imagination', p. 333.

64 Steven Justice, 'Did the Middle Ages Believe in their Miracles?', *Representations* 103.1 (2008): 1–29 (p. 15).

65 Justice, 'Did the Middle Ages Believe in their Miracles?', p. 13.

66 This distinction is similarly noted by Walker Bynum, 'Wonder', p. 13.

67 Walter Map, *De nugis*, pp. 128–29.

68 Walter Map, *De nugis*, pp. 128–29.

69 For example, in Map's account of Raso and his wife, the protagonist laments his imprudent actions (his trust in a woman) 'contra *fabulas et hystorias* et omnium ab inicio consilia sapientum' ('against *tales and histories* and all the counsel of wise men') (my italics). Walter Map, *De nugis*, pp. 266–67.

70 Geoffrey of Monmouth, *History of the Kings of Britain*, ed. Michael D. Reeve and trans. Neil Wright (Woodbridge: Boydell Press, 2005).
71 D. H. Green, *The Beginnings of Romance: Fact and Fiction, 1150–1220* (Cambridge: Cambridge University Press, 2002), p. 13.
72 Siân Echard, *Arthurian Narrative in the Latin Tradition* (Cambridge: Cambridge University Press, 2001), p. 70. For the initial ideological function of the *Historia*, see further, and in addition to Finke and Shichtman, *King Arthur and the Myth of History*: Stephen Knight, *Arthurian Literature and Society* (New York: Palgrave Macmillan, 1983), pp. 38–67; Geraldine Heng, *Empire of Magic: Medieval Romance and the Politics of Cultural Fantasy* (New York: Columbia University Press, 2004), pp. 17–62.
73 Ad Putter, 'Latin Historiography after Geoffrey of Monmouth', in *The Arthur of Medieval Latin Literature: The Development and Dissemination of the Arthurian Legend in Medieval Latin*, ed. Siân Echard (Cardiff: University of Wales Press, 2011), pp. 85–108; Brewer, *Wonder and Skepticism*, pp. 155–57.
74 For discussion of this motif, and its place in English and Welsh prophetic traditions, see Flood, *Prophecy, Politics, and Place*, pp. 35–37.
75 Nigel Bryant, ed. and trans., *Merlin and the Grail: Joseph of Arimathea, Merlin, Perceval: The Trilogy of Arthurian Prose Romances Attributed to Robert de Boron* (Cambridge: D. S. Brewer, 2008). For the status of this text as historical, see Richard Trachsler, 'A Question of Time: Romance and History', in *A Companion to the Lancelot-Grail Cycle*, ed. Carol Dover (Cambridge: D. S. Brewer, 2003), pp. 23–32.
76 William of Newburgh, *The History of English Affairs: Book 1*, ed. and trans. P. G. Walsh and M. J. Kennedy (Oxford: Aries and Philips, 1988), pp. 30–31. Hereafter William of Newburgh, *History*, I.
77 Karen Sullivan, 'On Recognizing the Limits of our Understanding: Medieval Debates about Merlin and Marvels', in *Uncertain Knowledge: Scepticism, Relativism, and Doubt in the Middle Ages*, ed. Dallas George Denery, Kantik Ghosh, and Nicolette Zeeman (Turnhout: Brepols, 2014), pp. 161–84 (pp. 167–70).
78 William of Newburgh, *History*, I, pp. 30–31.
79 Victoria Flood, 'Arthur's Return from Avalon: Geoffrey of Monmouth and the Development of the Legend', *Arthuriana* 25.2 (2015): 84–110.
80 William of Newburgh, *History*, I, pp. 34–37.
81 William of Newburgh, *History*, I, pp. 34–35.
82 Otter, *Inventiones*, p. 95.
83 Geoffrey of Monmouth, *Vita Merlini*, ed. and trans. John Jay Parry (Urbana, IL: University of Illinois, 1925).

84 Edward Peters, 'The Medieval Church and State on Superstition, Magic and Witchcraft: From Augustine to the Sixteenth Century', in *Witchcraft and Magic in Europe: The Middle Ages*, ed. Bengt Ankarloo and Stuart Clark (London: Athlone Press, 2002) pp. 173–245 (p. 207).

85 Harf-Lancner, *Les Fées au Moyen Âge*, pp. 203–04.

86 For the first attested appearance of the *tylwyth teg*, see 'Y Niwl Hudolus', in Helen Fulton, ed. and trans., *Dafydd ap Gwilym Apocrypha* (Llandysul: Gomer Press, 1999), pp. 118–21.

87 J. S. Brewer, James F. Dimock, and George F. Warner, eds, *Giraldi Cambrensis opera*, 8 vols (London: Green, Longman, and Roberts, 1861–91), IV, p. 49; Gerald of Wales, *The Journey through Wales and Description of Wales*, ed. and trans. Lewis Thorpe (Harmondsworth: Penguin, 1978), p. 286.

88 Flood, *Prophecy, Politics, and Place*, pp. 48–49; Victoria Flood, 'Prophecy as History: A New Study of the Prophecies of Merlin Silvester', *Neophilologus* 102.4 (2018): 543–59.

89 Siân Echard, 'Geoffrey of Monmouth', in *The Arthur of Medieval Latin Literature: The Development and Dissemination of the Arthurian Legend in Medieval Latin*, ed. Siân Echard (Cardiff: University of Wales Press, 2011), pp. 45–66 (p. 47).

90 See below, pp. 46–47. For distrust of the oral recitation of history, particularly poetic, in a continental context, see Spiegel, *Romancing the Past*, pp. 64–65. Spiegel dates the shift to the early thirteenth century, and it would seem that in my particular (slightly earlier) examples suspect orality is entirely dependent on the identification of the teller or source culture.

91 Augustine, *Works*, VI: *Letters*, trans. J. G. Cunningham (Edinburgh: T&T Clark, 1872), p. 16. Discussed in Alastair Minnis, 'Medieval Imagination and Memory', in *The Cambridge History of Literary Criticism*, III: *The Middle Ages*, ed. Alastair Minnis and Ian Johnson (Cambridge: Cambridge University Press, 2005), pp. 237–74 (p. 242). Minnis understands this reservation as one of the primary reasons for the absence of a fully developed medieval theory of 'imaginative aesthetics' (pp. 242–43). Unfortunately, there is no accessible Latin edition of Letter VII.

92 Brewer, Dimock, and Warner, eds, *Giraldi Cambrensis opera*, IV, p. 49; Gerald of Wales, *Journey through Wales*, p. 286.

93 Julie Orlemanski, 'Who Has Fiction? Modernity, Fictionality, and the Middle Ages', *New Literary History* 50.2 (2019): 145–70 (pp. 153–54).

94 Glyn S. Burgess, trans., and Elisabeth van Houts, ed., with Anthony J. Holden's text, *Wace: The 'Roman de Rou'* (St Helier: Société Jersiaise, 2002), pp. 236–37. The wider context of these lines, including analogous material in Chrétien de Troyes's *Yvain*, is discussed on p. 371.
95 See below, p. 153. For discussion of cross-cultural perceptions in relation to the *matière de Bretagne*, see Sharon Kinoshita, *Medieval Boundaries: Translating Difference in Old French Literature* (Philadelphia: University of Pennsylvania Press, 2006), pp. 105–32; Michael A. Faletra, *Wales and the Medieval Colonial Imagination: The Matters of Britain in the Twelfth Century* (New York: Palgrave Macmillan, 2014), pp. 99–133.
96 Douglas Kelly, *The Art of Medieval French Romance* (Madison, WI: University of Wisconsin Press, 1992), pp. 110–14. See further Spiegel, *Romancing the Past*, p. 63.
97 See, in particular, Ananya Jahanara Kabir and Deanne Williams, eds, *Postcolonial Approaches to the European Middle Ages: Translating Cultures* (Cambridge: Cambridge University Press, 2005), esp. 'Introduction: A Return to Wonder', pp. 1–21, which explores the complex conceptual relationship between the language politics of medieval and of modern postcolonialism, further to Ruth Evans, 'Historicizing Postcolonial Criticism: Cultural Difference and the Vernacular', in *The Idea of the Vernacular: An Anthology of Middle English Vernacular Theory, 1280–1520*, ed. Jocelyn Wogan-Browne, Nicholas Watson, Andrew Taylor, and Ruth Evans (University Park, PA: Pennsylvania State University Press, 1999), pp. 366–70. See further the essays collected in Jeffrey Jerome Cohen, ed., *The Postcolonial Middle Ages* (New York: Palgrave Macmillan, 2000), and works cited below in n. 102.
98 Bruce W. Holsinger, 'Medieval Studies, Postcolonial Studies, and the Genealogies of Critique', *Speculum* 77.4 (2002): 1195–1227.
99 Kabir and Williams, 'Introduction', pp. 1–2.
100 Homi K. Bhabha, 'Signs Taken for Wonders: Questions of Ambivalence and Authority under a Tree outside Delhi, May 1817', *Critical Inquiry* 12.1 (1985): 144–65 (p. 144); reprinted in *The Location of Culture*, 2nd edn (London: Routledge, 2004), pp. 145–74.
101 Bhabha, 'Signs Taken for Wonders', p. 147.
102 Helen Fulton, 'Romantic Wales: Imagining Wales in Medieval Insular Romance', in *Cultural Translations in Medieval Romance*, ed. Victoria Flood and Megan G. Leitch (Cambridge: D. S. Brewer, 2022), pp. 21–44. For accounts of medieval postcolonialism in relation

to the insular or archipelagic regions to which I am here indebted but which for the most part have not approached the question of Welsh co-creation, see Michelle R. Warren, *History on the Edge: Excalibur and the Borders of Britain* (Minneapolis, MN: University of Minnesota Press, 2000); Jeffrey Jerome Cohen, *Hybridity, Identity, and Monstrosity in Medieval Britain* (New York: Palgrave Macmillan, 2006); Jeffrey Jerome Cohen, ed., *Cultural Diversity in the British Middle Ages: Archipelago, Island, England* (New York: Palgrave Macmillan, 2008); Faletra, *Wales and the Medieval Colonial Imagination*.

103 For discussion of the association of supernaturalism with the 'Celtic', see Patrick Sims-Williams, 'The Visionary Celt: The Construction of an Ethnic Preconception', *Cambrian Medieval Celtic Studies* 11 (1986): 71–96; Helen Fulton, 'Matthew Arnold and the Canon of Medieval Welsh Literature', *Review of English Studies*, NS 63 (2011): 204–24; Byrne, *Otherworlds*, pp. 7–10.

104 Ana Pairet, 'Polycorporality and Heteromorphia: Untangling Melusine's Mixed Bodies', in *Melusine's Footprint: Tracing the Legacy of a Medieval Myth*, ed. Misty Urban, Deva Kemmis, and Melissa Ridley Elmes (Leiden: Brill, 2017), pp. 36–51 (pp. 40–41).

105 For recent discussion of the Middle English translations see Jan Shaw, *Space, Gender, and Memory in Middle English Romance: Architectures of Wonder in Melusine* (New York: Palgrave, 2016); Jan Shaw, 'Geographies of Loss: Cicilian Armenia and the Prose Romance of *Melusine*', in *Cultural Translations in Medieval Romance*, ed. Victoria Flood and Megan G. Leitch (Cambridge: D. S. Brewer, 2022), pp. 209–26; Jennifer Alberghini, 'Matriarchs and Mother Tongues: The Middle English *Romans of Partenay*', in *Melusine's Footprint: Tracing the Legacy of a Medieval Myth*, ed. Misty Urban, Deva Kemmis, and Melissa Ridley Elmes (Leiden: Brill, 2017), pp. 146–61. The English translations post-date the period of my study.

# 1

# 'Historia fabulosa': writing fairies in England and Wales

Wallia vero non a Walone duco, vel Wendoloena regina, sicut fabulosa Galfridi Arthuri mentitur historia.

(But 'Wallia' is not from Duke Gualo or Queen Guendolena as Geoffrey Arthur invents with fabulous history.)[1]

This chapter explores the politically contingent process of determining history from fiction in the Welsh-set fairy narratives of Walter Map's *De nugis curialium* (c. 1187–91) and Gerald of Wales's *Itinerarium Cambriae* (c. 1191). I suggest that both authors were reluctant to fully historicise Welsh legendary content, or at least those materials understood to be explicitly political (for which we might read: prophetic). This rests on a discomfort with Welsh background traditions understood by Walter Map and Gerald, however erroneously, to function analogously to the legend of Arthur's return from Avalon. In this context, the Avalon legend and its perceived analogues are not simply 'simulacra' of history, as has been suggested by previous critics, but rather are used to police the very limits of history.[2] This engagement with Welsh history-making and its disavowal is thrown into sharp relief in the final part of this chapter through comparison with the fairy *mirabilia* of William of Newburgh: marvellous narratives endorsed by their geographical localisation within England, and in relation to English witnessing communities, which present a clear example of the ways in which wonder and its limits were culturally determined.

Both Walter Map and Gerald have been associated, to use G. T. Shepherd's phrase, with the 'emancipation of the story': the twelfth-century movement of tale material from the monastery to the court, and across linguistic groups, by a new class of secular clerics.[3] This situation has been understood, most influentially by Otter, to have presented new possibilities for the interweaving of history with fiction, rooted in a new type of authorial self-awareness on the part of 'cleric-courtiers' whose sense of professional precarity fostered a certain loss of extra-textual meaning.[4] However, what seems to me most significant about the marvellous history-writing of this period is not necessarily the precarity of its authors, but the relationship of some of its most significant writers to Wales.[5] Both the *Itinerarium* and the Welsh-set narratives of *De nugis* are indicative of a late twelfth-century elite English interest in Welsh tale content – an extension of the colonial ambitions of this period, a claiming of the stories of Wales alongside its territory.[6] Narratives of the supernatural played an important part in this, for perceived Welsh supernaturalism demonstrated both the exceptional nature of the newly conquered Welsh territories (where marvels might be found) and the lack of sophistication of its people, and so a mandate for conquest.

## Arthurian precedents

In the twelfth century one of the chief categories of marvel through which the English appear to have approached Welsh narratives of the supernatural was the Arthurian. Further to discussion in the Introduction of the dimensions of the English-constructed legend of Avalon, we might note the very specific terminology and characteristics applied by authors working within England to Welsh historical narratives, coloured by supernaturalism. In his rejection of British (Breton or Welsh) oral accounts of Arthur, William of Malmesbury observed: 'Hic est Arthur de quo Britonum *nugae* hodieque delirant' ('This is Arthur of whose trifles the Britons rave'; my italics).[7] *Nugae* are, of course, the very business of Walter Map, so it is perhaps no surprise to see British trifles, among others, in *De nugis*. The word has been read previously in relation to fictionality, and as Shepherd notes it is also suggestive of the origins of tale content in oral cultures.[8] Notably, this is precisely how Welsh legendary material was conventionally understood by authors within England: of oral origin and dubious historical status. This perception does not appear to have been the product of a blanket distrust of orality, but rather, specifically, as we find in Map's Welsh-set anecdotes, of the narratives that might be recounted by Welsh witnesses, understood as the tellers of tall tales. (There may be a confusion here, on the part of English authors, between the fantastic narratives of the *cyfarwydd*, native storytellers, and historical content.)

Partial or total misunderstandings of aspects of Welsh legendary history in England appear to have informed a sense of the distinctiveness of Welsh accounts of the insular past – to which a third suspect quality was added, the poetic. William of Malmesbury continues his account of spurious Arthurian marvels associated with rejection of the legend of Arthur's return. He dismisses this as a fable, using another word commonly found in English rejections of Welsh legendary content, *naenia*: 'Sed Arturi sepulcrum nusquam visitur, unde antiquitas *naeniarum* adhuc eum venturum fabulatur' ('the sepulchre of Arthur is nowhere to be seen, whence ancient songs fable that he is still to come'; my italics).[9] Writing over fifty years later, William of Newburgh similarly referred to Merlin's prophecies as British 'nenias'.[10] P. G. Walsh and M. J. Kennedy translate this comment, 'divinationum illarum nenias' ('trifling songs of these prophecies'), as 'infantile stories of these prophecies', which certainly captures the spirit of these lines.[11] Yet the allusion to *nenias* may in both contexts have a double function, operating in relation to elegy, as we find in its classical usage.[12] It is certainly possible that these English authors may have been aware of a particular emotive context in which Arthurian and other legendary contents were consumed in Wales, such as *Englynion y Beddau* – which incorporate an account of the marvellous graves of Welsh heroes – and include potentially, the earliest account of Arthur's absent grave (although this is not necessarily suggestive of a legend of the hero's return) of the type with which William of Malmesbury may have been acquainted.[13] As Jenny Rowland has noted of Welsh saga poetry more broadly, the *Englynion* are intended to inspire a particular mode of elegiac affect than to precisely document historical events.[14] I do not mean to imply that medieval Welsh historical material was universally constructed in this vein, rather that certain aspects of lyric, legendary Welsh traditions may have been known, in limited forms, to English authors, and were received as embodying a set of historiographical and emotional cues in some respects alien, and anti-historical.

The association of Welsh elegy with fantasies of fairies appears to have emerged in the late twelfth century, not just in relation to legends of Avalon but in Geoffrey of Monmouth's account of the marvellous parentage of Merlin. The addition of the incubus to the Merlin legend was Geoffrey's innovation entirely; demons and fairies are not an explicit feature of Welsh historical-prophetic discourse. This is not to say that marvels were absent from Welsh legendary narratives – their distinctive character has been remarked by Fulton as a kind of 'magic naturalism', invested in the marvellous properties of Welsh flora, fauna, and landscape.[15] Among these we might include the Welsh *gormesoedd*: legendary supernatural plagues associated with different periods of the island's occupation and the disenfranchisement of the Welsh, which incorporated the contestation between the red dragon of the Britons and the white of the Saxons in Snowdonia, as reimagined in Geoffrey's *Omen of the Dragons*.[16] Discussed immediately prior to Merlin's revelation of the dragons of the *Omen* and the ensuing prophecies of insular gain and loss, Geoffrey's incubus is a true demonic marvel associated with presentiments of the fall of kingdoms (Vortigern's), a supernatural portent in the fashion of a *gormes* constructed for a non-Welsh audience. The incubus signifies in relation to a broader historical field. This is how Vortigern's magus positions the prophet's father in the *Historia*:

> In libris philosophorum nostrorum et *in plurimus historiis* repperi multos homines huiusmodi procreationem habuisse. Nam ut Apulegius de deo Socratis perhibet, inter lunam et terram habitant spiritus quos incubos daemones appellamus. Hii partim habent naturam hominum, partim uero angelorum, et cum uolunt assumant sibi humanas figuras et cum mulieribus coeunt. Forsitan unus ex eis huic mulieri apparuit et iuuenem istum in ipsa generauit.
>
> (I have discovered in the books of our philosophers and *in very many histories* that many people have been born in this way. As Apuleius records in *De Deo Socratis*, between the moon and the earth there

live spirits whom we call incubi. They are part human, part angel, and take on human form at will and sleep with women. Perhaps it was one of them who fathered this youth.) (VI. 544–50; *my italics*)

Although the magus, later bested by Merlin, speaks of false histories (Apuleius's position on the divinity of *daemones* was rejected by Augustine), the discourse invoked by Geoffrey is nonetheless clearly one of historiographical deliberation.[17] The historical incubus recurs in Geoffrey's later *Vita Merlini*, there not associated with Merlin's parentage but rather situated within the cosmic vision of the prophet Thelgesin (Taliesin). In his account of the order of creation, largely drawn from Isidore, Thelgesin observes of *cocodemons* (derived from the Greek *kakodaímōn*, bad spirits), the term here used for incubi:[18]

> Et sibi multociens ex aere corpore sumpto
> Nobis apparent et plurima sepe sequuntur
> Quin etiam coitu mulieres agrediuntur
> Et faciunt grauidas generantes pore prophano.
>
> (Often they assume a body made of air
> and appear to us and many things often follow.
> They even hold intercourse with women
> and make them pregnant, generating in an unholy manner.)
> (lines 781–84)

Although it is debatable just how historical Geoffrey understood material included in his ludic, poetic *Vita* to be, this passage is consistent with Augustine's understanding of the incubus (the aery bodies of demons) and the qualified historicity of demonic *mirabilia*. Thelgesin's account is given in the terms of historical reportage: after the demon is visible to us ('nobis'), 'plurima sepe sequuntur' ('many things often follow').

While it is sometimes argued that Geoffrey's legend of Merlin marks the beginning of medieval romance, I would suggest that in his use of the incubus Geoffrey is more interested in demonic history – an interest which precipitated a twelfth-century historiographical shift (albeit one with Augustinian and Isidorean precedents).[19] The *Historia* signifies the introduction of demonic elements into historical-prophetic narratives, particularly those tracing histories of loss. This was a model which, given the ontological indeterminacy of the works of demons (either material or illusory), could marginalise and discredit as much it might endorse. Depending on the point of application, it was either the subject of a profound misperception or a true historical event. This is one facet of the broader English co-option of Galfridian historiographical strategies into the later twelfth century, understood to be erroneous in application to Welsh subjects but largely credible in application to English.

## A Galfridian fable

Map had little interest in directly revisiting Geoffrey of Monmouth's material, but he does appear to have drawn on recognisable features of Galfridian historiography, held in conjunction with fairy (incubus/succubus) narratives and accounts of territorial-historical change.[20] In Distinctio I he writes of the British king Herla's journey to a subterranean otherworld at the invitation of a king described as a pan and a pygmy, from which he emerges generations later to find that the age of the Britons has passed and the people of the island speak a new language, English. Map concludes that spectral appearances of Herla's company, hereafter undying, were attested by Welshmen until the first year of the reign of Henry II when the spectres disappeared into (or were drowned in) the Wye.[21] Herla's unsettled court is presented as a counterpart to the court of Henry in a manner characteristic of the exemplary uses of *fabula* alongside *historia* elsewhere in Map's work, 'Vnam tamen et solam huic nostre curie similem fuisse fabule dederunt' ('One court and one only do stories tell of that is like our own').[22] The narrative functions as part of a fabulous sequence in which Map similarly compares the court to the infernal wheel of the classical Ixion. Yet what is most notable is the Britishness of this *fabula*, through which Map deliberates in meta- and intertextual terms on precisely what history is and is not.

The legend was almost certainly Map's own invention. There was no British King Herla and the name is rooted in a false etymology for the wild hunt, the Harlequin. It is, as Joshua Byron Smith notes, most feasibly an Anglo-Norman addition to the Matter of Britain, based on a continental tale type.[23] The fabulous anecdote draws on, and manipulates, historiographical cues familiar to twelfth-century readers of Geoffrey of Monmouth.[24] Although nowhere in this anecdote is Map's sense of insular history synchronous with that of Geoffrey, it has much in common with Galfridian historiographical strategy as it was understood by authors in England. For example, the rejection of content from Geoffrey's *Historia* in part appears to have been predicated on both fabulous monarchs and fabulous etymologies much like Map's Herla and Harlequin. In the roughly contemporary *Descriptio Cambriae*, Gerald of Wales queries the Galfridian etymology of Wales (Guales) from the British queen Guendolen, who ruled the Britons contemporary with their retreat into Wales in the face of Saxon advances. Gerald designates Geoffrey's account of the queen as 'fabulosa' rather than historical on the basis that no such ruler ever lived among the Welsh – although we might note that immediately prior to his rejection of the reality of Guendolen, Gerald draws on Geoffrey's account of Brutus, eponymous founder of Britain, as the stuff of history and true etymology.[25] This is the rejected truth claim which appears in the epigraph to this chapter, where Geoffrey, notably, takes the name of his most fabulous king, 'Arthur'. Gerald's term for this type of invention or fraud, 'historia fabulosa', presents a neat encapsulation of the hostile (and uneven) response to Galfridian *mirabilia* that appears to have emerged towards the end of the twelfth century: at once *historia* and *fabula*.

The observation of Herla's Saxon interlocutor at the end of the account may even be a direct nod to the controversial status of Guendolen (if we can assume that Gerald's critique reflects a familiar challenge to Geoffrey's *Historia* in this period). Like the concluding passages of Geoffrey's *Historia*, the Saxon's response stages the diminishment of British power in the island. He notes that by the time of Herla's return, the Saxons have been in the ascendency for two hundred years, and the earliest inhabitants of the island have fled, presumably, as we find in Geoffrey, to Wales. When Herla asks after the fate of his (unnamed) queen, the Saxon replies that he has never heard of a queen of that name except in fables: 'nomen autem illius non audiui regine, nisi quod aiunt hoc nomine dudum dictam reginam antiquissimorum Britonum que fuit uxor Herle regis, qui fabulose dicitur ...' ('but the name of that Queen I have never heard, save that they say that long ago there was a Queen of that name over the very ancient Britons, who was the wife of King Herla; who, the fable says ...').[26] The account of the pan follows. Again, wonder appears to be at the centre of this: the Saxon shepherd looks upon Herla with amazement ('admiracione'), while Herla is similarly amazed by the shepherd's revelation of his history, or rather his status as *fabula*. This is a moment of disjunction: a creature of fable here, briefly, asserts his reality, only to find himself fiction. In an episode which explicitly contests the historicity of (pseudo-) Welsh legendary imaginings, Map's Herla learns that he is as fabulous as the pan.

Map's concern, much like that of William of Malmesbury and William of Newburgh, is not just with the presence of marvellous content in Welsh representations of the past, but with a perception of the Welsh historical method itself as erroneous. The account of Herla reads in relation to contemporary rejections of the Avalon legend: the return of a preternaturally long-lived hero of the legendary British past from a mysterious otherworld. Indeed, the pan, elsewhere used in *De nugis* as a synonym for fairy, may here directly recall the discrediting twelfth-century fairy associations of Avalon.[27] Welsh history, understood in the Galfridian fashion, emerges as a space of marvels beyond credibility.

### The fairy mother in English history

Before we explore Walter Map's construction of a Welsh fairy mother, a narrative treated as a *fabula* in the vein of Map's pseudo-historical legend of Herla, I first approach Map's English fairy mother narrative as a standard of comparison. While within this framework scepticism is necessarily entertained, it is resolved as the anecdote reveals itself as wonderfully and inexplicably true, even aligned with the miraculous, all the while making use of distinctive Galfridian cues relating to the pattern of insular history.

Map writes of the encounter of the Saxon thane, Eadric Silvaticus (Wild), Lord of Ledbury North, who returning from a hunting trip passes through a forest and encounters a group of superhumanly large dancing ladies at a banqueting house (*fata* – fates or fairies). Filled with lust, Eadric abducts and rapes one of the dancers, despite the violent reprisals of her companions. As suddenly as they appeared, the dancers vanish, and only Eadric's abductee remains. The fairy then issues a prohibition, or more properly a prophecy, informing Eadric that while he does not chide her by mentioning her sisters, or the place in which he found her, he will have good fortune.[28] The couple marry, children are born, and word of Eadric's remarkable marriage reaches the court of William 'bastardus' (William I), then newly king, and the thane sees fresh honour. However, eventually Eadric offends his wife in the manner of the prophecy, and she disappears with all the children except one, a holy man named Alnoth. This departure marks a sudden decline in Eadric's fortune, and he ends his life poor and isolated. Alnoth, afflicted with paralysis, later receives a miracle cure from the relics of St Ethelbert at Hereford and makes a significant endowment of his patrimonial inheritance, in the saint's name, at Ledbury North.

Dimensions of the anecdote may well have had their origins in material in genuine local circulation, known by clerics at Hereford Cathedral, as with many of Map's narratives from the March.[29] The final movement of the narrative reads as an origin tale for the church of St Ethelbert in Ledbury, and in addition to a contracted version of the narrative in Distinctio IV at least one other legend of the church's endowment appears in this period, in association with another dynasty of the pre-Norman past: Gerald of Wales attributes it to Edwin, an earlier lord of Ledbury North, in the age of Offa.[30] A genuine historical figure, Eadric was remembered in the March, as throughout England, as a leader of English resistance against William.[31] In the early years of Norman rule he waged war in the March and laid siege to the Norman garrison at Shrewsbury in alliance with Bleddyn ap Cynan of Gwynedd.[32] He has been identified with 'Edric Salvage' who appears in the Domesday Book, who before the conquest held manors in Shropshire and Herefordshire. By the 1080s these lands were no longer in his possession, and neither had they passed to his heirs (if indeed he had any). It is uncertain whether these losses were due to the king's displeasure or Eadric's death.[33]

Following defeat at Chester in 1070, the culmination of a wave of resistance to Norman rule across northern England and Shropshire between 1069 and 1070, Eadric submitted to William. History does not record whether he broke this subsequent vow, but Map's anecdote suggests that he may have been remembered as having done so; if we understand Eadric's broken vow to his fairy bride as a re-imagining of his vow to William.

It has long been suggested that Map's narrative is related to a local saga of Eadric, and the anecdote has been tentatively compared to the post-conquest representation of Hereward's resistance to the Normans.[34] It is certainly possible that Eadric's supernaturalised account might be understood, as Elisabeth van Houts writes of the twelfth-century *Gesta Herewardi*, as a Latin record or reworking of a vernacular narrative that made 'an attempt to cope with the trauma of defeat' through a 'romanticisation' of the past.[35] Marvellous material would seem to be particularly well suited for such a purpose, if we follow Catherine A. M. Clarke's thesis that the marvels of twelfth-century historiography, which trouble and disrupt the chronicler's understanding of the natural world, have an explicitly metaphorical function, a testament to the limitations of language in the context of post-conquest trauma.[36] Yet this particular anecdote cultivates an impression of post-conquest continuity, not least in the naturalised appearance of William I as Eadric's king, who appears without comment. There is a sense of coherence in terms of the community within which, and about which, the account was generated, at once English and Norman, and we might recognise the presence of ciphers of a certain type of nostalgic Englishness carried into the Norman period, like the name of St Ethelbert and indeed Eadric himself. This, as we shall see similarly in the fairy narratives of William of Newburgh, is characteristic of early English fairy accounts.

For all its marvellous content, and its political allegorical function, the narrative is still presented as historical. It was presumably understood as mimetic in the respect that it memorialises a history of loss within living memory, *modernitas* – for Map the period of recent history (within one hundred years of the present) that might be recounted by oral reporters with an element of certainty.[37] Notably, the narrative uses Galfridian conventions, which we might regard as markers of historicity, however apparently fabulous. First and foremost among these is that most Galfridian of historiographical strategies, prophecy. The wording of the fairy's reproach is important: 'a die uero illa decides a felicitate, meque sublata detrimento frequenti deficies, diemque tuum inportunitate tua preuenies' ('In truth, from that day you will fall into ruin, and from my removal of good fortune you will suffer frequent defeat, and through your own impatience anticipate your day of death'). This functions not only as a curse but as an *ex euentu* prophecy related to Eadric's historical position: 'detrimentum' refers not only (as we find in James, Brooke, and Mynors's translation) to diminishment, or material loss, but to military defeat (the alternative translation I offer here; both meanings may well have been implied).[38]

Although his interest in the fantastic has been understood as evidence of his fiction-making – a self-conscious presentation of a collection of lurid *fabulae* – Map's prophetic fairy shares with Geoffrey's incubus an explicitly historical concern.[39] Map also shares his terminology ('a fantasia, quod est aparicio transiens, dicitur fantasma') with medieval Aristotelian understandings of sense perception.[40] For Aristotle the *phantasm* (*fantasma*), the likeness of sensory stimuli, especially visual images, impresses upon the imagination, like a signet ring upon wax, an impression thereafter stored in the memory (the term thus also refers to the 'memory image').[41] The material composition of the stimulus (what Aristotle terms its identity) is largely insignificant when it comes to the effect of the impression, the phantasmatic quality of which is always the same. This presents a striking analogy to the fairy – her own ontology is in many respects of less significance than that of the impression she leaves (here literalised): her offspring. In the account of Eadric, an impression is retained not in the individual memory but the collective: Alnoth's place in the historical record. Map's Aristotelianism is in this sense meta-historical. This point of genealogical/Aristotelian metaphor may not be Map's innovation alone. Although the heyday of medieval Latin Aristotelian translation and reception post-dates Map's period of writing – he wrote prior to Albertus Magnus and Thomas Aquinas's discussions of Aristotelian imagination, as well as significant Latinate interest in the Arabic translation of *De anima* by Ibn Sina (Avicenna) – he was near-contemporary with thinkers like William of Conches, teacher of another writer at the court of Henry II, John of Salisbury.[42] William extended the classical understanding of sense impression and imaginative and memorial retention in relation to maternity. A variation on Aristotle's wax seal, he wrote of the womb as a mint for coins by which the permeable imagination of the mother might change the shape or features of the child (or by which her infidelities might be revealed through multiple births which bear the impressions of different partners – a common medieval distrust of the mothers of twins).[43] Maternity is utilised more generally in medieval textual demonstrations of the material effects of visual stimuli upon the imagination and subsequently the body, such as the famous example of the pregnant woman who sees a strawberry and gives birth to a child with a strawberry birthmark: a thesis which finds a hyperbolic extension in concepts of the fairy's mother mark, in relation to which the later *Mélusine* romances have productively been read.[44]

The account of Eadric's fairy bride is not alone in Map's construction of the historical record. Map asks not only what we might make of Alnoth but 'ille Britonum de quo superius, in quo dicitur miles quidam uxorem suam sepellisse reuera mortuam, et a chorea redibuisse raptam?' ('the other narrative of the Britains [sic] told above, in which a knight is said to have buried his wife, who was really dead, and to have recovered her by snatching her out of a dance?').[45] This is an allusion to a knight of Brittany, who appears elsewhere in *De nugis*, who recovers his apparently dead wife from a fairy dance and has sons with her, the descendants of whom endure into the present age.[46] In its operations, this account comes very close to Augustine's formulation of wonder, where the marvellous is fundamentally indistinct from the miraculous, demonstrating the power of God who works effects beyond the limits of human understanding:

> Audienda sunt opera et permissiones Domini cum omni paciencia, et ipse laudandus in singulis, quia sicut ipse incomprehensibilis est, sic opera sua nostras transcendunt inquisiciones et disputaciones euadunt, et quicquid de puritate ipsius a nobis excogitari potest aut sciri, si quid scimus, id uidetur habere, cum totus ipse sit uera puritas et pura ueritas.

(Surely the acts and permissions of the Lord are to be hearkened to with all patience, and he is to be praised in every one of them; for as he is incomprehensible, so his works transcend our questioning and escape our discussion, and whatever can be thought or known by us about his purity (if we know anything at all) he is seen to possess, since he is wholly true purity and pure truth.)[47]

Much as Augustine invokes wonder at Etna as a testament to the divine inventiveness of God, and a reminder of the pains of hell, so do these paired fairy narratives demand contemplation of a God whose wonders are beyond rationalisation. The Breton narrative also has the additional effect, if the Augustinian correspondence might be understood as a broadly recognisable one, of cautioning the reader to remember his own soul and its post-mortem capacity for sensory experience: the Breton wife after all is among the material but phantasmatic dead.

Map's narrative entertains the doubt that forms a prelude to the confirmation of a marvellous historical event as a proper object of wonder. Just as the account of the Breton knight, apparently rooted in a reliable chain of witnesses, provides supporting evidence for the narrative of Eadric, there are other comparable narratives which, in the manner of Augustine's lamps of Venus, are noted by Map as the site of false wonder. Upon sighting the fairy company, Eadric recalls erroneous beliefs in classical gods:

> Gencium errores audierat, nocturnasque phalanges demonum et mortiferas eorum uisiones, Dictinnam et Cetus, Driadum et Lares, edoctus offensorum uindictam numinum, quomodo subitis eorum uisoribus subitas inferant penas.
>
> (He had heard the gentile errors, and nocturnal phalanxes of demons and deadly visions of them, of Diana and Cetus, of dryads and lares; he had learnt of the vengeance of the offended gods, how they might suddenly punish those who suddenly see them.)[48]

This is not only an invocation of classical *fabula* (the episode most obviously recalls the myth of Diana and Actaeon) but a paradigmatic medieval example of false belief: the 'Canon episcopi'. Named after its incipit, the 'Canon' first appears in Regino of Prüm's *Libri de synodalibus causis* (*c.* 906), denouncing the belief of certain wicked women seduced by the illusions of demons and by phantoms ('demonum illusionibus et fantasmatibus seductae') that they had ridden (or flown) by night on beasts in a hunt with Diana or Herodias, traversing great distances.[49] Again, we see a familiar engagement with apparently embodied demonic apparitions, the materiality of which is here denied – these demonic *phantasmata* are located in the interior world of the imagination alone. The 'Canon' was incorporated around 1140 in Gratian's *Decretum*, which became the primary body of teaching material for medieval canon law, and by the twelfth century it appears in conjunction with discussions of fairies.[50] Although the 'Canon' has been associated by some historians with genuine systems of popular belief, all the re-use of the motif can tell us with any certainty is the continued utility of the *Decretum*.[51] Indeed, in much of medieval Europe the night flight may never have been a subject of genuine folkloric belief. As Watkins notes, intended to encompass every possible conceivable religious deviation that might be encountered by the faithful, penitential traditions are rooted in the accretion of disparate sources, drawn from a medley of different times and places.[52]

The hunt of the 'Canon' is a purely illusory demonic experience, erroneously accepted as a material reality by women who, among the most unstable of medieval reporters, were the victims of demonic fictions.[53] The 'Canon' appears in a penitential context roughly contemporary with the production of *De nugis*. Writing between 1161 and 1184, Bartholomew Iscanus, the Bishop of Exeter, required one year's penance from those who believed it.[54] It was known among other writers of the Angevin court; for example, in his *Policraticus*, warning against dream interpretation, John of Salisbury wrote of Diana's dream as a demonic deception to which the uneducated and gullible were especially susceptible.[55] Eadric's very epithet might be understood to be synonymous with erroneous belief. In the twelfth century *silva* and its derivatives appear in a close relationship to ignorance. 'Sylvaticus' is a coinage from the earlier part of the century, in the writings of Orderic Vitalis, meaning 'agrestis, incultus, aspero ingenio' ('wild, uncultured, rude of wit'). As Ad Putter has observed, the twelfth-century revival of the classical distinction between the civilisation of the city (of which the court or castle is a later substitution) and the de-civilisation of the countryside (for which we might read forest or wasteland) prefigures (and informs) the association of the forests of Arthurian romance with the rustic, the violent, and the religiously deviant.[56]

But what is Eadric's possible error or deviation? Like the dreamers of the 'Canon' he perhaps mistakes a demonic illusion for reality and seeks material contact with it. In fact, he seeks the most material of all contact, the sexual, the genealogical, and the dynastic, the historical. Yet this contact does not prove to be an impossibility, and Eadric's experience is of a very different nature from that of the dream: it occurs within the boundaries of the historical real. What is more, as opposed to the delusions of the female dreamers of the 'Canon', in the logic of high medieval English historiography, Eadric's encounter would appear to be endorsed by its association with the experiences, and testimonies, of high-status men: not only Eadric himself, but William I, who witnesses the fairy's beauty, and the comparable account of the Breton knight.[57] In fact, Eadric's epithet might suggest not error (even as Map plays with this possibility), but a heightened state of corporeality. Map writes that Eadric takes the name 'sylvaticus' from his 'corpore agilitate et iocunditate uerborum et operum' ('bodily activity and rollicking words and deeds').[58] Quite what we might do with the term 'iocunditate' is a slightly vexed question; if we regard Eadric as the first in a chain of English reporters, it positions him as an unreliable witness and destabilises the credibility of the narrative.[59] But I suspect that Map's concern in these lines is not to destabilise the authority of his text so much as to emphasise the material, experiential, historical qualities of Eadric – a far cry from the ephemeral Herla.

This is not to say, however, that the episode is fully immersed in historiographical conventions. Its execution is multi-discursive. This is even and especially in Map's representation of Eadric's embodiment and engagement with sense impressions. In his description of Eadric's lovesickness, Map borrows from the conventions of the love lyric and early romance. At the sight of the fairy Eadric is struck by Cupid's arrow and wounded to the heart (the Aristotelian seat of memory):

> Hac uisa, miles accipit uulnus in cor, arcuque Cupidinis impressos uix sustinet ignes; totus accenditur, totus abit in flammas, et a feruore pulcherrime pestis aureique discriminis animosus efficitur.

(At the sight the knight received a wound to the very heart, and ill could bear the fires driven in by Cupid's bow; the whole of him kindled and blazed up, and from the fever of that fairest of plagues, that golden peril, he drew courage.)[60]

There is something fabulous about the classical frame of this allusion, which sits interestingly with the presumably intended parity of the episode as a whole with the myth of Diana and Actaeon, invoked in Map's account of gentile fables. The allusion to Diana in the 'Canon' itself, of course, drew on the fabulous resonance of classical mythology. Further, the suddenness of Eadric's desire is a familiar trope in early romance, not least in relation to the female fairy who is a fictionalised magnification or exaggeration of the presentation of the courtly lady within *fin'amor* conventions.[61] However, love at first sight is a type of embodied wonder response with some measure of extra-textual referentiality. An arresting experience tied to ocular stimuli, and a secularisation of divine affect, it was an expression of wonder entirely familiar to Map's courtly audience. Indeed, courtly love is a prime example of a set of culturally constructed emotional cues or scripts, with a clear set of recognisable bodily responses.[62] We might read it similarly to its less benign counterpart (to which it is very close in its operation) the evil eye, which Karnes eloquently observes as an excellent example of 'the realness – the sheer bodiliness – of imaginative effect'.[63] It is a component of the experiential, in the sense that it represents an encoding (however fictionalised) of love and desire familiar to Eadric's readers. Notably, this representation of love and wonder finds no parallel in Map's Welsh fairy analogues, where emotional cues and processes are situated outside the familiar codes and conventions of his Plantagenet readership.

I do not mean to suggest in the above analysis that Map's account of Eadric and his fairy bride is straightforwardly historical; rather it draws on historiographical components and emerges, however complexly, in a plausible relationship to the historical real – or rather, is entertained as a phantasmatic historical event. In the composite allusions of the narrative, history does on occasion meet romance, although the fairy is not herself necessarily first and foremost here a romance component. Once accepted as a demon, and what is more a prophetic one, she has a place within history, even as a historical signifier – not least in relation to a history of loss.

## A Welsh fairy portent

In comparison to the history of Eadric, the first 'aparicio' of Distinctio II is framed as pure *fabula*, and in many respects its emotional cues and analogical comparisons are far less complex. Map positions the narrative as a 'portentum nobis Walenses referunt' ('a portent related to "us" [presumably, an audience in England] by the Welsh').[64] Given Map's uses of Isidore elsewhere in *De nugis* (not least in his figure of the pan), he may have had in mind Isidore's gloss on the portent. For Isidore, as it seems for Map, while 'portentum' is read in relation to foreshadowing ('portendere'), the portent is not necessarily historical, and Isidore gives a wealth of fabulous classical examples including gorgons and chimeras, drawn from Augustine's examples of the *fabulae* that populate the undiscerning poetic imagination.[65] Certainly, as we shall see presently, Map approaches the final component of the tale as a mendacious fiction. Indeed, Map asserts at the very beginning of the account that it is not a miracle, the result of divine intervention, but another class of phenomena entirely: 'Aliud non miraculum sed portentum' ('Another not miracle but portent').[66]

The account opens with Wastin Wastiniauc's consecutive visions on three clear moonlit nights of bands of women dancing in his field by 'stagnum Brekeniauc' (Llyn Syfaddon). Acting upon clues from the women themselves, Wastin catches one of them, marries her, and has children with her. The lady places an otherworldly prohibition on the union: if Wastin rushes towards the sounds of shouting beyond the River Llynfi and strikes her with his bridle, she will return to the water. In due course the taboo is broken, and the lady flees to the lake with all the children, save one named Triunein Nagelauc ('crooked Triunein'), presumably a comment on physical stature or health: we might note Triunein as an analogue to Alnoth, and their remarkable physicalities may well be a variation on the mother mark as we find it in the later *Mélusine* romances, although certainly here less obviously romanced.⁶⁷ (*Triunein*, 'thirteenth', suggests that he is one of a large family). Triunein grows up to serve the King of Deheubarth, a geographical designation originally covering the whole of south Wales. The king boasts of the strength of his raiding parties, to which Triunein replies that the force from Deheubarth is not equal to the power of his own countrymen, the men of Brycheiniog. After being imprisoned for his impudence, it is elected that Triunein use his knowledge of his home kingdom to lead the raiding party. Here Brycheiniog is identified as the kingdom of the legendary Brychan (here named 'Breauc'), orientating the tale firmly in the pre-Norman insular past. Brychan defeats the raiding party with savage barbarity, and builds three monuments: from their left hands, their right hands, and their penises – the latter not simply a signifier of the emasculating capacities of defeat, but a figure of genealogical foreclosure.

The final part of the tale is most interesting for what it might tell us about the boundaries of *historia* and *fabula*. Map reports a rumour that Triunein was rescued from the battle by his mother and lives with her in the lake, but dismisses this as an 'error' concerning a missing man:

> Quod autem aiunt Triunein a matre sua seruatum, et cum ipsa in lacu illo uiuere unde supra mencio est, imo et mendacium puto, quod de non inuento fingi potuit error huiusmodi.
>
> (But whereas they tell that Triunein was saved by his mother and still lives with her in the lake I mentioned, I think it must even be called a lie, for such a fiction could easily be invented about a man who was missing.)⁶⁸

This term recalls the 'gencium errores' known to Eadric, but there is, potentially, a specifically Welsh dimension to this, and the tale may show us one of the ways in which Map is reading Welshness.⁶⁹ He invokes some very particular cultural-linguistic cues about the boundaries of history, in which Welsh fictions are fundamental. His concern with Welsh 'mendacium' echoes pervasive attitudes about another ostensibly Welsh otherworld, and a hero's marvellous survival of a mortal battle: the legend of Arthur and Avalon. These are precisely the terms that William of Newburgh applied to the demonic prophecies of Geoffrey's Merlin, which he understood to be invented by Welsh liars, 'mendacibus esse conficta', for the benefit of the curiosity ('curiositatem') of a Welsh audience without wisdom ('minus prudentium').[70]

The connection between the Welsh and deception is pervasive in *De nugis*. In a sequence of materials on Wales (separate from his account of Wastin and Triunein), Map recounts various negative national characteristics of the Welsh: vengefulness (we might think of Brychan), boastfulness (of which Triunein is guilty), and gullibility (the Welsh audience who believe in Triunein's survival).[71] It has been suggested, given Map's reference to 'compatriote nostri Walenses' at the very beginning of his Welsh sequence, that here we see an overture to the fictionality of *De nugis* through the destabilisation of its author's authority. As Otter has suggested, like the words of the Cretan who maintains that all Cretans are liars, can the words of Walter the Welshman be trusted?[72] However, a distinction between Map and the Welsh is made explicit, and he identifies himself, much as does Gerald, as a man of the March, 'qui marchio sum Walensibus' ('who is a dweller on the marches of Wales'), more closely aligned with the Norman, later English, colonial project in Wales than with the Welsh.[73]

Throughout *De nugis*, Map does not appear to deploy his Welsh content with the playful de-centring of his historical authority primarily in mind. Rather, I suggest that he approaches Welsh content as particularly instructive in his interpretation of marvels, the limits of wonder, and his meditations on doubt and belief. We might note similarly his account of the credulity of the Welsh king Llewellyn ap Gruffydd, who took a report of a dream of his wife's adultery as a reality and demanded recompense from the dreamer. He was paid not in the cows demanded by the Welsh laws, but in the reflection of the same in the lake of Brycheiniog, the location of the account of Wastin and Triunein.[74] The account is simultaneously a testament to Welsh gullibility and literalism, an inability to distinguish dreams from reality, and fact from fiction. It also stages the ways in which in a Welsh context, the inability to discern fact from fiction inspires violent responses, even political crises – a common trope that we shall see in Gerald of Wales's writing also.

The differentiation between *historia* and *fabula* is a competency that Map understands to be fundamental to his audience in England. Throughout *De nugis*, Map emphasises the powers of discernment that his elite readers must necessarily employ. In a specific invocation of the *humilitas* topos, excusing his rough style, Map makes clear precisely the type of active reading he expects from his courtly audience:

> Singuli lectores appositam ruditatem exculpant, ut eorum industria bona facie prodeat in publicum. Venator uester sum: feras uobis affero, fercula faciatis.
>
> (Every reader must cut into shape the rough material that is here served up to him, that thanks to their pains it may go forth into the world with a fair outside. I am but your huntsman. I bring you the game, it is for you to make dainty dishes out of it.)[75]

Like a huntsman who has brought meat for the table, the author is not required to determine how his text will be consumed: his courtly audience must decide what to make out of, and how to deploy, his material (and we might think of Map's understanding elsewhere of both *fabula* and *historia* as sites of moral and behavioural exempla). While, as Echard notes, this is a suggestively metafictional manoeuvre, it also rests on a practice of historical discernment in which Map understands his readers to be engaged.[76] It is perhaps no surprise that this passage concludes Distinctio II of *De nugis*, which contains the text's most sustained account of apparitions; and it is certainly possible that the figure of the huntsman recalls the *fabula* of Herla in Distinctio I. Yet in his Welsh material – in which his register is both ethnographic and colonial – Map is quick to provide a moral and political gloss, identifying the lie, the fable, for his readers in highly charged terms. This identification must be understood as aligned with the pre-existing suspicions and prejudices of an audience in England. The author tells his audience what they already know.

For Map the bad faith of the Welsh operates in a double sense, both political and religious. Remembering that the account of Wastin is not a miracle, we might compare Map's dismissal of the possibility of Triunein's marvellous survival to the movement of faith we find in the account of the knight of Brittany, who restores his fairy-taken wife from the dead, read in relation to the account of Eadric. These episodes, beginning with Wastin's succubus bride, read in *De nugis* as a part of a sequence, and we might assume, given the connective nature of the work's commentary and titles (if we can understand the latter to be Map's own), that they were intended to be read cumulatively. This accretion of evidence traces a movement towards belief, which necessarily incorporates a component of scepticism. As Steven Justice notes of the treatment of medieval miracles, doubt is an essential predicate of belief, exercised as part of a process of compiling, and combining, evidence. Justice finds in Thomas Aquinas's thirteenth-century analysis of belief a neat encapsulation of the parameters of belief and doubt from Augustine onwards:

> Aquinas endorses Augustine's definition of 'believe' (credere) as 'think with assent' (*cum* assensu cogitare), because *cogitare est simul coagitare*: roughly, 'to think is to bang things together.' ... Simultaneous with and inseparable from the act of believing, 'a certain motion of doubt befalls the believer'.[77]

Like the author of the medieval miracle, in the context of a collection of ostensibly corroborating material, Map necessarily broaches scepticism (his Welsh-set fairy narrative) before he can approach belief (in his English and Breton narratives).

The introduction of doubt reads most obviously as a response to anxieties about the Welsh cultural field of the narrative. Map distinguishes between those British materials concerning marvellous survivals and post-mortem returns which he is prepared to credit, and those which he is not. The Breton material, concerning the dead wife, is somehow more palatable as a miracle than its Welsh analogue, the survival of Triunein. Perhaps this is because it concerns the survival of a wife rather than a warrior-son; or perhaps Map, writing in England, associated politically volatile British material concerning post-mortem survival with Wales rather than Brittany. Most obviously, however, the Welsh tale is necessarily a fabulous *portentum* precisely because it threatens to be a political prophetic one. Triuenin is, like Arthur, a hero from the remote insular past returning from an aquatic otherworld – not over the water, but under it. Although it is likely to bear no relationship to any genuine Welsh construction of Arthurian prophecy, there are legends of supernatural mothers in Welsh-language contexts, such as the otherworldly Rhiannon, mother of Pryderi, Prince of Dyfed, who appears in the *Mabinogi*, and brief literary allusions to the mother of Gwyn ap Nudd, Lord of Annwfn, the Welsh Otherworld, which in a number of its representations is, like the fairy's home, underwater.[78]

The plausibility of a Welsh-language background source for the tale of Wastin has seen in-depth discussion by Brynley F. Roberts, who notes the use of the Welsh territorial suffix, -iauc, -iawg, in the name Wastin Wastiniauc, a variation on the name Brychan Brycheiniog (who therefore appears in doubled form in the tale); and the odd inclusion of the place name 'Reynos, id est Brecheniauc', a plausible corruption of the Welsh 'Rheinwg'. This is suggestive of the scrambling of Welsh names in oral transmission to a non-Welsh-speaking author or informant. Roberts has suggested that we might draw on Welsh background material of this type to arrive at something approaching Map's Welsh legendary-historical source. He proposes a narrative of Wastin Wastiniauc, lord of the region around Llangorse Lake who became the protagonist of a 'Melusina-type legend' in order to explain the conception of a local hero, Triunein, regarded as an opponent of the new dynasty of Brychan. His disappearance suggests that he marks a terminal line and the ascendency of the children of Brychan.[79] Brychan appears as the subject of Welsh literary, and almost certainly oral, hagiographic interests in this period, and so it is perhaps remarkable that Map denies any hagiographic function to the narrative. In the twelfth-century *Vita Sancti Gundleii* (the life of the father of St Cadog), Brychan is a warrior opponent of Arthur, Kai, and Bedevere.[80] In *De nugis* Map's Brychan material follows a legend of St Cadog, and Map may have been aware of the *Vita*, although equally he may simply have perceived a commonality in terms of the localisation of both narratives in south Wales. Material on Brycheiniog also appears in Gerald's *Itinerarium Cambriae*, which corresponds to Welsh Triads concerning the king's saintly descendants.[81] Gerald notes local customs he witnessed in Brycheniog celebrating the feast day of Brychan's daughter, St Eluned;[82] and his opportunity to see the unbreakable torque of St Cynog (Brychan's son), which cursed a thief who tried to break it for its gold.[83] An association between

Brychan and hostilities with the kingdom of Deheubarth are a matter of clerical interest in an early thirteenth-century Cambro-Latin text, *De situ Brechaniauc*, which was probably based on a twelfth-century original. This includes an account of the Irish origins of Brychan and the deeds of his son Clytguin, who invaded the whole of south Wales and is commonly identified as 'Conqueror of Deheubarth'.[84] Map's narrative appears to present a variant of this historical tradition, where Brychan himself is seen to defeat the men of Deheubarth. Although the place name Deheubarth was an anachronistic designation in the age of Brychan, it is a feature not only of Map's tale but of Welsh Brychan material also.[85]

Brycheiniog occupied an important place in the geo-political imaginary of post-conquest south Wales in the late twelfth century. Map appears to have been aware of an itinerary of marvels very similar to that described by Gerald of Wales, who writes of Llyn Syfaddon as a site of a marvel associated with Welsh or regional sovereignty. Gerald notes a tongue-in-cheek exchange between the Welsh prince Gruffydd ap Rhys and a small company of Marcher lords in the reign of Henry I, concerning Welsh beliefs in an omen of Welsh rule connected with the lake.[86] Certainly, the waters of the region do appear to have been connected with notable portents. Elsewhere in the *Itinerarium*, Gerald observes that where the River Llynfi meets the Wye, we find an area called 'Glasbury', where the water turns green during periods of violence. The water changed colour most recently, Gerald writes, before the invasion of Hywel ap Maredudd in 1136.[87] Gerald probably has, characteristically, a confected Welsh etymology in mind (the medieval Welsh use of the word 'glas' encompasses green and sea-green), although this association may not necessarily have been original to the author.

In the late twelfth century this complex of wonderful and legendary, highly specifically geographically situated, content may have seemed particularly timely. The cantref was held by the English crown and came under threat from raiding parties led by Rhys ap Gruffydd and his sons in the late 1180s, as in Map's anecdote, from Deheubarth.[88] Wastin's otherworldly encounter might be understood in relation to the changing shape of political power in a contested region of south Wales – a regional violence that took new forms in the late twelfth century, and may well have inspired new re-imaginings of old material. There is potentially a strategy of genuine memorialisation at work in Map's tale, of not only the legendary past but more recent history, much as we find in his account of Eadric, which is similarly elegiac. The likely common function of these tales, and their tonal correspondence in this final respect, is notable, and yet one is understood as credible while the other is not – which is to say, one 'emotional community' might memorialise its history, while the other's is nothing more than fantasy. In the rejection or acceptance of this material, the question is precisely who has the right to such narratives, whose history might be mourned or celebrated.

## False prophecies

From an English perspective, Welsh legendary-historical content of a type with the Triunein narrative was understood as a sphere of false wonders, analogous to the rejected Avalon legend. However, a twelfth-century association between the wonders of Geoffrey of Monmouth's writings and Welsh historiography may not have been an English fabrication entirely. Galfridian content is brought into a suggestive proximity with Welsh oppositional cultures in Gerald of Wales's anecdote concerning the Caerleon soothsayer Meilerius (a Latinisation of the Welsh name Meilyr), in his *Itinerarium Cambriae*.[89] The anecdote treats events of the early 1170s, told in relation to Gerald's journey through Caerleon with Archbishop Baldwin in the spring of 1188.[90] It moves between English-occupied Caerleon and the largely Welsh-populated surrounding territory of Nether Gwent, and recalls the marvellous events that preceded Hywel ap Iorwerth's seizure of Caerleon Castle in 1173 and his defeat by the Earl of Pembroke in 1174.

Gerald's account relates the demonic encounters of Meilerius, who in the conclusion of the narrative appears in the retinue of Hywel at Caerleon. Like Map's accounts of Wastin and Eadric, the anecdote traces the rise and fall of the fortunes of a particular historical, or legendary-historical, individual associated with the influences of a succubus (or fairy), and in this case incubi also.

The composition of Gerald's account is roughly contemporary with Walter Map's, and it is Gerald's longest treatment of demonic encounters in the *Itinerarium*. Gerald writes of Meilerius's ability to discern truth and falsehood through the activities of demons. Upon possessing the Welshman, they flee at the appearance of St John's Gospel; at the introduction of Geoffrey's *Historia*, however, the demons surround the pages of the book, a characteristic mark of suspicion of Geoffrey's text, at least when situated in a Welsh context.[91] Just as Merlin's prophetic powers were understood to have a demonic provenance, so do Meilerius's – although here we find not an incubus father but a succubus lover. Meilerius derives his occult abilities from a sexual encounter with a demon, who appears to him in the form of a beautiful woman the prophet has long desired, before revealing herself to be 'hispidam et hirsutam', a recollection of the pans and *pilosi* of Isidore – from the perspective of a Latin cleric of the 1180s, a fairy (*fata*). Following his account of Meilerius's succubus encounter, Gerald notes the soothsayer's interaction with further demons, beginning with an incubus who frequented Nether Gwent. The appearance of the incubus was understood as a portent of war, and 'patriae turbationem magnam'. In this case, the upset it heralds is an attack by Hywel.[92] Meilerius encounters demonic manifestations at monasteries across south Wales also, before he and his demons accompany Hywel to Caerleon, where, despite his demons' prophetic assurances to the contrary, Meilerius dies in the siege.

Otter has suggested that the doubt that accompanied some aspects of Geoffrey's *Historia* by this period was fundamental to Gerald's account of Meilerius, which is not simply indicative of Gerald's inconsistent relationship to Galfridian source material but is executed as an intertextual joke. Reading Meilerius and his demons as a 'multilayered Liar joke', Otter perceives a destabilisation of Gerald's double sources – the demonically inspired Meilerius and the lying Geoffrey – and so of the authority of Gerald himself.[93] However, as Laurie A. Finke and Martin B. Shichtman note, we might tread with care in assuming that Gerald's work contains deliberate forays into fiction-writing, which are intended to be understood as distinct from history: 'Of course the historian is free to call into question her own truth claims, even to undermine them in the name of irony, but in doing so, she risks being understood by audiences to be doing something entirely different from history.'[94] Rather, while truth-claims might be understood as rhetorical strategies, they correspond to a mode of history-writing intelligible to an intended audience who share the frame of reference of the author, not least in terms of the distinction between (and again, Finke and Shichtman's terminology is in keeping with my own) 'valid and invalid truth claims; in other words, how they distinguish between fact and fiction'.[95] This is first and foremost, I suggest, in relation to the authority of witnesses and source texts, and in this account Gerald engages directly with Welsh historical and prophetic discourses, understood in relation to Geoffrey's Welsh political intersections and, potentially, early oppositional uses.[96]

The precedent of the *Historia* is fundamental to Gerald's account of Meilerius, which echoes the movement from the incubus narrative of *Historia* VI to the prophecies of *Historia* VII. The events detailed in the anecdote are not necessarily solely the product of Gerald's Galfridian interests but may even be suggestive of the early Welsh assimilation of Galfridian content within a pre-existing prophetic and historical culture, or at the very least, a perception of common political prophetic investments. As Jean Blacker observes, the *Prophetiae* appear to have been approached by some contemporary commentators in, or working in the orbit of, post-conquest England as a potentially seditious Welsh text – an apprehension similar to that of William of Newburgh, noted above.[97] While this is in part a prejudicial and reductive English construction (there was more to Welsh political culture than Geoffrey!), elements of the *Prophetiae* do cohere relatively closely with a Welsh prophetic tradition forecasting the exile of the English from the island and the territorial re-conquests of the Welsh princes.[98] We might note in particular also the Galfridian associations of Caerleon, Meilerius's home and the site of the narrative's conclusion. Arthur's principal court in *Historia* X, Caerleon, was, Juliette Wood has argued, a focus of relatively early Welsh imaginings of independence after Geoffrey.[99] Although we can only hypothesise here, it is not impossible that genuine Welsh engagements with Galfridiana were in place prior to the earliest attested Welsh translations of the *Historia*, the *brutiau* (c. 1250). Certainly, there is evidence of one Welsh translation of the prophecies, integrating an engagement with the Latin commentary tradition, which we might tentatively place in the first half of the thirteenth century.[100] This also reads suggestively in relation to Meilerius's engagements with Cistercian houses in Wales, important locations in the dissemination of Galfridian translation and native prophecy into the later Middle Ages.[101] Certainly, Meilerius's situation in the proximity of a physical book of the *Historia* (if we understand this to be more than a rhetorical strategy) feels significant.

The Welsh relationship to prophecy, Galfridian or not, is explored in the narrative in relation to an erroneous wonder response. Gerald remarks how peculiar it is that Meilerius could see the prophetic demons when others could not and concludes that he must have had a particular quality of vision. Although this might be read as a claim for Meilerius's fraudulence, Gerald's understanding of his false prophecy is more subtle than this. He writes that 'spiritus' cannot be seen with 'oculis corporalibus', unless they themselves have assumed bodily form ('assumptis corporibus'), as presumably is the case in Meilerius's demonic sexual encounter – potentially the same phenomenon of which Map writes in his account of Eadric. Poised between belief and doubt, what matters is the meaning of the invisible movement of spirits, for which Gerald notes a familiar biblical precedent:

> Sed forte corporali visione miraculosa visi sunt haec. Cuiusmodi visione rex Balthasar in Daniele vidit manum scribentis in pariete, 'Mane, Techel, Phares', hoc est, appensum, numeratum, divisum; qui et eadem nocte regnum partier et vitam amisit.

> (Possibly they could be seen only by some miraculous sort of physical vision, rather like that in the Book of Daniel, when King Belshazzar saw the writing on the wall: 'Mene, Tekel, Peres', which means 'numbered, weighed, divided'. That same night Belshazzar lost both his kingdom and his life).[102]

This is not a straightforward exegetical reading of the episode at Caerleon. Although like Belshazzar, Hywel loses his kingdom, Meilerius is emphatically not a second Daniel. Negative comparisons to Daniel were invoked by Gerald's contemporaries, such as

John of Salisbury, in relation to the false, potentially demonically inspired, interpretations of dreams.[103] Meilerius's prophetic vision is 'miraculosa', in the sense that demonic power operates, as Map reminds us also, under licence from God, but Meilerius's faith in the demon (rather than God) is misplaced. This process might be understood in relation to 1 Corinthians 12.10, a passage much discussed from the Church Fathers onwards, concerning the practice of spiritual discernment, which asks whether a prophet is inspired by God or by the devil.[104] This is here applied not simply to the individual prophet, but to the marvellous occurrences associated with him, and the value at which they ought to be held. Gerald gestures to a process of phenomenal discernment: some marvels are an exercise in faith; while others are demonic forgeries and reveal bad faith, both political and religious.

Gerald's specific formulation of Meilerius's vision is almost certainly indebted to Augustine's commentary on Genesis, *De Genesi ad litteram*, which was much used in high medieval exegesis to comment on biblical prophecy and its interpretation.[105] Augustine outlines a concept of spiritual vision, the apprehension not of bodies 'but the likeness of bodies'.[106] This is distinct from bodily vision and the intellectual vision by which we grasp abstract principles, but like bodily vision spiritual vision is necessarily subject to intellectual vision in its interpretation. Gerald suggests that Meilerius, while in possession of spiritual vision, is lacking in intellectual vision, and mistakes demonic fictions for truth. This is the more interesting, given that Meilerius is, or at least his demons are, associated in the wider anecdote with a very clear process of spiritual and historical discernment (in their reaction to the pages of the *Historia*); it is, however, misdirected, and the anecdote exemplifies the demonic appeal of the false or fabulous as a kind of inverted spiritual discretion. What is at issue is not the reality of the demonic phenomenon itself, then, but the dangers of belief in mendacious demonic prophecy, as a point of intellectual and spiritual misidentification. Meilerius and indeed Hywel are the paradigmatic misguided Welsh audience of history and prophecy: like William of Newburgh's naive Welshmen, they are deceived by the false prophecies of demons.[107]

## Galfridian fables

There is a further example suggestive of Gerald's use of Augustinian concepts of wonder and perception in his treatment of ostensibly Welsh fairy narratives. Elsewhere in his *Itinerarium*, Gerald writes of the Swansea priest Elidorus (Elidyr), who wandered into the underground kingdom of little men the size of pygmies (a synonym for fairies, as we find in Map's account of Herla) and who, after stealing a piece of their treasure, was banished from their company forever.[108] Gerald notes that the fairies speak a form of 'curuum Graecum' ('crooked Greek') close to Welsh. The narrative functions in a clear relationship to a false Welsh etymology Geoffrey of Monmouth gives in *Historia* I, which attributes the origins of the Welsh language to the period the Trojans spent in Greek captivity following the fall of Troy, reading *Cymraeg* as 'curuum Graecum', from the Welsh *cam* (crooked) and *Graeg* (Greek, which in this compound lenites).[109] As Michael Faletra has noted, this narrative constructs a fantastic representation of the otherness of Wales and the Welsh language, grounded in Galfridian principles, but I suspect that the account is also invested in the dimensions of Welsh belief and its relationship to historical narrative.[110] Galfridian history, understood as Welsh *mirabilia*, is aligned with classical fable. Like Herla and Triunein, Elidorus emerges as a cipher for Welsh credulity, tied to fantasies of fairyland.

Unable to determine the reality status of the event, Gerald concludes with an overture to Augustinian wonder:

> Sin autem interpositae relationis de veritate quid sentiam scrupulosus investigator inquiras, cum Augustino respondeo, admiranda fore divina miracula, non disputatione discutienda: nec ego negando divinae potentiae terminos pono, nec affirmando eam quae extendi non potest insolenter extendo.

> (If scrupulous reader, you inquire about the truth of this account, I respond with Augustine that divine miracles are there to be wondered at, not disputed or discussed. If I reject it, I place a limit on God's power. If I affirm it, I presumptuously go beyond the bounds of credulity, and that I am not able to do.)[111]

It has been suggested that this assessment stages an epistemological crisis. Gerald, like Gervase of Tilbury, whose fairy narratives are discussed in Chapter 2, has been associated with the new Platonism of the late twelfth and early thirteenth centuries, and has been understood to be interested not in the world as a space of Augustinian marvel or miracle but in the regularity of nature: a pattern-drawing which narratives of this type frustrate.[112] Yet Gerald's wonder is not necessarily uncritical, and, indeed, neither was that of Augustine. For Augustine not all apparent marvels were truly wonderful, and the historian must exercise his best judgement based on personal experience and the credibility of his reporters.

Gerald's stated source for the anecdote is David II, Bishop of St David's (Gerald's uncle), who, Gerald writes, spoke with Elidorus. Although Gerald gives no sense of the bishop's assessment of the anecdote, it is telling that David is not invoked as an authenticating witness who speaks to the truth-claim of the phenomenon; rather he emerges as an investigator of a type with Gerald, who questions Elidorus on the details of the fairies' language. In approaching this anecdote, we cannot but note Gerald's personal investment in the bishopric, and his conviction that St David's needed a bishop with sufficient knowledge of Welsh practices, such as his uncle, or Gerald himself.[113] The primary implication of the narrative would appear to be that it takes a bishop who recognises the (false) marvels of the Welsh to perform his pastoral role to the fullest. (We might note Gerald's concerns elsewhere in his writings about religious deviations among the Welsh houses, on occasion associated with demonic or marvellous signifiers. For example, in his account of Meilerius, Gerald notes the prophet's role in the fall of the abbot of Strata Marcella, exposing, through his demonic knowledge, the abbot's sexual improprieties.[114])

Gerald concludes that, as Augustine observes, this is a type of narrative which 'nec affirmanda plurimum, neque neganda decreverim' ('cannot be greatly affirmed, nor may it be denied').[115] Gerald's allusion to the pygmies reads in relation to the uncertainty that Augustine expressed about the existence of the Plinian peoples. In Book XVI of *De civitate Dei*, Augustine asks whether we ought to believe in 'quaedam monstrosa hominum genera, quae gentium narrat historia' ('certain monstrous races of men described in pagan history').[116] Among those he notes, 'alios statura esse cubitales, quos Pygmaeos a cubito Graeci vocant' ('There are men only a cubit high whom the Greeks call pygmies from their word for cubit').[117] This interest in Greek origins and etymologies reads suggestively with Gerald's fairy account, and it is certainly possible that Gerald has an Augustinian as much as a Galfridian precedent in mind. Notably, Augustine concludes his discussion of the Plinian peoples:

> Quapropter ut istam quaestionem pedetemtim cauteque concludam: aut illa quae talia de quibusdam gentibus scripta sunt, omnino nulla sunt; aut si sunt, homines non sunt; aut ex Adam sunt, si homines sunt.
>
> (Let me then tentatively and guardedly state my conclusion. Either the written accounts of certain races are completely unfounded or, if such races do exist, they are not human; or, if they are human, they are descended from Adam.)[118]

As I suggested in the Introduction, Augustine appears to have engaged in an understanding of optional belief as concerns those marvels from pagan antiquity that cannot be substantiated but do not directly contradict scripture.[119] The Plinian peoples belong to this category, and belief in them would be a matter of taste, even whimsy, and, we might assume, not particularly deeply held. As Lorraine Daston and Katharine Park note, the existence of such creatures, situated on the margins of the world, was impossible to prove or disprove, and so the 'facticity' of their existence does not appear to have been a particularly fraught question. However, when situated closer to home, marvels were subject to greater scrutiny.[120]

Localisation, therefore, matters. While Gerald's uncertain conclusion might be suggestive of optional belief in the manner of Augustine's account of the Plinian peoples, his language more obviously corresponds to the scrutiny that we find in Augustine's accounts of those near-marvels that ought to be corroborated or rejected as *fabulae*. The truth is one that a 'scrupulosus investigator', properly educated in the distinction between history and fiction, will be able to discern, for all the familiar fabulous cues are present: Welshmen who believe in insular otherworlds, populated by *panae*, pygmies, and fairies. Gerald's Welsh believers become Augustine's credulous Romans.

## The cultural limits of wonder

The historical status of twelfth-century fairy marvels was determined in relation to the location and community context of the reported (or allegedly reported) phenomenon. This appears particularly illuminatingly in the writings of one of Gerald's and Walter Map's contemporaries, William of Newburgh. While William rejected the Welsh *fabulae* of Geoffrey of Monmouth, he credited the plausibility of other marvels rooted in English localities and witnessing communities. In a sequence of English-set *mirabilia* towards the end of Book I of his *Historia rerum Anglicarum*, William gives a brief narrative concerning a peasant of Northumberland who, much like Gerald's Elidorus, stumbles into a fairy feast inside a hill. The peasant, returning home from the next village a little drunk, hears singing within a hillside, and wonders at ('miratus') the sound. Stepping through a door in the hill, he sees a fairy feast, from which he steals an unusual cup, which finds its way to Henry I, and subsequently the kings of Scotland, before it is returned to Henry II (for William, the marvel, and its material proof, rightly belong in an English context). Although the peasant's drunkenness might seem to discount the episode as a properly historical object of wonder – or at least serve as a caveat similar to the rusticity of Map's Eadric – like Map, William provides a number of authenticating details, including high-status witnesses, and in conclusion notes, 'Haec et hujusmodi incredibilia viderentur nisi a dignis fide testibus contigisse probarentur' ('these and similar stories would appear incredible were they not proved to have happened by witnesses worthy of belief').[121] Like Map, William establishes a reliable chain of reportage and material historical evidence (the cup) and concludes, much as does Map, that we might understand such events in relation to demonic activity under God, which credibly might be held as components of the historical real as long as we are duly aware of their demonic origins.[122]

The chapter that immediately precedes the account of the fairy cup in the *Historia* is a richer and more complex case in terms of the function of wonder and delineation of belief, which, William suggests, rests on something other than demonic activity. We might read this in relation to what James Wade terms the 'adoxic' position of the fairy, here held at a remove from demonic signification.[123] This is the account of the green children of 'Vlfputes' (Wolf Pit, later Woolpit), which although little noted has a close functional similarity to Map's fairy mother narratives. William's account of the green children might be (and indeed has been) understood as a paradigmatic example of the operation of medieval wonder and, I would suggest, its culturally determined limits.[124] With a mind to the latter, it has been previously read in relation to concerns about sex and marriage across cultural lines and the 'fragility of English identity', most notably in relation to Welsh indigeneity.[125] However, this account appears to carry none of the same anxieties about Welsh *fabulae* that we find elsewhere in this period, and William is precisely the type of author (given his account of Geoffrey's *Historia*) who we might expect to be animated by this. Rather than detecting in this tale a crisis of English identity, I suggest that we might read it as an Augustinian embrace of wonder, reflecting the limits of reason and a movement of faith – a reading rooted in the Englishness of William's scene and, relatedly, of his reporters.

William repeats an apparently widespread oral report of the discovery of two green children in a field in East Anglia during a harvest in the reign of King Stephen. The children, who speak no English, initially reject the food of the villagers, and can eat only beans. After some time, they adapt: their skin pigmentation changes, and they acquire both the English language and Christianity. They later identify themselves as the inhabitants of St Martin's Land, a subterranean realm beyond the light of the sun, who have followed the sound of the bells of St Edmund's Cathedral in Bury to Woolpit. After baptism, the male child sickens and dies, but the female child, the older of the two, survives:

> ... sorore incolumi permanente et nec in modico a nostri generis feminis discrepante. Quae nimirum postea apud Lennam, ut dicitur, duxit maritum, et ante annos paucos superstes esse dicebatur.
>
> (... the girl continued unaffected, differing not even in the slightest way from the women of our own kind. She certainly took a husband and Lynn, according to the story, and was said to be still living a few years ago.)[126]

There is a clear thematic correspondence between William's account of the green girl's survival and Map's allusion to the fairy-born, such as Alnoth, 'bona se successione perpetuant' ('[who] themselves endure in good succession').[127] Functionally aligned both with the children of the fairy or succubus mother and with the mother herself, the green girl endures, potentially even as part of a branch on a family tree.[128]

The introductory sentences of the anecdote are worth quoting in full for William's somewhat fraught, but nonetheless definitive, sense of his account's validity within his wider historical project:

> Nec praetereundum videtur inadutium a seculis prodigium quod sub rege Stephano in Anglia noscitur evenisse. Et quidem diu super hoc, cum tamen a multis praedicaretur, hesitavi, remque vel nullius vel abditissimae rationis in fidem recipere ridiculum mihi videbatur, donec tantorum et talium pondere testium ita sum obrutus ut cogerer credere et mirari quod nullis animi viribus possum attingere vel rimari.

> (I think that I should not omit mention of a prodigy unprecedented since the world began which is known to have occurred in England during Stephen's reign. I myself had protracted doubts over this, though it was reported by many, and it seemed to me absurd to accept as genuine an event whose rational basis was non-existent or most obscure. But finally I was so overwhelmed by the weighty testimony of so many reliable people that I was compelled to believe and marvel at what I cannot grasp and investigate by any powers of the mind.)[129]

William's terminological choices matter: from Isidore onwards we read that *prodigia* belong in the realm of *historia*.[130] As William wrote in the 1180s, the reign of Stephen fell within the range for which one would conventionally expect (within the norms of medieval historiography) oral rather than written records. As Partner observes, to William's doubts about the reality status of the children 'the resolution is testimony', the weight of oral evidence from trustworthy reporters.[131] William concludes that the girl lives still, 'ut dicitur' ('according to the story'). As Spiegel notes of this phrase, it functions as a familiar tag in the writing of recent history among high medieval Latin authors, indicating a 'received stock of stories [which] there was practically no sound ground for banishing from the narrative'.[132] Indeed, this is precisely the point: this anecdote is part of the received stock of English oral history, in a way in which Welsh prophecy, of course, is not.

The unanchored alterity of the green children presents William with an opportunity to reflect on English custom, food, language, and even skin colour as here normatively perceived (English children are not green). We might note also the English geography of the account. Woolpit, William notes, is only four or five miles from the monastery and cathedral of St Edmund, which take their name and foundation narrative from a pre-conquest English saint, and the bells of which can be heard in the village. William appears to invoke a scene of pseudo-pre-colonial, even nostalgic, Englishness that we might read in relation to Map's account of Eadric, although as there, the events of the Norman invasion are perhaps not forgotten. As Jeffrey Jerome Cohen has noted, St Martin's Land recalls the name of the abbey at Battle, the walls of which bleed each year on the anniversary of the Battle of Hastings – a phenomenon recorded by William elsewhere in his chronicle.[133] Further, as Clarke has astutely observed, we might also read this narrative, set in the reign of Stephen, in relation to the traumas of the English Anarchy, expressible only in marvel and metaphor.[134] Yet as much as the unclosed marvel signifies the uncertainties and ruptures of recent history, it also frames a distinct conceptualisation of Englishness, and of English narrative and emotional communities. The credibility of the marvellous account is rooted in its local source culture, which is understood as continuously English on both sides of 1066. Even the place name itself, William assures his reader, is suitably English: he begins his account with the English etymology of 'Wlfpittes'.

For William, the reality or truth status of marvellous phenomena depends on the credibility of the historian's reporter(s). Nonetheless, his account is coloured by an awareness of the apparent impossibility of the phenomenon in question. Watkins suggests that like a number of episodes in twelfth-century historical writing that might be understood to be in some sense ambiguous (within which he includes Map's fairy materials), William finds himself 'prisoner' to the ambiguities of the account of the green children.[135]

However, William is adamant that the anecdote is worthy of record and deserves a place in his history – and this is not in spite of its anomalous status but because of it. As in the case of the Augustinian marvel, the cause of the event lies beyond human knowledge, although it appears to signify in relation to a deeper truth, relating to divine wonders that inspire a movement of faith: a supreme example of the affective qualities of medieval wonder. Indeed, the central wonder within William's account is the supra-rational nature of religious belief itself. It reads as a literalised movement of faith, conceived in geographical terms. The green children are drawn from St Martin's Land to East Anglia by the sound of the bells of St Edmund: 'cumque in sonitum illum quem admirabamur animo intenderemus, repente, tanquam in quodam mentis excessu positi, invenimus nos inter vos in agro ubi metebatis' ('When we turned our attention to the sound which caused us surprise [wonder], it was as though we were out of our minds, for we suddenly found ourselves among you in the fields where you were harvesting').[136] Wonder in the Augustinian tradition is, of course, perspectival, and the sound of the bells is as much a source of wonder for the green children as the children themselves are for the people of Woolpit. (Incidentally, we might note William's particular interest in the wonder-provoking capacity of aural phenomena, as opposed to the purely ocular – we might think similarly of the voices that draw his Northumbrian peasant towards the fairy hill.) The perspectival re-orientation the anecdote achieves is fundamental to its wider function: through the wonder of the children, the reader is invited to wonder at the bells, that is, their deeper significance.

It is, in a very distinctive way, a conversion narrative, and these connotations are certainly not subtle. The scene of the harvest recalls the Parable of the Sower in Matthew 13 and its apocalyptic interests in the status of souls. However, the movement of the children towards the bells functions as more than an exegetical metaphor: it is a comment on the place of wonder within medieval history-writing. William presents the reading of historical event, and subsequently the writing of history, as enacting an invisible movement of faith: the children wonder (and indeed, wander) and reach towards the church bells, much as William and his readers wonder and strive towards the mysterious divine workings that the anecdote exemplifies. This is a celebration of an Augustinian wonder response, which draws on a distinctively religious mode of affect. Wonder is here distinct from curiosity, and we might remember William's concern elsewhere with the unthinking *curiositas* of the Welsh. William engages with wonder in the vein of medieval thinkers like Bernard of Clairvaux, who warned of the dangers of idle curiosity. In his distinction between *admiratio* and *imitatio* (a caution against inappropriate mimicry of the asceticism of saints), Bernard described wonder in relation to a golden goblet from which we absorb the drink (the virtues of wonderful exempla) but give back the cup (that is, wonder without imitation).[137] We might here think in very literal terms of the fairy cup stolen by William's Northumbrian peasant, which ought to have been given back (and this is precisely the type of literalism I suspect we find in William's metaphors); but also of the status of the green girl, which is beyond rationalisation. The function of this, if applied to William's narratives, of course, is not to admire the secular wonder as one would a saint, but to seek its deeper, Augustinian meaning – drink it deep, and give it back unrationalised. This type of positive reflection on the wonder response is not found in accounts of analogous Welsh fairy narratives by historical writers working in England, where wonder is always misplaced and offers nothing revelatory for the historian beyond its denial.

## Conclusion

This chapter has explored the ways in which authors in England determined the credibility of fairy narratives and their place in the historical record. I have suggested that the discernment practised by these authors rests on a culturally determined construction and rejection of wonder. This analysis presents a departure from previous work on the politics of 'common emotions', for it traces not emotional cues in the political sphere but rather the reading of wonder itself as the grounds of political contestation, determined by the status of the historiographical conventions of one community when received by another.[138] This occurred in line with a very specific conceptualisation rooted in Augustinian wonder, with a particular utility in application to Welsh, or perceived Welsh, historical content: inappropriate wonder. This material demands a reappraisal of previous hypotheses concerning the relationship between the supernatural mother narratives of medieval Wales and those of England – approached not as sources but as analogues.[139] The first chapter in the development of the historiographical fairy by authors in England is not a straightforward appropriation of Welsh supernatural content but a rejection of Welsh discourses of wonder, both real and perceived, which determined the parameters of the English fairy tradition.

## Notes

1 Brewer, Dimock, and Warner, eds, *Giraldi Cambrensis opera*, VI, p. 179. My translation.
2 Wade, *Fairies in Medieval Romance*, pp. 39–72.
3 Shepherd, 'Emancipation of the Story'.
4 Otter, *Inventiones*, p. 127.
5 For a succinct statement on commonalities in the cultural backgrounds, educations, and careers of Gerald and Walter Map, see A. K. Bate, 'Walter Map and Giraldus Cambrensis', *Latomus* 31 (1972): 860–75, although Bates's claims of Gerald's plagiarising of Map have been disputed. Gerald belonged to a Marcher family, descended from the Norman lord Gerald de Barri and Nesta, a Welsh princess of Deheubarth. Gerald's cultural context is discussed in Michael Richter, *Giraldus Cambrensis: The Growth of the Welsh Nation* (Aberystwyth: National Library of Wales, 1996); Michael Richter, 'Gerald of Wales: A Reassessment on the 750th Anniversary of his Death', *Traditio* 29 (1973): 379–90; Brynley F. Roberts, *Gerald of Wales* (Cardiff: University of Wales Press, 1982); Robert Bartlett, *Gerald of Wales: A Voice of the Middle Ages* (Stroud: Tempus, 2006). While Gerald on occasion made much of his Welsh heritage, this was done selectively and his cultural sympathies for the most part appear to have been aligned with English interests, and later French. See further Flood, *Prophecy, Politics, and Place*, pp. 20–22, 44, which argues for the political strategies that governed Gerald's Welsh engagements, beyond previous understandings of Gerald's hybridity as a state of cultural crisis. Walter Map's background is less certain, but like Gerald he came from the March and his cultural affiliations

were largely Anglo-centric, although it has been suggested that his surname may be a version of the Welsh patronymic 'mab'. For a summary of relevant scholarship on Walter's name, see Joshua Byron Smith, *Walter Map and the Matter of Britain* (Philadelphia: University of Pennsylvania Press, 2017), p. 13.

6 The writings of Latin clerics present a viable, even a dominant, mode of transmission of Welsh material into English and French contexts during this period, potentially more so than the model of the Breton *conteur*, for which we do not possess the level of evidence that scholars once assumed. See further Echard, *Arthurian Narrative in the Latin Tradition*; Byron Smith, *Walter Map and the Matter of Britain*; Patrick Sims-Williams, 'Did Itinerant Breton "Conteurs" Transmit the Matière de Bretagne?', *Romania* 116 (1998): 72–111.

7 Thomas Duffus Hardy, ed., *Willelmi Malmesbiriensis Monachi Gesta regum Anglorum atque historia novella*, 2 vols (London: Sumptibus Societatis, 1840), I, p. 51.

8 Shepherd, 'Emancipation of the Story', p. 54.

9 Hardy, ed., *Willelmi Malmesbiriensis Monachi Gesta regum Anglorum*, II, p. 110.

10 William of Newburgh, *History*, I, pp. 30–31.

11 William of Newburgh, *History*, I, pp. 30–31. For attestation of the term's use as 'trifling song, popular song, or nursery rhyme', see 'nenia', in D. Howlett and R. Ashdowne, eds, *Dictionary of Medieval Latin from British Sources*, 17 vols (Oxford: Oxford University Press, 1975–2013); online edition compiled by R. E. Latham, https://logeion.uchicago.edu/nenia [last accessed 31 March 2021].

12 'Nenia', glossed as a 'funeral song, a song of lamentation', in Charlton T. Lewis and Charles Short, eds, *A Latin Dictionary* (London: Harper Brothers, 1898), www.perseus.tufts.edu/hopper/text?doc=nenia&fromdoc=Perseus%3Atext%3A1999.04.00599 [last accessed 31 March 2021].

13 For discussion of this *englyn*, which describes Arthur's grave as 'anoeth bid' ('the world's wonder'), and its possible meanings (an absent grave *or* a marvellous one) see Patrick Sims-Williams, 'The Early Welsh Arthurian Poems', in *The Arthur of the Welsh: The Arthurian Legend in Medieval Welsh Literature*, ed. Rachel Bromwich, A. O. H. Jarman, and Brynley F. Roberts (Cardiff: University of Wales Press, 1991), pp. 33–72 (pp. 49–50). For comment on its relationship to William of Malmesbury see Flood, 'Arthur's Return from Avalon', p. 93.

14 Jenny Rowland, *Early Welsh Saga Poetry: A Study and Edition of the Englynion* (Cambridge: D. S. Brewer, 1990), p. 2. For discussion

of the absence of narrative poetry from Middle Welsh, its relationship to oral performance, and its 'emotional charge' see Brynley F. Roberts, 'Oral Tradition and Welsh Literature: A Description and Survey', *Oral Tradition* 3/1–2 (1988): 61–87 (pp. 63–64). As Oliver Padel has suggested, in its origins Welsh Arthuriana may have always been intended to be legendary rather than strictly historical – a space of marvellous stories rather than recollection of historical events. O. J. Padel, 'The Nature of Arthur', *Cambrian Medieval Celtic Studies* 27 (1994): 1–31.

15 Helen Fulton, 'Magic and the Supernatural in Early Welsh Narrative: *Culhwch ac Olwen* and *Breuddwyd Rhonabwy*', *Arthurian Literature* 30 (2013): 1–26. See further Victoria Flood, 'The Supernatural Company in Cultural Translation: Dafydd ap Gwilym and the *Roman de la Rose* Tradition', in *Cultural Translations in Medieval Romance*, ed. Victoria Flood and Megan G. Leitch (Cambridge: D. S. Brewer, 2022), pp. 65–84.

16 Rachel Bromwich, ed. and trans., *Trioedd Ynys Prydein: The Triads of the Island of Britain* (Cardiff: University of Wales Press, 2014), pp. 90–93. For further discussion of the *gormesoedd* and their relationship to the *Omen of the Dragons*, see Patrick Sims-Williams, 'Some Functions of Origin Stories in Medieval Wales', in *History and Heroic Tale: A Symposium*, ed. Tore Nyberg, P. M. Sorensen, and A. Trommer (Odense: Odense University Press, 1989), pp. 91–131 (pp. 105–06); Brynley F. Roberts, 'Geoffrey of Monmouth and Welsh Historical Tradition', *Nottingham Medieval Studies* 20 (1976): 29–40 (p. 33). For detailed discussion of imaginings of historical loss in Wales, see Aled Llion Jones, *Darogan: Prophecy, Lament and Absent Heroes in Medieval Welsh History* (Cardiff: University of Wales Press, 2013).

17 Augustine, *City of God*, III, pp. 152–55.

18 For discussion of this terminology see Michael J. Curley, *Geoffrey of Monmouth* (New York: Twayne Publishers, 1994), p. 124.

19 Heng, *Empire of Magic*, p. 49.

20 For notice of the absence of directly Arthurian material in *De nugis*, see Elizabeth Archibald, 'Arthurian Latin Romance', in *The Arthur of Medieval Latin Literature: The Development and Dissemination of the Arthurian Legend in Medieval Latin*, ed. Siân Echard (Cardiff: University of Wales Press, 2011), pp. 132–45 (p. 143).

21 For discussion of this alternative translation, see Byron Smith, *Walter Map and the Matter of Britain*, p. 92. This is read in relation to a short narrative of the Herlethingus in Distinctio IV (Walter Map, *De nugis*,

pp. 370–71), a nocturnal company of the dead who are attacked by Welshmen. We might note the apparent credulity of a Welsh attempt to kill creatures of fable.

22  Walter Map, *De nugis*, pp. 30–31.
23  Byron Smith, *Walter Map and the Matter of Britain*, pp. 97–103. For the association of Map with French-language content, in his own time, see an address from Gerald of Wales to Walter Map in Brewer, Dimock, and Warner, eds, *Giraldi Cambrensis opera*, III, p. 165. Discussed by Spiegel, *Romancing the Past*, pp. 66–67.
24  Watkins, *History and the Supernatural*, p. 208, suggests that the generic indeterminacy of *De nugis* gives Map some freedom in whether he is dealing with *historia* or *fabula*, but Map appears to for the most part have a clear sense of what he is doing with each of these categories – and their combining presents a deliberate comment on the boundaries of the historical and the credible.
25  Brewer, Dimock, and Warner, eds, *Giraldi Cambrensis opera*, VI, p. 179. This is offered by Geoffrey alongside the etymology that Gerald here accepts, the derivation of Welsh from the Old English *welas* (foreigner), a 'barbarous' term which is distasteful to Gerald, who elsewhere in this passage makes much of the Trojan origins of the Welsh.
26  Walter Map, *De Nugis*, pp. 30–31.
27  We might note, for example, the account of fairies, also identified as neutral angels and demons in Map's account of the fairy helper of the heretic knight Eudo, Olga. Olga speaks of the illusions of such beings, who assume new forms to trick humans: 'Nos antiquitus populi decepti dixere semideos aut semideas, pro forma corporis assumpti uel apparicionis nomina ponentes discretiua sexus. Ex locis autem incolatus uel permissis officiis distinccius appellamur Monticole, Siluani, Driades, Oreades, Fauni, Satiri, Nayades, quibus ex eorum inposicione presunt Ceres, Bacus, Pan, Priapus et Pales' ('In old times the deluded people called us demi-gods or demi-goddesses, giving us names distinctive of sex, agreeable to the shape of the body or the appearance we put on: and from the places we dwelt in or the functions allowed to us we are called Hill-men, Wood-men, Dryads, Oreads, Fauns, Satyrs, Naiads, and our rulers (thus christened by the people) Ceres, Bacchus, Pan, Priapus, and Pales') (Walter Map, *De nugis*, pp. 320–21). A similar account of fairies as 'neutral' angels (those who sided neither with God nor with Lucifer at the Fall) is found in *South English Legendary*, although these might return to heaven on Judgement Day. The latter is discussed by Firth Green, *Elf Queens and Holy Friars*, pp. 23–24.

28 For discussion of the operation of the fairy's 'taboo' on the level of the narrative logic of romance, see Wade, *Fairies in Medieval Romance*, pp. 109–46; Byrne, 'Fairy Lovers'. As Byrne notes, complete and lasting fulfilment is something of a narrative dead-end, and thus the narrative is contingent on the prohibition. Its *telos* here is also overtly historical (prophetic).

29 Juliette Wood, 'Walter Map: The Contents and Context of *De nugis curialium*', *Transactions of the Honourable Society of Cymmrodorion* (1985): 91–103 (p. 94).

30 Brewer, Dimock, and Warner, eds, *Giraldi Cambrensis opera*, III, pp. 422–23. Discussed in relation to the tale of Eadric in James Hinton, 'Notes on Walter Map's *De nugis curialium*', *Studies in Philology* 20 (1923): 448–68 (p. 453). For discussion of the hagiographical interests of both accounts, see Joshua Byron Smith, 'Gerald of Wales, Walter Map, and the Anglo-Saxon Past of Ledbury North', in *New Perspectives on Gerald of Wales: Texts and Contexts*, ed. Georgia Henley and Joseph McMullen (Cardiff: University of Wales Press, 2018), pp. 63–77.

31 Hinton, 'Notes on Walter Map's *De nugis curialium*', pp. 452–53; Susan Reynolds, 'Eadric Silvaticus and the English Resistance', *Bulletin of the Institute of Historical Research* 54 (1991): 102–05 (p. 103).

32 Reynolds, 'Eadric Silvaticus and the English Resistance'; Ann Williams, *The English and the Norman Conquest* (Woodbridge: Boydell Press, 1992), pp. 91–92; Ann Williams, 'Eadric the Wild', *Oxford Dictionary of National Biography* (Oxford, 2005), www.oxforddnb.com/index/101008512/Eadric-the-Wild [last accessed 31 May 2020]; Hinton, 'Notes on Walter Map's *De nugis curialium*', pp. 451–54.

33 Hinton, 'Notes on Walter Map's *De nugis curialium*', p. 452.

34 Hinton, 'Notes on Walter Map's *De nugis curialium*', p. 452; Reynolds, 'Eadric Silvaticus and the English Resistance', p. 104.

35 Elisabeth van Houts, 'The Memory of 1066 in Written and Oral Traditions', *Anglo-Norman Studies* 19 (1996): 167–79 (p. 173).

36 Catherine A. M. Clarke, 'Signs and Wonders: Writing Trauma in Twelfth-Century England', *Reading Medieval Studies* 35 (2009): 55–77 (esp. pp. 61–65).

37 Walter Map, *De nugis*, pp. 122–25. For the customary expectation of oral, rather than literary sources, in the writing of recent history in the Anglo-Latin tradition, see Partner, *Serious Entertainments*, pp. 186–87.

38  Walter Map, *De nugis*, pp. 156–57.
39  Tony Davenport, 'Sex, Ghosts, and Dreams: Walter Map (1135?–1210?) and Gerald of Wales (1145–1223)', in *Writers of the Reign of Henry II: Twelve Essays*, ed. Ruth Kennedy and Simon Meecham-Jones (New York: Palgrave Macmillan, 2006), pp. 133–50 (pp. 136–37).
40  Walter Map, *De nugis*, pp. 160–61. For the full quotation see above, p. 15.
41  Aristotle, *On the Soul, Parva naturalia, On Breath*, trans. W. S. Hett (Cambridge, MA: Harvard University Press, 1957). See Mary Carruthers, *The Book of Memory: A Study of Memory in Medieval Culture* (Cambridge: Cambridge University Press, 2008), pp. 18–19; Janet Coleman, *Ancient and Medieval Memories* (Cambridge: Cambridge University Press, 1991), p. 20. For discussion of medieval reception of this concept from Ibn Sina to Thomas Aquinas see Carruthers, *Book of Memory*, pp. 58–89.
42  Dorothy Elford, 'William of Conches', in *A History of Twelfth-Century Western Philosophy*, ed. Peter Dronke (Cambridge: Cambridge University Press, 1988), pp. 308–27.
43  Elliott, *Fallen Bodies*, p. 41. This remained a feature of deliberations on foetal development, particularly relating to the birth of monsters, into the early modern period. For an overview of the literature concerning this later period see Daston and Park, *Wonders and the Order of Nature*, p. 415.
44  Douglas Kelly, 'The Domestication of the Marvelous in the Melusine Romances', in *Melusine of Lusignan: Founding Fiction in Late Medieval France*, ed. Donald Maddox and Sara Sturm-Maddox (Athens, GA: University of Georgia Press, 1996), pp. 32–47 (pp. 40–41).
45  Walter Map, *De nugis*, pp. 160–61.
46  Walter Map, *De nugis*, pp. 344–45.
47  Walter Map, *De nugis*, pp. 160–61.
48  Walter Map, *De nugis*, pp. 156–57. Departing from Brooke and Mynors's translation, I translate 'Cetus' as the name of the classical aquatic god, a counterpart to Diana, and presumably to be read in association with the dryads.
49  Quotations from Aemilius Ludwig Richter, ed., *Corpus juris canonici*, 2 vols (Leipzig: Tauchnitz, 1879), I, p. 1030. My translation. See also John T. McNeill and Helena M. Gamer, eds. and trans., *Medieval Handbooks of Penance* (New York: Columbia University Press, 1938), p. 331; Alan Charles Kors and Edward Peters, eds and

trans., *Witchcraft in Europe 400–1700: A Documentary History* (Philadelphia: University of Pennsylvania Press, 2001), p. 189. The meaning of the second name given in the 'Canon', Herodias, remains obscure: it has been suggested, variously, that it is a reference to a Germanic deity or to the biblical wife of King Herod. See further Edward Peters, *The Magician, the Witch and the Law* (Philadelphia: University of Pennsylvania Press, 1978), pp. 71–78.

50 Kors and Peters, eds and trans., *Witchcraft in Europe*, pp. 60–63; McNeill and Gamer, eds and trans., *Medieval Handbooks of Penance*, pp. 314–21. For a brief discussion, see also Kors and Peters, eds and trans., *Witchcraft in Europe*, pp. 203–04; Saunders, *Magic and the Supernatural*, p. 82.

51 The most famous argument for the relationship of the dream to the world of popular belief is that of Carlo Ginzburg, who positioned the night flight as a component of a long-enduring vein of trans-Eurasian shamanism, which informed the inquisitorial construction of witchcraft. This position is carefully and convincingly critiqued by Michael Bailey, 'Medieval Concept of the Witches' Sabbath', *Exemplaria* 8.2 (1996): 419–39 (pp. 424–26). For an overview of Ginzburg's findings, see Carlo Ginzburg, 'Deciphering the Sabbath', in *Early Modern European Witchcraft: Centres and Peripheries*, ed. Bengt Ankarloo and Gustav Henningsen (Oxford: Clarendon Press, 1993), pp. 121–38.

52 Watkins, *History and the Supernatural*, pp. 77–78.

53 For discussion of the status of different types of witness, see Partner, *Serious Entertainments*, p. 118; Watkins, 'Memories of the Marvellous in the Anglo-Norman Realm', pp. 99–101.

54 McNeill and Gamer, eds and trans., *Handbooks of Penance*, p. 349.

55 John of Salisbury, *Frivolities of Courtiers and the Footprints of Philosophers: Being a Translation of the First, Second, and Third Books and Selections from the Seventh and Eighth Books of the 'Policraticus' of John of Salisbury*, ed. and trans. Joseph B. Pike (New York: Octagon Books, 1972), p. 87. For discussion of John's distrust of dream interpretation, see Steven F. Kruger, *Dreaming in the Middle Ages* (Cambridge: Cambridge University Press, 1992), p. 16.

56 Ad Putter, *Sir Gawain and the Green Knight and French Arthurian Romance* (Oxford: Clarendon Press, 1995), pp. 41–44.

57 The authenticating invocation of a high-status witness is similarly discussed in relation to William of Newburgh by Partner, *Serious Entertainments*, p. 123. See further Otter, *Inventiones*, p. 105.

58 Walter Map, *De nugis*, pp. 154–55.

59 Notably, Map does write at least one joke into his account of Eadric (Brooke and Mynors have suggested that it was most likely directed at Gerald of Wales: *De nugis,* p. 155, n. 2). He identifies the house of the dancing women with an English 'Ghildhus', a place where much liquor might be consumed. Encounters with fairies are often associated with drunkenness in works from this period, which is no surprise given the association of the fairy with the illusory. We might note, for example, William of Newburgh's drunken peasant who stumbles upon a fairy hill, from where he steals a remarkable cup. This is discussed further above, p. 76. Map's use of the term, however, appears most obviously to cement the Englishness of the narrative's context and the community within which he understands it to have been generated.

60 Walter Map, *De nugis,* pp. 155–57.

61 For a roughly contemporary example, we might note Marie de France's Lanval, of whom we read upon meeting his fairy, 'Amurs le puint de l'estencele / Que sun quor alume e esprent' ('Love's spark pricked him so his heart was set alight'; lines 119–20). Glyn S. Burgess and Keith Busby, eds and trans. *The Lais of Marie de France* (London: Penguin, 2003). Uncomfortable as it may seem, this trope is not entirely at odds with the rape that follows in Walter Map's account of Eadric; we might, for example, compare the Old French romance *Partonopeus de Blois* and the first encounter between the hero and his fairy lover Melior. Nonetheless, there may be a moral or legal reading of this episode in the context of the wider narrative. As Corinne Saunders notes of the post-conquest law codes, the most extreme punishment for rape was the loss of property and goods – exile and outlawry, which would appear to correspond with the decline in Eadric's fortunes after the fairy's departure. Corinne Saunders, *Rape and Ravishment in the Literature of Medieval England* (Cambridge: D. S. Brewer, 2001), p. 49. However distasteful it is, we might also understand the allusion to rape as something of a joke: within the framework of the succubus/incubus convention, it is the human who is under assault, not the demon.

62 Boquet and Nagy, *Medieval Sensibilities,* pp. 109–13. As Boquet and Nagy note, medieval authors do not have a singular conception of courtly love, but the conventions of *fin'amor* developed by Occitan poets were developed in relation to other tropes across Europe, and it is this broader tradition which Map presumably, like Marie de France, has in mind. For discussion of courtly love, and its reception among twelfth-century clerical authors and chroniclers, which even informed

their comprehension of historical events, see William M. Reddy, *The Making of Romantic Love: Longing and Sexuality in Europe, South Asia, and Japan, 900–1200 CE* (Chicago: University of Chicago Press, 2012), pp. 168–220. For discussion of medieval psychology, and theories of the imagination, in the embodied response of romance heroes and heroines, see Corinne Saunders, 'Mind, Body and Affect in Medieval Arthurian Romance', in *Emotions in Medieval Arthurian Literature: Body, Mind, Voice*, ed. Frank Brandsma, Carolyne Larrington, and Corinne Saunders (Cambridge: D. S. Brewer, 2015), pp. 31–46.
63  Karnes, 'Marvels in the Medieval Imagination', p. 331.
64  Walter Map, *De nugis*, pp. 148–49.
65  Isidore of Seville, *Etymologies*, pp. 243–44.
66  We might note that Map's scepticism concerning miracles was applied not only to Welsh content but to other subject matter in *De nugis*, such as a reputed miracle of Bernard of Clairvaux which he elsewhere rejects as an obscene joke. *De nugis*, pp. 80–81; discussed by Walker Bynum, 'Wonder', pp. 12–13.
67  Walter Map, *De nugis*, p. 150, n. 1. For discussion of the epithet in the Welsh Triads, see Brynley F. Roberts, 'Melusina: Medieval Welsh and English Analogues', in *Mélusines continentales et insulaires: actes du colloque international tenu les 27 et 28 mars à l'Université Paris XII et au Collège des Irlandais*, ed. Jeanne-Marie Boivin and Proinsias MacCana (Paris: Honoré Champion, 1999), pp. 281–95 (pp. 287–88).
68  Walter Map, *De nugis*, pp. 154–55.
69  Faletra notes that the Hereford context of the account of Eadric might suggest the fairies themselves as ciphers for the Welsh if we read the tale in line with anxieties concerning cross-cultural sexual contact and marriage. Faletra, *Wales and the Medieval Colonial Imagination*, p. 81. However, while Eadric's *raptus* is broadly in line with the abductions associated with the moment of colonisation, this medieval practice is broader than this historical context, and does not necessarily signify colonial activity. For the relationship between the seizure of territory and *raptus* see David R. Wyatt, *Slaves and Warriors in Medieval Britain and Ireland, 800–1200* (Leiden: Brill, 2009), pp. 117–27 (with reference to Eadric, p. 114).
70  William of Newburgh, *History*, I, pp. 34–35.
71  The whole sequence runs from *De nugis*, p. 182 to p. 205.
72  Otter, *Inventiones*, pp. 124–25.
73  Walter Map, *De nugis*, pp. 194–95.

74 Walter Map, *De nugis*, pp. 186–89.
75 Walter Map, *De nugis*, pp. 208–09.
76 Siân Echard, 'Map's Metafiction: Author, Narrator and Reader in *De nugis curialium*', *Exemplaria* 8.2 (1996): 287–314 (pp. 313–14).
77 Justice, 'Did the Middle Ages Believe in their Miracles?', p. 13.
78 P. C. Bartrum, 'Fairy Mothers', *Bulletin of the Board of Celtic Studies* 19 (1962): 6–8; Juliette Wood, 'The Fairy Bride Legend in Wales', *Folklore* 103 (1992): 56–72. For discussion of *annwfn* and its associations with aquatic depths, see John Carey, 'The Location of the Otherworld in Irish Tradition', in *The Otherworld Voyage in Early Irish Literature*, ed. Jonathan Wooding (Dublin: Four Courts Press, 2000), pp. 113–19 (Welsh material is discussed on pp. 118–19). This essay was first published in *Éigse* 19 (1982–83): 36–43. See further Patrick Sims-Williams, *Irish Influence on Medieval Welsh Literature* (Oxford: Oxford University Press, 2010), pp. 57–58.
79 Roberts, 'Melsuina', p. 292.
80 'Vita Sancti Gundleii', in A. W. Wade-Evans, ed., *Vita sanctorum Britanniae et genealogiae* (Cardiff: University of Wales Press, 1944), pp. 172–93.
81 Bromwich, ed. and trans., *Trioedd Ynys Prydein*, pp. 294–95. This is found in Triad 70 (pp. 195–97), Triad 81 (pp. 211–13), and Triad 96 (p. 243).
82 For a discussion of these customs in relation to popular practice see C. S. Watkins, '"Folklore" and "Popular Religion" in Britain during the Middle Ages', *Folklore* 115.2 (2004): 140–50 (pp. 142–43).
83 Brewer, Dimock, and Warner, eds, *Giraldi Cambrensis opera*, IV, p. 26.
84 A. W. Wade-Evans, 'The Brychan Documents', *Y Cymmrodor* 19 (1906): 18–50 (pp. 25, 33, 38).
85 The fourteenth-century scribe of Oxford, Bodleian Library, MS 851 misidentifies Deheubarth as north Wales, presumably by means of simplifying the conflict between the kingdoms which follows.
86 Brewer, Dimock, and Warner, eds, *Giraldi Cambrensis opera*, VI, p. 34; Gerald of Wales, *Journey through Wales*, p. 94.
87 Gerald of Wales, *Journey through Wales*, p. 81.
88 For possible references to the Lord Rhys in *De nugis*, see Neil Cartlidge, 'Masters in the Art of Lying? The Literary Relationship between Hugh of Rhuddlan and Walter Map', *Modern Language Review* 106.1 (2011): 1–16 (pp. 10–11). Cartlidge notes that similar material is found in another Welsh-border author of this period, Hugh of Rhuddlan.

89 It is possible that the name may be a reference to Walter Map's *De nugis*. In his account of the custom of Welshmen, on New Year's Day, to steal or to go by houses and listen for information, he records the listening of Theudus (Tewdys) at the house of one Meilerius (Meilyr), where he gained a prophecy of Welsh kingship. Walter Map, *De nugis*, pp. 188–91.
90 Brewer, Dimock, and Warner, eds, *Giraldi Cambrensis opera*, VI, pp. 3–152 (pp. 55–61); Gerald of Wales, *Journey through Wales*, pp. 114–21.
91 Brewer, Dimock, and Warner, eds, *Giraldi Cambrensis opera*, VI, p. 58; Gerald of Wales, *Journey through Wales*, pp. 117–18.
92 Brewer, Dimock, and Warner, eds, *Giraldi Cambrensis opera*, VI, p. 60; Gerald of Wales, *Journey through Wales*, p. 119.
93 Otter, *Inventiones*, pp. 152–53; see further Faletra, *Wales and the Colonial Imagination*, p. 154; Watkins, *History and the Supernatural*, pp. 209–11.
94 Finke and Shichtman, *King Arthur and the Myth of History*, p. 14.
95 Finke and Shichtman, *King Arthur and the Myth of History*, p. 14.
96 For a previous reading of anxieties about Welsh prophecy in this account, see Julia Crick, 'The British Past and the Welsh Future: Gerald of Wales, Geoffrey of Monmouth, and Arthur of Britain', *Celtica* 23 (1999): 60–75 (pp. 71–75).
97 Brynley F. Roberts, 'Geoffrey of Monmouth, *Historia regum Britanniae* and *Brut y Brenhinedd*', in *Arthur of the Welsh: The Arthurian Legend in Medieval Welsh Literature*, ed. Rachel Bromwich, A. O. H. Jarman, and Brynley F. Roberts (Cardiff: University of Wales Press, 1991), pp. 97–116; Katherine Himsworth, 'Brut y brenhinedd', in *Arthur in the Celtic Languages: The Arthurian Legend in Celtic Literatures and Traditions*, ed. Ceridwen Lloyd-Morgan and Erich Poppe (Cardiff: University of Wales Press, 2019), pp. 95–109; Jean Blacker, 'Where Wace Feared to Tread: Latin Commentaries on Merlin's Prophecies in the Reign of Henry II', *Arthuriana* 6.1 (1996): 36–52.
98 Most famously, the prophecies re-negotiate a familiar Welsh prophetic motif of the returning heroes Cynan and Cadwaladr, which is representative not of personal returns of the type found in English traditions of Arthur but of the successes of contemporary military leaders from Brittany and north Wales. From a Welsh perspective, the Conanus and Caduladrus of *Prophetiae*, lines 110–14, who slaughter the 'alienigenarum' and fill the rivers of Britain with blood, might apply to any number of historical and contemporary Welsh figures opposed to English rule. Flood, *Prophecy, Politics, and Place*, pp. 21–43.

99 Juliette Wood, 'Caerleon Restaurata: The Narrative World of Early Medieval Gwent', in *The Gwent County History*, I: *Gwent in Prehistory and Early History*, ed. Miranda Green and Ray Howell (Cardiff: University of Wales Press, 2004), pp. 317–30 (pp. 319–21).

100 Brynley F. Roberts, 'Copïau Cymraeg o Prophetiae Merlini', *National Library of Wales Journal* 20.1 (1977): 14–39.

101 For a fuller discussion of the evidence for genuine Welsh prophetic practice in this and other Galfridian-inspired accounts from the period see Victoria Flood, 'Political Prodigies: Incubi and Succubi in Walter Map's *De nugis curialium* and Gerald of Wales's *Itinerarium Cambriae*', *Nottingham Medieval Studies* 57 (2013): 21–46.

102 Brewer, Dimock, and Warner, eds, *Giraldi Cambrensis opera*, VI, p. 61; my translation based on Thorpe's in Gerald of Wales, *Journey through Wales*, pp. 120–21.

103 John of Salisbury, *Frivolities of Courtiers*, p. 87.

104 Kruger, *Dreaming in the Middle Ages*, pp. 50–53.

105 Minnis, 'Medieval Imagination and Memory', pp. 245–46. Minnis notes a similar use of Augustine in Gerald's contemporary Caesarius of Heisterbach, who, however, as we shall see in Chapter 2, appears to have been influenced by Gerald's writings. For discussion of the relationship between prophecy and medieval theories of the imagination, see Karnes, 'Marvels in the Medieval Imagination', pp. 333–48, which gives an overview of material drawn from medieval Arabic and Latin sources. These perspectives are far more developed than anything we see in Gerald's Augustinian engagements.

106 Augustine, *The Literal Meaning of Genesis II*, ed. and trans. John Hammond Taylor (New York: Newman Press, 1982), pp. 213–14. For discussion of the Neoplatonic origins, and later medieval influence, of this formulation, see Coleman, *Ancient and Medieval Memories*, p. 111.

107 For discussion of William of Newburgh's rejection of prophecies of Arthur's return, as a point of Welsh naivety, see Introduction, pp. 20–21.

108 Brewer, Dimock, and Warner, eds, *Giraldi Cambrensis opera*, VI, pp. 75–78; Gerald of Wales, *Journey through Wales*, pp. 133–35.

109 Geoffrey of Monmouth, *History*, I, lines 458–62.

110 Faletra, *Wales and the Medieval Colonial Imagination*, p. 171.

111 Brewer, Dimock, and Warner, eds, *Giraldi Cambrensis opera*, VI, p. 78; Gerald of Wales, *Journey through Wales*, p. 136.

112 For the influence of new Platonism in this period, see Watkins, *History and the Supernatural*, pp. 27–33.

113 For an overview of Gerald's investment in St David's, including its claim as a historical archbishopric, independent of Canterbury, see Bartlett, *Gerald of Wales*, pp. 44–53. This historical claim to St David's metropolitan status, as drawn on by Gerald, was rooted in *Prophetiae*, lines 48–49, where St David is associated with the 'pallium', although Geoffrey situates a Welsh see in Caerleon. In the 1130s, the bishops of both Llandaff and St David's made a case for their sees as historical archbishoprics, and Geoffrey appears to deny both claims.
114 Gerald of Wales, *Journey through Wales*, p. 118.
115 Brewer, Dimock, and Warner, eds, *Giraldi Cambrensis opera*, VI, p. 78; my modified translation based on Thorpe's in Gerald of Wales, *Journey through Wales*, p. 136.
116 Augustine, *City of God*, V, pp. 40–49. For discussion of the long reception history of the Plinian peoples, see John Block Friedman, *The Monstrous Races in Medieval Thought and Art* (Syracuse, NY: Syracuse University Press, 2000).
117 Augustine, *City of God*, V, pp. 42–43.
118 Augustine, *City of God*, V, pp. 48–49.
119 See Introduction, p. 14.
120 Daston and Park, *Wonders and the Order of Nature*, pp. 21–66.
121 William of Newburgh, *History*, I, pp. 118–21; Partner, *Serious Entertainments*, p. 123.
122 For a discussion of the 'authorizing capacity of otherworld objects' in relation to the fairy cup, see Byrne, *Otherworlds*, pp. 108–09.
123 Wade, *Fairies in Medieval Romance*, p. 81.
124 Walker Bynum, 'Wonder', p. 23.
125 Jeffrey Jerome Cohen, 'Green Children from Another World, or the Archipelago in England', in *Cultural Diversity in the British Middle Ages: Archipelago, Island, England*, ed. Jeffrey Jerome Cohen (New York: Palgrave Macmillan, 2008), pp. 75–94.
126 William of Newburgh, *History*, I, pp. 114–15.
127 Walter Map, *De nugis*, pp. 160–61.
128 A variant account by Ralph of Coggeshall locates the narrative in relation to named, presumably verifiable, persons in the region: the girl serves as a wayward servant in the house of a local knight, Richard de Calne. Ralph of Coggeshall, *Chronicon Anglicanum*, ed. Joseph Stevenson (London: Longman, 1875), pp. 118–20.
129 William of Newburgh, *History*, I, pp. 114–15.
130 Isidore of Seville, *Etymologies*, p. 244.
131 Partner, *Serious Entertainments*, p. 115; discussed also by Otter, *Inventiones*, pp. 102–03.

132 Gabrielle M. Spiegel, 'Genealogy, Form and Function in Medieval Historical Narrative', *History and Theory* 22.1 (1983): 43–53 (p. 46).
133 Cohen, 'Green Children from Another World', p. 87. For a fuller discussion of the marvel at Battle, in relation to post-conquest trauma, see Clarke, 'Signs and Wonders', pp. 60–61.
134 Clarke, 'Signs and Wonders', p. 68.
135 Watkins, *History and the Supernatural*, p. 64.
136 William of Newburgh, *History*, I, pp. 116–17.
137 Walker Bynum, 'Wonder', p. 12.
138 For discussion of the political function of emotional cues in the courts of medieval princes, see Boquet and Nagy, *Medieval Sensibilities*, pp. 158–80.
139 I refer here to previous assumptions regarding the 'Celticity' of the fairy of English and French romance, for which see Introduction, p. 28.

# 2

# 'Relatum ueridica': wonderful history from Gervase of Tilbury to Philippe Mousket

Scio equidem mihi pridem relatum ueridica naratione ... missam

(For my part, I know of a happening of which I was once given a reliable account)[1]

The distinction between *fabula* and *historia* remained a feature of historiographical treatments of marvels into the early thirteenth century, and it appears in Gervase of Tilbury's *Otia imperialia* (1214). Directing his work to the Holy Roman Emperor, Otto IV, grandson of Henry II and Eleanor of Aquitaine, Gervase might be oriented in broadly the same circles as Walter Map and Gerald, although *Otia* is coeval with the end of Gerald's career and stands roughly a generation apart from Map. It has been suggested that Gervase's approach to *mirabilia* exhibits a fuller awareness than the work of previous historians of a distinction between the natural and the supernatural, grounded in 'a strong sense of the value of empirical data'.[2] A number of Gervase's marvels have even been read as precursors to post-Enlightenment scientific observation, and his approach has been understood as a modification of Augustine's near-limitless wonder: a process of observation and explanation representing a precocious 'disenchantment of the world'.[3] However, for Gervase in some ways the world remains as enchanted as it was for Gerald and Walter Map, and he integrates fairy narratives in a recognisably Augustinian framework of wonder, as remarkable historical occurrences that ultimately frustrate the search for causation, although they might be credibly believed.

Following an overview of Gervase's approach to recording *mirabilia*, and the principles of discretion applied throughout the fairy content of *Otia*, this chapter addresses Gervase's conflation of the fairy with another figure who appears in marvellous, and indeed miraculous, episodes in chronicles and *mirabilia* collections from the late twelfth and early thirteenth centuries, the heretic, and the subsequent reception of this tradition in the thirteenth-century anti-Angevin histories of Gerald of Wales and Philippe Mousket. In this material, as in the previous chapter, we see a concern with the proper subject and limits of wonder that constitute a community of wonder. These narratives are remarkable in their incorporation of components that extend the plausible limits of Augustinian wonder as we find it in *De civitate Dei*, the prohibitions of the 'Canon episcopi', and the earlier insular historiographical tradition, integrating direct allusions to both the night flight and, an associated idea, human–animal metamorphosis. While the fairies of these narratives are presented as components of the historical real (they are, as in Chapter 1, progenerative), my authors' primary interests are nonetheless in the extent and limits of the fairy's wonder-working (presented both as analogous to, and on occasion identified with, the false marvels of the heretic), and the power of the eucharist, the cross, or St John's Gospel to compel her departure. The demonic fairy appears as a source of abject, although properly historical, wonder, mobilised in the narrative service of wonderful meditations on the power of God and the boundaries of the Christian community, applied – in the final examples with which I am concerned – in explicitly dynastic terms.

## Wonder and discretion

Wonder, approached with knowing discretion, presents the very occasion for the compilation of Book III of *Otia*, the preface to which establishes an overtly Augustinian framework in which the object of wonder is necessarily endorsed, if not by the weight of scripture, by reliable reportage. Gervase presents marvels as appropriate refreshment for the ears of an emperor, a discerning listener ('deliciosis auribus') attuned to the properties of true marvels as distinct from false:

Enimuero non ex loquaci ystrionum garrulitate ocium decet imperiale imbui, sed potius, abiectus importunis fabularum mendaciis, que uestustatis auctoritas comprobauit aut scripturarum firmauit auctoritas aut cotidiane conspectionis fides oculata testatur ad ocium sacri auditus sunt ducenda.

(To be sure, it is not proper that an emperor's leisure should be contaminated with the prating babbling of players; on the contrary, the crude falsehoods of idle tales should be spurned, and only those things which are sanctioned by the authority of age or confirmed by the authority of scripture, or attested by daily eye-witness accounts, should be brought to his venerable hearing in his leisure hours.)[4]

*Mirabilia* compiled for an emperor are chosen with care, with a mind to a veracity that is understood to go hand in hand with an economy of words. There is a close connection here between the garrulous speaker and fabulous lies ('fabularum mendaciis') which we have seen already in relation to the figure of the British storyteller. Gervase reiterates this principle in the final lines of the preface, adding that he does not write 'fabulosa' content, distinct from the lies of performers ('mimorum mendaciis'), and the accounts of storytellers ('auctorum') who have no knowledge of the true condition of the marvels ('miranda') he recounts.[5] Although this is in part a claim for the emperor's attention, the allusion may also refer to (among others) the British storytellers rejected by Gervase's contemporaries in England (which, regardless of any genuine interest in the Avalon legend among Breton *conteurs*, was a familiar trope). Gervase uses the same vocabulary that we find in William of Newburgh's rejection of the British hope: a concern with 'fabulosa' material, 'medacium', and 'fallaces', the subject of false 'miranda', drawing on a commonly constructed cultural distinction between the true marvel and the false.

Like Gerald and Walter Map, Gervase applied different levels of plausibility to different fairy narratives, and similarly, on occasion, used the fairy as a signifier of improper credulity, and a lack of intellectual sophistication. Writing on the basis of either Gerald's 1198 account of the discovery of Arthur's bones or the *Vita Merlini* directly, elsewhere in *Otia* Gervase rejected the 'fabulose' beliefs held by the 'Britones' of Arthur's return from Avalon, where (in line with Geoffrey's *Vita*) he is watched over by

'Morganda fatata' – a familiar combining of the fabulous and the fairy in a (perceived) British narrative context (Arthur's mysterious end is recorded in 'uulgarem Britonum traditionem').[6] Gervase here exhibits a familiar distrust of British orality, although, unlike William of Newburgh, he appears to have had no particular concerns regarding the authority of Merlinian prophecy, at least as it might be read in application to the events of the *Historia* as a genuinely historical document (this exercise informs the preceding Arthurian section of *Otia*).[7] Gervase also does not appear to have been apprehensive of accounts of Arthur's survival when removed from a British context. He repeats an alternative narrative of Arthur's rule over a beautiful plain filled with riches, reached by passing through Mount Etna.[8] He notes testimonies of the people ('indigenis') of the region of the many gifts that Arthur sends from his home within the mountain to the bishop. Gervase here characteristically combines testimony with doubt, in a formulation which associates wonder with a lack of full knowability: 'que a multis uisa et a pluribus fabulosa nouitate admirata fuerunt' ('Many people have seen these gifts, and even more have wondered at the extraordinary [*fabulosa*] story of their origin').[9] It is no surprise that this marvel is ascribed a greater (albeit still tentative) truth value than Gervase's account of Avalon and Morgan. Etna was a volcanic analogy for the fires of purgatory from Augustine onwards (certainly, Gervase's account has been read in relation to thirteenth-century conceptualisations of purgatory) and was itself a paradigmatic example of a true Augustinian marvel.[10]

Regardless of his precise intended target in the principles of discernment established in the opening of Book III, Gervase makes it clear that marvels are not to be accepted unquestioningly but are to be subjected to due scrutiny. He outlines his distinction between miracles and marvels – the former the product of divine intervention, the latter occurring in nature but with causes beyond our comprehension:

> Que inaudita percipiuntur amplectimur, tum ex mutatione cursus naturalis quam admiramur, tum ex ignorancia cause cuius ratio nobis est imperscrutabilis, tum ex assuetudine nostra quam in aliis uariari sine cognitione iudicii iusti cernimus. Ex hiis, duo proueniunt:

miracula et mirabilia, cum utrorumque finis sit admiratio. Porro miracula dicimus usitatius que preter naturam diuine uirtuti ascrimibus, ut cum uirgo parit, cum Lazarus resurgit, cum lapsa membra reintegrantur. Mirabilia uero dicimus que nostre cognicioni non subiacent, etiam cum sunt naturalia; sed et mirabilia constituit ignorantia reddende rationis quare sic sit.

(When anything strange is observed we seize on it, partly because of the inversion of the natural order, which surprises us, partly because of our ignorance of the cause, whose working is a mystery to us, and partly because of seeing our expectation cheated in unfamiliar circumstances of which we lack a proper understanding. From these causes arise two things, miracles and marvels, though they both result in wonderment. Now we generally call those things miracles which, being preternatural, we ascribe to divine power, as when a virgin gives birth, when Lazarus is raised from the dead, or when diseased limbs are made whole again; while we call those things marvels which are beyond our comprehension, even though they are natural, in fact the inability to explain why a thing is so constitutes a marvel.)[11]

This is distinct from the relatively loose definition of the miraculous that we have seen in Walter Map, and significantly pre-empts Aquinas's distinction between the marvellous (occurrences within the bounds of nature but beyond explanation) and the miraculous (the result of divine intervention). Within the Thomist framework, the marvellous was similarly understood as perspectival: it was thought to be remarkable only because of the limited knowledge of the beholder.[12] However, Gervase's point is not that the marvel is a site of ignorance but that it is a site of knowledge, acquired through a discerning relationship to credible sources. The remainder of the passage delineates a catalogue of Augustinian marvels including the peacock's incorruptible flesh, the fires of Sicily, and the marvel of lime. Gervase, as throughout his work, supplements Augustine's observations with personal witness testimonies. Just as Augustine witnessed the incorruptibility of roast peacock in Carthage first-hand, Gervase writes that when in Rome he observed the marvellous properties of the salamander nourished by fire (notably, the salamander is the first marvel listed by Augustine in *De civitate Dei* as an analogue to spiritual corporeality).[13]

In contrast to the later writings of Thomas Aquinas, and other investigators of apparent wonders, like Roger Bacon and Albertus Magnus, the goal of Gervase's enquiry was not the discovery of causation itself: rather, a marvel is to be subjected to scrutiny, and its status confirmed only when no single cause can be discovered.[14] Gervase found a clear precedent for reaffirmed uncertainty in Augustine's discussion of demonic pro-generation, to which he returns throughout his treatment of demonic *mirabilia*, confirming only that he understands the phenomenon to be demonic and a necessary focus of an exercise in discretion which is as religiously and morally charged as it is historical.

## Lares

Gervase's fullest discussion of demonic pro-generation and associated concepts is found in chapter 86 of the third book of *Otia*. As Edward Peters notes, the multiple possible rationalisations of the incubus given here by Gervase read as a defence of 'legitimate wonder' – for a single cause, beyond the mysterious operations of the divine, is unknown.[15] Unlike Gerald and Walter Map, Gervase provides, among possible causes, a medical definition of the incubus as a nocturnal hallucination resulting from a thickening of the humours. Yet his primary interest, despite his engagement with what we might consider to be more conventional scientific observation, is with the historical record of analogous demonic encounters, among which he includes *larvas*, manifestations of *lares* (household spirits) who assume bodily forms apparently capable of working good or ill effects. Gervase is invested in the sexual, genealogical, and domestic familiarity of phantasmatic encounters of this type, as well as the double sense in which the phenomenon might be made familiar by common report:

> Si queritur quid sibi uelint hec audita sepissime ac miranda, respondeo quod ait beatissimus omnium questionum inuestigator Augustinius, id totum diuini iudicii secretis attribuendum, quia: 'Facit angelos suos spiritus et ministros suos ut flamman ignis.' Sicut enim bonos angelos aereis corporibus induit ad ministerium suum familiarius excercendum, ita et demones corporum formis fantasticis et laruatis, quasi

larium, hoc est domorum, familiaritatem in figura tenentibus indui sustinet, ut quod mandatum in bonis operator ad bonum, hoc eius pacientia mali operentur ad nostre infirmitatis illusionem ac penam.

(If anyone asks the meaning of these wonders which one so often hears, I reply with the words of Augustine, that most blessed investigator of all questions; he says that the whole matter should be referred to the mysteries of divine justice. 'He makes his angels spirits and his ministers a burning fire.' Just as he endows the good angels with airy bodies to enable them to fulfil their ministry in closer communion with us, so too he allows demons to put on *fantasticis* and *laruitis* bodily shapes, the shapes as it were of *lares*, that is of household spirits, so that they present a familiar appearance. This means that the mandate which works for good in good spirits, evil spirits use by his leave to mock and punish our weakness.)[16]

This passage includes a direct citation of Augustine's discussion of angelic and demonic bodies in *De civitate Dei* (although Augustine remains unresolved as to whether the fiery ministry of the angel is literal or metaphorical).[17] Gervase continues, in the passage that follows, that like Augustine he cannot speculate on the precise composition of the bodies of demons and angels, but demonic pro-generation – however uncertain its causation – remains a possibility. A verbatim quotation from Augustine's account of the Dusii follows. Gervase makes much in this section of Augustine's role as an 'investigator' of wonders, and of the uncertain nature of phantasmatic materiality. The Augustinian acceptance of wonder was not understood to be unquestioning but discerning, even and especially when the results of investigations are open-ended and so speak most fully to the glory of God. The reality of such occurrences, Gervase further comments, in a sentence which echoes across the later *Mélusine* tradition, is obscure but nonetheless plausible, for the limits and extent of creation are unknowable. Gervase concludes that when quizzed on such occurrences, all he might answer is: 'Iuditia Dei abissus multa' ('The judgements of God are a great deep'; Psalm 35.7).[18] Nonetheless, if such pro-generation does occur, the only interpretation that Gervase expresses with any certainty is that, as Augustine similarly contended in his account of the Dusii, it is surely demonic – the work not of angels but of those who fell with the devil and were (in Gervase's words) 'ad huiusmodi illusiones reseruati sunt ad hominum penam' ('reserved to provide phantoms of this nature to punish humankind').[19] It is essential that one knows how to read such potentially ambiguous accounts, not least in regard to their demonic connotations.

Gervase is engaged in his own Augustinian investigations. He records that like Augustine's Dusii, *lares*, also known as *fada* (the Provençal term for fairies), are attested by credible common reportage and are evidenced by the phenomenon's visible and known material effects – significant personal gain followed by loss:

> Hoc equidem a uiris omni exceptione maioribus cotidie scimus probatum, quod quosdam huiusmodi laruarum, quas fadas nominant, amatores audiuimus, et cum ad aliarum feminarum matrimonia se transtulerunt, ante mortuos quam cum superinductis carnali se copula immiscuerint; plerosque in summa temporali felicitate uidimus stetisse, qui, cum ab huiuscemodi fadarum se abstraxerunt amplexibus aut illas publicauerunt eloquio, non tantum temporales successus sed etiam misere uite solatium amisserunt.

> (But here is something we do know, confirmed daily as it is by men who are above all reproach: we have heard that some men have become the lovers of *larvas* of this kind, which they call *fada*, and when they have transferred their affections with a view to marrying other women, they have died before they could enjoy carnal union with their new partners. And we have seen many men who had attained the summit of worldly happiness, but then, as soon as they renounced the embraces of *fada* of this kind, or spoke about them in public, they lost not only their worldly prosperity, but even the solace of a wretched life.)[20]

Like Map, Gervase's fairy narratives explore the relationship between the material and the imaginary, and might best be approached, like the fairy encounter of Map's Eadric, as an imaginative event. Like Map, Gervase draws on structures of courtly love to convey phantasmatic materiality. The suffering of the unfaithful lovers of fairies is not a feature of Gervase's supernatural mother accounts themselves (discussed below), and although it is possible that he may have known Marie de France's *Lanval*, Gervase may well have got here, potentially like Marie, through an awareness of the principles of courtly love as pastiched, or parodied, by

Andreas Capellanus, who famously observes that 'love, when named, flees'.[21] We might consider whether, like Andreas, Gervase writes here in a comic, or at least an ironic, register, and the speech prohibition and languishing lovers is something of a joke, a piece of clerical misogyny.[22] Gervase certainly understands fairy phenomena in relation to secular love and desire cast in decidedly negative terms, and his uses of fairy material are often inflected by a rejection of *fin'amor*. Yet however ironically executed, Gervase's fairy narratives are engaged not simply with metaphorical or symbolic applications but with the collection of testimony, and the fairy's prohibition conveniently offers a rationale for those areas in which evidence might be lacking. The prohibition against speaking of a fairy's love places a clear limit on the volume of available testimony – a point of explanation as to why seemingly common report is not necessarily so common after all.

### The lady of Chateau-Rousset

The materiality of visionary experiences, coloured by a concern with the dangers of *fin'amor*, is a feature of Gervase's first fairy bride narrative, in Book I of *Otia*: the account of the Lady of Chateau-Rousset. This is a Provençal dynastic origin legend, functionally analogous to Walter Map's account of Eadric – not least in its interest in the material proof of the marvel presented by the existence of the fairy's children. Drawing on 'relatum ueridica' ('a reliable account'), Gervase writes of the encounter of Raymond, a lord of Chateau-Rousset, with a beautiful, richly dressed woman by the (perhaps tellingly named) River Lar. The mysterious woman calls Raymond by name, and consents to marry him on the condition that he never see her naked. If he breaks this prohibition, Raymond will lose any material prosperity his new wife might bring him. Inevitably, he spies on his wife bathing, and watches her turn into a serpent. The fairy disappears from her husband forever, although she is said by the nursery maids to return at night to visit her children. Concerning the perpetuity of the fairy's descendants we read of a single daughter, who married into Provençal nobility – an authenticating detail in terms of the material effects of the demon mother, formulated in very similar terms to Walter Map's account of Alnoth and the descendants of the dead wife of Brittany:

> Sane miles felicitate ac gratia pro maxima parte minoratus, filiam illius domine cuidam nostro affini ex nobilibus Prouince oriundo postea dedit in uxorem, que inter coetaneas et confines suas plurimum extitit graciosa, et eius iam successio ad nos usque peruenit.
>
> (The knight was indeed in large measure deprived of his prosperity and favour. He subsequently gave a daughter of that lady in marriage to a certain kinsman of ours, a scion of the Provençal nobility: she was well-loved among her contemporaries and neighbours, and descendants of hers survive to our own day.)[23]

Unlike the successors of Eadric, however, the line does not appear to be terminal, and although we might note the virtue and good acts of the supernatural mother's child, she is a married woman rather than a saint. The interest in the knight's daughter may, however, imply the decline of the patriline: the dynastic connection of interest here pertains to a female heir. Unlike in the Eadric account (although closer to that of the Breton knight's wife), Gervase does not historically locate the narrative or name the family, although a certain level of familiarity, and indeed familial connection ('nostro affini'; Gervase himself appears to have been of noble Angevin stock), is implied.[24] It is possible that the intended family, and historical context, may have been, in their own time and place, clear enough.

The cultural codes with which Gervase constructed this account, and those by which he presumably intended it to be read, must be understood in relation to a sense of relative credibility, closely connected to concepts of demonic materiality, as we find in his account of *lares* in Book III. Presented in the context of the first book of *Otia*, which sketches an account of the cosmography and early history of the world through a series of biblical glosses, the narrative is exemplary and exegetical. It is introduced as commentary on Genesis 3: 'De oculis apertis post peccatum' ('the opening of the eyes after sin').[25] The origins of humankind appear to have brought to Gervase's mind the marvellous origins of a Provençal dynasty, intimately connected to the matters of sin, prohibition, and sight. Yet there is a greater commonality still: both the biblical account and its marvellous gloss are concerned with the materiality of the imagination. The fairy narrative is preceded by an account of the female-faced serpent, drawn from Peter Comestor's gloss on Genesis in his *Historia scholastica* (c. 1170). Comestor's commentary presents a significant early chapter in (if not, indeed a point of origin for) the visual tradition of the female-faced serpent, which from the early decades of the thirteenth century appears in manuscript illustrations and stained glass across Europe.[26] It is a precedent that Gervase misidentifies, following Peter, as drawn from Bede – although it remains uncertain whether Peter intended to ascribe this material to Bede, or the part of his commentary that precedes it.[27] The association of this material with Bede may have been useful for Gervase's, like Comestor's, historical interests. We might remember, as we find in William of Newburgh, that Bede's name was synonymous with historical credibility.[28]

Gervase writes of Eve, seduced by a serpent with a woman's face – for, Gervase writes, echoing Comestor, 'similia similibus applaudunt' ('like approves like').[29] The motif rests on the particular susceptibility of female imaginations to demonic phenomena, as we find in near-contemporary and later clerical accounts of cognition, such as those of William of Auvergne and Vincent of Beauvais.[30] Comestor's commentary possessed a very clear utility for Gervase on the historiographical level, for in his concern with the imaginations of women, Comestor draws on the Aristotelian model of cognition and of memory, which we have seen played a role in historical imaginings, and indeed in the concept of the historical imagination, in the writings of Walter Map. Comestor writes that the serpent approached Eve rather than Adam, for the woman lacked the foresight of the man, and (he quotes Horace) was 'wax to be twisted by the vice'.[31] The sequence recalls the association of wax with sensory perception and memorisation, as we find in the Aristotelian model, which we have seen found a particular purchase in medieval imaginings of pregnancy and maternity.[32] This is rooted in a deeply misogynistic logic, in which, as Dyan Elliott has observed of later medieval discourses of spiritual discernment, women serve as negative exemplars for human failures of spiritual discretion more broadly.[33] Understood in their procreative function to be physically over-determined and affectively porous, female minds and bodies presented a model for approaching human frailty, including the lust of men for women. Indeed, in the narrative proper, Gervase depicts not a failure of female discernment, but the knight's misidentification of his bride, deceived by her beauty, through the very optical-cognitive (masculine) experience we might associate with *fin'amor*. 'Inflammatus' ('inflamed by the heat of passion'), the knight agrees to a hasty marriage and the condition that he never look upon his wife naked. His second mistake is similarly associated with fiery desire: burning ('accenditur') to see his wife naked, he draws back the curtain screening the bath, and witnesses her serpentine form.[34] The desire of Gervase's knight reads similarly to that of Map's Eadric. This is a re-imagining of courtly love or romance paradigms in a demonological context, most likely informed by the pre-conceptions of a vein of clerical misogyny, which emerges as a clear pattern across the early fairy mother narratives.

Like Map, Gervase is interested not simply in the disruption of courtly codes, but in an act of phenomenological and historiographical discernment that is particularly complex. While it is obvious (to author and reader) that the fairy is a demon, the precise mechanism by which she appears and disappears remains obscure. Gervase draws attention to the ontological uncertainty of demonic causation, poised between the illusory and the material, read in relation to a distinct category, metamorphosis.[35] Immediately prior to the account, he introduces two precedents from Augustine by which tales of female serpentine transformation might be read: the human–animal transformations of the witches of Greece and Jerusalem (a reference to the transformation of Lucian in Apuleius's *Golden Ass*) and the transformation of the rods of Pharaoh's magicians in Exodus 7. Both are demonic effects, although Augustine understands the latter as an acceleration of natural processes and the former as a dream or delusion.[36] The fairy account is presented as potentially confirmatory of either of these two positions, although Gervase's evidence is weighted towards a genuinely material engagement. For while the fairy appears to possess the quality of an illusion (a play not only on the vicissitudes of worldly fortune, but on the dangers of looking at women), through the very existence of her daughter and subsequent descendants she leaves a decidedly material trace and would appear to be emmeshed in the manipulation of matter itself.

In the same passage, and with the female-faced serpent in mind, Gervase raises the possibility of human–animal transformation, understood as a plausible historical and material process. He invokes the weight of common report:

> De serpentibus tradunt uulgares quod sunt quedam femine que mutantur in serpentes, que ita dinoscuntur: habent enim ligaturam albam quasi uittam in capite.
>
> Sane quod in serpentes mutari dicunt feminas mirandum quidem est, sed non destendum. Vidimus enim frequenter in Anglia per lunationes homines in lupos mutari, quod hominum genus 'gerulfos' Galli nominant, Angli uero *were wolf* dicunt; *were* enim Anglice uirum sonat, *wolf* lupum.
>
> (On the subject of serpents, the common people say that there are some women who change into them; they can be recognised by a white band or fillet which they have on the head.
>
> This allegation that women change into serpents is certainly remarkable, but is not to be repudiated. For in England we have often seen men change into wolves according to the phases of the moon. The Gauls call men of this kind *gerulfi*, while the English name for them is *werewolves*, *were* being the English equivalent of *vir* (man).)[37]

The first observation reads as a direct response to Comestor, who assumes that while God punished the Eden serpent, he did not extend the punishment to all serpents, and presumably, as Henry Angsar Kelly writes, he 'believed that there still existed serpents with virginal faces and voices, which could move in an upright position'.[38] For Comestor, the allusion appears to have functioned beyond allegory, and speaks to a perception of historical hybridity – a literalisation of a misogynistic metaphor.

Regardless of whether Gervase genuinely was in receipt of oral testimonies regarding female serpentine transformation, he employs the familiar posture of doubts entertained and on occasion overcome by the weight of testimony (itself a convention of writing *mirabilia* in this period) that we find in Gerald's and Walter Map's fairy mother narratives. Although it is remarkable, oral report testifies to a similar class of occurrences that are credibly 'mirandum'. We might note Gervase's allusion to the French and English etymologies of werewolf (*gerulfi*) which frame a claim to vernacular authority which we might compare with that of William of Newburgh's mode of community testimony in his Woolpit narrative (and we might note the apparent Englishness, etymologically, of the word *wulf*). Certainly, here we may well see something of the characteristic medieval investment in the revelatory powers of language that Laura Ashe has similarly observed in medieval historiography – presented here as a standard of localised proof.[39] Gervase writes in the Augustinian tradition of substantiated marvels, and elsewhere in *Otia* Gervase gives two examples of continental werewolves.[40] His allusion to the terminology of the Gauls may even be deliberately reminiscent of Augustine's discussion of the Dusii of Gaul (which we have seen appears elsewhere in *Otia*), an oral report that authenticates the experience of an ontologically uncertain occurrence. If so, Gervase extends the historiographical strategy found in Augustine's account of demonic pro-generation, and a wider twelfth-century fascination with hybrid bodies as a site of natural wonder, to an originally quite separate consideration of the limits of demonic materiality: metamorphosis.

There was a long historical rejection of the materiality of metamorphosis.[41] Augustine understood narratives of lycanthropy, Circe's porcine transformation of Odysseus's men, and the machinations of Apuleius's witches as highly convincing demonic illusions, produced by changes to 'phantasticum homini', a man's phantasmatic likeness:

> sed phantasticum hominis, quod etiam cogitando sive somniando per rerum innumerabilia genera variatur et, cum corpus non sit, corporum tamen similes mira celeritate formas capit, sopitis aut oppressis corporeis hominis sensibus ad aliorum sensum nescio quo ineffabili modo figura corporea posse perduci; ita ut corpora ipsa hominum alicubi iaceant, viventia quidem, sed multo gravius atque vehementius quam somno suis sensibus obseratis.

> (I hold instead that a man's phantom – which also in his thoughts and dreams is changed by the countless variety of objects it receives, and though it is not a body, still with astonishing swiftness receives shapes that are like material bodies – this phantom, I hold, can in some inexplicable way present itself to the senses of others in bodily form, when their physical senses are dulled or blocked out.)[42]

The materiality of metamorphosis was similarly rejected in the 'Canon episcopi', which held the night flight to be as impossible as the material transformation of species and likeness: both are dreams.[43] However, in the late twelfth and early thirteenth centuries, narratives of ostensibly historical transformation possessed a particular utility for secular clerics in the explanation of complex religious transformations. As Walker Bynum observes, medieval Christianity was a religion of paradoxes, which found explanatory analogues in figures of combining and of transformation. Perhaps the most widely discussed near-contemporary example of this is Gerald of Wales's account of the werewolf, commonly approached as an analogue to Gervase's brief allusion to lycanthropy.[44] Gerald writes of a priest who encounters a grievously ill female werewolf on the borders of County Meath in Ireland, once human but cursed alongside her husband by St Natalis and driven into exile in wolf form. Prior to receipt of the eucharist, to demonstrate her humanity, her husband (himself apparently capable of transforming back to his human form at will) peels off her wolfskin and she is revealed as an old woman.[45] Gerald writes that he learned of this from his Irish colleagues who, worried by the ethics of the priest's response, wrote to the author to hear his opinion on the matter. In his later recension of the account, Gerald positions the transformation of the wolf as a way of envisaging the transformation of the eucharistic bread to the body of Christ.[46] This type of transformation is not so much a total category change as a restoration, like miracles of the eucharist which make visible the body and blood of Christ (to quote Walker Bynum), 'an inverted (or counter) miracle ... a restoring of the normal relationship between interior and exterior'.[47] It is perhaps no surprise, then, that the second of Gervase's fairy narratives is account of a eucharistic miracle, in which the fairy narrative is introduced as an explicit analogy for transubstantiation: the account of the lady of L'Epervier.

## The lady of L'Epervier

In his second fairy narrative, concerned with the lady of L'Epervier Castle (located in the same region as Chateau-Rousset), Gervase repurposes the fairy mother motif in an account of the misbelief of the female heretic, who experiences an extreme aversion to the host. He begins the narrative with an allusion to 2 Corinthians 11.14, which warns of the appearances of Satan as an angel of light. This is part of Paul's broader consideration of spiritual discernment, and the structuring allusion of the 'Canon episcopi', treating the false transformation of bodies:[48]

> Siquidem ipse sathanas, qui transfigurat se in angelum lucis, cum mentem cuiusque mulieris ceperit, et hanc per infidelitatem sibi subiugauerit, illico transformat se in diuersarum personarum species atque similitudines ...
> 
> (Thus Satan himself, who transforms himself into an angel of light, when he has captured the mind of a miserable woman and has subjected her to himself by infidelity and incredulity, immediately changes himself into the likeness of different personages ...)[49]

This is essentially the transformation which for Gervase characterises the activities of *lares* (although their victims in *Otia* are typically male), but while the 'Canon' charges that the female victims of demonic subterfuge are 'in sompnis deludens',[50] deluded by dreams into belief in the bodily reality of their demonic engagements, for Gervase, as for Map, demonic encounters are not necessarily without material effect.

Gervase's account details how the lady, who following an encounter in a forest marries the lord of the castle, comes to church late every day and avoids participation in the mass. Her husband, hoping to discover the hidden cause of this, subjects his wife to questioning, but to no avail. While the language of early inquisitorial practices may here be perceptible (given the affinities of the behaviour of the fairy to that of the heretic), the knight might also be understood in relation to the Augustinian investigator who can find no explanation for the marvel: 'nec tante presumptionis causam sedulus inuestigator inuenisset' ('but in spite of persistent questioning he had not discovered the reason for such effrontery').[51] Like the writer, in his investigations the knight discovers marvels that cannot be explained but in their very obscurity speak to divine mysteries – here the power of the eucharist to repel demons. For finally, after she is physically restrained in the church by her husband and his servants, the lady hears the beginning of the eucharistic prayer and takes flight, aided by a demonic spirit. The flight is memorialised by a ruined tower next to the chapel, which Gervase notes is visible to his own day and bears witness to the historicity of the events here told. After warning his imperial reader against the dangers of heresy, and cautioning proper respect for the church, Gervase observes that the castle was destroyed, its name and that of its site was changed, and its inhabitants were moved to a new castle at Charpey.

Gervase integrates familiar cues related to contemporary constructions of, and legal punishments for, heresy. Rejection of the eucharist's miraculous significance, which the account is in large part intended to demonstrate, was understood to be one of the central aspects of European heresy in this period;[52] and the loss of the castle sits suggestively with the penalties applied to unrepentant heretics from 1184 onwards, which included the confiscation of property.[53] The fairy's own horror at the mass is a variation on the narratives of host abuse which were first associated with western Europe's Jewish populations in the early thirteenth century, who were held to be 'for all imaginative purposes ... interchangeable with heretics'.[54] The malevolent interest of Jews in the eucharist was an antisemitic fiction enthusiastically accepted by western Christian authors.[55] As Anthony Bale observes, antisemitic discourse appears across different medieval genres, including history-writing, charged with a distinctive truth status: 'antisemitic stories were implicitly "true" even as their distinctive power resides in their fantastical, evanescent, and unofficial elements ... the fantasy is more real, more true, than reality'.[56] The historical *mirabile* is similarly a space in which truth is not simply relative but contingent on commonly held values, and the incorporation of the stereotypical Jew is a component no realer but felt, where occasion suited, to be as deeply plausible as the fairy herself. Certainly, it is telling that (we might remember) for Gerald of Wales the two frameworks were conflated, and Morgan and Avalon were a component of British belief understood analogously to (rejected) Jewish messianism.[57]

Gervase's opening allusion to satanic misrepresentation in a beautiful form might even have been read in relation to those Jews who 'pass' as indistinguishable from Christians.[58] Jewish people were, after all, described by Augustine as once the favourite sons of God, now the sons of Satan.[59] The anxiety of the fairy's invisible difference underlies the account. Her origin remains unknown, as is typical of such narratives, and paired with a final, unambiguous revelation of difference. If not a direct allegory for Jewish misbelief, it is at the very least a narrative born out of the same concerns that prompted the thirteenth-century Lateran decrees which demanded visible distinctions between Christians, Jews, and Muslims, including the 'badge of shame'.[60] Such demarcations are related to concerns about the very substance of Gervase's narrative – marriage, children, and eucharistic rejection. The seductive power of (invisible) alterity informs a refashioning of the courtly lady of the fairy mother narrative, as the seductions of the heretic meet racialised difference. The conjunction of the two figures is not necessarily unexpected. After all, medieval Christian understandings of history were contingent on Christianity's Jewish past, and (not dissimilar to English attitudes towards narratives of the British past, surveyed in the Introduction and Chapter 1) commonalities are disavowed through invocations of the fantastic, employed as a distancing mechanism.[61]

Gervase's narrative is not purely representative: it also explicitly interrogates the historical status of the fairy and of the wonder tale. Gervase is at pains to note a clear point of material demonic engagement: demonic or demonically aided flight, the consequences of which are materially present in the ruined tower of the subsequently abandoned castle. The narrative approaches phantasmatic materiality in another respect also. It functions as an elaboration of (if not indeed a direct analogy for) the mystery of transubstantiation. It corresponds to the broader trend that Miri Rubin notes, the reporting of eucharistic miracles (including those with antisemitic components) with remarkable or memorable components as a way of 'teaching the symbolism of the eucharist'.[62] Gervase's account of transubstantiation, which appears in the conclusion to the chapter, is concerned with the divine revelation of hidden evil and its bringing to judgement:

> Tuba dominica sonat in ewangelio; uerum inter secreta sacerdotis opera Christus ipse descendit, tanto districtius occurentem te sibi diiudicans quanto secretius te uidet intus, renes et corda perscrutans.

> (The Lord's trumpet sounds in the gospel; but during the mysterious action of the priest, Christ himself comes down, judging you as you come before him, the more severely as he sees your inmost being, trying the hearts and reins.)[63]

The passage echoes Apocalypse 20.13, where each is rewarded according to their works. Gervase may also have had in mind Apocalypse 2, which tells of the false prophet Jezebel (2.20–24) and the 'synagogue of Satan' (2.9). Fairy material appears to have lent itself to interpretations of this passage, and in Geoffrey of Auxerre's fifteenth sermon on the Apocalypse (c. 1187–94), a version of the serpentine fairy mother narrative associated with an unnamed dynasty in Langres is used to exemplify the dangers of women preaching, with the fairy presented as an overt cipher for Jezebel.[64] The meaning of Gervase's account similarly appears to be that false believers (heretics, Jews, and overmighty women) are unmasked at the elevation of the host, and the eucharistic miracle prefigures the operation and culmination of history in its fullest sense: an apocalyptic drawing of the boundaries between the saved and the damned.

In the epilogue to the account of the lady of L'Epervier, Gervase cautions Otto to pick his advisors with discretion, and with a mind to due respect for the ministers of the church and the sacraments (from which the lady flees):

> Hinc tibi, felix Auguste, doctrina sumenda est circa eos qui circa diuina sacramenta deuoti sunt, et contra illos qui fornicantur a Deo, contempnentes sacramenta per manus nostri temporis sacerdotum ministra, quasi ad ueritatem uirtutemque sacramentorum dignitas aut indignitas operetur ministrancium. Profecto heretici sunt hii, qui solem contempnunt transeuntem per immunda loca.

> (From this, happy Augustus, you should take instruction, learning to favour people who are devoted to the divine sacraments, while shunning those who commit fornication against God and despise the sacraments administered at the hands of the priests of our time, as if the worthiness or unworthiness of the ministers decided the validity and effectiveness of the sacraments. They are heretics indeed, these people who despise the sun when it passes through unclean places.)[65]

The Arles setting of this eucharistic fairy narrative is surely no coincidence. Gervase appears to have had a particular interest in its recuperated presentation to Otto, and certainly the emperor was associated with the region – although he appears to have never visited. It was suggested, contemporaneously with his decline (he was finally deposed in 1215), that Otto might restrict his power to Arles alone, ceding imperial authority to the future Frederick II.[66] Gervase wrote in the years following Otto's excommunication by Innocent III, between 1210 and 1215, and his account of the decline of Otto's fortunes elsewhere in *Otia* reads very closely to the misfortune of the fairy-born in high medieval marvellous historiography: 'post multos arridentis tibi fortune applausus et uictorias de hoste possessas, iam rota tue prosperitatis ad deciduum flecti uidebatur' ('after the many plaudits which a smiling fortune had bestowed on you and the victories which you had gained over the enemy, the wheel of your prosperity seemed already to have started turning downwards').[67] The narrative and its religious-political *moralitas* are suggestive of the construction of a gendered opposition (or rather, an opposition that deploys gendered signs and signifiers): between the heretical or bad advisor, represented as the demonic figure of the female fairy (itself a clustering of misogynistic and antisemitic representations), and the sage advice of the churchman or cleric. One is a cipher for secular and sexual excess, the other for masculine clerical wisdom. Gervase redirects his reader's gaze, from the fairy in flight to the elevated host. The tale reveals history in its apocalyptic, and for Gervase its truest, sense – a history safeguarded and interpreted by secular clerics as historical exegetes.

## The heretics of Rheims

Gervase's conflation of the fairy with the figure of the eucharist-evading female heretic might be read in relation to a broader ideological shift identified by R. I. Moore in clerical writings of the twelfth and early thirteenth centuries, which increasingly positioned Jewish people, women, and other potentially marginalised groups in relation to heretical threats.[68] While this understanding of the period (and the magnitude of this historical change) has been nuanced in recent years, the uses of *mirabilia* in the writings of Gervase and his contemporaries certainly belong to a wider intellectual context keenly engaged with the threat of heresy, and associated misogynistic and antisemitic constructs, which, I suggest, conditioned the uses of marvellous content.[69] We find a useful measure of this in another historical account of a lady who vanished through a window: a heretic of Rheims who appears in the chronicle of Ralph of Coggeshall, which, as Peters observes, might be understood as an analogue to the lady of L'Epervier and, notably, places Gervase within those same circuits of ecclesiastical oral reportage on which he draws in *Otia*.[70] Ralph records an anecdote told to him by Gervase concerning a heretic he discovered in Rheims in the late twelfth century. In his youth, and while travelling in the company of the Bishop of Rheims, Gervase encountered, and propositioned, a young woman. The woman resisted Gervase, citing her fear of the damnation that meets lost virginity. Gervase understood this as an identifying feature of the 'Publicani' heresy (the Cathar distinction between the spiritual good and the evil of the flesh), and the woman was arrested.[71] She subsequently identified an older female member of the sect, who was arrested and condemned alongside the younger woman, but escaped burning through aerial ascent through a window, with the aid of malevolent spirits which she summoned with the word 'Recipe' ('catch') while throwing a ball of thread.[72] This is presented as the same demonic process that aided Simon Magus in his flight and speaks to both demonic–material interactions and demonic limitations. This would appear to be an early representation of that issue which most vexed later witch-theorists: transvection, the basis of the witches' night flight and an example of the (uncertain) extent and limits of demonic power over the material world.[73]

As Peters has observed, Ralph's anecdote combines different registers, among them the Latin *pastourelle* and the wonder tale, told as a caution against the wiles of heretics.[74] Indeed, Ralph is exercised by the very status and function of the wonder tale itself. The older heretic's flight is presented as a subject of improper wonder taken as holy by the credulous Albigensians, for the heretic is heir to Simon Magus, a false Christ. Ralph's account continues with the proper wonder of the crowd not at the older heretic's escape but at the burning of the younger, who would not recant her beliefs and was consumed entirely by the flames – unrepentant, and without screams of pain, to 'admiratione multorum' ('the wonder of the crowd').[75] The anecdote is followed by an itemisation of the articles of faith in which the heretics do not believe, among them that most Augustinian example of wonder, the fires of purgatory, which presumably we are invited to read in relation to the figure of the burning heretic.[76] Here we see something of the utility of the wonder tale in this period, as a self-conscious co-option of the wonder discourse understood to be used by the false prophets and marvel-workers among the heretics. Ralph's pious wonder tale corrects and redirects its reader's attention. However, as across the narratives in this chapter, we appear to see an engagement with the complex materiality, and the possibility of genuine wonder, that accompanies these demonic manifestations. This position again is with Augustinian precedent. In his discussion of the 'signa et prodigia mendacii' with which heretics (and one day, the servants of Antichrist) are led astray, Augustine reflects:

> Quae solet ambigi utrum propterea dicta sint signa et prodigia mendacii, quoniam mortales sensus per phantasmata decepturus est ut quod non facit facere videatur, an quia illa ipsa, etiamsi erunt vera prodigia, ad mendacium pertrahent credituros non ea potuisse nisi divinitus fieri, virtutem diaboli nescientes, maxime quando tantam quantam numquam habuit acceperit potestatem.
>
> (It is common matter of dispute whether these are called 'signs and lying portents' because he [Satan] is to deceive human senses by *phantasmata*, so that he may seem to do what he does not actually do, or because they are to be true wonders, but such as will lead men into falsehood, since men will believe that they could have been performed only by divine agency, for they will not know the power of the devil, above all when the devil has gained such power as he never had before.)[77]

The question is whether demons delude the imagination through false wonders or achieve true wonders that might inculcate among the foolish a false sense of demonic divinity, as is apparently the case with the flight of the heretic.

It is in respect of the true demonic wonder that Gervase appears to engage with the potentially wonderful reality of flight. In his own writings Gervase had a wider interest in demonically aided flight beyond that of the lady of L'Epervier. In a direct allusion to the night flight of the 'Canon episcopi', Gervase writes of the nocturnal flight of men and women as a subject on which disbelief might be suspended:

> Vt autem moribus ac auribus hominum satisfaciamus, constituamus hec esse feminarum ac uirorum quorundam infortunia, quod de nocte celerrimo uolatu regions transcurrunt.
>
> (But to gratify custom and my listeners' ears, let us allow that it is the wretched lot of some men and women to cover great distances in a swift, nocturnal flight.)[78]

Integrated in Gervase's lengthy account of incubi (discussed above), which briefly incorporates a medical rationalisation of sleep demons as hallucinations brought on by humoral imbalance, Gervase's 'gratification' of his readers' ears with this apparent overture to folklore has been understood by his most recent editors as an inclusion for pure entertainment only.[79] Yet this is not necessarily so simple: throughout this section of his work Gervase is far more interested in nocturnal demonic behaviours than he is in indigestion. His allusion to gratification would appear to suggest an element of common belief (however partial or knowing) and a satisfaction of expectations on at the very least the narrative level. This is to say that it is an overture to narrative, which, we see, is presented as historical. Indeed, these lines are followed by a corroborating story of a singular female nocturnal demon whose harassment of infants was witnessed, and the demon subsequently exorcised, by no other authority than the Archbishop of Arles.[80]

In his discussion elsewhere in Book III of further nocturnal 'fantasiis' ('visionary phenomena', although these might work material effects), another set of contemporary testimonies cluster. Alongside reiteration of Augustine's account of the demonic illusions that might be wrought using a man's likeness (his *phantasma*), Gervase writes of the accounts of his neighbours of the night flight of half-naked men and women. This is a flight which is presumably demonically aided, for upon hearing the name of Christ, its participants fall from the sky. Gervase adds to this what appears to be a personal witness testimony (although the use of the first-person plural may suggest localised common report, in the vicinity of Gervase, who in this period held office in Arles): 'Vidimus equidem in regno Arelatensi mulierem e castro Belliquadri oriundam ex consimili causa inter medias Rodani undas cecidisse' ('We ourselves saw, in the kingdom of Arles, a woman from the town of Beaucaire who fell into the midst of the waters of the Rhone for this very reason').[81] As Watkins notes, in this passage the prohibited belief in the night flight of the 'Canon episcopi' here appears to have become real for Gervase, in a way largely unprecedented in the works of previous authors.[82] This is a striking defence of the reality of such phenomena centuries before the night flight's better noted invocation in the writings of later witch-theorists.[83]

## Map's heretics and the Pierleoni

Gervase's approach is not entirely new, and it finds an earlier precedent not only in Ralph of Coggeshall's account of the two female heretics of Rheims, but also in Map's anecdote about the Paterines and the unmasking of their demonic strategies in Distinctio I of *De nugis*. Here the wonder of the reader is similarly redirected from the false wonder that might meet the heretics' demonically aided displays of power to the proper wonder inspired by the miraculous properties of consecrated salt and water. The account is organised around paired false and true wonders. It begins with notice of the Paterines' rejection of the Gospel of John and denial of the reality of the eucharist (two features of Gervase's account of the lady of L'Epervier also). Here a true wonder is supplanted by a false, and Map writes of the heretics' assembly, a 'sinagogis' where all worship a wonderful black cat, kissing its feet, tail, and 'pudenda'. Like the heretic's flight, this is one of the early motifs associated with heresy later repurposed by witch-theorists, but is also chillingly indicative of the transference of narratives of false wonder associated pejoratively with Judaism.[84]

Map then writes of a prince of Vienne, whose nephew is led into heresy by the Paterines through enchanted food, which the prince reveals – once sprinkled with consecrated salt – is no more than hare's dung. Again, we have a juxtaposition of the improper wonder of the heretics and Christian miracle. The heretics' wonder is, indeed, improper in the fullest sense, for they consume the most abject substance believing it delightful. Finally, we read of the sentence carried out against the Paterines – to be burned alive – the first attempt at which they survive, in what is taken by the common people as a sign of their sanctity, a prodigy that nearly begins a riot. However, once holy water is applied to the building in which the heretics are to be burned, the fire spreads and the execution is successfully carried out. A true marvel counters the false, and we read that the crimes of the Paterines are burned away: the stake survives the flames, while the bodies of the heretics are burned to ashes.[85] We might note, as in Ralph of Coggeshall's heresy account, that the successful burning of heretics, in spite of their wiles, is presented as something of a marvel. This is a type of historical wonder tale which even while its focus is anchored in materiality denies the humanity of the bodies burned.

A similar redirection is found in another of Map's fairy bride narratives. Although Gervase's rationalisation of the historicity of metamorphosis is more developed than Map's (in part, it seems driven by a very particular concern with the female heretic – an association that Map does not directly make, although it may be implied), Map's interest in the fairy theme appears to have been similarly informed by Comestor's antifeminist gloss, and has a similar point of application to that of Gervase: the use of secular marvels to read or position miracles. Map writes of the chance meeting of Henno, lord of an unnamed territory in Normandy, with a mysterious and beautiful woman in a forest near to the coast. The woman is alone, with a large store of treasure – she tells Henno that she was on her way to marry the King of France but was shipwrecked. Henno falls in love with the woman, and they marry and have children who are remarkable for their beauty. Henno's mother-in-law notices that the mysterious lady of the castle avoids elements of the mass, in this case the sprinkling of holy water and communion. Curious, she spies on her daughter-in-law bathing, and sees that she has assumed the form of a dragon. Informed of this by his mother, Henno, with the aid of a priest, contrives to sprinkle holy water on his wife, who, alongside a female servant who has helped to hide her transformation, disappears through the roof. Map notes that the offspring of Henno and his supernatural wife endure to this day.

The editors of *De nugis* entertain the possibility that by Henno Map may have meant Haimo Dentatus, a Norman baron killed in rebellion against William of Normandy (later William I) in 1047, whose overweening pride is noted by contemporary chroniclers.[86] While this certainly fits with Map's association of fairy narratives with rebellion and loss, unlike the account of Eadric, Map is not here interested in a personal fall, but, as we find in Gervase's second fairy narrative, in the exegetical applications of the account. Map draws on the 'apparicione', apparently historicised (with living descendants), to endorse the historicity of biblical miracles: the ascension of Christ. Map writes, 'Ne miremini si Dominus ascendit corporaliter, cum hoc pessimis permiserit creaturis' ('Marvel not that the Lord ascended to heaven with his body, since he has permitted such abominable creatures to do so').[87] Map presents a remarkable phantasmatic body that can disappear entirely into a spiritual realm, whether heaven or hell. We might note here an engagement, as we find in Gervase and Ralph of Coggeshall, with marvellous and miraculous flight; and an exegetical comparison between the flight of evil women and Christ which, as Walter Stephens notes, was to become commonplace in later centuries.[88] Indeed, in the presence of two, rather than one, demonically associated women in the narrative, Map may have had in mind a configuration of a type with Ralph's heretics; there is certainly a whiff of female heretical conspiracy here, although Map does not state this directly.

Map also pre-empts Gervase in the association he draws between the succubus, *fin'amor*, heresy, and antisemitism. In Distinctio IV Map writes of the encounter of Pope Silvester, also known as Gerbert, with a 'fantasticum illusionem' ('a fantastic or imaginary illusion').[89] A figure of great learning (not least, in his knowledge of Arabic astronomy), Gerbert appears to have inspired all manner of anxieties, and his legend was conflated with that of Theophilus, a proto-Faust. Map's account of Gerbert is by no means the first, although it is the only one of which I am aware in which Gerbert's demon is feminised.[90] Gerbert falls in love with a daughter of the Provost of Rheims; when this love is not reciprocated he declines into lethargy and debt, until one day he encounters in a forest at noon a demon in the form of a beautiful lady in possession of great wealth, identified as Meridiana (a name suggestive of the noon-day demon of the Psalm 90.6) or Mariana (the latter presumably a point of Marian inversion). With the aid of the demon's preternatural foreknowledge, Gerbert advances in the world, although his fidelity to the demon is compromised by his sexual encounter with the provost's daughter, now besotted. Meridiana apparently forgives him, and he achieves the highest ecclesiastical office – the papacy. Here, however, his use of the demon's knowledge proves ultimately self-defeating. Gerbert, believing himself safe until he celebrates mass in Jerusalem (a place he never intends to visit), finds himself in a church in Rome of that name, and dies. Drops of sweat which appear on the marble of his tomb are understood to have a predictive function, auguring the death of wealthy Romans.

This account depicts not only the illusory nature of worldly glory, wealth, and power, but the dangerously metamorphic qualities of love. This is fundamental not simply to the Luciferian promise of the demon, but to the account of lovesickness with which the narrative begins, understood as the consequence of an ill-fated looking at a wonderful woman. The daughter of the provost is the 'admiratio' (wonder) of the city. When Gerbert looks upon her – 'uidet, admiratur, cupit' ('he saw, wondered, desired') – he experiences an extreme set of embodied responses, under the power of the woman's 'veneno' (poison or love potion).[91] This reads in relation to the terms in which the demon describes the provost's daughter, a gorgon:

> que Minerue peplo uelauit Affroditem, et sub tue pretextu repulse in suam alii diuaricacionem appulerunt. Proh dolor! expulsa Pallade tegitur sub egide Gorgon.
>
> (Under her pretended robe of Minerva, she sheltered Aphrodite, and under pretext of rejecting you she has been made by others a partner in their iniquities. Alas, Alas! Pallas was driven out and a Gorgon was covered by her mantle.)[92]

The demon's identification of female falseness in speech and presentation, which hides a bitter poison, introduces an obvious point of parity between Gerbert's first love and the succubus. The gorgon (another female serpentine allusion) is a particularly interesting model for Aristotelian understandings of the material effects of visual stimuli: her look turns bodies to stone. Gerbert appears to be damned twice by his looking upon beautiful female bodies. His first love is even compared to the *striga*. We read of the effects of her poison: 'cuius uirtute degenerat in asinum, ad onera fortis, ad uerbera durus, ad opera deses, ad operas ineptus, in omni semper miseria petulcus. Non ei sentitur inflicta calamitas ...' ('by its power he sank to be an ass, strong to bear burdens, impervious to blows, sluggish to toil, stupid in skilled labour, ever prone to kick at any hardship. He did not feel the calamity that fell on him ...').[93] This is a reference to the work of the witches of Apuleius's *Metamorphoses*, which we have seen informed Gervase's later deliberations on the same subject. Gerbert is enchanted before he ever meets his demon lover, who would appear to be a magnification of his previous experience of love.

As we find in Gervase's accounts, the machinations of demonic women provide a context for the development of heresy – and devotion of the demon (or the courtly lady whose position she usurps) is represented not simply as enchantment but as idolatry. Map writes of Gerbert's successors much as he records the fortunes of the heirs to fairy dynasties, noting the significant loss of papal possessions in the generations following Gerbert: 'ut dicitur possessionibus omnium successorum suorum temporibus aliquit defluxit' ('it is said in the times of each and all of his successors something has dropped away from their possessions').[94] The narrative concludes with the decline of papal estates, through the granting by Pope Leo of the castle of Crescentius to the Jewish convert Peter Leonis, which remains still in the possession of his heirs. On the margins of the narrative is the figure of Pope Anacletus (1130–39), descended from Peter Leonis; and indeed, the narrative pauses on the matter of demonic inheritance, for the demon herself professes to come from a most noble stock ('et generosissimo producta stemate').[95] In the context of the Pierleoni, there is an explicitly antisemitic register to the tale's demonism (we might note similarly the 'sinagoga' of Map's Paterines), and a concern with the relationship between the material inheritance of the papacy, and the property and riches transmitted trans-generationally by the converted Jews of Rome. This material appears to articulate a very early version of an antisemitic conspiracy that was given new life in far more recent history: the demonological origins of Jewish power.[96] Again, we see the drawing of the boundaries of a community of wonder that brings together the author and his audience, defined in relation to the boundaries of faith. This is the pejorative work of the marvel.

### The Countess of Anjou

Given the circulation of historical wonder tales of the supernatural bride and mother among secular clerics working in the Plantagenet sphere, it need not surprise us to see in the years following 1200 a shift in its uses as a wonder tale mobilised against heretics (for the most part, women) to an explicitly anti-Angevin legend, expressing opposition – both coded and overt – to a familiar figure of misogynist attack: Eleanor of Aquitaine. We first find this in Gerald of Wales's early thirteenth-century *De principis instructione*, which recounts the remarkable appearance and disappearance of the fairy wife of an unnamed count of Anjou (the precise period to which this belongs remains unclear). The narrative presents a mode of political commentary similar to that of Gervase of Tilbury, and indeed, it has been argued that Gerald was inspired by Gervase's material.[97] A case has also been made for the influence of Map's account of Henno, and parity has long been noted between the fairy bride of Henno, due to be married to the King of France, and Eleanor of Aquitaine, of whom the fairy of Anjou presents a dark double.[98] However, the narrative type appears to have been relatively broadly disseminated within this clerical network, and sources remain irreducible. That this material was held in common was presumably a point of endorsement for it: we see among the clerics of this period something of a community of credible wonder, re-using and repeating narrative content, presumably both oral and literary (even serving as each other's witnesses). This is to say that, tautologically, clerical authority confers clerical authority. Like Gervase and Walter Map in their accounts of the heretical fairy and her false marvels, Gerald presents a distinction between false and true wonders, which is of utility for his construction of a very particular, anti-Angevin, version of the political past and present.

De principis is directed to the future Louis VIII of France and belongs to the period of Gerald's intense disillusionment with the Plantagenets, and his support for the extension of Capetian rule in England, a line free from the taint of demonism which, we shall see, Gerald associated with the Plantagenets.[99] Its first book sets out instructions for rule drawn from a wealth of biblical, classical, and antique authorities and examples in the mirror for princes' tradition. The second and third books draw on accounts of more recent history where, as we might expect, *mirabilia* cluster. For the most part, these are in the form of dreams, visions, and prophecies, indicative of antipathy towards the Angevin kings. Towards the end of Book III, Gerald writes of a nameless countess of Anjou, of unknown 'nacione', a creature who, in the manner of the female-faced serpent, 'facie pulcrior quam fide' ('was more beautiful in her face than her faith').[100] The lady was married to the count for her beauty but showed little sign of religious devotion and consistently left the church prior to the elevation of the host, leaving immediately after the gospel (this is probably an allusion, as we find in Gerald's account of Meilerius, to the uses of St John's Gospel to expel demons). At last, four knights restrain her in the church, grabbing her cloak, which the countess casts off and flies through the church window with two of her children.

The location of wonder in the anecdote is not where we might expect. It is articulated not as a response to the flight of the demon (although this is surely understood to be remarkable), but rather to her aversion to the mass, 'cum admiracione notato' ('noticed with amazement') by the court.[101] The demon's religious aversion is a site of wonder, to be contemplated, and resolved in the flight itself, figuring, as it does, a point of ejection from the religious and political community; and we might note here the multiple available uses of corporate worship to draw such boundaries, which were as political and social as they were religious. Gerald implies that we must distrust those for whom such occurrences, or impulses, are naturalised (i.e. are not a source of wonder). He writes of Richard I's rhetorical lack of wonder at retellings of the event, and its wider genealogical significance:

Istud autem rex Ricardus sepe referre solebat, dicens *non esse mirandum*, si de genere tali et filii parentes et sese ad inuicem fratres infestare non cessent; de diabolo namque eos omnes uenisse et ad diabolum dicebat ituros esse.

(King Richard often used to refer to this, saying that *it was no wonder if, coming from such stock, the sons do not cease from attacking the parents nor the brothers from attacking each other; for*, he said, *from the devil they had all come and to the devil they were all going*.)[102]

Fairy lovers are consistently associated with rebellion throughout the historical *mirabilia* of this period, not only because the caprice of the fairy is representative of a sudden downturn in fortune, but because the fairy was also associated with demonic overreaching; that is, Luciferian feudal rebellion. Yet although the reader might share Richard's logic, they would surely baulk at his lack of wonder at such occurrences. Richard's status here as a reporter is interesting, and previous scholars have suggested that, if taken on face value, it may even indicate longstanding Plantagenet uses of a legend in the vein of *Mélusine*.[103] However, Richard's relative normalisation of the supernatural mother would appear to testify to the various evils that the sons of Henry II have naturalised; this is to say that Richard does not class the anecdote as a wonder devalues his identification as a genuine testator; or at least, the manner of his (reported) reporting is itself a component of Gerald's anti-Angevin presentation. Further, the uses of this allusion correspond with satirical material in circulation in the late twelfth century, drawing on supernatural flight as a cipher for the phantasmatic instability of the royal court. Map, for example, associates the hypocrisies and instabilities of Henry II's court with the transformations of the *strigae*. He refers to the officers of the court as 'germina noctis, noctua' ('creatures of the night, screech-owls'), who hate the light and seek the darkness (we might recall that Gervase applied the allusion similarly to the bad advisors of the emperor in his account of the lady of L'Epervier).[104] A supernatural mother, with the ability of demonically aided flight, is certainly not out of place within this discourse.

The episode entered the historical record as a *mirabile*, on occasion reported with relative neutrality. Caesarius of Heisterbach, for example, notes that the kings of England are descended from a 'matre phantastica', a demonic origin they share with the prophet Merlin.[105] Caesarius argues that demons make use of human seed to father children, and that those born in this manner are thus truly human and will experience resurrection on the Day of Judgement. Caesarius's interest in *miracula* must not be understood at a divorce from historiographical impulses: the claims of his (for the most part near-historical) miracles are rooted in local reportage, and, as John Finlayson has observed, derived their credibility from their apparent local plausibility.[106] Caesarius's historical vision was, however, even longer than this: he begins his account of incubi with the origin legend of the Huns, conceived by the exiled women of the Goths through demonic encounters.[107] We see here the power of phantasmatic encounters to shape history, in both a deep and an immediate sense. In many respects, Caesarius's assessment presents an accurate understanding of the register and discursive intention of Gerald's account, which does appear to be historical.

The Angevin fairy episode is integrated within a series of more recent historical anecdotes, a number of which draw on a historical discourse marker in common with fairy *mirabilia*: prophecy. Gerald writes of Eleanor of Aquitaine's similarly troubled origins: the abduction of the wife of the Viscount of Châtellerault by the Count of Poitou, Eleanor's father (actually, her grandfather). Attendant upon this marriage is a prophetic warning, issued by a holy hermit, cautioning against the marriage: 'Si nuncius Dei sum et michi fidem non habueris, nunquam proles de uobis et ipsa suscipienda, uel propaginaliter inde prouentura, felices fructus facere posset!' ('If I am God's messenger, and you do not have faith in me, no offspring will be born from you and her, or, if offspring are born, they will not be happy fruit!'). Gerald appends the hermit's prophecy with an account of the dwindling promise of the Plantagenets, 'de quibus in flora tanta spes fuerat, quomodo citra fructum eius emarcuerunt' ('of whom there was such hope in the flower, withered without fruit').[108] All share the same dark outcome attendant on the fairy mother narrative as we have encountered it across the examples surveyed in the first two chapters. Here the fairy is not associated with a terminal line, although the prophecies certainly make use of the grammar of this, but rather an unfortunate one.

The anecdote of the demon mother is thematically aligned with another of Gerald's prophetic *mirabilia* associated with Henry II. Gerald writes of a panel long left blank in a royal chamber at Winchester, which towards the end of his life Henry ordered to be completed:

> ubi postmodum aquilam depingi iussit et quatuor aquile pullos ei insidentes, duos aliis duabus et tercium renibus, parentem unguibus et rostris perfodientes, quartum nec minorem aliis in collo residentem et paternis acris oculis effodiendis insidiantem. Requisitus autem a familiaribus suius quidnam hec pictura portenderet: 'Quatuor', inquit, 'aquile pulli quatuor filii mei sunt, qui me usque ad mortem persequi non cessabunt. Quorum minor natu, quem tanta dileccione nunc amplector, mihi denique longe grauius aliis omnibus et periculosius nonnunquam insultabit.'

> (Here he [Henry] afterwards ordered that an eagle should be painted, and the four chicks of the eagle sitting on it, two on the two wings, the third on the kidneys, piercing their parent with their claws and beaks, while the fourth, no less than the others, sat on the neck and waited for the opportunity to tear out the father's eyes violently. When he was asked by his household what this picture meant, he said: 'The four eagle chicks are my four sons, who will not cease persecuting me to death. The youngest of them, whom I now love with such affection, will eventually attack me more seriously than all the rest and sometimes more dangerously.')[109]

The blank panel, filled by the treachery of Henry's sons, is a cipher for the blank page of history, on which the king's prophecy sheds light. This political prophetic vision (likely to have been Gerald's own invention) shares a notable aspect with the account of the demon mother which follows: both are scenes of eucharistic subversion and inversion. Just as the fairy mother rejects the eucharist, in Henry's pictorial prophecy the pelican breast of Christ becomes the torn body of the Angevin eagle. Here we see a fundamentally dynastic historical reflection on the eucharist, an affinity in common with the intersection between dynastic marvel and eucharistic miracle also entertained by Gervase and Walter Map. Its historical function is, however, realised more fully by Gerald than in any previous developments of this theme. It presents a particularly striking example of the close conceptual relationship that Spiegel has noted between secular historiography (as genealogical) and the 'central generative myths of Christianity'. Spiegel understands the 'internal structure' of high medieval history-writing as operating in an explicit relation to 'agnatic lineages focused on the transmission of property, name, and status from father to son':

> What connects them directly to the central generative myths of Christianity is the extent to which they replicate the patrilineal origin of mankind itself. As recounted in Genesis, God creates *man* (Adam), from whom alone woman (Eve) derives. This patrilineal generation, of course, is repeated in the regeneration of mankind through the creation of the (new) man, Christ, this time explicitly designated as a Son to God, also explicitly designated as God the father. ... Historical myth and historiographical *mythos* are one and the same expression of an underlying Christian metaphysics which explains the generation of mankind in patriarchal terms, and which thereby seeks a supernatural foundation for the continuance of patriarchy as an exemplary structure of social order.[110]

The disrupted mass attended by the supernatural bride shares the symbolism of Henry's subverted, or abortive, Passion. Both suggest a truncated genealogical narrative: a disrupted or even terminal line, foreclosing its fullest (positive) historical realisation, the smooth, uninterrupted, and timely transfer of patrilineal inheritance. The allusion invites an exegetical historical reading, concerning disrupted or problematic lineages – and it is no surprise that throughout the early versions of the legend surveyed in this chapter disruptions to the mass recur. We might recall the loss of the castle that concludes Gervase's account of the lady of L'Epervier, which similarly associates disruption to the mass with disrupted inheritance. In this material, we see particularly acutely an interest that recurs throughout the first century and a half of the fairy mother tradition, one which we might read in a particular relationship to female perfidy and its detrimental effect on the community cohesion represented by eucharistic ritual. Yet more than this, if we understand the Passion (with Spiegel) as a moment of historical realisation, the fairy's disruption of the mass, in symbolic terms, forestalls the culmination of history itself. She is an anti-historical principle, even as she is integrated into the historical record.

The logic of Gerald's anecdotes is inescapably genealogical: from bad beginnings come troubled dynasties. Indeed, Gerald comes very close to positioning Eleanor as the matriarch of a terminal line (or lines plural) in the manner of Henry's remote fairy ancestor, although again he cannot elide the existence of the Plantagenets. Presented as a realisation of the hermit's prophecy to Eleanor's parents, Gerald details the fate of her daughters, Joanna of Sicily and Matilda, Duchess of Saxony, 'quarum alteram sine liberis, alteram sine leticia' ('one without children, one without joy');[111] the death of her grandsons in Greece and Jerusalem; and declares that the fortunes of her descendants in Spain, Germany, and Brittany remain unclear. Yet despite his prophetic interest in the decline of Eleanor's progeny, like, and indeed potentially as, that of the fairy, Gerald treads with care in his treatment of some of Eleanor's descendants and hopes for the good of the 'Hispanica', into which line Louis, the intended dedicatee of the work, had married. The disruption to the patriline of one dynastic line is here presented to the benefit of another, an interest Gerald shares with the later Mélusine tradition, as we shall see in Chapters 3 and 4. Indeed, it is notable that while Gerald's account is hostile, it is also explicitly imperial, for even as he traces the decline of the various branches of Eleanor's family, Gerald charts a vast geo-political reach, across the Mediterranean and the Holy Land – one even to rival that of Eleanor's later romance counterpart, Mélusine.

## A duchess of Aquitaine

The anti-Angevin application of the fairy mother motif next appears in Philippe Mousket's *Chronique rimée*, composed in Tournai, Flanders, in the first half of the thirteenth century. A work perhaps better known for its incorporation of Charlemagne materials, including an Old French version of the *Pseudo-Turpin Chronicle*, it is also one of the most significant early vernacular witnesses of the dynastic fairy mother legend.[112] Although once erroneously identified with Philippe of Ghent, the Bishop of Tournai, Mousket is generally understood to have been a layperson, although he appears to have shared not only the narrative material but also the gendered and religious antipathies of his clerical counterparts. The account appears to be a reworking of Gerald's episode in *De principis*, although it may have been inflected by other available models.[113] We have already noted the integration of Gerald's version of the Angevin fairy mother into historical writings of the thirteenth century as an ostensibly historical event, and Mousket is similarly a historical author. In this passage he identifies himself as a 'trouvère', the author of a poetic epic. On a formal level, we find across the *Chronique* the patterns of stress, rhyme, and assonance of the laisse of the *chanson de geste*. *Chansons* often feature a recognisable class of historiographical marvel, or rather miracle: the demonic or angelic, in relation to which we might read the demon/fairy who flees the mass. Nonetheless, the intended historicity of the text is by no means a given. Mousket's *Chronique* has previously been read in relation to the self-contained truth of its form, common to both historical and less obviously historical works. Paul Zumthor writes:

> The function of these texts was not to bear witness to truth, but to expound their own truth, which they created intrinsically within themselves in the telling. The rhythm imparted by the verse form (octosyllabic rhyming couplets) implies the same poetic manipulation of data in both kinds of texts.[114]

Although Zumthor suggests that to seek a significance beyond this, on the level of presumed (or constructed) mimesis, is anachronistic, we cannot deny that the contextualisation of this material does appear to be ostensibly historical. The demon mother passage presents a truth beyond the impressionistic or symbolic, an engagement with the movement of history, even its rationalisation, in the manner of the analogous episode in *De principis*.

Mousket's is the earliest known version of the legend in which the demon mother is identified as an ancestor not of Henry but of Eleanor and is localised in Aquitaine. The comparison between Eleanor and the demon is, I have suggested, invited by Gerald, not least in his connection of both with the disrupted patriline. This association, more fully realised by Mousket, can by no means be understood as the product of Mousket's singular ingenuity, but rather as a deeply entrenched set of associations that we find in demonic fairy *mirabilia* and constructions of heresy from the late twelfth century onwards.

We might note, like the fairy of the *mirabilia*, the foreignness of Eleanor to her English and northern French subjects, and the particular impression of Aquitaine, as R. W. V. Turner has put it, 'as an ungovernable land of rebels and heretics'.[115] Read in relation to the various rumours of Eleanor's sexual transgressions; her status as the paradigmatic courtly lady (double to the demonic fairy), granddaughter of the 'troubadour-duke' William IX; and her rebellion (as it was perceived) not only against one but two royal husbands, the identification of Eleanor with the fairy assumes its own misogynistic logic and, indeed, inevitability.[116]

Mousket writes of a count of Aquitaine who while hunting becomes separated from his hounds and men and discovers a young woman of marvellous ('mira') beauty, but of unknown origin, beside a fountain. He is seized by desire for her, marries her, and has children. However, the girl's true nature is diabolical, and she consistently finds a reason to leave the church at the Evangel of St John (a gospel with an especially apotropaic function, as we have seen in Gerald's accounts of Meilerius and the Countess of Anjou), prior to the elevation of the host. Eventually, she is restrained in church, and when threatened with holy water flies through the roof, damaging part of the building. The author concludes, reflecting on her departure, carried away – like the lady of L'Epervier and Ralph's heretic of Rheims – by an invisible demonic power:

> Si l'emporta et si l'esprist
> De sa malice et de son fu,
> Voïant le peule ki là fu.
>
> (Thus she was carried away and thus she might burn
> For her wickedness and her folly,
> In sight of the stake that was there.)
>
> (lines 18807–09)[117]

While the lady's burning surely has figurative connotations regarding her demonism, these lines explicitly recall the fate of the heretic, which the lady might otherwise have met. She is in this respect a very clear counterpart to the escaped heretic of Rheims, and certainly the narrative draws a close connection between flight and *maleficium* ('malice') of a type with this, as well as folly ('f[o]u' in line 18808, a play also on 'feu', fire), the inability to distinguish between divine and demonic phenomena characteristic of the undiscerning imaginations of the gullible and the heretical. Like the marvellous executions of heretics recorded in twelfth-century chronicles and historical *mirabilia*, the wonder of the demonic countess's discovery is endorsed by common report, invoked in the very public witness of the event in the internal world of the text. Demonic flight is here presented as a public spectacle either accompanying or analogous to the very public uncovering and destruction of heretics, which, like the telling itself, is intended to redirect the attention of both the reader and the in-text community from the demonic marvel of flight to the wonder of the mass.

As Daniel Power argues, Mousket's association of the motif with Eleanor is potentially suggestive of the chronicler's reception of Angevin calumnies in cross-channel circulation.[118] The anecdote corresponds to a broader tradition of bearing witness to the demonism (or otherwise) of the queen's body. Elsewhere in his *Chronique*, Mousket recounts a narrative found also in late thirteenth-century English manuscripts (with which Power has suggested it may share a common source) concerning Eleanor's disrobing before the French king's barons, to prove by her beauty that she is not the demon the king has held her to be.[119] While Eleanor's disrobing may have recalled the nudity taboo of Gervase's legend of the lady of Chateau-Rousset,[120] we might also note the broader dangers of sight, of the fairy or demon who inspires men's lusts, as we find across twelfth- and thirteenth-century uses of the narrative. The cultural codes and conventions of romance are here visible, and we might wonder to what extent this episode recalls the undress of the fairy of Marie de France's *Lanval*, who has been understood by at least one critic as a cipher for Eleanor.[121] Yet Mousket's account of Eleanor's demonic ancestor is rooted not in romance but in an earlier historiographical rejection of the cultural codes of romance, and a suspicion that the courtly lady, with all her enchantments, might really be a heretic or a demon.

Mousket also draws on the historical strategies of his predecessors in his defence of demonic materiality and maternity. As we find in Latin historiography, the reference to public witness of the demon's flight is followed directly by an allusion to her maternal materiality: 'VII enfans ot éus del conte, / Ki remèsent, ce truis el conte' ('They had seven infants in the province, / who endured, as I found in the story'; lines 18810–11). The (second) 'conte', a word with a wide field of meaning but potentially including written historical narrative, may be a reference to Gerald's *De principis*, which we have seen contains a lengthy account of the fates of the fairy's descendants through Eleanor and Henry, but it also (in the most likely meaning of its first use of 'conte', a reference to the locality) is engaged with narratives in regional circulation.[122] Mousket continues (in a departure from Gerald) that the children are situated outside the devil's power, following their baptism ('baptisiet, / Crestiénet et présigniet', lines 18812–13; an allusion to the apotropaic qualities of the sign of the cross also). This is precisely the same assurance given concerning Merlin's demonic parentage and baptism from Robert de Boron onwards, and Mousket may well invoke this as a recognisable cultural cue associated with insular history, here situated in a mutually affirming relationship to apparently local reportage.[123]

## Conclusion

This chapter has traced the marvellous discernment practised by historical authors of the late twelfth century and thirteenth century: a refocusing of the attention of the reader and in-text communities from marvels associated with demonic material manipulations (demonic flight and transformation) towards marvels which might properly be called miraculous (eucharistic) – even if it is the wonderful qualities of the former that allow considered engagement with the complexities of the latter. This is not quite the same contestation of history, and its parameters, that predominates in the examples explored in Chapter 1, although there are certain basic principles in common between the two – not least the importance of the system of values in relation to which the marvel signifies. Here the question is not so much what marvels ought to be included in, or excluded from, the writing of history, but first and foremost how the historical marvel ought to be read in moral or religious terms. In these texts the departure of the fairy is a demonstration of the limited power of the heretical or demonic wonder-worker, who disappears with the sign of the cross, the sprinkling of holy water, or the reading of St John's Gospel. Nonetheless, the genealogical effects the fairy works might endure, and are testament, to quote the Psalms via Gervase, to the 'abissus multa' of divine wisdom, a familiar Augustinian embrace of the affective qualities of wonder here understood in relation to the mysteries of demonic pro-generation. This is a distinctive cultural moment, for into the fourteenth century the marvels associated with the heretical fairy – flight or transformation – were no longer consistently aligned with the dangers of heresy, and imaginings of such spectacular occurrences might even be divorced from eucharistic analogies altogether. It is this to which we now turn, in Jean d'Arras's *Mélusine*, where we see the emergence of a new type of historical discernment, associated with knowing belief in the sophisticated marvels of the house of Lusignan.

## Notes

1 Gervase of Tilbury, *Otia imperialia: Entertainment for an Emperor*, ed. and trans. S. E. Banks and J. W. Binns (Oxford: Clarendon Press, 2002), pp. 90–91.
2 Watkins, *History and the Supernatural*, pp. 211–12, 219–20; Walker Bynum, 'Wonder', p. 13.
3 Watkins, *History and the Supernatural*, pp. 27–33, 219. The prime example of this is Gervase's report concerning the properties of the lodestone, although he derives much of this from Augustine. We might note the symbolic value of the magnet for modern scholars concerned with the 'scientific rationalism' of the Middle Ages. See, for example, Finlayson, 'The Marvellous in Middle English Romance', p. 368, which positions Roger Bacon's account of the lodestone as of a type with post-Enlightenment scientific rationalism.
4 Gervase of Tilbury, *Otia*, pp. 558–59.
5 Gervase of Tilbury, *Otia*, pp. 562–63.
6 Gervase of Tilbury, *Otia*, pp. 428–29.
7 Gervase of Tilbury, *Otia*, pp. 418–19.
8 Gervase of Tilbury, *Otia*, pp. 336–37.
9 Gervase of Tilbury, *Otia*, pp. 336–37.

10 See above, pp. 9–10. For discussion of the limits of Gervase's understanding of purgatory in his treatment of this material, see Le Goff, *The Birth of Purgatory*, p. 204.
11 Gervase of Tilbury, *Otia*, pp. 558–59.
12 Daston and Park, *Wonders and the Order of Nature*, pp. 120–22.
13 Augustine, *City of God*, VII, pp. 14–15.
14 Although his writings are just too early to show the sustained influence of Aristotle's *Metaphysica*, the influential commentaries on which were produced in the middle part of the century (most notably by Thomas Aquinas and Albertus Magnus), for Gervase, like Aristotle, wonder is the beginning of knowledge – but not as a process of rationalisation; rather, marvels are themselves a source of knowledge that might be investigated and classed as true or untrue. As Daston and Park note, Aristotle's was a principle that scholastic commentators struggled to navigate in their association of wonder with ignorance; there is no such issue with Gervase, for whom *mirabilia* are integrated in taxonomies of knowledge. *Wonders and the Order of Nature*, pp. 111–20. For discussion of the development of medieval scepticism in this vein in relation to wonder, see Brewer, *Wonder and Skepticism in the Middle Ages*.
15 Edward M. Peters, 'The Lady Vanishes: Gervase of Tilbury on Heresy and Wonders', in *Mind Matters: Studies of Medieval and Early Modern Intellectual History in Honour of Marcia Colish*, ed. Cary J. Nederman, Nancy Van Deusen, and E. Ann Matter (Turnhout: Brepols, 2010), pp. 177–90 (p. 189).
16 Gervase of Tilbury, *Otia*, pp. 728–29.
17 Augustine, *City of God*, IV, pp. 548–49.
18 Gervase of Tilbury, *Otia*, pp. 730–31.
19 Gervase of Tilbury, *Otia*, pp. 730–31; Augustine, *City of God*, IV, pp. 554–55. In both cases this is a response to the patristic gloss that Genesis 6.2 concerns angels who fell after sinning with women.
20 Gervase of Tilbury, *Otia*, pp. 730–31. While the edition here translates 'fada' as 'fays', I here retain the original.
21 For notice of intersections between Marie de France's understanding of courtly love and that of Andreas Capellanus, see Sharon Kinoshita and Peggy McCracken, *Marie de France: A Critical Companion* (Cambridge: D. S. Brewer, 2012), p. 64.
22 For discussion of Andreas Capellanus's misogyny, found specifically in his invective against women in Book III of *De amore*, see Don A. Monson, *Andreas Capellanus, Scholasticism, and the Courtly Tradition* (Washington, DC: Catholic University of America Press,

2005), pp. 116–20; Reddy, *The Making of Romantic Love*, p. 183. For discussion of the clerical misogyny of Andreas Capellanus alongside another author of Latin *mirabilia*, Walter Map, explicitly understood in relation to female speech, see R. Howard Bloch, *Medieval Misogyny and the Invention of Western Romantic Love* (Chicago: University of Chicago Press, 1991), pp. 55–57.

23 Gervase of Tilbury, *Otia*, pp. 90–91.

24 This is similarly the case in Gervase's account of the *lamia*, a trustworthy account told to him by Imbert, Archbishop of Arles, 'affini nostro'. Gervase of Tilbury, *Otia*, pp. 724–25.

25 Gervase of Tilbury, *Otia*, pp. 84–85.

26 This is a long tradition, which in this chapter I necessarily treat only briefly. There is a broader visual tradition of the motif which lies beyond the scope of my argument, for which see Henry Ansgar Kelly, 'The Metamorphosis of the Eden Serpent during the Middle Ages and Renaissance', *Viator* 2 (1971): 301–27 (p. 321). See further Nona C. Flores, '"Effigies amicitiae ... veritas inimicitiae": Anti-Feminism in the Iconography of the Woman-Headed Serpent in Medieval and Renaissance Art and Literature', in *Animals in the Middle Ages: A Book of Essays*, ed. Nona C. Flores (New York: Garland, 1996), pp. 167–95; Peggy McCracken, *In the Skin of a Beast: Sovereignty and Animality in Late Medieval France* (Chicago: University of Chicago Press, 2017), pp. 103–04. For discussion of its association with the legend of Mélusine, see E. Jane Burns, 'A Snake-Tailed Woman: Hybridity and Dynasty in the *Roman de Mélusine*', in *From Beasts to Souls: Gender and Embodiment in Medieval Europe*, ed. E. Jane Burns and Peggy McCracken (Notre Dame, IN: University of Notre Dame Press, 2013), pp. 185–220; McCracken, *In the Skin of a Beast*, pp. 113–17.

27 Gervase is following Comestor's commentary on Genesis, in which Comestor claims Bede's commentary on the same as his source (no such work survives). See Gervase of Tilbury, *Otia*, p. 87, n. 7; Agneta Sylwan, ed., *Petri Comestoris Scolastica historia: liber Genesis* (Turnhout: Brepols, 2005), pp. 40–41.

28 See above, p. 21.

29 Gervase of Tilbury, *Otia*, pp. 84–85.

30 Saunders, *Magic and the Supernatural*, p. 114; Elliott, *Fallen Bodies*, pp. 40–45; Karnes, 'Marvels in the Medieval Imagination', p. 344.

31 Sylwan, ed., *Petri Comestoris Scolastica historia: liber Genesis*, pp. 40–41.

32 Kelly, 'The Metamorphosis of the Eden Serpent', p. 308.

33 Dyan Elliott, 'Seeing Double: John Gerson, the Discernment of Spirits, and Joan of Arc', *American Historical Review* 107.1 (2002): 26–54 (p. 38). See further Nancy Caciola, *Discerning Spirits: Divine and Demonic Possession in the Middle Ages* (Ithaca, NY: Cornell University Press, 2006), pp. 126–75.
34 Gervase of Tilbury, *Otia*, pp. 87–90.
35 For discussion of the distinction between hybridity and metamorphosis in the intellectual culture of the twelfth and thirteenth centuries, see Walker Bynum, *Metamorphosis and Identity*, p. 152. Hybridity appears to have been a more common point of interest and representation, for reasons which we shall see presently.
36 The discussion of the transformation of Lucian is treated at length in Augustine, *City of God*, V, pp. 422–25. For discussion of the false wonders of Pharaoh's magicians, a favourite subject of Augustine across his works, see Gregory D. Wiebe, *Fallen Angels in the Theology of St Augustine* (Oxford: Oxford University Press, 2021), pp. 136–37.
37 Gervase of Tilbury, *Otia*, pp. 86–89.
38 Kelly, 'The Metamorphosis of the Eden Serpent', p. 309.
39 Ashe, *History and Fiction in England*, pp. 16–17.
40 Gervase of Tilbury, *Otia*, pp. 812–15. The wider intellectual context of Gervase's allusions is discussed in David I. Shyovitz, *A Remembrance of his Wonders: Nature and the Supernatural in the Medieval Ashkenaz* (Philadelphia: University of Pennsylvania Press, 2017), p. 151.
41 For discussion of the changing reality status of the werewolf, see Dennis M. Kratz, 'Fictus Lupus: The Werewolf in Christian Thought', *Classical Folia* 30 (1976): 57–78.
42 Augustine, *City of God*, V, pp. 424–25.
43 For a modern English translation of this section of the 'Canon', see Kors and Peters, eds and trans., *Witchcraft in Europe*, pp. 62–63.
44 Walker Bynum, *Metamorphosis and Identity*, pp. 104–05; David I. Shyovitz, 'Christians and Jews in the Twelfth-Century Werewolf Renaissance', *Journal of the History of Ideas* 75.4 (2014): 521–43; Shyovitz, *A Remembrance of his Wonders*, pp. 145–53; Lisa Lampert-Weissig, *Medieval Literature and Postcolonial Studies* (Edinburgh: Edinburgh University Press, 2010), pp. 48–49.
45 Gerald of Wales, *The History and Topography of Ireland*, trans. John O'Meara (Harmondsworth: Penguin, 1982), pp. 69–72.
46 Shyovitz, *A Remembrance of his Wonders*, pp. 149–50.
47 Walker Bynum, *Metamorphosis and Identity*, p. 104.

48 This is a stock application to demonic illusion. We find it, for example, in Walter Map's tale of Eudo. *De nugis*, pp. 332–33.
49 Richter, ed., *Corpus juris canonici*, I, p. 1031; Kors and Peters, eds and trans., *Witchcraft in Europe*, p. 62.
50 Richter, ed., *Corpus juris canonici*, I, p. 1031; Kors and Peters, eds and trans., *Witchcraft in Europe*, p. 62.
51 Gervase of Tilbury, *Otia*, pp. 664–65.
52 Miri Rubin, *Corpus Christi: The Eucharist in Late Medieval Culture* (Cambridge: Cambridge University Press, 1991), pp. 219–24.
53 Peters, 'The Medieval Church and State on Superstition, Magic and Witchcraft', p. 211. For an argument for the association of Gervase's account of the lady of L'Epervier with the historical decline of an aristocratic house in the region of Charpey as consequence of heresy, see Robert Chanaud, 'Le Chevalier, la fée et l'hérétique. Une ancêtre valentinoise de Mélusine, la dame du château de l'Épervier', *Le Monde alpin et rhodanien: revue régionale d'ethnologie* 13 (1985): 31–54.
54 R. I. Moore, *The Formation of a Persecuting Society: 950–1250* (Oxford: Basil Blackwell, 1990), p. 90.
55 Miri Rubin, 'Desecration of the Host: The Birth of an Accusation', *Studies in Church History* 29 (1992): 169–85; Rubin, *Corpus Christi*, p. 126; Moore, *Formation of a Persecuting Society*, pp. 38–39.
56 Anthony Bale, *The Jew in the Medieval Book: English Antisemitisms 1350–1500* (Cambridge: Cambridge University Press, 2006), p. 7, and further, pp. 23–54. The study of medieval antisemitism, in particular in the context of the writings of English authors, is a growing field of scholarship. For significant monograph-length publications in the last two decades, see Steven F. Kruger, *The Spectral Jew: Conversion and Embodiment in Medieval Europe* (Minneapolis, MN: University of Minnesota Press, 2006); Kathy Lavezzo, *The Accommodated Jew: English Antisemitism from Bede to Milton* (Ithaca, NY: Cornell University Press, 2016). For two significant stand-alone publications, see Jeffrey Jerome Cohen, 'The Flow of Blood in Medieval Norwich', *Speculum* 79.1 (2004): 26–65; Sylvia Tomasch, 'Postcolonial Chaucer and the Virtual Jew', in *The Postcolonial Middle Ages*, ed. Jeffrey Jerome Cohen (New York: Palgrave Macmillan, 2000), pp. 243–60. None, to the best of my knowledge, however, have noted the antisemitic uses of the fairy mother narrative, excepting Heng's significant, contextualising discussion of the late Middle English romance *Richard Coer de Lyon* in *Empire of Magic*, pp. 63–114.

57 See above, p. 24.
58 For discussion of 'passing' in a medieval context, see Linda Lomperis, 'Medieval Travel Writing and the Question of Race', *Journal of Medieval and Early Modern Studies* 31.1 (2001): 147–64 (p. 153); Lomparis draws on Sara Ahmed, *Strange Encounters: Embodied Others in Post-Coloniality* (London: Routledge, 2000), p. 128.
59 Norman Cohn, *Warrant for Genocide: The Myth of the Jewish World Conspiracy and the Protocols of the Elders of Zion* (London: Serif, 1996), p. 25.
60 Moore, *Formation of a Persecuting Society*, p. 45. The complaints of the Fourth Lateran Council in 1215, and similar contemporary anxieties, have been read in relation to *Richard Coer de Lion* by Heng, *Empire of Magic*, p. 88.
61 This is the more notable given David I. Shyovitz's compelling study of the common interests in *mirabilia* between the Jewish Pietists and Christian exegetes during precisely this period, which proposes the possibility of Gervase's encounters with learned Ashkenazic Jews in the context of his travels across the Empire. *A Remembrance of his Wonders*, p. 152.
62 Rubin, *Corpus Christi*, p. 113.
63 Gervase of Tilbury, *Otia*, pp. 668–69.
64 Harf-Lancner, *Les Fées au Moyen Âge*, pp. 143–50; Geoffrey of Auxerre, *On the Apocalypse*, trans. Joseph Gibbons (Kalamazoo, MI: Cistercian Publications, 2000), pp. 149–57. In the same sermon, Geoffrey also includes an account of the demonic wife of a young man in Sicily, whose speech interdiction relates to herself: when speech is forced, she vanishes. For Geoffrey, a good woman is a silent one.
65 Gervase of Tilbury, *Otia*, pp. 664–65.
66 Gervase of Tilbury, *Otia*, p. xxxii.
67 Gervase of Tilbury, *Otia*, pp. 466–67.
68 Moore, *Formation of a Persecuting Society*. For a brief discussion of misogyny as a given in polemics against heresy during this period, see Walker Bynum, *Resurrection*, p. 216.
69 For a nuanced reassessment of Moore's position, and defence of its continued relevance, see John H. Arnold, 'Persecution and Power in Medieval Europe: *The Formation of a Persecuting Society*, by R. I. Moore', *American Historical Review* 123.1 (2018): 165–74.
70 Peters, 'The Lady Vanishes'.
71 'Publicani' is a catch-all term, encompassing the Cathar and Albigensian heresies, among others – although, as R. I. Moore notes, the

distinction between these is by no means fixed, not least as a category externally imposed in the context of heretic hunting. For discussion of Ralph's report and the historical contexts of the events described (as these may, or may not, represent genuine beliefs in the region) see Moore, *The War on Heresy: Faith and Power in Medieval Europe* (London: Profile Books, 2014), pp. 3–5.

72  Ralph of Coggeshall, *Chronicon Anglicanum*, p. 122.
73  Stephens, *Demon Lovers*, pp. 125–44. For broader discussion of the relationship between tropes associated with heretics from the twelfth century onwards to those later associated with witches, see Cohn, *Europe's Inner Demons*; Richard Kieckhefer, *European Witch Trials: Their Foundation in Popular and Learned Culture, 1300–1500* (London: Routledge, 1976), p. 15.
74  Peters, 'The Lady Vanishes', p. 182.
75  Ralph of Coggeshall, *Chronicon Anglicanum*, p. 124. An English translation of the account is edited in Kors and Peters, eds and trans., *Witchcraft in Europe*, pp. 79–81.
76  Ralph of Coggeshall, *Chronicon Anglicanum*, p. 124.
77  Augustine, *City of God: Volume VI*, trans. William Chase Greene, Loeb Classical Library 416 (Cambridge, MA: Harvard University Press, 1960), pp. 364–65. I leave 'phantasmata' here untranslated, where the edition gives 'illusion'.
78  Gervase of Tilbury, *Otia*, pp. 722–23. My translation, modified from Banks and Binns.
79  Gervase of Tilbury, *Otia*, p. 723.
80  Gervase of Tilbury, *Otia*, pp. 724–25.
81  Gervase of Tilbury, *Otia*, pp. 742–43.
82  Watkins, *History and the Supernatural*, pp. 222–23.
83  The most famous example of this is found in the *Malleus maleficarum* (c. 1487), in which it is maintained that just because the 'Canon episcopi' is engaged with a point of demonic hallucination, demonically aided flight is not in and of itself necessarily an impossibility, as witch testimonies corroborate. Christopher S. Mackay, ed. and trans., *Malleus maleficarum*, 2 vols (Cambridge: Cambridge University Press, 2006), e.g. I, p. 219; II, p. 45; I, p. 409; II, p. 251.
84  Cohn, *Europe's Inner Demons*, pp. 40, 146. For analogous formulations of this in the twelfth century, associated with Jewish gatherings, see Moore, *Formation of a Persecuting Society*, p. 64.
85  Walter Map, *De nugis*, pp. 118–25.
86  See also Watkins, *History and the Supernatural*, p. 204.
87  Walter Map, *De nugis*, pp. 348–49.

88  For a discussion of the uses of the witch's transvection in relation to that of Christ, see Stephens, *Demon Lovers*, pp. 150–54.
89  Walter Map, *De nugis*, pp. 350–51.
90  The most recent full discussion of the Gerbert legend and its development, traced in relation to changing western European attitudes towards Arabic astral sciences, is found in E. R. Truitt, *Medieval Robots: Mechanism, Magic, Nature, and Art* (Philadelphia: University of Pennsylvania Press, 2015), pp. 71–82.
91  Walter Map, *De nugis*, pp. 350–51.
92  Walter Map, *De nugis*, pp. 354–55 (modernised translation).
93  Walter Map, *De nugis*, pp. 350–53.
94  Walter Map, *De nugis*, pp. 363–64.
95  Walter Map, *De nugis*, pp. 354–55. Anacletus's Jewish descent was understood by some as a disqualifying factor for this very highest ecclesiastical office, an example of the suspicion often attached to converts. Bernard of Clairvaux, for example, wrote of his accession: 'it is well known that Jewish offspring now occupies the see of St Peter to the injury of Christ'. Kruger, *The Spectral Jew*, p. 105.
96  Cohn, *Warrant for Genocide*, esp. pp. 25–27.
97  Daniel Power, 'The Stripping of a Queen: Eleanor of Aquitaine in Thirteenth-Century Norman Tradition', in *The World of Eleanor of Aquitaine: Literature and Society in Southern France between the Eleventh and Thirteenth Centuries*, ed. Marcus Bull and Catherine Léglu (Woodbridge: Boydell Press, 2005), pp. 115–36 (p. 131).
98  Robert L. Chapman, 'A Note on the Demon Queen Eleanor', *Modern Language Notes* 70.6 (1955): 393–96. For discussion of pejorative treatments of Eleanor of Aquitaine in contemporary insular historiography, see Power, 'The Stripping of a Queen', pp. 115–36, with discussion of the supernatural bride narrative on pp. 131–33.
99  Bartlett, *Gerald of Wales*, pp. 74–85.
100  Gerald of Wales, *Instruction for a Ruler: De principis instructione*, ed. and trans. Robert Bartlett (Oxford: Clarendon Press, 2018), pp. 688–89.
101  Gerald of Wales, *Instruction for a Ruler*, pp. 688–89.
102  Gerald of Wales, *Instruction for a Ruler*, pp. 688–89. My italics.
103  Power, 'The Stripping of a Queen', p. 131.
104  Walter Map, *De nugis*, pp. 12–13.
105  Caesarius of Heisterbach, *Dialogus miraculum*, ed. J. Strange, 2 vols (Cologne: J. M. Heberle, 1851), I, p. 124.
106  Finlayson, 'The Marvellous in Middle English Romance', pp. 372–73.
107  For discussion of early versions of the marvellous maternity of the Huns, including their association with witchcraft and with Amazons,

see Patrick J. Geary, *Women at the Beginning: Origin Myths from the Amazons to the Virgin Mary* (Princeton, NJ: Princeton University Press, 2006), pp. 22–27. The legend also appears in William of Auvergne's *De universo*, in the context of a rationalisation of the methods by which demonic pro-generation might occur, largely pre-empting the conclusions of Aquinas. See Elliott, *Fallen Bodies*, p. 58.

108 Gerald of Wales, *Instruction for a Ruler*, pp. 684–85. This corresponds very closely to a Merlinian prophecy concerning the murder of Thomas Becket and the rebellion of the princes found in Gerald's *Expugnatio Hibernica* (*c.* 1189): 'Patris iniuria prosternet filios quorum primus regni culmen ascendens subito tamen & quasi flos uernus citra fructum emarescet' ('The wrongs of the father will lay low the sons, of whom the first climbs to the summit of the kingdom, and yet suddenly will wither away like a spring flower before fruit is produced'). A. B. Scott and F. X. Martin, eds and trans., *Expugnatis Hibernica: The Conquest of Ireland by Giraldus Cambrensis* (Dublin: Royal Irish Academy, 1978), pp. 124–25.

109 Gerald of Wales, *Instruction for a Ruler*, pp. 680–81.

110 Spiegel, 'Genealogy, Form and Function', pp. 51–52.

111 Gerald of Wales, *Instruction for a Ruler*, pp. 686–87.

112 'Philippe Mousket', in *The Narrative Sources from the Medieval Low Countries* (Royal Historical Commission, Brussels, 2009), https://www.narrative-sources.be/naso_link_en.php?link=1136 [last accessed 5 January 2022].

113 Philippe Mousket's account is contextualised in relation to many of the texts surveyed in this chapter, although sensibly without offering an absolute textual genealogy, in Ralph V. Turner, *Eleanor of Aquitaine: Queen of France, Queen of England* (New Haven, CT: Yale University Press, 2009), pp. 299–313.

114 Zumthor, *Towards a Medieval Poetics*, p. 287.

115 R. W. V. Turner, 'Eleanor of Aquitaine, Twelfth-Century Troubadours, and her Black Legend', *Nottingham Medieval Studies* 52 (2008): 17–42.

116 Eleanor's various crimes have now been understood to be as much a construction as the legend of her fairy ancestor. These rumours, chiefly of her incestuous adultery with her uncle, Raymond of Antioch, while in Palestine, were understood to be so well known as to in some cases require only the most oblique allusion. Gerald of Wales, for example, writes that much is known about Eleanor's conduct in Palestine, but he does not go into detail. *Instruction for a Ruler*, pp. 688–89. In the same work, Gerald notes that Eleanor had sexual relations with

Geoffrey of Anjou while still married to the French king, a double crime as it also made her marriage to Henry II (Geoffrey's son) incest of the second degree. For recent reassessments of Eleanor see the essays collected in Bonnie Wheeler and John C. Parsons, eds, *Eleanor of Aquitaine: Lord and Lady* (New York: Palgrave, 2003).

117 Frédéric Auguste Ferdinand Thomas de Reiffenberg, ed., *Chronique rimée de Philippe Mouskes*, 2 vols (Brussels: M. Hayez, 1836–38), II. My translation. I am immensely grateful to Dr Jo Bellis for discussing these lines with me and assisting me with my translation questions. Any mistakes that remain are my own.

118 Power, 'The Stripping of a Queen', p. 133.

119 These appear in two late thirteenth-century manuscripts. Transcriptions are printed in Power, 'The Stripping of a Queen', pp. 134–35.

120 Power, 'The Stripping of a Queen', p. 133.

121 M. A. Pappano, 'Marie de France, Alienor d'Aquitaine, and the Alien Queen', in *Eleanor of Aquitaine: Lord and Lady*, ed. Bonnie Wheeler and John C. Parsons (New York: Palgrave, 2003), pp. 337–67; discussed by Power, 'The Stripping of a Queen', p. 126.

122 Although Zumthor suggests that *conte* may have been used as a synonym for 'fable', in contrast to the truth-claims of *estoire* and *dit*, two neologisms coined c. 1200, these terms all appear to have taken on an expanded meaning relatively early, and their use is no certain indication of intended fictionality or historicity. Zumthor, *Towards a Medieval Poetics*, p. 119.

123 For discussion of the historical status of this text in a continental context, see Trachsler, 'A Question of Time'.

# 3

# 'Le Noble hystoire': romance and history in Jean d'Arras's *Mélusine*

> Or vous ay dit et devisé, selon les vrayes croniques et la vraye histoire, comment la noble foteresse de Lusengen en Poictou fut fondee.
>
> (I have given you an account, based on the authentic chronicles and the true story, of how the noble fortress of Lusignan in Poitou was founded.)[1]

This chapter addresses a work that we can position in direct textual descent from the Latin *mirabilia* explored in the previous chapters: Jean d'Arras's Middle French prose romance *Mélusine* (c. 1392), which traces the origins and fortunes of members of the house of Lusignan, beginning with their eponymous fairy founder.[2] The text tells of the fairy ancestor of the house who is cursed to turn into a serpent once a week until the Day of Judgement, but whose humanity might be restored through marriage to a human, if he were able to abide by her prohibition: not to look upon her in her serpentine transformation. The narrative takes its cue from Gervase of Tilbury's account of common report of serpentine metamorphosis and associated narratives. Gervase appears as a stated source in Jean's prologue, which also includes a potted account of the lady of Chateau-Rousset, from which Jean's hero, Raymondin, takes his name. Although the text, and the fairy herself, are commonly understood as one of the paradigmatic wonders of medieval romance (and indeed, the heroine's name is presented as a synonym for *merveille*), the generic and discursive affiliations of Jean's construction of wonder, and their political connotations, have attracted surprisingly little attention.[3]

An exploration of the heterogenous nature of the text, this chapter suggests that *Mélusine* stands at an important juncture in the relationship between vernacular romance and the interests of Latin historiography. The marvels of the text are presented as historical events, the significance of which is made clear to Jean d'Arras's aristocratic and royal patrons, whose belief, or rather suspension of disbelief, is a quality of a noble heart. These are marvels which invoke fear and trembling in those outside the community of wonder affiliated with the line of Lusignan – most notably, the English. This distinction reaffirms the historical importance, and political value, of the fairy to those – in the world beyond the text – capable of divining her meaning. The fairy is intelligible to a community of readers which is constituted both emotionally and politically.[4] This overtly political application of fairy *mirabilia* represents an extension and magnification of the tendencies detectable in earlier fairy narratives, constructing communities of wonder and historical belief and policing their boundaries.

## Romance and history

Although it has been argued that the truth-claims of early romance may have influenced the truth-claims of historical and topographical *mirabilia*, my sense is that we might orient the trope in both contexts within a long Augustinian tradition, and on some occasions the influence is more obviously the reverse.[5] As Kelly argues, on the basis of the terminology used by the authors of French romance, romance presents a balance between 'marvellous and frequently enigmatic, unclear, or meaningless narrative *matiere*' and 'the author's *san* or conception of that *matiere*'.[6] Although this position assumes the existence of source marvels beyond the text (traditions which may, in certain circumstances, have been no more than self-contained authorising fictions), conceptually this works very well for those romances which draw on Latin *mirabilia*, such as *Mélusine* – though the historiographical marvel is, I have suggested, rarely without meaning, even if that meaning is a divine enigma. Certainly, however, romance deploys a different mode of marvellous interpretation, a mode of 'topical invention' (to reorient Kelly's phrase)[7] beyond mere glossing, that magnifies the extraordinary while pointing towards the marvel's social, psychological, or symbolic truth.

Located between history and romance, Jean d'Arras's *Mélusine* explicitly invokes not only the truth status of the psychological, ethical, and class-based values contained within the romance marvel, but truth – at least, the politically contingent presentation of truth – in an immediately historical sense. In his epilogues, Jean incorporates testimonies of contemporary apparitions of the fairy of a type with those in the insular and continental historiographical tradition. These are among the historiographical discourse markers that appear throughout the text, incorporated alongside the less obviously referential cues of romance. My analysis in this chapter rests on a recognisable distinction between the *merveilleux* of romance and the *mirabilia* of the Latin historical tradition. Although from Jacques Le Goff onwards the two have largely been understood as synonymous, first and foremost as a class of secular marvels, I suggest that they rest on two distinctive sets of conventions.[8] This is not to deny that on the level of allusion the romance *merveille* owes a profound debt to the historical *mirabile* – indeed, Jean's very activity rests on this correspondence – but the key question for my current purpose is the extent to which the fairy carries with her a sense of historicity, that is, a function as a historical discourse marker.

I am not necessarily implying that the text is consistently historiographical. As has been argued of other Old and Middle French romances, *Mélusine* was likely to have been intended to be read as a 'blend of fiction and fact', qualities emphasised in varying degrees in subsequent versions.[9] This makes it a particularly important text in the study of the relationship between history and romance. Its engagement with history is complex, and even where it does employ historical (as opposed to historiographical – that is, discursive) allusions, these are often romanced. In his integration of relatively distant, but nonetheless recognisable, historical characters, Jean is less concerned with historical facts and timelines than with a series of metonyms that are broadly representative of dynastic history. Mélusine's son Guyon, a crusader who becomes King of Armenia, bears a lose affinity to the twelfth-century King of Jerusalem Guy of Lusignan; while Geoffroy, who murders his brother Froimont along with the monks of Maillezais, has been associated with Geoffroy, Viscount of Châtellerault, a lord of Lusignan who attacked the monastery in 1232.[10] Although revisionist in some of its accounts of recent history, when taken as a whole the history of *Mélusine* is not revisionist so much as it is symbolic, drawing dynastic symbols of the house into new configurations – and in this respect it is typical of dynastic romance, in that it represents an obviously imaginary past that is not directly mimetic. However, Jean's text draws on another set of narrative conventions which are presented as possessing a level of real-world referentiality: a centring of the historicity of the fairy, however fraught this proposition might seem. For the fairy is not ancillary to the text's history-making but fundamental to it.

## Patrons and sources

Jean d'Arras dedicates his romance to the third son of Jean II of France, Jean, Duke of Berry, prolific literary and artistic patron and builder (the latter an interest notably shared with the romance's heroine); and to Jean's sister Marie de Bar.[11] The overtly political rationale of *Mélusine* turns not on the family's royal French genealogy but on its maternal line, traced through Bonne of Luxembourg to the fairy founder of the house of Lusignan, Mélusine, the half-serpent daughter of the fairy Presine and Elinas, King of Albany (Scotland).[12] The legendary genealogy that the romance traces in association with Jean de Berry was remote, and as Jane H. M. Taylor has observed, the text constructs 'a geographical genealogy feeding off a biological one'.[13] The greater part of the romance concerns the deeds of Mélusine's sons, who build an empire which extends from Poitou into central Europe and the Mediterranean. In its interest in the marriages of Mélusine's children, the romance traces the formation of various local European dynasties, and the potential political utility of its geographically and dynastically expansive history was by no means unique to Jean de Berry.[14] Jean d'Arras's account was considered potent enough to inspire an alternative version of the legend in octosyllabic French verse, Couldrette's *Mélusine*, produced about 1400, discussed in Chapter 4. Couldrette revised Jean d'Arras's prose original in line with the interests of Guillaume l'Archevêque, the Lord of Parthenay, another claimant to Lusignan. There the Parthenays are identified as the descendants of Mélusine's youngest son, Thierry.[15]

The house of Lusignan appears to have been associated with an un-named founding fairy of Poitou (specifically, Parthenay) from the early fourteenth century onwards, but as Laurence Harf-Lancner has observed, the legend saw its greatest prominence contemporaneously with the decline of the main branches of the house at the end of the century.[16] The prominence of the legend is best understood as both a symptom and a rationalisation of decline in the context of the claims of new political actors to the mantle of Lusignan. The occasion for Jean's composition is the Duke of Berry's claim to territory in Poitou and the fortress of Lusignan – the seizure of which from the English in 1374 is the subject of one of the romance's epilogues, endorsed by a spectral vision of Jean de Berry's fairy ancestor contemporary with the English loss of the castle. It has been suggested that Jean d'Arras's *Mélusine* might be aligned with a propaganda campaign in support of the duke's control over the region, conducted on the popular level.[17] In his prologue Jean writes of stories passed down from 'noz anciens' ('our elders'), of things seen 'ou paÿs de Poictou et ailleurs' ('in the land of Poitou and elsewhere'), although his chief authority for tales of fairies is identified in the same passage as Gervase of Tilbury.[18] Whether mention of Mélusine really did function as an appeal to the fairy legends of the people of Poitou will remain forever obscure, but Jean's work is overtly positioned both in relation to common report and personal testimonies, particularly those from aristocratic actors, which cluster thickly in the work's epilogues.

Near-contemporary fairy testimony presents a valuable strategy for Jean, integrating the dynastic claims of the text into the political fabric of the world beyond the text. This is alongside his stated textual sources, which serve as a reminder of the lines of patronage, as well as the historiographical conventions, that contextualise his composition. The prologue introduces the work as a compilation of 'vrayes coroniquez' ('true chronicles'), provided by Jean de Berry and the Earl of Salisbury, John Montagu.[19] We see in this brief allusion the clear association of historical truth with the most reliable of reporters: elite male political actors. The precise texts here meant remain obscure, although functionally this extends the authorising strategy applied to oral sources, both subsequently in Jean d'Arras's text and in the earlier Latin tradition: the introduction of credible reporters (here, the providers of written testimony). Library records show that two now-lost dynastic chronicles of the house of Lusignan were in Jean de Berry's possession, but their dimensions remain uncertain, although it has been suggested also that he may have provided Jean d'Arras with a French translation of Gervase's *Otia imperialia*.[20] The nature of Montagu's contribution is more unclear still, although similarly feasible. He was a favourite of the English king Richard II, was involved in brokering the king's marriage to Isabella of Valois, and is understood to have composed (now-lost) literary works of his own, praised by none other than Christine de Pisan.[21] This inclusion is not so much suggestive of a favouring of textual elite authority above popular orality as an extension of strategies applied to oral authorities to literary patrons. Jean locates his patrons within circuits of narrative exchange, in much the way we find in my twelfth- and thirteenth-century examples.

## Wonder

Jean d'Arras is not the first author to make use of Gervase's fairy narratives. The lady of L'Epervier appears in the fourteenth-century *Gesta Romanorum*, glossed with a *moralitas* which reads the lady as a symbol for worldly desires, and cautions the reader to attend mass regularly.[22] We might also note the thirteenth-century and early fourteenth-century French translations of Gervase, which integrated additional 'merveilles' essentially as a vernacular *mirabilia* collection.[23] Like that of the French translators of *Otia*, Jean d'Arras's treatment of the marvellous must be understood in relation to a broader source tradition of Latin historical writing. It is within this discursive context that we might approach the interest in *emerveillement* in Jean's prologue. Jean glosses the fairy marvel in relation to Old Testament prophecy concerning the mystery of God's design:

> David le prophet dit que les jugemens et punicions de Deiu sont comme abysme sans rive et sans fons et n'est pas saige qui les cuide

comprendre en son engine. Et croy que les merveilles qui sont par universel terre et monde sont le plus vrayes, comme les choses dictes faees comme de pluseurs autres. Doncques la creature ne se doit pas pener par oultrageuse presumption que les jugemens et fais de Dieu vueille comprendre en son entendement, mais y penser et soy esmerveillier et, en soy esmerveillant, considerer comme il saiche doubter et glorifier cellui qui si celeement juge.

(The prophet David says that the judgements and punishments of God are like a boundless, bottomless abyss, and that he is unwise who attempts to understand them through his intellect. And I believe that the marvels which occur on earth and throughout all creation are eminently true, including those things that are said to be the work of fairies or enchantment, and a variety of others as well. Thus we mortals should not, through outrageous presumption, strive to fathom the judgements and works of God with our human understanding, but rather think on them and marvel, and in so doing consider how we may fear and glorify Him who judges in such impenetrable ways.)[24]

Fairies are located within the created world but with causes beyond direct human cognition. They are part of the impenetrable wisdom of God, visible through marvels which occur on earth. This passage is taken, nearly verbatim, from Gervase's Augustinian account of the curious bodies of fairies (as demons), and the question of progeneration, glossed by Gervase with Psalm 35.7.[25] Jean d'Arras's passage reads as the final link in a long textual chain relating the operation of marvels within nature, which the reader is invited not to explain but to contemplate.

In the passage that immediately follows, Gervase's Augustinian formulation of wonder is drawn by Jean into proximity with one of the most significant authorities on wonder for late medieval authors: Aristotle's *Metaphysica*. Aristotle positioned wonder (as Denise Schaeffer glosses it, 'a particular kind of *not* knowing') at the very beginning of scientific investigation – the impetus for the discovery of the operations of the cosmos.[26] Jean's citation from Aristotle reads: 'Le creature de Dieu raisonnable doit entendre, selon que dit Aristote que des choses invisibles, selon la distinction des choses qu'il a faictes ça jus, et que par leur presence de leur estre et nature le certifie' ('According to Aristotle, the rational creature of God should realise that invisible things, according to the distinctions among the entities created here below, attest to Him by their nature and manifestations').[27] Jean appears to see no contradiction between Aristotelian investigation stemming from wonder as a type of ignorance, and Augustinian acceptance of wonder. Certainly, both rest on an exercise in discernment, and, as discussed in the previous chapter, Gervase's Augustinian applications touch on matters of causation. Jean plausibly uses Aristotle's comment on 'invisible things' (forces within the created order) to refer to the activities of demons under God; certainly, this is how it reads in conjunction with the preceding passage on fairies. This appears to be a strategic misreading of Aristotle, whose treatment of 'invisible things' is not a demonological principle, but refers to the orderly motions of the cosmos.[28] (Jean's only other direct reference to Aristotle in the text is in his description of the Count of Poitiers, who knows more of astronomy than any man since Aristotle.[29]) The hidden rationality of the invisible offers an inviting, and indeed, authorising, comparison, and Aristotle here (briefly) emerges as an authority on the phantasmatic. Jean wrote roughly contemporaneously with the clerical interest in diabolism that Richard Kieckhefer has understood to have coloured interests in the figure of the witch in the late fourteenth century and fifteenth century.[30] While Jean's work pre-dates the 1398 condemnations by the faculty of theology at the University of Paris concerning twenty-eight articles understood to be sorcery and *maleficium* – including a refutation of the neutral or benevolent status, or prophetic omniscience, of certain demons (by which we might read fairies) – he belongs to a similar intellectual context.[31] As Kieckhefer notes, the construction of *maleficium* in the condemnations rests on an implicitly Aristotelian understanding of the causal relationship of the *maleficium* of the witch to the effective powers of demons: a world view shaped by an Aristotelian interest in hidden powers that Jean himself shares.[32]

Yet the demonic is only ever a covert presence in the French text. In a significant departure from his Latin sources and analogues, Jean's fairy is never explicitly identified as demonic.[33] Unlike the demonic fairies of Latin *mirabilia*, Mélusine is aligned with those fairies of medieval romance who declare their Christian faith.[34] In this respect, Jean's text is most obviously a romance, although this is not to deny that it is engaged in a search for meaning such as we find in fairy *mirabilia*. The romance quest or adventure might be understood as a search for significance, which – in the most satisfactorily concluded of romances – ends in knowledge and recognition. As Kelly puts it, the authorial response (*sens*) to the *matière* of romance might be understood as 'first *emerveillement*, then inquiry'.[35] In this way the quest of the knight is analogous to the investigative or revelatory practices of the author, as the narrative itself builds a cumulative contextualisation of (or commentary on) the romance *merveille*: 'Both knightly quest (*matière*) and authorial inquest (*san*) seek marvels.'[36] This is a juxtaposition that we have seen also in Gervase's representation of the knight of L'Epervier, an investigator of a type with the author.[37] Jean's Raymondin is similarly positioned, although his error is the inverse of that of his earlier Latin counterpart – in his rejection of Mélusine, he does not mistake the demonic for the divine but rather misreads the complex moral and physical ontology of Mélusine.

While fairy *phantasmata* might be probed in the manner of the demonic investigations of Gervase and Walter Map, for Jean d'Arras the phenomenon signifies in relation not to the mysterious mechanics of demonic intervention but rather to the marvellous might of the house of Lusignan. This complicates the historical status of the fairy in the text. When divorced from demons, fairies exist outside familiar theological and phenomenological frameworks, and therefore it is perhaps no surprise that in late medieval marvellous historiography, non-demonic fairies often serve as a marker of credulity and superstition. This is a superstition from which Jean d'Arras, with his elite reporters, appears to distance himself even as he uses it in his prologue as an element of local colour. We might note, for example, the account of Morgan le Fay in the *Prose Lancelot* – a text ascribed by medieval readers, apparently with a level of plausibility, to Walter Map, and which appears to draw on Gerald of Wales's allusion to the 'goddess' Morgan.[38] We read of 'Morgue la dieusse' ('Morgan the goddess'), who was regarded as such only by those without the sophistication to realise that her knowledge was acquired through the study of sorcery and enchantment – that is, those who cannot tell the true history from fiction.[39] The denial or rationalisation of the fairy occurs even in less obviously historical romances, such as the Old French *Partonopeus de Blois*, in which the mysterious heroine Melior is revealed not as a fairy but as a Byzantine princess.[40]

Yet for Jean fairy belief is a marker of the highest intellect, and a subject appropriate to the study of natural philosophy. In his reiteration of Augustine in the prologue, we see acclaim for those with wisdom enough to accept the limits of their knowledge:

> Et que plus sera la personne grossiere et plus a enviz le croira, et plus sera deliee de engin et de science naturelle et plustost y aura affection que ce soit chose faisable combien que les choses secretes de Dieu ne puet nulz savoir au cler.
>
> (The coarser intellects will be the most reluctant to believe it, while those with more subtle intelligence and an innate grasp of science will more readily intuit that such things are possible, although no one can clearly know the secret workings of God.)[41]

In the context of the dedicatees of Jean d'Arras's work, this is an act of overt class positioning. Belief, or rather the willingness to entertain belief, in the marvellous is a sign of a noble heart. As Daston and Park observe of Augustine, so might we understand Jean's work: 'Scepticism was the hallmark of the narrow-minded and suspicious peasant, trapped in the bubble of his limited experience, while belief characterised the pious, the learned, and the theologically informed.'[42] This is the very knowledge of the aristocratic heroes of romance. As in the revelations of the grail quest, we see 'explicit class distinctions made in romance between those capable of understanding and thus knowing the context of the marvellous adventure on the one hand, and those explicitly excluded and thus unable to know it on the other'.[43] This might be understood as one of the organising principles of Jean d'Arras's text and the principles of inclusion and exclusion it constructs.

## Hybridity and fiction-making

In terms of its mixed discursive affiliations to romance and history, *Mélusine* has often been approached by previous critics as a hybrid text, a double to the fairy's own hybridity.[44] While this is a compelling metaphor from the perspective of the modern critic, it is not necessarily of a piece with the author's own conceptual context. Similarly, while there are excellent previous analyses of the relationship between the fairy's hybrid and metamorphic body and imaginings of female abjection, or indeed the abject nature of identity itself, these speak less obviously to questions of genre or discourse.[45] As Ana Pairet suggests, an awareness of medieval understandings of bodily transformation and mixed forms demands a certain attentiveness to narrative contexts, and, I would add, discursive cues.[46] Pairet's own analysis explores the rhetorical function of Mélusine's 'polycorporality' and 'heteromorphy', the fairy's movement between, and simultaneous occupation of, different forms. However, I suggest that there is another avenue through which we might consider the semantics of corporeality, with pertinence for the text's complex claims to truth: the relationship of hybridity to fiction-making.

From Augustine and Isidore onwards hybridity was situated in a close relationship to the fantasies of pagan poets and their *fabulae*. Although in the late twelfth century this fabulous association appears to have been to an extent destabilised in the historicised figure of the female-faced serpent, hybrid forms appeared as stock examples in a long tradition of deliberation about the powers, and fictionalising properties, of the imagination, into the later Middle Ages. We might note, for example, Ibn Sina's widely circulated example of the powers of the sensory imagination to combine images to create new entities, such as a chimera – a combining of the image of a lion's head with a goat's body and a serpent's tail.[47] This position was reiterated by Albertus Magnus in his *Summa de creaturis* (*c*. 1240–44):

> Phantasia appellatur vana compositio imaginum, sicut in corpore hominis caput leonis & cauda equi, eodem modo quo imaginamur tragelaphum & hircoceruum & chimeram.
>
> (*Phantasia* is called the false composition of the imagination, such as the body of a man with the head of the lion and bottom of a horse, in the same way are imagined tragelaphum and hircocervum [two synonyms for the same creature, half goat, half stag] and chimeras.)[48]

Albertus writes here of the creative power of *imaginativa* or *phantasia*, which in its summoning of such unreal images possesses the power to override the faculty of reason to which it ought to be subject. As Alastair Minnis notes, the terminology used, and precise processes implied, by Ibn Sina and Albertus are by no means one and the same, but both broadly regard fiction-making as combinative.[49] We might note similarly the combinative interests of some of the early illustrators of Jean d'Arras's text. The fairy is represented in hybrid form in some (although by no means all) of the early French illustrations. As Lydia Zeldenrust's research into the illustrations and woodcuts of the fairy shows, fairly early in the reception of Couldrette's text Mélusine acquired not only a mermaid's tail but wings.[50] Potentially, this is not only a reading across the text(s) (an allusion to Mélusine's final flight) but a combining of distinct animal attributes, in the fashion of the chimera; and similarly, we might note that the classical siren, iconographically aligned with Mélusine, was sometimes represented in medieval images as winged.[51]

Hybridity was not, however, synonymous simply with fiction but also with divine allegory, allowing a focusing of the mind on paradoxical formulations understood as analogous to the mysteries of the incarnation and the eucharist.[52] This is very much a legacy of the twelfth- and thirteenth-century *mirabilia* tradition discussed in Chapter 2, as well, as Walker Bynum has noted, as a wider theological context at work in the earlier period exemplified in the writings of Bernard of Clairvaux (a thinker, we have seen, who was particularly engaged with wonder), regarding Christ as a hybrid, a *mixtio*, of divine presence in a human womb.[53] As I suggest below, Jean d'Arras treats a similar movement of faith in paradox, and it is interesting that in both cases, the phenomenon discussed is glossed in relation to medicalised discussions of the remarkable generation of remarkable children.[54] This appears most clearly in *Mélusine* in relation to the fairy's sons. The first children of the house of Lusignan are similarly hybrid, born with various extraordinary features, including tusks and marks in the shape of lion paws.[55] Although these descriptions correspond to the heroic epithets of romance, prophecy, panegyric, and heraldry, these are not figurative allusions but bodily applications.[56] The text offers medical rationalisations for the hybrid such as the 'mother mark', the impression the mother's imagination makes upon the child in the womb, which we might read in relation to the fairy's weekly transformation that continues throughout her pregnancies.[57] This rests on medieval Aristotelian understandings of the womb as a site of the reception and retention of images, although the image received would here seem to be the fairy herself.[58] The concept finds direct reference in Raymondin's first, private, rejection of Mélusine as 'fantosme', where he observes that her children have been born bearing 'estrange signe' ('strange signs'), evidence of the fairy's materiality that runs counter to his sense of her spectrality.[59]

Hybridity is here not (or at least, not only) a theme of chimerical fiction, but a marvellous adaptation of medical theory related to a wider theological conceptualisation of divine *mixtio*. Yet although the hybridity of her sons might be explained through an explicitly stated genealogical-medical context, the precise nature of Mélusine herself remains marvellously inexplicable, an uncertainty which is a predicate of the fairy of romance. There is a fine line in the text between the material and the immaterial, the imaginative and the experiential, and there is, potentially, something of an intellectual game at work here. The fairy presents an exercise in discernment which is unanswerable or irreducible, and this would seem to be precisely the point.

## Fantosme

The wonderful reality status, and materiality, of *phantasmata* is a structuring interest of the romance. We find an explicit treatment of this in two parallel episodes: Raymondin and Mélusine's first and last encounters. In a forest at night, directly following his role in the death of his uncle, the Duke of Poitou, in a hunting accident, Raymondin encounters three fairies, one of whom is Mélusine, at 'la Fontaine de Soif' ('the Fountain of Thirst'). Mélusine addresses Raymondin in terms which, while typical of the Christian fairy of romance, are also aligned with the vocabulary, and conceptual interests, of Latin fairy *mirabilia*:

> Et saiches que je sçay bien que tu cuides que ce soit fantosme ou euvre dyabolique de mon fait et de mes paroles, mais je te certiffie que je suiz de par Dieu et croy en tout quanque vraye catholique doit croire.
>
> (I know, too, that you believe my words and deeds result from some phantasm or diabolical power, but let me assure you: I am on God's side and believe everything a true Catholic must believe.)[60]

The Old and Middle French *fantosme* is cognate with the Latin *phantasma*. Like the Latin *phantasma*, *fantosme* has a demonic resonance, but the term is also here functioning as a synonym for fairy (a point of longstanding conceptual affinity with the demonic), just as it appears alongside *fata* in Latin *mirabilia*, most notably in Map's account of Eadric Wild.[61] As we see in this earlier fairy narrative, the knight's encounter with the fairy is understood as a physical engagement with a marvellous phenomenon, and an embodied response to a marvel. However, unlike Eadric, another hunter in a forest alone at night, Raymondin is not assailed by the arrows of love. As Jan Shaw notes, the initial point of sensory engagement in this episode is not sight but touch, although this is followed by perception of the fairy's beauty as an optical-cognitive experience.[62] Raymondin is roused from a stupefying grief, in itself a type of marvel ('menant telle doulour que c'estoit merveilles'),[63] by Mélusine's touch, which awakens him to a new order of marvellous beauty:

> Lors le prent par la main et le tyre fort et ferme en disant. 'Sire vassaulx, dorméz vous?'
> Et Remondins fremist tout ainsi comme uns homs qui s'esveille en seursault, et met main a l'espee comme cil qui cuidoit que les gens du conte lui venissent courir sus. Et quant la dame l'apperçoit sis sçot bien qu'il ne l'avoit pas encores apperceue et lui dist tout en riant, 'Sire vassaulx, a qui voulez vous commencier la bataille? Voz ennemis ne sont pas cy present! Beau sire, je suis de vostre partie'. Et quant Remondin l'ouy, si la regarde et perçoit la grant beauté qui estoit en la dame. Si s'en donne grant merveille et ne lui semble mie qu'il eust oncques mais veu si belle.
>
> (She seized his hand and gave it a strong, firm tug, then asked, 'Sir vassal, are you asleep?'

Raymondin shuddered like a man startled from a deep slumber; he laid his hand to his sword, as if he thought the count's men were upon him. Realizing that he hadn't yet noticed her, the lady laughed: 'Sir knight, with whom would you do battle? Your enemies are not here! Fair lord, I am on your side!' Raymondin turned toward the voice and perceived the great beauty of the lady. Her beauty was a great marvel, the likes of which he had never beheld before.)[64]

This fairy encounter is a point of concrete material engagement from its very beginning, where immediate physical contact initiates a cognitive or psychological transformation. Here we see the state change that Fradenburg has suggested is typical of romance, texts 'fascinated' with wonder as a space of possibility that provokes attentiveness (for reader and character alike), and which, accordingly, includes among its topoi a 'characteristic juxtaposition between sleeping and waking'.[65] The meeting of Mélusine's parents, the fairy Presine and Elinas the King of Scotland (similarly, an encounter of a hunter with a fairy by a fountain), is characterised in very similar terms: upon hearing the fairy's singing, 'il ne scet s'il est jour ou nuit ou s'il dort ou veille' ('he knew not whether it was day or night, or whether he was awake or sleeping').[66] We might approach this as one particular facet of the metamorphic effects of the romance marvel – a capacity reinforced by the comparison of Presine's song to that of the siren ('seraine'). As Fradenburg writes (albeit with a different set of metamorphic examples), 'Romance turns these shifts of sentience into a life-world, in which the dead or the mechanical come to life and powerful men change into pigs.'[67]

Raymondin's 'shift of sentience' presents a variation on the physically transformative properties of love and desire that we have noted in the earlier fairy narratives. Nonetheless, the historiographical motif is not one and the same as the romance. In the context of earlier historical writings, an allusion to the experiential (that is, to somatic experience) would appear to function as a signifier of the historical real and a refutation of the charge of *fabula*, but this is complicated by the multi-discursive affinities of Jean's text. Romance imagines somatic cognitive experiences, including love and grief, the intensity of which might be understood as romance marvels in and of themselves; but while both

Raymondin's grief and the fairies in the fountain are *aventure* generating marvels typical of romance, they are also historicised.[68] We read of the Fountain of Thirst: 'Et aucuns la nommerent la Fontaine faee pour ce que mainte aventure y est avenue du temps passé et avenoit de jour en jour' ('which some called the enchanted [or fairy] fountain because of the myriad adventures that had been occurring there for a long time').[69] While this might be understood as a piece of 'internal folklore' (to borrow Wade's phrase), or a generic marker of romance (we might think of the marvellous fountain of Chrétien's *Yvain*, or the Fountain of Barenton in Brocéliande disproved by Wace), this particular fountain is presented as possessing a historical life beyond the text.[70] Jean d'Arras includes in his second epilogue the testimony of a servant of the family who, prior to Jean de Berry's seizure of Lusignan, encounters Mélusine at the castle's well, once her fountain.[71] The fountain, subsequently the well, marks the site on which the castle of Lusignan was built, and the romance aventure that occurs there is written into the very beginnings of a historical dynasty. Similarly material is the fountain's presence in the landscape of Poitou, enduring into the present and future as a setting of prophetic and prodigious revelations.

As it functions in a referential relationship to the world beyond the text, the phantasmatic is also the real. For Jean d'Arras, let us not forget, belief is the quality of a noble heart. As Rupert T. Pickens has suggested, the text operates in part as an intellectual exercise in which the reader is invited to balance impossibilities which prove to be true.[72] This is precisely where, in his final encounter with Mélusine (as opposed to his first), Raymondin falls short: apparently, he does not possess the competency of the text's audience in their reading of the fairy (although his misreading arguably teaches one how to read marvellously). His adjuration of Mélusine is a striking failure to balance contrary, but nonetheless true, propositions:

> Hee, tresfaulse serpente, par Dieu, ne toy ne tes fais ne sont que fantosme ne ja hoir que tu ayes porté ne vendra a chief en la fin.
>
> (Ah! You deceitful serpent, by God, you and your deeds are nothing but phantoms, nor will any heir born of you come to a good end.)[73]

As previous scholars have noted, *fantosme* is used here pejoratively, as a term of abuse.[74] Yet Raymondin is not exactly wrong: Mélusine is in the final event phantasmatic, appearing as a spectre (although one apparently capable of nursing her youngest children) following her departure from her human life, but her actions have had the most material of consequences. Prior to her departure from the castle at Mervent, following Raymondin's rejection of her, she addresses the assembled company of nobles, with an encapsulation of the text's central historical paradox, the phantasmatic family tree:

> Et toutesfoiz, je vueil bien que vous sachiéz qui je sui ne qui fu mon pere, afin que vous ne reprouvéz pas a mes enfans qu'ilz soient filz du mauvaise mere ne de serpente ne de faee. Car je suiz fille an roy Elinas d'Albanie et la royne Presine, sa femme.

> (Still, I want you to know who I am and who my father was, so that my children will not be stigmatized as the sons of a demon mother, a serpent or a fairy. For I am the daughter of King Elinas of Scotland, and Queen Presine, his wife.)[75]

Mélusine does not exactly deny that she is any of these things, rather that they ought not to be understood as her primary designation. Jean's use of these three designations ('mauvaise mere ne de serpent ne de faee') may well be an allusion to the various synonyms (witches, serpents, fairies) at work in his Latin source context(s), and it might even be an attempt at a taxonomy in the manner of Gervase. Indeed, these words precede Mélusine's flight through the castle window, and the impression left, in the manner of Gervase's fairy, by her footprint. However, unlike the earlier fairy women whose nature she shares, Mélusine (as she here reminds us) possesses a known point of origin, and in this respect she is unique among the fairies of both the insular and continental traditions. Further, the materiality of her sons, the (historical) extent of Lusignan-held territory, and the castles she herself builds are testament to that reality, and that perpetuity, beyond the terminal or unfortunate lines of the earlier Latin works. Indeed, the good end of one of Mélusine's heirs – Jean de Berry – is the very rationale behind the romance. The phantasmatic is also the historical, and there is a truth to the paradox that Raymondin is, initially, unable to grasp.

Although there are various scholarly deliberations on how we might approach the underlying meaning of the paradoxical truth of the text (which I understand as Mélusine's simultaneous embodiment and ephemerality), unlike its earlier Latin counterparts, the text contains no obvious guide to an exegetical reading. The fairy is not, for example, placed in juxtaposition with the mass; nor is her flight compared to the bodily assumption of Christ or the Virgin, although some critics have suggested that such correspondences might be covertly present.[76] The absence of an exegetical gloss, of a type with Gervase or Gerald's earlier texts, is, I suspect, largely because all such comparisons are, in the earlier tradition, facilitated by the fairy's demonism. Yet Jean returns to the same basic principle: the ability to entertain, and to accept, the fairy paradox (material *phantasmata*) is analogous to faith. In his prologue, alongside Augustine, Gervase, and Aristotle, he quotes Romans 1.20, 'les choses qu'il a faictes seront veues et sceues par la creature du monde' ('these things enable His [God's] creations to be seen and known by worldly creatures').[77] In the wider context of the biblical verse itself, St Paul is not specifically engaged with the truth of the marvellous, but rather with the presence of God's invisible qualities within creation. Read by Jean in relation to his repositioned quotation from Aristotle, and through an Augustinian lens (via Gervase), this material, in sum, points to the divinity of *mirabilia*. To doubt Mélusine's historical reality is to doubt divine omnipotence, and to look upon her is to glimpse something of the complexity of creation and God's greatness.

## Prophecies of foundation

Among the historiographical markers of the text, contributing to the construction of its truth-claim, is political prophecy, a particular category of marvel that appears also in earlier fairy mother narratives, although the association is perhaps most overtly and fully realised in Jean's *Mélusine*. The relationship between romance and prophecy is an extension of the relationship between romance and history. As Cooper observes of prophetic insular and continental romances, including *Mélusine*, 'the foundation legends that so often took romance shape are themselves a form of prophecy of the future'.[78] This is, I suggest, one of the principal debts that continental romance owes to insular historiography. In the latter, the phantasmatic and the prophetic are closely connected, and, as we have seen from Geoffrey of Monmouth onwards, prophetic *phantasmata* find a concrete application to both the historical and the geographical. I suggest that prophecy is similarly fundamental to the ways in which Jean's continental narrative draws the emotional and geographical boundaries of a particular community and conceptualisations of dynastic identity (of the house of Lusignan), in a manner that is in part Galfridian. In its Galfridian affinities, Jean d'Arras's text looks back to the very origins of the historiographical fairy narrative – which pairs demonic or phantasmatic pro-generation, or its plausibility, with political prophecy.

The first dynastic prophecy of the romance is given by the heroine's mother, Presine, in the context of her serpentine curse upon her daughter, following the murder of King Elinas (their father) by Mélusine and her sisters:

> ... et non contretant de toy ystra noble lignie moult grant et qui feront de grans et haultes prouesces ... Et t'apparras trois jours devant que la forteresse que tu feras et nommeras de ton nom devra muer seigneur et aussi quant ly uns des hoirs qui de ta lignie ystront devra mourir.
>
> (... and in any case, a very great and noble lineage shall descend from you and accomplish many great acts of prowess ... and whenever the fortress that you shall build and endow with your name is to change lords, or whenever one of your descendants is about to die, you shall reappear there three days beforehand.)[79]

Presine's prophecy is mirrored by the astrologically informed prediction of Raymondin's uncle, Count Aimery, in the origin narrative of Mélusine's husband, presented as parallel to her own – a prophecy issued in relation to a romance 'aventure':

> Et l'aventure si est telle que, se a ceste presente heure, uns subgiéz occioit son seigneur qu'il devendroit ly plus riches, ly plus puissans, ly plus honnouréz qui feust oncques en son lignaige, et du lui ystroit si tresnoble lignie qu'il en seroit mencion et remembrance jusques en la fin du monde.

(For this is the adventure: if, at this very hour, a subject were to kill his lord, he would become the richest, most powerful, and most honoured man of all his lineage, and from him would issue such a noble lineage that it would be spoken of and remembered until the end of time!)[80]

Although certainly we might approach this 'aventure' in terms of the wish fulfilment of the romance marvel, and of fairies in particular (a promise of future prosperity), these prophecies allude to events beyond the romance marvel's ordinary historical scope. In their interests in dynastic beginnings, both prophecies are not only of Galfridian descent in a generalised sense (by virtue of their use of political prophetic discourse), but contain reminiscences of the prophetic legend of Brutus and the foundation of Britain in *Historia* I. Telling of an island of immense fertility and bounty in the west beyond Gaul, once inhabited by giants, the goddess Diana instructs Brutus to go forth:

> Hanc pete; namque tibi sedes erit illa perhennis.
> Hic fiet natis altera Troia tuis.
> Hic de prole tua reges nascentur, et ipsis
> tocius terrae subditus orbis erit.
>
> (Sail to it; it will be your home forever.
> It will furnish your children with a new Troy.
> From your descendants will arise kings, who
> Will be masters of the whole world.)[81]

New Troy is the name Brutus gives the new city of London; and his descendants, like the land itself, will take his own name: the Britons. The relationship of Geoffrey's Brutiad to Trojan foundation legends circulating in medieval France have been well noted.[82] There are at least two fifteenth-century examples of (very close) French translations of the British settlement narrative as a stand-alone text.[83] However, in *Mélusine* this material does not overtly frame a claim for the Trojan descent of the house of Lusignan – although perhaps tellingly, Raymondin's first act as Lord of Lusignan is the reconquest of his ancestral Breton territories. Rather, Galfridian cues were a natural feature of dynastic history-writing with supernatural elements.

Geoffrey's *Historia* appears to have been a far less fraught point of historical inclusion in France than it was in England.

Although among readers in England, the *Historia* was understood (depending on the particular historian) both as fabulous and as the very foundation of British history, in France Galfridian material was received as more or less historical.[84] The *Prophetiae* appeared in the context of a vernacular Galfridian chronicle tradition related to, and derived from, Wace's *Brut*, with an active tradition of copying and commentary into the fifteenth century.[85] Géraldine Veysseyre has identified three versions of the French *Brut* containing the *Prophetiae*, all of which possess a common debt to Wace, although they were independently produced.[86] These are the *Estoire des Bretons*, a thirteenth-century anonymous prose translation which survives only in Paris, Bibliothèque nationale de France, Français MS 17177; an anonymous prose translation, *Les Croniques des Bretons*, preserved in manuscripts from the early fifteenth century onwards, including a significant witness in circulation at the Valois court; and Jehan Wauquelin's mid-fifteenth-century *Roman de Brut*, produced in a Burgundian, pro-English context.[87] While the *Estoire* significantly pre-dates *Mélusine*, and the *Roman de Brut* is later and belongs to an entirely different political context, the *Croniques* are a product of a period very close to Jean d'Arras's literary activity, if not indeed precisely contemporary with it. As found in the fifteenth-century Paris, Bibliothèque nationale de France, Français MS 2806, the commentary contains a reference to the defeat of the French at the Battle of Poitiers in 1356, suggesting a date of textual composition in the late fourteenth or early fifteenth century.[88] It offers a significant precedent for the application of Galfridian historiographical models to independent French political contexts, in a manner very similar to the prophecies of *Mélusine*. I am not suggesting that *Mélusine* necessarily stands in a direct source relationship to a French *Brut*; rather that the *Historia* (whether in Latin or French) and related traditions presented a model for Jean in his writing of the legendary history of Lusignan, which, when viewed in the context of contemporary courtly French vernacular translations of Geoffrey, suggests a prophetic activity entirely in keeping with the historical interests of Jean's primary audience.

The British foundation legend, derived from Geoffrey, was a feature of *mirabilia* collections, including Jean d'Arras's stated source, Gervase's *Otia*. Gervase gives a potted account of *Historia* I:

> Et autem Britannia a Bruto, primo ipsius habitatore, dicta, qui cum esset filius Siluii, filii Ascani, filii Enee, expulsis gigantibus ipsam suo regno ad instar Troiae constructo Trinouanto decorauit, et nomine suo in posterum nuncupandam instituit.
>
> (Britain takes its name from Brutus, its first settler, who was the son of Silvius, son of Ascanius, son of Aeneas. After driving out the giants he adorned Britain with his royal seat of Trinovantum [London], built to resemble Troy, and ensured that the country would be called after him from then on.)[89]

These components – a first settler of noble lineage, who founds and builds a kingdom which takes his own name and who defeats the monstrous men of a previous age (the giants, to whom we shall return presently) – find distinctive reformulations in *Mélusine*. In the *Historia* Geoffrey writes of Brutus's role in the death of his father, Silvius, which precedes his period of Greek captivity and journeying across Asia and Europe to Britain (the same narrative which finds oblique allusion in *Otia*). Aged fifteen, like both Raymondin and Mélusine at the time of their parricidal acts, Brutus offends through a stray arrow in a hunt upon cornering a deer, while Raymondin's misplaced sword stroke slays both his uncle and the boar they hunt in the forests of Poitou. Aimery's prophecy reads closely to the prophecy Geoffrey gives concerning Brutus, prior to his birth. Magicians (*magi*) foretell that the child will be a boy who '... patrem et matrem interficeret, pluribus quoque terris in exilium peragratis ad summum tandem culmen honoris perueniret' ('would kill his father and mother, wander many lands in exile and in the end receive the highest honour').[90] This is not to suggest that the moral implications of parricide in *Mélusine* are absent: as Megan G. Leitch notes, the romance is particularly interested in treason; but the event itself assumes a distinctly legendary historical and prophetic resonance within a Galfridian framework, depicting the formation of new lines.[91]

Like the prophecy of Diana, the prophecies of Aimery and Presine articulate dynastic claims to a particularly significant, geographically privileged place. In *Mélusine* Poitou assumes certain features in common with Brutus's Britain. On Raymondin's return from Brittany (a site with its own place in Galfridian legendary history), Poitou is re-imagined as a *locus amoenus* in the Galfridian tradition, conceptualised in suggestively coastal terms:

> Et tant chevaucha qu'il entra en la terre de Poictou, la ou il trouva grant foison de haultes forests non habitees en aucuns lieux, grant foison de sauvagine comme cerfs, bisches, dains, chevreulx, porcs et autre bestes sauvaiges. Et en moult d'autres lieux belles plaines, belles praieries et belles rivieres. 'Par foy,' dist Remondin, 'c'est grant dommage que cest paÿs n'est habitéz et peupléz, car moult y est grasse la contree.' Et en pluseurs lieux treuve sur la marine moult de belles places non habitees lesquelles, a son semblant, feussent moult prouffitables a habiter.
>
> (He [Raymondin] rode back into Poitou, where he found an abundance of tall, uninhabited forests, in some places teeming with game – stags, hides, roebucks, boars, and other wild animals – and in many other places magnificent prairies and rivers. 'What a terrible shame,' he said, 'that such a fertile land is not inhabited!' And in several places along the coast he came upon lovely uninhabited areas that he thought could be very profitably settled.)[92]

Raymondin encounters Poitou as if for the first time: uninhabited but full of resources. It assumes a positive liminality, framed by the description of Raymondin's journey along the coast. Moving through Poitou, space which will in the course of the romance be claimed for the house of Lusignan, Raymondin reaches Lusignan itself. He arrives at the new fortress, which Mélusine has constructed with preternatural speed and, it appears, with the aid of supernatural helpers (a feature of the Latin *mirabilia* tradition).[93] He sees the newly built town and the Clarion Tower and finds the project so developed that he marvels ('esmerveille') and doubts whether it is Lusignan. But, as we customarily find in the operation of the marvel, doubt is met with confirmation.

This marvel follows a formula very similar to that of Brutus's first journey to Britain from Gaul: arrival at a well-resourced coastal site, and a rapid programme of building, and in this case cultivation, which gives the impression of longstanding occupation (although it is not, in the case of *Historia* I, the result of supernatural intervention, a sense of destiny surely plays a role):

> (Prosperis quoque uentis promissam insulam exigens, in Totonesio littore applicuit. Erat tunc nomen insulae Albion; quae a nemine, exceptis paucis gigantibus, inhabitabatur. Amoeno tamen situ locorum et copia piscorum fluminum nemorisbusque praeelecta, affectum habitandi Bruto sociisque inferabat. ... agros incipiunt colere, domos aedificare, ita ut in breui tempore terram ab aeuo inhabitatam censeres.)

> (Favourable winds brought him to the promised isle, where he came ashore at Totnes. The island was at that time called Albion; it had no inhabitants save for a few giants. The choice position of this pleasant land, its numerous rivers, good for fishing, and its woods led Brutus and his companions to want to settle there. ... They began to till the fields and build homes so that, in a short time, the country appeared to have been occupied for many years.)[94]

Just as Mélusine builds a tower and a town with great rapidity, so are the homes of Britain built so quickly (although not preternaturally so) that it is as if they have always been there. In Galfridian terms, this is a clear signifier of a dynastic line endorsed by the inexorable logic of a prophetic-historical narrative.

In *Mélusine*, this forms the very basis of an authorising community of wonder, who bear witness to the truth value of the narrative's central marvel. This is situated for Jean in relation not simply to place but to the evidential function of etymologies. Following her wedding to Raymondin, the Earl of Poitiers asks Mélusine to name the castle and town that will become Lusignan:

> 'Monseigneur,' dist Melusigne, 'puisqu'il ne puet estre autrement et que je voy que c'est a votre plaisir que je lui mette son nom, or ait a nom Lusignen'. 'Par foy,' dist le conte, 'ce nom lui affiert tresbien pour deux cas, car vous estes nommee Melusigne d'Albanie et Albanie en gregois vault autant a dire comme chose qui ne fault et Melusigne vault autant a dire merveilles ou merveilleuse. Et aussi ceste place est fondee merveilleusement ne je ne croy mie que jamais, tant comme elle durra, que on n'y treuve de merveilleuses choses.'

> ('My lord,' said Mélusine, 'since that is your wish, let it be called Lusignan'. 'Indeed,' said the count, 'that name is doubly appropriate,

because you are called Mélusine of Scotland [Albany], and because Scotland [Albany] in Greek means "an infallible thing", while Mélusine means "marvels" or "marvellous". And this place has been marvellously founded, and I do believe that marvellous things will never cease to occur here, for as long as it endures.')[95]

Although this episode is largely characteristic of the interest in appellation that we find in romance (which marks out a hero or heroine as exceptional), as well as the generative power of the romance marvel as the source of *aventure*, it also carries a clear historiographical, and political, logic.[96] The naming suggests that the territory was always meant to be Mélusine's, which is to say a possession of the house of Lusignan, in a movement that reaches beyond the text. This perpetuity is endorsed by the recurrence of marvels at the site into the age of the author. This model also utilises a historical-textual precedent, and the inclusion of Greek is a marvellous historiographical cue, if not indeed a metatextual allusion to Brutus's linguistic context. Brutus's first settlement is followed closely by an account of the naming of the island, its people, and their language, which memorialises Brutus for all time:

Denique Brutus de nomine suo insulam Britanniam appellat sociosque suos Britones. Volebat enim ex diriuatione nominis memoriam habere perpetuam. Vnde postmodum loquela gentis, quae prius Troiana siue curuum Graecum nuncupabatur, dicta fuit Britannica.

(Brutus named the island Britain after himself and called his followers Britons. He wanted to be remembered forever for giving them his name. For this reason the language of his people, previously known as Trojan or 'crooked Greek', was henceforth called British.)[97]

This paradigm, and its etymological interests, are utilised by Jean in much the way we have seen etymologies employed in earlier texts, by William of Newburgh and Gervase of Tilbury. They speak to the historical credibility of the marvel.

The final element *Mélusine* shares with the Galfridian origin narrative is the defeat of the giants, which occurs in the second generation of Jean d'Arras's text. Geoffroy fights and subdues the giants who live in the caves of his mother's homeland, Albany, who were invited by Presine to guard the tomb of the murdered Elinas but have multiplied and terrorise the people of that kingdom.

Found in the mountain caves of Northumberland, these giants present a marked similarity to the giants of the *Historia*, driven by the Britons to 'cauernas montium', prior to their extinction.[98] This episode is conceptualised in part as a romance *aventure* (after all, giants are not the prerogative of Galfridian history alone), yet there are Galfridian cues here. Of Mélusine's own ancient origins there may be an intentional parity between 'Albany' (Scotland) and the pre-settlement name of Britain in the *Historia* and apocryphal Galfridian history, 'Albion'.[99] Albion has a long association in Galfridian apocrypha not only with giants but with phantasmatic conceptions. The story of how the giants came to occupy Albion attracted particular attention from insular authors from the early fourteenth century onwards, when the *Historia* acquired a prequel in the legend of Albina, versions of which circulated in both Latin and insular French.[100] I am not the first critic to suggest that Jean may have made use of the Albina legend to frame a claim for the fairy's historicity, although the correspondence has yet to be fully addressed.[101] Like Mélusine and her sisters, Albina and her sisters rebel against their father, for which they are exiled from their homeland (Greece in some versions, and Syria in others).[102] This brings them to Albion, where they couple with incubi and birth the first generation of giants, who populate the island until the arrival of Brutus. None of this is to imply that Jean understood his giants as one and the same as those of the Galfridian tradition, Geoffroy as Brutus, or Mélusine as Albina. Rather, I suggest that in the *Historia* and related traditions, Jean finds a point of historiographical inspiration, and integrates and re-orders Galfridian components. To a reader familiar with the conventions of Galfridian history (as I suggest Jean's courtly audience very plausibly to have been), this operates as an authenticating sign of historicity. Indeed, if we are alert, as we assume were medieval readers, to the biblical intertext behind the Albina legend, it recalls the much-commented upon parentage of the pre-diluvian giants of Genesis 6.2, the occasion of Augustine's discussion of the Dusii.[103]

It has been suggested by Stephen G. Nichols that Jean made use of the Albina legend as the grounds of national contestation: 'a Francocentric fantasy ... play[ing] upon the pathological and British (a conjunction encouraged by the text) origins of the dynasties that have ruled in the southwest of France'.[104] Nichols here refers to the role of Galfridian content in English dynastic self-casting. We might think most notably of the Arthurian self-representation of the kings of England from Henry II onwards: an association that appears in a particularly virulent strain of English jingoism mobilised in the fourteenth century in the wars against France.[105] Although this allusion, and the others here surveyed, may stage a conscious French appropriation and subversion of an English historiographical discourse, we might also note the endorsing presence of a conceptual framework in which the invocation of a very specific legendary-historical scene is transplanted to a new continental locale, understood in relation not simply to the French crown but to a genealogical group with a geographically expansive reach. While on occasion it comes close to an 'imagined community' in a national or proto-national sense, the emotional community of the text is unmistakably class-based (aristocratic) and is enmeshed in a network of cross-border affiliations.

## Prophecies of imperium

The international contexts of the romance's communities of wonder must be understood in relation to the imperial fantasies the text constructs. These are articulated explicitly in the text's initial prophecies, borne out by subsequent historical events beyond the scope of the text, the realisation of which cements the truth status of the fairy. We might note the prophecy that Mélusine issues to Raymondin as she departs her mortal existence:

> Sachiéz que aprés vous jamais homs ne tendra ensemble le paÿs que vous tenéz et auront moult voz hoirs apréz vous a faire. Et sachiéz que aucuns par leur folie decherront moult d'onneur et de heritaige.
>
> (Know that after you no man will ever hold all the land you now hold, and your heirs will face many difficulties; some of them, through their folly, will decline greatly in honour and estate.)[106]

There is a contemporary aspect to this prophecy of the family's territorial losses. From 1385 to his death in 1393 (roughly contemporary with the writing of *Mélusine*), Leon V, the last Lusignan king of Armenia, then in exile in Paris, actively appealed to the kings of France and England for their assistance in a new crusade against the Mamluk Sultanate, incorporating the recovery of the Armenian kingdom alongside the conquest of Palestine.[107] This contemporary context, of later Lusignan loss and a renewed crusading interest, forms the basis of a series of connected prophecies in the romance. We might note the political prophecy of Mélusine's sister, Melior, made to the ill-fated King of Armenia generations after Mélusine's departure from Lusignan, itself a realisation of Presine's earlier curse upon her second daughter. Melior is to remain in a castle in Armenia as keeper of a sparrowhawk. Any knight who can keep vigil there for three days without sleep may ask anything of Melior except her love or her body, a prohibition broken by a king of Armenia (a double taboo, in that the ill-fated king is also Melior's nephew). The curse will endure for nine generations, understood in Melior's prophecy to culminate in Leon, identified, in the Galfridian fashion, through an animal cipher:

> Fol roy, par ta musardie te mescherra. Toy et les tiens decherront de terre, d'avoir, d'onnour et de heritaige jusques a la ix$^e$ lignie. Et perdra par ta fole emprise le ix$^e$ de ta lignie le royaume que tu tiens, et portera cellui roy nom de beste mue.
>
> (Foolish king, your impulsiveness will bring you grave misfortune. You and yours will lose land, wealth, prestige and patrimony until the ninth generation, and because of your foolhardy undertaking the ninth of your line will lose the kingdom you now hold. That king will bear the name of 'mute beast'.)[108]

This prophetic and historiographical strategy is by no means unique to Jean d'Arras's text. Galfridian prophecies often depict trans-generational loss following from the moral shortcomings of a particular monarch. This appears also in prophetically inflected English histories of this period. We might note, for example, the *Prophecy of the Six Kings*, which was integrated in the Anglo-Norman and later the Middle English *Brut* as Merlin's response to Arthur's question concerning the last six kings to rule in England. The final king of the English is the 'moldwerp', a cursed mole who deposes his predecessor (one of the main reasons why this figure was later associated with Henry IV), during whose time England is conquered by the Welsh and Scots: 'After þis lambe shal come a Moldewerpe acursede of Godes mouþ, a caitif, a cowarde as an here, he shal haue an elderliche skyn as a goot; and vengeance shal fal vppon him for synne.'[109] I mention this not as a source for the prophecy of the 'beste mue', but as an analogue, carrying out very similar historiographical work. This correspondence is suggestive of common conceptualisations of prophetic history on both sides of the English Channel, and indeed, in the context of the *Brut* the *Six Kings* did see continental circulation, although among partisans of the English king rather than the French.[110] Once we recognise the cross-channel flow of historical literary materials in the context of the Hundred Years War, it is not surprising that the political prophetic strategies of *Mélusine* in part mirror those of the English *Brut* tradition.

Jean d'Arras's prophecies are not exclusively accounts of loss, and there is an implicit hope of territorial restoration and expansion in the third prophetic curse of Presine placed on her third daughter, Palestine, who is confined within the mountain of Canigou in Aragon (a space of wonder as early as Gervase's *Otia*), with a vast store of her father's treasure, until 'uns chevaliers de vostre lignie y vendra, lyquelz aura le tresor et en aidera a conquerir la Terre de promission' ('a knight of your own lineage shall come; he shall use the treasure for the conquest of the Promised Land').[111] In an act of nominative determinism (in keeping with Jean d'Arras's broader interest in naming and territorial claims), Palestine is an embodied claim to the role that Lusignan might play in the conquest of the Holy Land.[112] This crusading prophecy, which follows directly from Presine's foreshadowing of Armenian loss delivered in relation to Melior's punishment, is not realised in the romance itself, and, in contrast to Couldrette's later version, none of Mélusine's sons ever profess to attempt it. It points to a political world beyond the text and the anticipation of the involvement of the house of Lusignan in a new crusade, hundreds of years after the family's active association with the kingdom of Jerusalem.[113]

## Belief and exclusion

The text imagines a partisan reader who shares the author's sense of appropriate wonder, aligned with an overtly articulated dynastic ideology. We find this most clearly in the multiple epilogues of the text recounting the various appearances of Mélusine at Lusignan, or to members of the house, in recent historical memory. These are presented in terms of 'proof' supplementary to the textual traditions Jean references: 'Ces preuves, et autres pluseurs, ont esté clerement sceues sans ce que les vrayes croniques et les livres des histoires en dient' ('All these proofs, and many others, have become very well-known, even without what the authentic chronicles and the books of history tell of them').[114]

Perhaps the most illuminating of the near-contemporary episodes for our understanding of the community of wonder here constructed is Jean d'Arras's account of Mélusine's appearance in the bedroom of the last English castellan of the fortress, John Creswell, on the eve of the English departure from Lusignan and the passing of the fortress to the French: 'Il vit, ce disoit il, apparoir presentement et visiblement devant son lit une serpente grande et grosse merveilleusement, et estoit la queue longue de vii a viii piéz, burlee d'azur et d'argent' ('He said that he very clearly saw before his bed a dragon that was extraordinarily large, with a tail some seven or eight feet long banded in azure and silver').[115] Mélusine's extraordinary tail represents a reassertion of the Lusignan line at the site in the person of Jean de Berry. At the end of the anecdote, the duke claims the fortress from Creswell and receives this account of his vision. Jean d'Arras presents the duke as his historical informant for this episode, and in a suggestively metatextual move, the patron comes to endorse the historicity of the romance as a credible historical witness. As Firth Green has noted, this is a decidedly revisionist treatment of recent history: the castle came into French possession as part of a ransom exchange, and during this period Creswell was in a French prison rather than at Lusignan.[116] The historical claim is here an ostentatious fiction in which both author and patron are complicit.

However, the framing of the marvel is perhaps most interesting in terms of the exclusion of Creswell from a community of wonder, even as he serves as the first reporter in a chain. He is at once a credible witness and an uncomprehending one – a foil to the perceiving community of Lusignan partisans, in both its textual and extra-textual forms. The English castellan is unable to make sense of the appearance of the dragon and is frozen in terror: he does not possess the cultural codes by which he might understand it, and needs to have it explained by his mistress, Alixandre, a woman of Sancerre (in Poitou). We read of his reaction:

> Et dist de certain a monseigneur qu'il n'avoit onques en sa vie eu ne ot depuis si grant paour. Et dist qu'il se dreça en son seant et prist l'espee qui estoit a son chevéz. Et lors lui dist, si comme il recordoit a monseigneur, celle Alixandre, 'Comment, Cersuelle, vous qui avéz esté en tant de bonnes places, avéz vous paour de celle serpente? Certes, c'est la dame de ceste forteresse et qui la fist fonder, et sachiéz qu'elle ne vous fera ja mal. Elle vous vient monstrer comment il vous dessaisir de ceste place.' Et dist Cersuelle que celle Alixandre n'en ot oncques paour, mais il disoit bien qu'il n'en fu onques asseur.
>
> (Creswell told my lord that he had never before or since been so afraid. He said that he sat up and took the sword that was at his bedside. Then Alixandre said to him, 'What, Creswell, you who have seen so much service, are you afraid of that dragon? It is surely the lady of this fortress, she who had it built, and you can be sure that she will not harm you; she has come to show you that you must give up this place.' Creswell said that Alixandre was not afraid even for an instant, but he himself was not much reassured.)[117]

Creswell does not understand the nature of the experience and attempts to fight the phantom – an inappropriate reaction that recalls Raymondin's unsheathing of his sword upon his first encounter with Mélusine, although there the misperception is not necessarily the fairy's materiality but a misreading of her intent. Creswell has no available point of reference; he is situated outside the community for whom the phenomenon is intelligible. Alixandre, notably, is unafraid. Yet the code by which Jean d'Arras invites his readers to approach and interpret the episode is rooted not only in a sense of the customs and beliefs of the region, but in a familiarity with textual precedents. We read of the dragon that 'elle se mua en figure de femme aulte et droicte, et estoit vestue d'un gros burel et ceinte dessoubz les mamelles, et estoit affublee de blans cuevrechiéz a la guise du viel temps' ('she metamorphosed into the figure of a tall, upright woman, wearing a dress of coarse cloth bound under her breasts, and coiffed with a white head covering in the old-fashioned style').[118] This is an allusion not simply to pastness in Mélusine's appearance (as Fradenburg suggests, the romance marvel might be understood as nostalgic),[119] but to the white head-dresses by which Gervase understands his serpent-women to be recognisable: 'habent enim ligaturam albam quasi uittam in capite' ('they can be recognised by a white band or fillet which they have on the head').[120] Jean d'Arras draws the text into alignment with common report as it is textually attested, although he seems to be aware of the relative historical remoteness of Gervase's account (the head-dress is antiquated). Concluding his accounts of Mélusine's spectral visitations to near-historical actors, Jean asserts that these endorse the events of the romance proper, itself based on the writings of Gervase and other credible 'philosophes'.[121]

This marvel sits notably in the broader context of the balance of French and English interests in the text, in relation to which dragon omens present an important precedent. The Mélusinian dragon appears to be overtly Galfridian. We might note, for example, Mélusine's appearance in her dragon form to her sons before the death of Raymondin:

> fut Melusigne grant espace sur la Tour Poictevine en guise de serpente, et quant elle vit ses enfans plourer, si ot grant douleur et gecta un cry grant et merveilleux, et sembla a tous que la forteresce fondist en abysme. Et pour lors sembla a ceulx qui la furent qu'elle plourast moult tendrement. Et lors prist son chemin parmy l'air et s'en va le droit train d'Arragon. Et avoit la queue longue a merveilles, toute burlee d'azur et d'argent.
>
> (Mélusine, in dragon's guise, remained for a long time on the Poitevin Tower, and her children's tears caused her great pain. She let out such a great and marvellous cry that it seemed to everyone as if the fortress were collapsing, and as if she herself were weeping very tenderly. Then she rose into the air and flew straight towards Aragon: her tail was wondrously long, and banded with azure and silver.)[122]

The sons function as credible witnesses, but the cry Mélusine issues, apparently audible to all, ensures further opportunities for testimony. 'Issues' would, incidentally, appear to be precisely the right word here, for the fairy's 'cry grant et merveilleux' is a counterpart to the 'grant et merveilleux' line of Lusignan itself, and certainly it is the fortunes of the family which in part she mourns. This omen functions in relation to prophecy as a public discourse, and indeed a public marvel, in the Galfridian tradition. We find a very similar conceit in the opening of Geoffrey of Monmouth's *Prophetiae* where another prophetic figure, Merlin, is moved to tears as he contemplates the shaky foundations of Vortigern's fortress before the king and his magi, before explaining the meaning of the dragons who – like the transformed fairy – are omens of territorial loss and restitution.[123] In a not terribly subtle metaphor in which a shaky tower stands for a shaky territorial hold, the dragon omen is in both cases intimately connected to the fate of a particular (dynastic) community and the space it claims as its own. Again, here there is a feasible debt on Jean d'Arras's part to the strategies of Galfridian history-writing, not necessarily as a self-conscious intertextual allusion (although this could well be the case) but rather as a precedent for a type of fantastic history-writing.[124] Indeed, as in Geoffrey's work, it is not only to the in-text audience that the prophet and/or the omen speak(s), but to the elite audience of the text. I understand this implicit external audience to constitute a community of wonder, constructed around not the apparently historical plausibility of the dragon *mirabile* but the historical truth of its prophecy.[125]

Jean d'Arras's *Mélusine* pre-dates the virulent anti-English applications of the *Prophetiae* that we find into the fifteenth century (most notably, the prophetic propaganda associated with Jeanne d'Arc), but stands roughly contemporary with the *Croniques des Bretons*, which makes use of anti-English content.[126] As it appears in Français MS 2806, the prophecy and commentary of the *Croniques* represent a significant departure from the English historiographical tradition. As Veysseyre notes, Français MS 2806 is far more interested in interpreting the futurist portions of the *Prophetiae* as critiques of contemporary French moral and political decline than it is in insular political affairs. Nonetheless, the author notes the anti-English potential of certain passages of Geoffrey's text, as they were mediated by Geoffrey from an oppositional tradition active in Wales, forecasting British (Welsh) restoration and English decline. We find this most notably in its representation of the white dragon of the Saxons. *Prophetiae*, line 112, a brief period of Saxon resurgence, is glossed by the author in relation to 'le blanc dragon de Germanie', and the commentary notes the relationship between the (religious) sins of the 'Angloiz' and their Saxon forefathers ('peres Saxons').[127] The allusions to non-Christian Saxon religious practices in the *Historia* and *Prophetiae* appear to have been read by the commentator in line with representations of English apostacy in invectives of the Hundred Years War.[128] The interpretation of the *Omen of the Dragons* in oppositional terms reads suggestively with Jean d'Arras's representation of the dragon Mélusine, who, as she appears before Creswell, chases the English from Lusignan; the silver and azure dragon of Lusignan emerges as a counterpart to the red dragon of the Britons.[129]

Certainly, the dragon of Lusignan appears to have been invoked in the context of opposition to English claims to the fortress in the early fifteenth century. One of the images for March in *Les Très Riches Heures* (produced *c*. 1412–16), which alongside *Mélusine* is one of the most significant artistic and literary productions associated with Jean de Berry's patronage, appears to recall the romance.[130] In the background of the illustration Mélusine, here a golden dragon, flies above the walls of the fortress below the zodiac frame. It is perhaps no coincidence that Mélusine appears in the month which signals the beginning of agricultural labour for the year, drawn into a clear conceptual relationship in the image with the prosperity of the fortress and of Jean de Berry. She is after all, as Le Goff notes, the 'fairy of economic growth', who – we might add – shares the interests of the romance's patron in the expansion of buildings and lands.[131] Like the romance, this image in the *Heures* appears to be as interested in the history of cultivation as it is in the textual production of wonder as an ennobling cultural enterprise. Yet there is also a political utility to this image beyond the local, thrown into national focus. The *Heures* was produced roughly contemporaneously with the re-articulation of a new English claim to Poitou during the reign of Henry V and is a clear assertion of Jean de Berry's territorial right.[132]

We might note a final telling allusion to an appearance of the dragon as Jean d'Arras imagines the departure of the English from the fortress. Jean invokes another historical witness: 'Item Yvain de Galles jura a mon tresredoubté seigneur, le duc dessus dit, que il l'avoit veue par deux foiz sur les murs de Lusegnen, trois jours devant que la forteresse feust rendue' ('In the same way, Yvain de Galles swore to my most respected lord the duke that he saw the dragon twice on the walls of Lusignan three days before the fortress was surrendered').[133] While the name 'Yvain', the French version of the Welsh Owain, presents a clear overture to the world and nomenclature of Arthurian romance and its marvels (we might think of Chrétien's *Yvain*), only one historical Owain can have been in Jean's mind: Owain Lawgoch. An exiled Welsh nobleman who fought on the French side in the Hundred Years Wars and received active French royal support in his ambitions for Welsh recovery, Owain was murdered by an English agent in Poitou in 1378.[134] While likely to be a component of a revisionist history in the romance, his presence in the region during the period of the castle's transfer from English hands to French is not implausible. Certainly, Owain's presence speaks to a broader network of anti-English alliances, drawn into a common framework of wonder. Unlike Creswell, Owain can interpret the marvel unaided. There may well be an authorising element of Britishness in Jean's account, that is, of Welshness, a detail that authenticates prophecy in both symbolic and literal terms. Like Merlin, Owain is a Welshman capable of divining the meanings of dragons in relation to a prophetic discourse oppositional to English occupation. This might suggest an awareness of the association of Galfridian historiographical strategies not simply with England but with Wales. It sits intriguingly with Owain's associations with the French court and may even suggest an awareness of the Welsh dragon as a live political discourse in Valois contexts. Most notably, however, when read in the long historical view of the previous chapters of this book, it suggests the emergence not of the British subject position as a cipher for unthinking credulity, but of the Britons as interpreters of high political marvels, a competency in common with those who read the history and prophecies of Lusignan.

## Conclusion

Jean d'Arras's *Mélusine* presents a new application of British *phantasmata* as an object of noble French belief. His fairies step into the pages of an audaciously re-imagined history. They are the progenitors of a dynastic history which cultivates recognisable points of affinity to the *Brut*, its heroine authorised by Merlinian prophecies and corresponding marvels – of which she is chief – understood as a series of signs and symbols fundamentally antagonistic to English control in central and southern France, although imagining a more specific dynastic *imperium* than national ambition alone. I suggest that this may well present a knowing transference of oppositional strategies from the Welsh tradition, although these were mediated in large part via the English, a site of overt ideological contestation through discursive co-option. The text not only stages an engagement with the initial question of my study – the matter of whose histories might be believed – but contests and shifts the grounds of dynastic and history through use of a paradigm both marginalised and utilised on the other side of the English Channel.

## Notes

1 Jean d'Arras, *Mélusine*, ed. Vincensini, p. 808; *Mélusine*, ed. and trans. Maddox and Sturm-Maddox, p. 227.
2 For the most comprehensive discussions of Jean d'Arras's text, see Donald Maddox and Sara Sturm-Maddox, eds, *Melusine of Lusignan: Founding Fiction in Late Medieval France* (Athens, GA: University of Georgia Press, 1996); and Misty Urban, Deva Kemmis, and Melissa Ridley Elmes, eds, *Mélusine's Footprint: Tracing the Legacy of a Medieval Myth* (Leiden: Brill, 2017). For the only monograph-length discussion of the English *Mélusine* to date, see Shaw, *Space, Gender, and Memory*. For discussion of *Mélusine* in insular and continental perspectives, see Jeanne-Marie Boivin and Proinsias MacCana, eds, *Mélusines continentales et insulaires: actes du colloque international tenu les 27 et 28 mars à l'Université Paris XII et au Collège des Irlandais* (Paris: Honoré Champion, 1999); and for its Spanish translation, see Ivy A. Corfis, 'Empire

and Romance: *Historia de la linda Melosina*', *Neophilologus* 82.4 (1998): 559–75.

3 For discussion of Jean d'Arras's 'epistemology of wonder' in relation to the gender dynamics of the text, see Shaw, *Space, Gender, and Memory*, pp. 23–57. (Shaw writes of the *c.* 1500 Middle English translation, which is largely a faithful translation of the French.) For a brief account of Jean d'Arras's marvellous historical precedents, see Stephen G. Nichols, 'Melusine between Myth and History: Profile of a Female Demon', in *Melusine of Lusignan: Founding Fiction in Late Medieval France*, ed. Donald Maddox and Sara Sturm-Maddox (Athens, GA: University of Georgia Press, 1996), pp. 137–64; and for the marvellous nature of the text's crusading accounts, see Daisy Delogu, 'Jean d'Arras Makes History: Political Legitimacy in the *Roman de Mélusine*', *Dalhousie French Studies* 80 (2007): 15–28.

4 For discussion of the relationship between romance and 'emotional communities' of readers (with a particular mind to manuscript circulation), see Raluca Radulescu, 'Performing Emotions in the Arthurian World', *Arthuriana* 29.4 (2010): 3–7.

5 Daston and Park, *Wonders and the Order of Nature*, p. 62.

6 Kelly, *Art of Medieval French Romance*, p. 147.

7 Kelly, *Art of Medieval French Romance*, p. 147.

8 Le Goff, *The Medieval Imagination*, pp. 27–30; Kelly, *Art of Medieval French Romance*, p. 156; Michelle Sweeney, *Magic in Medieval Romance from Chrétien de Troyes to Geoffrey Chaucer* (Dublin: Four Courts Press, 2000), p. 32. Generally, the conceptual association is taken as implicit, and the *mirabilia* of Gervase of Tilbury are frequently cited as precursors of the marvels of medieval romance.

9 This is discussed in relation to the Old French *Partonopeus de Blois* and its later versions by Matilda Tomaryn Bruckner, *Shaping Romance: Interpretation, Truth, and Closure in Twelfth-Century French Fictions* (Philadelphia: University of Pennsylvania Press, 1993), p. 115.

10 Sidney Painter, 'The Lords of Lusignan in the Eleventh and Twelfth Centuries', *Speculum* 31.2 (1957): 27–47; Emmanuele Baumgartner, 'Fiction and History: The Cypriot Episode in Jean d'Arras's *Mélusine*', in *Mélusine of Lusignan: Founding Fiction in Late Medieval France*, ed. Donald Maddox and Sara Sturm-Maddox (Athens, GA: University of Georgia Press, 1996), pp. 185–200. In the contexts of early print Jean d'Arras's text appears to have been split into two sections, one telling of Mélusine and the other of the deeds of Geoffroy; one a (penitential) romance and the other closer to a history. Zeldenrust, *The Mélusine Romance in Medieval Europe*, pp. 23–24.

11 For an account of Jean de Berry's cultural interests, as well as his building and renovation projects across the large part of central France in his possession, see Jean Longnon, Raymond Cazelles, and Millard Meiss, eds, *Les Très Riches Heures du duc de Berry* (London: Thames and Hudson, 1989), pp. 15–19.

12 For further comment on the importance of maternal genealogy in *Mélusine*, see Burns, 'A Snake-Tailed Woman'; E. Jane Burns, 'Magical Politics from Poitou to Armenia: Mélusine, Jean de Berry, and the Eastern Mediterranean', *Journal of Medieval and Early Modern Studies* 43.2 (2013): 275–301; Ana Pairet, 'Melusine's Double Binds: Foundation, Transgression, and the Genealogical Romance', in *Reassessing the Heroine in Medieval French Literature*, ed. Kathy M. Krause (Gainesville, FL: University Press of Florida, 2001), pp. 71–86. For a recent discussion of the Luxembourg connection see Pit Péporté, 'Mélusine and Luxembourg: A Double Memory', in *Melusine's Footprint: Tracing the Legacy of a Medieval Myth*, ed. Misty Urban, Deva Kemmis, and Melissa Ridley Elmes (Leiden: Brill, 2017), pp. 162–82 (pp. 162–71).

13 Jane H. M. Taylor, 'Melusine's Progeny: Patterns and Perplexities', in *Melusine of Lusignan: Founding Fiction in Late Medieval France*, ed. Donald Maddox and Sara Sturm-Maddox (Athens, GA: University of Georgia Press, 1996), pp. 165–84 (p. 166).

14 For a discussion of some of the local historical dynastic movements romanced in the text, see Péporté, 'Melusine and Luxembourg', p. 163.

15 For discussion of the relationship between the two French *Mélusines*, see Jean d'Arras, *Melusine*, ed. and trans. Maddox and Sturm-Maddox, pp. 12–14; Zeldenrust, *The Mélusine Romance in Medieval Europe*, pp. 17–63 (which notes erroneous earlier scholarly arguments for a single Latin source from which both romances were derived, made on the basis of a fifteenth-century cataloguing error concerning the Castilian translation, p. 17). See also Matthew W. Morris, eds and trans., *A Bilingual Edition of Couldrette's Mélusine or Le Roman de Parthenay* (Lampeter: Edwin Mellen Press, 2003). Morris identifies Couldrette's version as an adapted versification of Jean d'Arras's prose text. See further Chapter 4 below.

16 Laurence Harf-Lancner, 'Littérature et politique: Jean de Berry, Leon de Lusignan et le *Roman de Mélusine*', in *Histoire et littérature au Moyen Âge: actes du colloque du centre d'études médiévales de l'Université de Picardie 1985*, ed. Danielle Buschinger (Göppingen: Kümmerle, 1991), pp. 161–71. In his *Reductorium morale* (c. 1340–50), the

Franciscan homilist Pierre Bersuire, born in Poitou, wrote of a 'fada' associated with the house and castle of Lusignan, seen in the form of a serpent. Extract, with date, quoted by Claude Lecouteux, 'Zur Entstehung der Melusinensage', *Zeitschrift für deutsche Philologie* 98 (1979): 73–84.

17 For an understanding of the legend as courting popular support, see Morris, ed. and trans., *A Bilingual Edition of Couldrette's Mélusine*, pp. 22–23.

18 Jean d'Arras, *Mélusine,* ed. Vincensini, p. 116; *Melusine*, ed. and trans. Maddox and Sturm-Maddox, p. 20.

19 Jean d'Arras, *Mélusine*, ed. Vincensini, pp. 111, 113; *Melusine*, ed. and trans. Maddox and Sturm-Maddox, p. 19.

20 Harf-Lancner, 'Littérature et politique', p. 162; Firth Green, *Elf Queens and Holy Friars*, p. 30. One of the two surviving French translations was produced between 1320 and 1330 by Jean de Vignay, who worked under the patronage of the French royal family. Cinzia Pignatelli and Dominique Gerner, eds, *Les Traductions françaises des Otia imperialia de Gervais de Tilbury par Jean d'Antioche et Jean de Vignay* (Geneva: Droz, 2006), pp. 97–98.

21 Nigel Saul, *Richard II* (London: Yale University Press, 1997), p. 359; J. C. Laidlow, 'Christine de Pizan, the Earl of Salisbury and Henry IV', *French Studies* 36 (1982): 129–43.

22 Hermann Osterley, ed., *Gesta Romanorum* (Hildesheim: Georg Olms Verlagsbuchhandlung, 1963), pp. 540–41.

23 Jean d'Arras's romance appears to have been read back onto the French translations of *Otia*. In the sole surviving manuscript of Jean de Vignay's translation, Paris, Bibliothèque nationale de France, Rothschild MS 3085, fol. 26v, the account of the lady of Chateau-Rousset is glossed, in a later hand: 'Rémondin, Mélusine'.

24 Jean d'Arras, *Mélusine*, ed. Vincensini, pp. 112, 114; *Melusine*, ed. and trans. Maddox and Sturm-Maddox, p. 19.

25 See above, p. 102.

26 Denise Schaeffer, 'Wisdom and Wonder in *Metaphysics* A:1–2', *Review of Metaphysics* 52.3 (1999): 641–56. For medieval application, see Daston and Park, *Wonders and the Order of Nature*, pp. 111–20.

27 Jean d'Arras, *Mélusine*, ed. Vincensini, p. 114; *Melusine*, ed. and trans. Maddox and Sturm-Maddox, p. 20.

28 For the distinction between Aristotle's understanding of wonder and medieval *mirabilia*, see Daston and Park, *Wonders and the Order of Nature*, pp. 116–17, which positions Gervase's engagements with paradox in contrast to Aristotle.

29 Jean d'Arras, *Melusine*, ed. and trans. Maddox and Sturm-Maddox, p. 28. This may have been intended as a compliment to Jean de Berry, whose personal library is known to have included books of astrology. Longnon, Cazelles, and Meiss, eds, *Les Très Riches Heures du duc de Berry*, p. 17.
30 Kieckhefer, *European Witch Trials*, pp. 19–20.
31 Kors and Peters, eds and trans., *Witchcraft in Europe*, pp. 129–32. For association of the neutral or benevolent angels in the prohibitions with fairy-belief, see Firth Green, *Elf Queens and Holy Friars*, p. 25.
32 Kieckhefer, *European Witch Trials*, pp. 22, 79–80. Jean even appears to have been associated with an interest in demonism and antifeminism typical of late medieval clerical writings on witchcraft, although it lacks the full condemnation of such beliefs and practices that we find in witch-theory. I refer to the *Évangiles des quenouilles*, an account of the occult knowledge of rural women reported to a male scribe, which in the fifteenth-century Chantilly, Musée Condé MS 654, is ascribed to one 'Jehan d'Arras' (among others). For discussion of *Les Évangiles* as something of an outlier in its tolerance of medieval superstitions, in the context of early witch writings, see Michael D. Bailey, 'Superstition and Sorcery', in *The Routledge History of Medieval Magic*, ed. Sophie Page and Catherine Rider (London: Routledge, 2019), pp. 487–501 (p. 488); Madeleine Jeay and Kathleen Garay, eds and trans., *The Distaff Gospels: A First Modern English Edition of 'Les Évangiles des quenouilles'* (Peterborough, Ontario: Broadview Press, 2006), pp. 246–47.
33 Although this list is by no means exhaustive, for a discussion of Mélusine's demonic and divine affinities see, in particular, Nichols, 'Melusine between Myth and History'; Chera A. Cole, 'Passing as a "Humayn Woman": Hybridity and Salvation in the Middle English *Mélusine*', in *Melusine's Footprint: Tracing the Legacy of a Medieval Myth*, ed. Misty Urban, Deva Kemmis, and Melissa Ridley Elmes (Leiden: Brill, 2017), pp. 240–58; Tania M. Colwell, 'Mélusine: Ideal Mother or Inimitable Monster?', in *Love, Marriage and Family Ties in the Later Middle Ages*, ed. Isabel Davis, Miriam Müller, and Sarah Rees Jones (Turnhout: Brepols, 2003), pp. 181–203; Burns, 'A Snake-Tailed Woman'; Taylor, 'Melusine's Progeny'; Zeldenrust, *The Mélusine Romance in Medieval Europe*, pp. 26–33.
34 Cooper, *English Romance in Time*, p. 179. For Mélusine's affinity to the fairies of romance (including those of the lai) as it sits alongside her relationship to the fairies of the Latin tradition (specifically Gervase), see Sara Sturm-Maddox, 'Configuring Alterity: Rewriting

the Fairy Other', in *The Medieval Opus: Imitation, Rewriting, and Transmission in the French Tradition: Proceedings of the Symposium Held at the Institute for Research in Humanities, October 5–7 1995, the University of Wisconsin-Madison*, ed. Douglas Kelly (Leiden: Brill, 1996), pp. 125–38.
35 Kelly, *Art of Medieval French Romance*, p. 150.
36 Kelly, *Art of Medieval French Romance*, p. 156.
37 See above, p. 111.
38 Harf-Lancner, *Les Fées au Moyen Âge*, pp. 418–19. The plausibility of Walter Map's authorship, if not its reality, is discussed by Byron Smith, *Walter Map and the Matter of Britain*.
39 Harf-Lancner, *Les Fées au Moyen Âge*, pp. 418–19.
40 Cooper, *English Romance in Time*, p. 186.
41 Jean d'Arras, *Mélusine*, ed. Vincensini, p. 816; *Melusine*, ed. and trans. Maddox and Sturm-Maddox, p. 229.
42 Daston and Park, *Wonders and the Order of Nature*, pp. 61–62.
43 Kelly, *Art of Medieval French Romance*, p. 202.
44 See, for example, Zeldenrust, *The Mélusine Romance in Medieval Europe*; Donald Maddox and Sara Sturm-Maddox, 'Introduction: Melusine at 600', in *Melusine of Lusignan: Founding Fiction in Late Medieval France*, ed. Donald Maddox and Sara Sturm-Maddox (Athens, GA: University of Georgia Press, 1996), pp. 1–11; Kevin Brownlee, 'Melusine's Hybrid Body and the Poetics of Metamorphosis', in *Melusine of Lusignan: Founding Fiction in Late Medieval France*, ed. Donald Maddox and Sara Sturm-Maddox (Athens, GA: University of Georgia Press, 1996), pp. 76–99; Angela Jane Weisl, 'Half Lady, Half Serpent: Melusine's Monstrous Body and the Discourse of Romance', in *Melusine's Footprint: Tracing the Legacy of a Medieval Myth*, ed. Misty Urban, Deva Kemmis, and Melissa Ridley Elmes (Leiden: Brill, 2017), pp. 222–39.
45 See, for example, Miranda Griffin, *Transforming Tales: Rewriting Metamorphosis in Medieval French Literature* (Oxford: Oxford University Press, 2015), pp. 146–60; Sylvia Huot, 'Dangerous Embodiments: Froissart's Harton and Jean d'Arras's Melusine', *Speculum* 78.2 (2003): 400–20.
46 Pairet, 'Polycorporality and Heteromorphia'. Although Pairet suggests that hybridity presents an anachronistic point of application to medieval texts, it is the closest category term we have for composite bodies of the type with which I am here concerned, and I retain it here.
47 Minnis, 'Medieval Imagination and Memory', p. 242.

48 *Beati Alberti Magni Summa de creaturis diuisa in duas partes* (Lyon: Claude Prost, Claude Rigaud, Jean Antoine Huguetan, Jérôme de La Garde, Petrus Jammy, and Pierre Rigaud, 1651), p. 181 (Part II, Qu. 36). My translation.

49 The distinction rests on the activity and passivity of the imaginative processes by which images are received and new configurations created, and the separation or otherwise between 'phantasia' and 'ymaginativa'. Minnis, 'Medieval Imagination and Memory', p. 242.

50 Zeldenrust, *The Mélusine Romance in Medieval Europe*, p. 41. For discussions of illustrations and woodcuts of Mélusine, in addition to Zeldenrust, see Laurence Harf-Lancner, 'L'Illustration du Roman de Mélusine de Jean d'Arras dan les éditions du XVe et XVIe siècle', in *Le Livre et l'image en France au XVIe siècle*, ed. Nicole Cazauran (Paris: Presses de l'École Normale Supérieure, 1989), pp. 29–55.

51 Burns, 'A Snake-Tailed Woman', p. 191.

52 For a brief discussion of the relationship between hybridity, monstrosity and the sacred, see Asa Mittman, *Maps and Monsters in Medieval England* (London: Routledge, 2006), pp. 175–76.

53 Walker Bynum, *Metamorphosis and Identity*, pp. 122–23.

54 Walker Bynum, *Metamorphosis and Identity*, p. 123.

55 Jean d'Arras, *Mélusine*, ed. Vincensini, pp. 292, 294; *Melusine*, ed. and trans. Maddox and Sturm-Maddox, pp. 70–71 (modified).

56 For the function of these designations as heroic epithets, see Zeldenrust, *The Mélusine Romance in Medieval Europe*, p. 54. This is also a feature of the treatment of the account of the adult Geoffroy in the later split editions where, as Zeldenrust notes (pp. 60–61), Geoffroy's name is treated as an epithet by illustrators, who represent him without any exceptional characteristics. As a mode of heroic endorsement, these signifiers are certainly double-edged: Geoffroy's tusk, for example, presents a resurfacing of his father's hidden crime.

57 Kelly, 'The Domestication of the Marvelous', pp. 39–40. For a discussion of the facial *tares* in medieval French literature, see Jean d'Arras, *Mélusine*, ed. Vincensini, pp. 40–41. For discussion of the text's biological interests, including the monstrosity of multiple births, see Gabrielle M. Spiegel, 'Maternity and Monstrosity: Reproductive Biology in the *Roman de Melusine*', in *Melusine of Lusignan: Founding Fiction in Late Medieval France*, ed. Donald Maddox and Sara Sturm-Maddox (Athens, GA: University of Georgia Press, 1996), pp. 100–24.

58 Elliott, *Fallen Bodies*, p. 41.

59 Jean d'Arras, *Mélusine*, ed. Vincensini, p. 688.

60 Jean d'Arras, *Mélusine*, ed. Vincensini, p. 164; *Melusine*, ed. and trans. Maddox and Sturm-Maddox, p. 33.
61 We might note the Middle English context for this that we find in the roughly contemporary *Sir Gawain and the Green Knight*, where we read of the first appearance of the Green Knight, interpreted by the court at Camelot: 'For fantoum & fayryȝe þe folk þere hit demed' (line 240) – another phantom capable of working decidedly material effects. The meanings conveyed by the word are multiple, and this is indeed precisely the point: the reader is left to determine the nature, and the reality status, of the marvel. J. R. R. Tolkien and E. V. Gordon, eds, *Sir Gawain and the Green Knight* (Oxford: Oxford University Press, 1967).
62 Shaw, *Space, Gender, and Memory*, pp. 76–77.
63 Jean d'Arras, *Mélusine*, ed. Vincensini, p. 158; *Melusine*, ed. and trans. Maddox and Sturm-Maddox, p. 32. This might be read in relation to the 'stupefying' power of the prodigy, the experience of wonder detailed in Albertus Magnus's commentary on Aristotle. See further Daston and Park, *Wonders and the Order of Nature*, p. 113. In the context of the narrative, the terrible wonder experienced by Raymondin, prior to his encounter with the fairy, would be the realisation of astrological prophecy in the youth's murder of his uncle.
64 Jean d'Arras, *Mélusine*, ed. Vincensini, p. 162; *Melusine*, ed. and trans. Maddox and Sturm-Maddox, p. 32. I here give a more literal translation of the final two sentences.
65 Fradenburg, 'Simply Marvelous', pp. 5–6, 23.
66 Jean d'Arras, *Mélusine*, ed. Vincensini, p. 122; Jean d'Arras, *Mélusine*, ed. and trans. Maddox and Sturm-Maddox, p. 22.
67 Fradenburg, 'Simply Marvelous', p. 6.
68 For discussion of the romance motif of the fairies in the fountain, see Neil Cartlidge, 'The Fairies in the Fountain: Promiscuous Liaisons', in *The Exploitations of Medieval Romance*, ed. Laura Ashe, Ivana Djordjevic, and Judith Weiss (Cambridge: D. S. Brewer, 2010), pp. 15–27.
69 Jean d'Arras, *Mélusine*, ed. Vincensini, p. 158; *Melusine*, ed. and trans. Maddox and Sturm-Maddox, p. 31.
70 Wade, *Fairies in Medieval Romance*, p. 3.
71 Jean d'Arras, *Mélusine*, ed. Vincensini, p. 814.
72 Rupert T. Pickens, 'The Poetics of Paradox in the *Roman de Melusine*', in *Melusine of Lusignan: Founding Fiction in Late Medieval France*, ed. Donald Maddox and Sara Sturm-Maddox (Athens, GA: University of Georgia Press, 1996), pp. 48–75. For an earlier assessment of

the competing propositions of truth and illusion in the romance, see Michèle Perret, 'Invraisemblable verité: témoignage fantastique dans deux romans du XIVe et XVe siècles', *Europe: revue littéraire mensuelle* 61 (1983): 25–34; Michèle Perret, 'Writing History/Writing Fiction', in *Melusine of Lusignan: Founding Fiction in Late Medieval France*, ed. Donald Maddox and Sara Sturm-Maddox (Athens, GA: University of Georgia Press, 1996), pp. 201–25.
73 Jean d'Arras, *Mélusine*, ed. Vincensini, p. 692; *Melusine*, ed. and trans. Maddox and Sturm-Maddox, p. 191.
74 Colwell, 'Melusine', p. 200.
75 Jean d'Arras, *Mélusine*, ed. Vincensini, p. 702; *Melusine*, ed. and trans. Maddox and Sturm-Maddox, p. 194. My modified translation taking 'mauvaise mere' as 'demon mother' rather than 'bad mother'.
76 For a discussion of the fairy in relation to the maternity of the Virgin see Colwell, 'Mélusine', pp. 193–97; Burns, 'A Snake-Tailed Woman', p. 187. More broadly, Burns suggests that the heroine might present a secular inversion of Eve and the Eden serpent, with paradise restored.
77 Jean d'Arras, *Mélusine*, ed. Vincensini, p. 114; *Melusine*, ed. and trans. Maddox and Sturm-Maddox, p. 20.
78 Cooper, *English Romance in Time*, p. 188. For a discussion of prophecy as a feature of both history and romance, see Helen Cooper, 'Thomas of Erceldoune: Romance as Prophecy', in *Cultural Encounters in the Romance of Medieval England*, ed. Corinne Saunders (Cambridge: D. S. Brewer, 2005), pp. 171–88 (pp. 183–84).
79 Jean d'Arras, *Mélusine*, ed. Vincensini, p. 136; *Melusine*, ed. and trans. Maddox and Sturm-Maddox, pp. 25–26.
80 Jean d'Arras, *Mélusine*, ed. Vincensini, pp. 152, 154; *Melusine*, ed. and trans. Maddox and Sturm-Maddox, p. 30.
81 Geoffrey of Monmouth, *History*, I, lines 309–12.
82 Jean-Yves Tiliette, 'Invention du récit: la "Brutiade" de Geoffroy de Monmouth (*Historia regum Britanniae*, § 6–22)', *Cahiers de civilisation médiévale* 39 (1996): 217–33.
83 Richard Trachsler, 'L'*Historia regum Britannie* au XVe siècle. Les manuscrits New York, Public Library, Spencer 41 et Paris, Bibliothèque de l'Arsenal, 5078', in *L'Historia regum Britanniae et les 'Bruts' en Europe*, I: *Traductions, adaptations, réappropriations (XIIe–XVIe siècle)*, ed. Hélène Tétrel and Géraldine Veysseyre (Paris: Classiques Garnier, 2015), pp. 193–205. The account of Brutus's foundation legend, in conjunction with Diana's prophecy, also circulated as a separate text in Latin prophetic collections in late medieval England –

for example, in the late fifteenth-century British Library, Cotton MS Cleopatra C.iv, for which see H. L. D. Ward, *Catalogue of Romances in the Department of Manuscripts in the British Museum*, 2 vols (London: British Museum, 1883), I, p. 311.

84 For discussion of the English *Brut* tradition, which takes Geoffrey's *Historia* as its foundation, see Lister M. Matheson, *The Prose Brut: The Development of a Middle English Chronicle* (Tempe, AZ: ACMRS Press, 1998). For the historical status of the *Historia* in France, see Trachsler, 'A Question of Time', pp. 23–25.

85 For discussion of the Anglo-Norman translations of the *Prophetiae*, and their relationship to Wace, see Jean Blacker, ed. and trans., *Anglo-Norman Verse Prophecies of Merlin* (Dallas, TX: Scriptorium Press, 2005).

86 Géraldine Veysseyre, 'Metre en roman: *les prophéties de Merlin*. Voies et détours de l'interprétation dans trois traductions de l'*Historia regum Britannie*', in *Moult obscures paroles: études sur la prophétie médiévale*, ed. Richard Trachsler, Julien Abed, and David Expert (Paris: Presses de l'Université Paris-Sorbonne, 2007), pp. 107–66 (esp. pp. 108–10). See also Géraldine Veysseyre and Clara Wille, 'Les Commentaires latins et français aux prophetie Merlini de Geoffroy de Monmouth', *Médiévales* 55 (2008): 93–114.

87 Alongside these, we might note the inclusion of the *Prophetiae* in the Vulgate *Merlin* as it appears in the Didot-*Perceval* manuscript (Paris, Bibliothèque nationale de France, Nouvelles acquisitions Françaises MS 4166). This is the only version of the romance of *Merlin* (in either French or English) in which the *Prophetiae* are included. It incorporates a commentary invested in the Scottish campaigns of Edward I and appears to have been produced in a Plantagenet context, in either England or northern France. See Julien Abed, 'La Traduction française de la *Prophetia Merlini* dans le Didot-*Perceval*', in *Moult obscures paroles: études sur la prophétie médiévale*, ed. Richard Trachsler, Julien Abed, and David Expert (Paris: Presses de l'Université Paris-Sorbonne, 2007), pp. 81–105. For an edition of Français 17177, see Géraldine Veysseyre, ed., *L'Estoire de Brutus: la plus ancienne traduction en prose française de l'"Historia regum Britannie" de Geoffroy de Monmouth* (Paris: Classiques Garnier, 2015). For a further itemisation of medieval French manuscripts containing the *Prophetiae*, see research on the French contexts of the *Prophetiae* produced by Jaclyn Rajsic for the Crossing Borders database, *Crossing Borders in the Insular Middle Ages* (Newcastle University, 2018), https://digitalcultures.ncl.ac.uk/projects/crossingborders/#/db [last accessed 11 March 2021].

88 Veysseyre, 'Metre en roman', pp. 155–56. The manuscript was presented to Francis I of France (*d*. 1547), probably by one of his royal counsellors, Aimar de Raconet. Irene Fabry-Tehranchi has suggested that its political pessimism regarding French affairs may indicate its original circulation among the Burgundians, but this remains difficult to substantiate, and aspects of the commentary are consistent with the anti-English interests of pro-Valois French political prophecy. Irene Fabry-Tehranchi, 'Merlin as a Prophet in the Manuscripts of the *Chroniques des Bretons* and Jean de Wavrin's *Chroniques d'Angleterre*', *Reading Medieval Studies* 44 (2018): 81–143 (p. 103).

89 Gervase of Tilbury, *Otia*, pp. 306–07.

90 Geoffrey of Monmouth, *History*, I, lines 58–59.

91 For discussion of parricide in the romance as a 'heinous deed deser[ving] of capital punishment', which is necessarily hidden from public knowledge in both Jean d'Arras's original and its Middle English translation, see Megan G. Leitch, *Romancing Treason: The Literature of the Wars of the Roses* (Oxford: Oxford University Press, 2015), pp. 85–86. For a brief discussion of Mélusine's obfuscation of knowledge of Raymondin's crime, and the role of this fairy circumvention of mortal processes of justice in his 'path to wealth and greatness', see Cooper, *English Romance in Time*, p. 197. Jan Shaw has read this act of parricide as essential for the end of patrilineage and the beginning of 'the matriline'. *Space, Gender, and Memory*, p. 204.

92 Jean d'Arras, *Mélusine*, ed. Vincensini, p. 284; *Melusine*, ed. and trans. Maddox and Sturm-Maddox, p. 68.

93 Zeldenrust, *The Mélusine Romance in Medieval Europe*, p. 37.

94 Geoffrey of Monmouth, *History*, I, lines 451–59.

95 Jean d'Arras, *Mélusine*, ed. Vincensini, pp. 216, 18; *Melusine*, ed. and trans. Maddox and Sturm-Maddox, p. 48. For discussion of the translation of 'Albanie', see below, n. 99.

96 Kelly, *Art of Medieval French Romance*, p. 198.

97 Geoffrey of Monmouth, *History*, I, lines 459–62.

98 Geoffrey of Monmouth, *History*, I, line 457.

99 Jean d'Arras, *Mélusine*, ed. Vincensini, pp. 216, 18; *Melusine*, ed. and trans. Maddox and Sturm-Maddox, p. 48. Although Burns has argued that 'Albanie' may have been intended as a reference to Albania, this is most convincingly translated as Scotland, and I here follow Maddox and Sturm-Maddox. See Burns, 'A Snake-Tailed Woman', p. 214.

100 For discussion of the various versions of the Albina legend, see Ruth Evans, 'The Devil in Disguise: Perverse Female Origins of the Nation',

in *Consuming Narratives: Gender and Monstrous Appetite in the Middle Ages and the Renaissance*, ed. Liz Herbert McAvoy and Teresa Walters (Cardiff: University of Wales Press, 2002), pp. 183–95. The Anglo-Norman version is edited by Georgine E. Brereton in *Des Grantz Geanz: An Anglo-Norman Poem* (Oxford: Blackwell, 1937). The Latin text has been edited and translated by James P. Carley and Julia Crick in 'Constructing Albion's Past: An Annotated Edition of *De origine gigantum*', *Arthurian Literature* 13 (1994): 41–144.

101 See Nichols, 'Melusine between Myth and History', p. 161, who suggests that 'it could not but signal to contemporary minds the pathological origins of Albany as recounted in the popular fourteenth-century Anglo-Norman poem, *Des grantz geanz*'.

102 If we understand Jean d'Arras to have been familiar with the version of the legend that situates the sisters in Greece, this might also be read in relation to the interest in Greek we have already noted. However, we cannot necessarily be so precise in terms of Jean's reading.

103 See above, p. 13.

104 Nichols, 'Melusine between Myth and History', pp. 160–61. We might also understand the operation of the legend in relation to the Greek origins of Albany (the kingdom of Mélusine's birth) as we find it in Scottish legendary content of this period relating to Scota. This was an origin legend which functioned in direct opposition to the Trojan origins of the Britons as mobilised in late medieval English historiography, although the matter of the dissemination of Scottish legendary historiography in France during this period remains a question for another time. For a discussion of the legend in its Scottish contexts see Emily Wingfield, *The Trojan Legend in Medieval Scottish Literature* (Cambridge: D. S. Brewer, 2014), pp. 25–26.

105 Flood, *Prophecy, Politics, and Place*, pp. 96–99.

106 Jean d'Arras, *Mélusine*, ed. Vincensini, p. 698; *Melusine*, ed. and trans. Maddox and Sturm-Maddox, p. 193.

107 Harf-Lancner, 'Littérature et politique', pp. 166–71.

108 Jean d'Arras, *Mélusine*, ed. Vincensini, pp. 804, 806; *Melusine*, ed. and trans. Maddox and Sturm-Maddox, pp. 225–26.

109 Friedrich Brie, ed., *The Brut, or the Chronicles of England*, 2 vols (London: K. Paul, Trench, Trübner, 1906–08), I, p. 75.

110 For discussion of the French circulation of the *Six Kings,* see Victoria Flood, 'Prophecy of the Six Kings: Translation and Transmission', in *Crossing Borders in the Insular Middle Ages* (Newcastle University, 2018), https://digitalcultures.ncl.ac.uk/projects/crossingborders [last accessed 11 March 2021]. This draws on research for the project

database undertaken with Jaclyn Rajsic, for whose cataloguing of the French manuscripts I am grateful.

111 Jean d'Arras, *Mélusine*, ed. Vincensini, pp. 136, 138; *Melusine*, ed. and trans. Maddox and Sturm-Maddox, p. 26; Gervase of Tilbury, *Otia*, pp. 684–87.

112 Michèle Perret suggests that the name Mélusine itself may recall a historical princess of the kingdom of Jerusalem, Mélisende. 'Attribution et utilisation du nom propre dans *Mélusine*', in *Mélusines continentales et insulaires: actes du colloque international tenu les 27 et 28 mars à l'Université Paris XII et au Collège des Irlandais*, ed. Jeanne-Marie Boivin and Proinsias MacCana (Paris: Honoré Champion, 1999), pp. 169–79 (p. 179).

113 I refer to Guy of Lusignan's role in the kingdom of Jerusalem in the twelfth century. For the association of Jean de Berry with crusading expectations, see Daston and Park, *Wonders and the Order of Nature*, p. 38.

114 Jean d'Arras, *Mélusine*, ed. Vincensini, p. 814; *Melusine*, ed. and trans. Maddox and Sturm-Maddox, p. 229.

115 Jean d'Arras, *Mélusine*, ed. Vincensini, p. 810; *Melusine*, ed. and trans. Maddox and Sturm-Maddox, p. 227.

116 Firth Green, *Elf Queens and Holy Friars*, p. 31.

117 Jean d'Arras, *Mélusine*, ed. Vincensini, p. 812; *Melusine*, ed. and trans. Maddox and Sturm-Maddox, p. 227–28.

118 Jean d'Arras, *Mélusine*, ed. Vincensini, p. 812; *Melusine*, ed. and trans. Maddox and Sturm-Maddox, p. 228.

119 Fradenburg, 'Simply Marvelous'.

120 Gervase of Tilbury, *Otia*, pp. 86–87.

121 Jean d'Arras, *Mélusine*, ed. Vincensini, p. 816; *Melusine*, ed. and trans. Maddox and Sturm-Maddox, p. 229.

122 Jean d'Arras, *Mélusine*, ed. Vincensini, p. 770; *Melusine*, ed. and trans. Maddox and Sturm-Maddox, p. 215. Modified translation: the edition translates 'un cry grant et merveilleux' as 'such a shrill cry'. I give here a more literal translation of this important, recurrent vocabulary in the text.

123 'Mox ille, in fletum erumpens, spiritum hausit prophetiae' ('He burst into tears and was inspired to prophesy'). Geoffrey of Monmouth, *History*, VII, line 32.

124 While the dragon of medieval romance is by no means necessarily a consistently Galfridian borrowing, Geoffrey's omen does appear to have presented a precedent for romance authors. For a suggestive association of another romance dragon, the lady of Synadoun in *Le*

*Bel inconnu*, with the dragons of the *Omen*, see Fulton, 'Romantic Wales', pp. 43–44.

125  For notice of prophecy as 'merveille' in the French translations of the *Prophetiae* see Fabry-Tehranchi, 'Merlin as a Prophet', pp. 87–88.

126  For a discussion of the prophecies associated with Jeanne, see Deborah A. Fraioli, *Joan of Arc: The Early Debate* (Woodbridge: Boydell Press, 2000), pp. 55–68, and the Galfridian prophecies mentioned in the charges raised against Jeanne by the English and the Burgundians: W. P. Barrett, ed., *The Trial of Jeanne d'Arc Translated into French from the Original Latin and French Documents* (London: Routledge, 1931), pp. 145–46. For a comparison of Jeanne's prophetic self-casting and the Mélusine legend see Nadia Margolis, 'Myths in Progress: A Literary-Typological Comparison of Mélusine and Joan of Arc', in *Mélusine of Lusignan: Founding Fiction in Late Medieval France*, ed. Donald Maddox and Sara Sturm-Maddox (Athens, GA: University of Georgia Press, 1996), pp. 241–66.

127  Veysseyre, 'Metre en roman', p. 150, n. 228.

128  We might note, for example, Christine de Pisan's *Ditié de Jehanne d'Arc*, which characterises the chastisement of the English in similarly prophetic terms: 'Et sachez que par elle Anglois / Seront mis jus sans relever, / Car Dieu le veult, qui oit les voiz / Des bons qu'ilz ont voulu grever! / [...] / En Christianté et l'Eglise / Sera par elle mis concorde. / Les mescreans dont on devise, / Et les herites de vie orde / Destruira, car ainsi l'acorde / Prophecie, qui l'a predit ...' ('And know that she will cast down the English for good, for this is God's will: he hears the prayers of the good whom they wanted to harm [...]. She will restore harmony in Christendom and the Church. She will destroy the unbelievers people talk about, and the heretics and their vile ways, for this is the substance of a prophecy that has been made ...'). Christine de Pisan, *Ditié de Jehanne d'Arc*, ed. and trans. Angus J. Kennedy and Kenneth Varty (Oxford: Society for the Study of Medieval Languages and Literature, 1977), pp. 36, 47.

129  Within insular and continental historiography, we do find new dragons in the Galfridian fashion, not least the dark dragon of the Normans. See further Anne F. Sutton and Livia Visser-Fuchs, 'The Dark Dragon of the Normans: A Creation of Geoffrey of Monmouth, Stephen of Rouen, and Merlin Silvester', *Quondam et futurus* 2.2 (1992): 1–19; Flood, 'Prophecy as History'. For a discussion of the various Merlinian dragons and their French reception, see Anne Berthelot, '*Dragon rouge / dragon blanc / dragons d'or / dragon d'airain*: les avatars du dragon dans le corpus merlinesque', in *Le Dragon dans la*

culture médiévale: colloque du Mont-Saint-Michel, 31 octobre – 1er novembre 1993, ed. Danielle Buschinger (Greifswald: Reineke-Verlag, 1993), pp. 11–25.
130 Chantilly, Bibliothèque du Château de Chantilly, MS 65, fol. 3v (Mars). See further Longnon, Cazelles, and Meiss, eds, *Les Très Riches Heures du duc de Berry*, pp. 4, 174.
131 Le Goff, *Time, Work, and Culture in the Middle Ages*, p. 219.
132 Péporté, 'Melusine and Luxembourg', p. 163.
133 Jean d'Arras, *Mélusine*, ed. Vincensini, p. 814; *Melusine*, ed. and trans. Maddox and Sturm-Maddox, p. 228.
134 R. R. Davies, *The Age of Conquest: Wales, 1063–1415* (Oxford: Oxford University Press, 1991), p. 438.

# 4

# 'En rime l'istoire': vanishing history in Couldrette's *Mélusine* and *Richard Coer de Lyon*

> Et afin qu'il en soit memoire,
> Vous mettrez en rime l'istoire
>
> (And so that it may be remembered,
> You will write a history in rhyme)
>
> (lines 79–80)

In the fifteenth century the fairy mother legend appears in Middle French and Middle English romances with reduced (although by no means entirely absent) historiographical features. I understand this not as an inevitable rejection of the materiality of *phantasmata* but as a discursive movement which speaks to the capabilities of Latin fairy *mirabilia* in the re-imaginings of romance. In the works discussed in this chapter we see a diminished claim to historicity. This is not to say that all considerations of discernment disappear from the narrative; rather, a different set of cultural cues is invoked, and a different type of reading is anticipated. This still rests on the distinction between history and fiction, but the primary interest here is in the operation of fiction and its knowing enjoyment within an ostensibly historical context. This type of text, which features historical characters but appears to be counter-factual and engages in only limited historiographical strategies, has presented a conceptual problem for critics. John Finlayson summarises this succinctly: 'Either we have a completely gullible audience or one which was concerned neither with absolute veracity or absolute unreality.'[1] I suggest that neither is quite the case; rather, we have a pre-modern audience capable of engaging with historical fiction, enjoying overtures to historical allusions, while they are also aware of a text's fictionality.

This type of fiction-making characterises Couldrette's *Mélusine*, which departs from Jean d'Arras's original in its explicit allusions to Arthurian romance. Couldrette's fairy is situated at the centre of an exemplary, politically directed romance which takes its cue from French Arthuriana beyond and distinct from the Galfridian elements that shaped Jean d'Arras's work. This conjunction is detailed in the first half of the chapter. The second half of the chapter explores a closely contemporary, similarly exemplary, use of the fairy in a Middle English context: the *a*-text of *Richard Coer de Lyon* (*c.* 1400). Here the fairy is re-imagined as a figure of paradoxography, poised between history and fiction, and juxtaposed with the author's pointed engagement with what he understands to be the utterly incredible fictions of Judaism and Islam. *Richard a* draws on pejorative tropes and stereotypes found also in medieval western European travel writing and crusading accounts, rooted in perceptions of the unthinking credulity of non-Christian communities. Wonder and its limits are again communally constructed, here as part of an explicitly articulated chauvinism.

## A new text for a new patron

Commissioned by Guillaume l'Archevêque, the Lord of Parthenay, Couldrette's *Mélusine*, also known as the *Romance of Parthenay*, presents a political relocation of Jean d'Arras's earlier text, foregrounding the rights of those descended from Mélusine's younger son, Thierry: the line of Parthenay. Occluding Jean d'Arras's status as source, Couldrette writes that he directly reworks Latin historical material translated into French verse:

> Dedens la tour de Mabregon
> Deux beaux livres furent trouvez
> En latin et tous approuvez,
> Qu'on fist translater en françois.
>
> (In the tower of Mabregon
> Two good books were discovered

In Latin which were fully verified,
And translated into French.)

(lines 102–05)[2]

This formulation is very clearly indebted to Jean d'Arras's French prose original, a debt made clear in Couldrette's allusion in the lines that follow to a third book in the possession of the Earl of Salisbury, the source noted in Jean d'Arras's prologue. The two Latin books are thus likely to be a fiction.[3] The tower of Maubergon (Mabregon) would appear to be a reference to Jean de Berry's palace in Poitiers, and although the duke is unnamed, the first source book of Jean d'Arras's prologue is clearly intended.[4] Aligned with a long historiographical tradition found most famously in Geoffrey of Monmouth's *Historia*, we again see the originating discovery (to borrow Bhabha's formulation once more) of a remarkable book, which emerges as a site of contested meaning making and the beginning of history.

This Galfridian context is particularly significant, and potentially complicated, in terms of the utility of verse as a quasi-historical medium in Couldrette's text. It is generally accepted that, in the context of the development of French historiography (rooted in Latin translation, as we find in Jean d'Arras's text), prose emerged from the thirteenth century onwards as a more authoritative medium for aristocratic history than verse.[5] Couldrette's form may invoke an earlier, distinctly Galfridian, historiographical precedent. He shares his octosyllabic couplets with Wace's *Roman de Brut*, a text which, despite the apparently historical status of the later French *Bruts*, occupied 'a literary space suspended between history and fable, where, Wace proclaimed, the author will find "ne tut meçunge, ne tut veir" [not entirely a lie, not entirely the truth]'.[6] This was also the customary metre of Old French verse romance, including the romances of Chrétien de Troyes – and if Couldrette is writing history, it would appear to be history in the vein of romance, with aural cues which, by the fourteenth and fifteenth centuries, were more overtly romanced than Jean d'Arras's text. Couldrette's phantasmatic theme and poetic delivery appear to have been understood as in some sense suspect by his early sixteenth-century English translator, who, in his original prologue to the translation, opposes his own poetic activities to the lies of classical poets: 'Poetes whilom som fantesied; / Som maligne gostes, ful of tyrannye' (lines 45–46), presumably with which the text might otherwise be aligned.[7] Couldrette's poetic history here comes all too close to the fantasies of pagan poets.

Yet historicity emerges as a powerful shared fiction in Couldrette's text – in many respects deployed as cynically as it is in Jean d'Arras's, similarly through a constructed patron–author complicity. Couldrette writes of his patron Guillaume as providing a model for his history, an origin narrative previously commissioned by Guillaume ('un livre qu'avoit a faire'; line 60). The precise nature of this book remains unclear, and it may be a strategic fiction like Couldrette's Latin sources. A taste of such an account, spurious or otherwise, follows – an invocation of Guillaume's own account of his supernatural origins:

> Le chastel fu fait d'une faée,
> Si comme il est partout retrait,
> De laquele je sui extrait,
> Et moy et toute ma lignie.
> De Partenay, n'en doubtez mie,
> Mellusigne fu appellée
> La fée que vous ay nommée,
> De quoy les armes nous portons,
> En quoy souvent nous deportons.

> (The castle [the fortress at Lusignan] was made by a fairy,
> So it is said everywhere,
> From whom I am descended,
> And all of my line
> Of Parthenay, there is no doubt.
> She is called Melusine
> The fairy who you name,
> Whose form is in the arms we wear
> And bear openly.)

(lines 70–78)

Guillaume's presumably imagined address (unless he was given to speaking in rhyming couplets!) ends with the command to his clerk Couldrette to write the history of Mélusine in verse, so that it might better be remembered – the command which forms this chapter's epigraph, and encapsulates a striking web of contradictions, in which fictive form appears, at least on a surface level, to counter historical intent. Couldrette's patron's imagined words present a very similar strategy to the oral testimony of Jean de Berry employed by Jean d'Arras in his second epilogue. Yet this occurrence is unique within Couldrette's text. Throughout, Couldrette does not cite oral testimony where Jean d'Arras does, and his patron is presented as an authority on Mélusine only in that he knows the story of the fairy and claims it as his own. Further, unlike the Duke of Berry, Guillaume is not positioned in a historiographical chain of witnesses to the fairy. While tied to concrete, material details – most notably the family's crest (to the best of my knowledge, the Parthenay blazon does not include the dragon, so this is presumably an allusion to the house of Lusignan) – the fairy is understood in relation not to contemporary or near-historical reportage but rather to contemporary interest, including the textual, presumably prompted by Jean d'Arras's text (an implicit presence in the prologue). Couldrette's imagined or reconstructed dialogue with his patron does not testify to the historical appearances of the fairy but rather the currency of her legend. This is presumably because Lusignan itself could not be invoked directly as a locale of contemporary knowledge specific to the patron (it was held by Jean de Berry, not Guillaume), and Couldrette's primary strategy of authorisation is therefore necessarily rooted in textual rather than oral report. This, I suggest, had a direct impact on the type of narrative precedents on which Couldrette drew, and the discursive contexts in which he located his fairy narrative.

## Couldrette's historical fiction-making

Couldrette's text has characteristically been understood to possess a certain 'heterogeneity' in its handling of historical content.[8] It appears to have been received by its early readers, and copyists, as a historical work. Where other texts are integrated in the early manuscripts of Couldrette these are consistently historical: the matter of Troy, *chansons de geste*, and chronicles.[9]

It may, then, seem counterintuitive to emphasise Couldrette's fiction-making; certainly so, if we assume the supernatural to be a signifier of fiction (an association which, however, my previous chapters have been intended to destabilise). Couldrette's work has been read as departing from the supernatural interests of Jean d'Arras.[10] In his abridgement he omits the discussion of fairies drawn from Gervase of Tilbury in Jean's prologue; the initial account of Presine and Elinas, and the curse under which the sisters must live; Mélusine's gift to Raymondin of the magic rings; and the supernatural builders of Lusignan.[11] Couldrette's omissions might be understood as a policy of successful abridgement, cutting sites of repetition and extraneous detail, but this practice also results in a discursive refocusing of the original, supplanting the historiographical marvel with the unclosed *merveille* of chivalric romance – although like Jean's text, it similarly operates in relation to multi-discursive cues. Many of the episodes omitted (although admittedly not all) are related to the Latin historiographical tradition of writing *mirabilia*, including both Jean d'Arras's framing interest in dynastic prophecy, and his rationalisation of the fairy's reality, derived from *Otia*. Their omission resituates the fairy, un-glossed, as a marvel of romance, the material effects and mechanics of which need no explanation.

The primary purpose of Couldrette's *Mélusine* is its protagonist's, and readers', moral or ethical instruction; whereas, as we have seen, for Jean d'Arras, the text explores the competing truths that a noble heart must necessarily contain, including, it would seem, fantastic history. For Couldrette like Jean d'Arras, Mélusine is an Augustinian wonder, indicative of the miraculous bounds of God's creation, but in Couldrette's text she is integrated in a framework invested in a primarily symbolic or moral meaning. Jean d'Arras's reference to Aristotle is retained and repurposed by Couldrette at the beginning of his new prologue:

> Le philozophe fu moult sage,
> Qui dist en la premiere page
> De sa noble Metaphisique
> Que l'umain entendement s'aplique
> Naturelmeut à concevoir
> Et à apprendre et à savoir.

(The philosopher was most wise,
Who said on the very first page
Of his noble *Metaphysics*
That human understanding strives
Naturally in conceiving,
Both to apprehend and to know.)

(lines 1–6)[12]

Couldrette uses a familiar convention, which appears across a number of different genres (although initially in a scholastic context) from the thirteenth century onwards: the Aristotelian prologue, which positions the author as the efficient cause of the text, conceived in relation to the four major causes which for Aristotle govern all action.[13] However, the passage is also a realignment of Aristotle's position concerning the wonder that compels the study of hidden forces (which similarly begins from an interest in, and interrogation of, first principles). For Couldrette, the Aristotelian perspective is read explicitly in relation to the kind of knowledge that can be gained from the study of the exemplary moral uses of chivalric romance:

> Les choses de long-temps passées,
> Plaisent quant ilz sont recordées,
> Mais qu'ilz soient bonnes et belles
> Trop plus que ne sont les nouvelles.
> Ne parlon tant du roy Artus,
> Qui voult esprouver les vertus
> Des nobles chevaliers et gens.
>
> (The things a long time passed
> Please when they are rehearsed,
> Provided they are also good and fair,
> Even more so than novelties.
> Much has been said of King Arthur,
> Who wished to test the virtues
> Of noble and honourable knights.)

(lines 13–19)

Couldrette rejects Gervase of Tilbury's, and Jean d'Arras's, taste for novelty ('les nouvelles'), actively eschewing the *mirabilia* tradition in favour of the remarkable endeavours of Arthur's knights. While the

Arthurian allusions of Couldrette's *Mélusine* have been understood as evidence of the Anglicisation of the romance, read in relation to Guillaume's Plantagenet sympathies during the 1360s and 1370s, as Tania Colwell observes, the text appears to have been commissioned during the period of Guillaume's reconciliation with the French crown, and, as Couldrette's epilogue notes, it was completed after his death.[14] To assume that Arthurian allusions are necessarily markers of Englishness is to deny the cultural capital of Arthurian content among elite audiences in France.

The aspects of Arthuriana which Couldrette appears to consider most appropriate to his prologue are the marvellous *aventures* of Lancelot, Gawain, and Percival – perhaps the least obviously historically tethered aspect of French Arthuriana. Elements of the *Mélusine* narrative (in its various forms after Jean d'Arras) might be understood as components of a religious allegory similar in its focus to the 'high devotional ground ... and the peaks of adventure' occupied by the Arthurian grail quest, an element which I argue below is significantly extended in Couldrette's text.[15] Narratives of this type take their value from the moral or exemplary quality of their fictions, for which the appearance of historical verisimilitude is not necessarily a prerequisite. This type of non-mimetic, allegorical construction has even been understood by at least one scholar as a paradigmatic example of the moralistic patterning of early fantasy (as a trans-historical genre).[16] Certainly, Couldrette's work coheres with Matilda Tomaryn Bruckner's analysis of Old and Middle French romance: 'within the heart of fiction itself there are matters of vital concern to the romance public, if only it knows how to take romance fictions properly to heart'.[17] We might remember that as far back as Walter Map, a reader might learn truths by which to live from *historia* and *fabula* alike. The type of discernment primarily needed here is moral rather than ontological. Couldrette's prologue guides its fifteenth-century aristocratic reader in the identification of the moral or ethical kernel of romance (its exemplary function as a behavioural model): a type of reading that calls for 'active recognition and interpretation' rather than passive consumption.[18] This is understood by Couldrette as superior to enjoyment of the marvel's novelty, with which he appears to have associated Jean d'Arras's original and his Gervasian model.

In Couldrette's prologue, romance is understood as the history of legendary heroes, produced for the edification and instruction of their aristocratic descendants:

> S'affiert à tout homme de bien
> S'enquerir moult fort des histoires
> Qui sont loingtaines memoires;
> Et tant plus est de hault degré,
> Doit-il de degré en degré
> Savoir don't il est descendus ...
>
> (It is fitting that every man of worth
> Enquire very strongly into histories
> That are long remembered;
> And the more he is of high degree, the more
> He should, little by little,
> Learn about those from whom he is descended ...)
>
> (lines 36–41)

This genealogical imperative, integral to the commissioning of the work itself, is characteristic of dynastic romance, where the line between romance and history is a porous one. A way of looking back to a legendary past constructed as fictionalised or quasi-fictionalised, genealogy is here at once material and ephemeral.[19] Although, noting Couldrette's interests in the Arthurian model of romance, we might ask what medieval line has ever claimed descent from Lancelot, Couldrette is open to precisely such imaginary genealogies, and towards the end of the text tells of the descendants of the Arthurian knight Tristran. The naming of Arthur's knights provides an appropriate setting for a romance *merveille*, abstracted from historical referentiality but overtly concerned with exemplarity and concepts of descent which might be understood as symbolic.

The marvellous encounters of the fellowship present an organising principle of Arthurian *matière*, divided into discrete or linked tales of the king's knights, as we find from Chrétien de Troyes onwards.[20] This operates in a clear conceptual relationship to the sequential representation of the chivalric activities of Mélusine's sons, as we find in Jean d'Arras's text also. As Daisy Delogu notes, these episodes subscribe to an ideal of chivalric adventure, in which the hero emerges not as a knight errant but at the head of an army, located in an ostensibly mimetic political and geographical space.[21] This is a capability to which Couldrette responds, yet while the political kernel of the original is retained and redirected, mimesis largely vanishes. This non-mimetic quality has famously been associated with French romance's use of ostensibly Breton marvels. In his seminal study of literature and representation, Erich Auerbach writes: 'It is from Breton folklore that the courtly romance took its elements of mystery, of something from the soil, concealing its roots, and inaccessible to rational explanation; it incorporated them and made use of them in the elaboration of the knightly ideal.'[22] As discussed in the Introduction, this critical position is one that only comparatively recently has been subject to due scrutiny and revision, and the supernaturalism of the Britons/Bretons is effectively a medieval French and English pejorative stereotype.[23] Yet it is a stereotype that was particularly powerful among English and French authors through to the end of the Middle Ages. I would suggest that in Couldrette's negotiation of Jean d'Arras's text, we see the culmination of a long historical reception of British, and importantly pseudo-British, allusions abstracted from any genuine earlier source functions or applications (where indeed these exist), invoked as fictions that a sophisticated audience might knowingly consume with a mind to their social or political significance. Couldrette's adaptation features not only recognisable Arthurian (largely pseudo-British) allusions but Arthurian characters and locations, including those long interpreted as phantasmatic.

## Avalon

There are overtures to Arthurian fictionality in Couldrette's text, including one which carries the weight of a long-lived association with the fables of the Britons: Avalon. On the one occasion when Avalon appears in Jean d'Arras's work, it is an overt signifier of a romance *aventure*. Jean writes of Presine's flight to Avalon, 'nommé l'ile Perdue, pour ce que nulz homs, tant y eust este de foiz, n'y sauroit rassenger fors par aventure' ('which was called the Lost

Isle, because no man, however many times he has been there before, could ever find it again except by chance').[24] The locale has all the marvellous uncertainty and ephemerality of the romance *merveille*. The 'ile Perdue' is almost certainly drawn from the *Lancelot-Grail*, where an island of the same name appears as a location visited on the grail quest, which is ruled over by Galehot of the Outer Isles (the Orkneys), approachable via a perilous causeway.[25] It is one of the familiar romance cues that we find in Jean d'Arras's text. Couldrette, however, gives Avalon a fuller textual presence as the site of a distinctive adventure, relocated from the earlier text. Couldrette identifies the site of Helmas's (Elinas's) tomb, and Geoffroy's subsequent adventures (adventures which would not be out of place in the grail legend), as Avalon: 'Qu'ilz encloirent par desroy / Cy, dedens Avalon on mont' ('They [the sisters] enclosed him [Helmas], with wickedness, in Avalon, in the mountain'; lines 4999–5000). This is a conflation of two marvellous mountains in Jean d'Arras's text: Eleneos, above Avalon, from where Presine and her daughters look over Albany and where the young fairies plot their father's demise, and the mountain in Northumberland, Brumblerio, where Elinas is imprisoned and entombed.

While, as is typical of Couldrette, this is a relatively obvious practice of abridgement and clarification – the removal of an unnecessary doubling of textual locations – its narrative effect goes beyond simplification and has a distinctively intertextual function. The locating of Helmas's golden tomb inside 'Avalon' recalls the bountiful Otherworld of Arthur in Gervase's Sicilian iteration of the legend, similarly a source of great treasure. Helmas's resting place is a golden chamber cut into the rock:

Qu'il arrive en une place
Où treuve une chambre moult belle;
Se faite fust toute nouvelle,
Elle ne péust plus belle estre:
Ouvrée à désire et à senestre,
En la roche fut entaillie;
Mais n'y avoit q'une saillie
Belle fu et gente à devise
Les richesces durement prise
Que dedens la chambre a véue:

Elle fu toute à or batue,
Plaine de riche pierrerie.

(He arrived at a spot where he found
A very beautiful room,
With a newly constructed look;
It couldn't have been more beautiful.
Great craftsmanship had gone into it,
Being cut into solid rock;
There was only one entrance to the place.
It was most fair and noble in design.
Anyone seeing its interior
Would have prized its great richness.
It was entirely of beaten gold
Studded with precious gems.)

(lines 4836–74)

The splendid chamber contains at its centre a tomb, studded with gemstones from within the mountain, with an effigy of a knight with a beautiful lady at his feet cast in alabaster who bears a tablet which recounts the fate of Helmas, from which Geoffroy learns of his family's supernatural origins. These details are consistent with the description of the tomb in Jean d'Arras's text (although the description in the latter is somewhat more florid) but are drawn into a sharper intertextual focus once associated explicitly with Avalon, the opulent resting place of another British king. The static figures of the fairy and the knight read as a re-imagining of Arthur and Morgan as in the version of the return legend in Geoffrey of Monmouth's *Vita Merlini*, and subsequently conjured, and rejected, by Gerald of Wales and later Gervase. Certainly, the allusion is recognisably fabulous.

Described by Couldrette as 'nouvelle', Helmas's tomb represents precisely the type of Gervasian *merveille* which he rejects in his prologue as incompatible with modern historical writing. Clearly it might, however, be integrated into those portions of the text which read as Arthurian *aventure*, invoked for the purposes of exemplarity. The bold knight, who quests for and discovers his remarkable origins – origins, importantly, which are encountered only in textual and/or visual form (the text in the tomb) – would appear to present a mirror to Guillaume himself, the bold reader of Couldrette's poem and truthful interpreter of its *fabulae*.

## A knight of Tristran's line

A similar act of discursive signposting is found in a distinctively Arthurian addition specific to Couldrette's version (although he claims its presence in his source chronicle). I refer to the account of the knight of Tristran's line. Towards the end of the work is the spurious history of a knight of 'Engleterre', 'de la lignie Tristran estrait' (line 6471), who takes on the Lusignan quest for the treasures of Palatine and the promise of a new crusade. In the context of this episode, following as it does from the activities of Geoffroy in Northumberland, Canigou is an extension, and clarification, of the pseudo-Arthurian trajectory there established – and its treasures present a counterpart to those of Avalon, another marvellous mountain.[26] The knight climbs the mountain facing bears and serpents – typical romance threats against which a knight might prove his prowess and at odds, as Zeldenrust notes, with the appearance of the Mélusinian serpent elsewhere in the romance.[27] These impediments may be an extension of the wonders associated with Canigou in Gervase's *Otia* – a steep-sided mountain in Catalonia, the ascent of which is nearly impossible, in which silver, gold, and crystal are mined. Gervase's mountain is perilous on account not simply of its size and shape, but also of the invisible demons found there.[28]

Although he climbs higher up the mountain than any man before him, the Arthurian knight cannot succeed, for it is prophesied, as we find in Jean d'Arras's text, that this treasure is reserved for the house of Lusignan alone. The Lusignan, or Parthenay, line is here endorsed by comparison to the glories, and the limitations, of other great genealogies. Yet the knight of Tristran's line only exists within the self-contained world of the text, for the romance includes an account of its own record. The knight has a page who survives the enterprise and lives to tell the tale, which is narrated by a clerk of some repute, with a quasi-clairvoyant reputation for truth-telling. We see here an interest in the fulfilment of events within the fictive frame of the text (much like the Arthurian prophecies of the Vulgate cycle):

En ce sçot-il par ung devin,
Qui fu jadis clerc de Merlin

> Et près d'ilecques demouroit.
> Tout le monde àla lui couroit;
> De quelconque necessité
> Il en diseit la verité,
> Et savoit tout entirement,
> Comme s'il y fust proprement,
> Ce qu'avenoit en la montaigne.
>
> (He learned from a divine,
> Who was once a clerk of Merlin,
> who lived near that place
> To whom all the world travelled;
> Of any event,
> He would say the truth,
> And knew everything well,
> As if he were there,
> What happened on the mountain.)
>
> (lines 6431–39)

A book written about the deeds of an English knight told by a clerk of Merlin sits suggestively with the precedent of the *Lancelot-Grail*, identified, in the internal world of the earlier Arthurian text, as the work of Merlin's mentor and scribe, Blaise. The allusion also suggests a level of intertextuality between the adventures of the English knight and those in the *Lancelot-Grail*, where the knights similarly face wild serpents and bears, in pursuit of great treasure with a place in the history of salvation. Interestingly, the clerk's training is understood in the early sixteenth-century English translation of Couldrette to be French: he is a clerk of Toulouse ('a scoler was of Tholouse certain'; line 5982); whereas in Couldrette, he is associated with the scientific learning of Toledo ('fu à l'escole de Tholette'; line 6441), which makes sense, given the episode's Iberian setting.[29] The English translator may well have assumed that a French-language Arthurian source was here meant.

There is surely some humour in the English knight who is unable to retrieve Palatine's treasure, in an early fifteenth-century text written when the English had no real foothold in France.[30] The failure of the knight is a less overtly politically directed variation on the English misperception, and overmighty territorial claims, of Jean d'Arras's epilogue and its account of the terror of the English castellan at the sight of the spectral Mélusine. It is a testament to the valour of the fairy's line. Yet in Couldrette's text, the knight's Englishness must also be understood first and foremost as a discourse marker: an overture to the insular origins of Arthurian romance.

## Prophecy

Despite his interests in Merlin and Avalon, one of the primary divergences of Couldrette's *Mélusine* from Jean d'Arras's text is the omission of the latter's prophetic frame – an explicitly historiographical convention, which demands a historical (futurist, if not directly mimetic) mode of reading. Presine's curses upon her daughters, with their relevant prophetic dimensions, which appear in the first chapter of Jean d'Arras's romance, are relocated to a much later point in Couldrette's text (Couldrette's version begins with Raymondin's murder of his uncle). They appear in the inscription on Presine's tablet in Helmas's tomb in Avalon, discovered by Geoffroy in the context of his romance *aventure*. In Couldrette's version, these events are there detailed for the first time, and although there is a certain economy to this, in line with Couldrette's practices of abridgement (the reminiscence of the murder of Elinas at this point in Jean d'Arras's text is repetitious), it mutes the role, and force, of prophecy in the history of Mélusine's descendants.

This is not to say, however, that this version avoids prophecy altogether: it informs, we have seen, the legend of the knight of Tristran's line, although this is most obviously at one with the prophetic resonances that characterise the Arthurian knight's quest more broadly, as a revelatory process, of expectations frustrated so that the destinies of other Arthurian actors might be realised (we might think, for example, of the failure of Gawain, Lancelot, and Percival in the grail quest, so that Galahad might succeed). The curse upon Palatine is the only one of Presine's three curses that in Couldrette retains a prophetic aspect with a historiographical function beyond the text: a prophecy of the discovery of the treasure that will fund the Lusignan conquest of Jerusalem. Presine's words regarding Mélusine and Melior have no obviously prophetic application other than the directly narratological. There is no reference to the foundation of the fortress of Lusignan and its perpetuity, or to the Armenian decline. While these episodes are relocated elsewhere, we are not taught to read prophetically in our approach to the text. Structure matters in terms of the reader's assumed horizon of expectations and intended response to available cultural cues. Given that Couldrette's readers have not hitherto been encouraged to read prophetically, it is perhaps no surprise that in the account of Melior's encounter with the ill-fated King of Armenia the meaning of her prophecy of the losses of the Armenian line are made explicit through clear biographical and historical detail:

> Je' vis le roy venir en France
> Que d'Ermenie l'en chassa,
> En France vint et trespassa;
> Le roy le soustint longuement,
> Et puis moru finablement
> A Paris, et fu, ce me semble,
> Oú moult de gens je vy ensemble,
> Aux Celestins mis en la terre.
>
> (I saw the king come to France,
> Who was chased from Armenie,
> Who came to France and passed away;
> The king sustained him for a long time,
> And finally he died,
> So I believe, it was in Paris,
> Many people I saw gather,
> At Celestine for the interment.)
>
> (lines 6114–21)

The passage continues to describe the dress of the mourners, who are clothed not in black but in white as is the custom of Armenia. This is a relatively rare moment of historical mimesis in the text, based on reportage, or witness testimony, of recent events that have taken place in Paris (knowledge that the author does not appear to have of Lusignan).

The omission of the foundation prophecy and prophecy of Mélusine's apparitional returns similarly demands a different reading of Mélusine's curse. Where elsewhere in the text the notion of Mélusine's spectral returns to the fortress is noted, it is in the words of Mélusine herself, in her final departure from Raymondin, rather than in more closely contemporary description of events at Lusignan:

> Ceulx qui après cent ans encore
> Naistront, bien en oront parler:
> Voire, qu'on me verra parler
> Entour le chastel de Luzignen
> Tousjours devant en cellui an
> Que le chastel changera maistre.
> S'en l'air on ne me puet congnoistre,
> Si m'apparay en terre plaine
> Ou au moins dessus la fontaine.
>
> (Many who, after a hundred years
> Are born, will speak of it:
> In truth, they will speak of me,
> About the castle of Lusignan
> In this year, three days before
> The castle will change master.
> They shall see me in the air,
> Or on the plain earth,
> Or at least beside the fountain.)
>
> (lines 3998–4006)

Although this passage makes truth-claims, these are unsubstantiated by concrete examples of the fairy's later apparition of the kind given by Jean d'Arras. Yet this passage is rooted in a renegotiation of Jean d'Arras's content, and so for readers of the two (presumably such as Guillaume), reading intertextually, it recalls the authority of the source. Alongside the prophetic aspects of Presine's curse in the original, it makes use of Jean's account of the omens given in the final epilogue of his work: the testimonies of Creswell and Owain, and of the servant who spotted Mélusine by the well (the fountain); but full details are necessarily occluded. One of the primary challenges for Couldrette in any direct reapplication of the historiographical model used by Jean d'Arras is that he cannot draw on testimony at Lusignan itself, the romance's site of dynastic origin. The place of extra-textual interest for the author is Parthenay, the site of Guillaume's tomb, rather than Lusignan. Mélusine observes that her many future appearances are verified by true testimony, and yet there are no authenticating examples, no chain of verifiable reporters in the historiographical fashion so explicitly invoked by Jean d'Arras, for there is no possible overture to contemporary or near-historical Lusignan except through an oblique allusion to the earlier version of the romance.

## The absent heir

Couldrette's marvellous phenomena are grounded in the non-mimetic, although sometimes intertextual, conventions of medieval romance, and the reader's familiarity with these codes. The meaning the reader takes from these is not obviously derived from attempts at occult rationalisation or interests in causation. This does not mean, however, that quest has come untethered from inquest: the fairy's teleological significance is still revealed to the attentive reader in the later parts of the text, as we find in Jean d'Arras – in prophecies of empire and crusade. For Couldrette, however, this possibility necessarily remains unclosed, without a viable contemporary referent for prophetic realisation. While Jean d'Arras's Lusignan prophecies are realised in Jean de Berry – whose seizure of Lusignan is presaged by the fairy with her tail in the colours of the house, positioned in the broader context of the romance as defeat of the English in France, and even the grounds of a new crusade – nowhere does Couldrette anticipate the specific realisation of these in Guillaume or his heir, Jean de Parthenay. Where in Jean d'Arras's text we find the account of the Duke of Berry's ominous and prophetic encounters at the fortress, in Couldrette's we read of the failures of the English knight in Aragon. Although certainly the line of Parthenay is endorsed by their favourable, prophetically ratified, comparison to the line of Tristran, it remains that the failure of one party does not necessarily imply the success of another. Indeed, following the knight's failure, we read of Geoffroy's plan to secure Palatine's treasure, a venture forestalled by his death. This leads Couldrette to an account of Guillaume's death in 1401, preceding a prayer (rather than a prophecy) concerning the fate of the house of Parthenay. In the first in a sequence of addresses to the saints, Couldrette asks that the apostles Peter, Paul, and Andrew protect the line of Parthenay:

> Par courtoisie
> N'oubliez mie celle lignie,
> Dont grant noblesce est saillie
> Et en mainte terre espartie;
> Car en maint lieu
> Ont-ilz conquis maint noble lieu
> Par leur noble chevalerie.
>
> (For courtesy,
> Do not overlook this line,
> From which great nobility is descended,
> And spread over many lands;
> Who have conquered
> Many a noble place
> With their noble chivalry.)
>
> (lines 6578–84)

The territorial holdings of Parthenay are presented as synonymous with the conquests of the fairy's sons, and the terminology used here recalls the *courtoisie* and *chevalerie* associated with the Arthurian fellowship in the prologue, to which the apostles are here re-imagined as a counterpart. As Colwell notes, there is something anxious about this insistence on the coherence of Parthenay territories. In this period, Jean de Parthenay, although married, was without a male heir, and in the event of his death, his patrimony would have been divided between his two sisters.[31] We see a concern about fragmentation not found in Jean d'Arras's *Mélusine*. Further, there is, of course, a difference between a prayer for prosperity and a prophecy of it; the good outcome of the one is less assured than that of the other, for after all, prophecy is really history written in the future tense.

Although the work was presumably commissioned by Guillaume in relation to its geographical and political utility (an appropriate legend for this region and this family), the tale type itself cannot but help speak to the instability of genealogical perpetuity and the vicissitudes of fortune. Let us not forget that Couldrette's *Mélusine* was completed for a dead patron, with (at the time) a terminal line. Whereas in Jean d'Arras's text moments of dynastic decline or uncertainty are tempered by the conquests of the Duke of Berry, in Couldrette's these are unanswerable. Even as a text that (as Colwell argues) responds to 'a contemporary crisis: the foreseeable extinction of an ancient baronial family', it also presents a rationalisation of that decline – the withdrawal of the fairy's favour (the same logic applied to the fate of the Armenian line in both romances).[32] Here we see a fracture in romance itself, a glimpse of the inexorable workings of history, and the surfacing of a decidedly historical pessimism in common with earlier historiographical uses of the fairy mother motif.

The text is, as I have suggested, multi-discursive, and although it is a fiction, Couldrette maintains its truth. The epilogue gives space to Couldrette's lengthy naming of the descendants of the fairy, in dynasties spread across Europe, from Armenia to Norway: a perpetuity that speaks to the fairy's material reality, and in some respects presents a counter to the anxieties the author expresses regarding Guillaume's own descendants. He uses the familiar recourse of the phantasmatic dream:

> Onc homme n'oÿt pareille
> Ne n'ouyt dire tel merveille,
> Et si ne l'orra de cest an,
> Com des enffans de Lusignen.
> Ne cuidez que ce soit mensonge;
> En verité c'est ung droit songe.
> Et qui n'auroit veü l'istoyre
> A paine le pourroit en croire,
> Mes l'istorye le nous racompte
> Tout ainsi comme je le compte.

> (No one ever heard the like of it
> Nor heard tell of such a wonder,
> Nor indeed is ever likely to,
> As of the offspring of Lusignan.
> Don't think it is a made up thing,
> In truth, it is a truthful dream.
> Anyone who'd not seen the chronicle
> Would hardly believe it,
> But the chronicle relates the tale
> Just as I am telling it now.)

(lines 6857–66)

Couldrette's evidence is self-reflexively textual, but it is also presented as mimetic or historically referential. Marvellous as it seems, the text possesses some level of reality status precisely because it is a dynastic chronicle. It must be read in relation to genealogical continuity, and both the bodies of the fairy's heirs and the text serve as forms of material witness, however phantasmatic the fairy might be understood to be (a dream, but a truthful one). This takes the place of the witness testimonies Jean d'Arras records, and in a movement away from the oral reportage of the earlier chronicle tradition, we see text as the primary means of authentication. The 'chronique' itself is the only point of authorisation beyond the fairy's living descendants, and the function of the former is entirely to inform how we might read the latter: it presents those descendants with an origin story. Nonetheless, through body and text, this is an engagement with materiality to which we might compare the footprint of Gervase's thirteenth-century version. The historicity of the marvel reasserts itself.

## New communities of wonder

The wider history of the *Mélusine* romances might be understood in relation to the construction of new communities of wonder, beyond the house of Lusignan. Among these are not only the house of Parthenay but communities of readers across late medieval and early modern Europe.[33] It is in this context that we see the return of the Mélusinian fairy (from her very beginnings the product of a transnational community of clerical authors) to an insular context.[34] The narrative was certainly known in aristocratic circles in England. Alongside Jean d'Arras's identification of the Earl of Salisbury as one of his patrons, we might note the history of London, British Library, Cotton MS Otho D.ii, a copy of Jean d'Arras's version generally understood to have been purchased by John, Duke of Bedford, from the library of Charles VI of France after the latter's death in 1422. It subsequently passed into the English royal library by the reign of Richard III at the latest, almost certainly via John's wife Jacquetta (mother of Elizabeth Woodville, wife of Edward IV), whose signature is understood to have been on the last folio, lost in the fire at the Cotton Library in the eighteenth century.[35]

An English translation of Jean d'Arras is found in London, British Library, Royal MS 18.B.ii (*c.* 1500), which was once in the possession of John Lumley and his father-in-law the Earl of Arundel and which subsequently, like Cotton Otho D.ii, was integrated into a royal library.[36] Zeldenrust has identified the source of the English prose version as most likely to have been the edition of the romance printed in Geneva in 1478.[37] This is in addition to surviving fragments of an early printed English translation of Jean d'Arras, tentatively associated with Wynkyn de Worde, representative of a version independent of that in Royal MS 18.B.ii, although potentially with a common exemplar.[38] Couldrette's text was also translated into English, with verse retained, during the same period (*c.* 1500–20), in incomplete form in Cambridge, Trinity College Library, MS R.3.17; its early provenance is unknown, although Walter Skeat's early theory that the translator was an Englishman in Poitou is now rejected, given the wide reach of the legend during this period.[39] The demand for the translation of both versions of the French *Mélusine*, as Zeldenrust notes, is likely to have been facilitated by existing printed English translations of thematically similar French romances such as *Partonopeus de Blois*.[40]

There is a conjunction between *Mélusine* and Middle English romance that pre-dates the English translations. The association of the fairy mother with English political figures recurs roughly contemporaneously with Couldrette's re-imagining of Jean d'Arras, in the *a*-text of *Richard Coer de Lyon* (*c.* 1400; hereafter *Richard a*). *Richard a* survives in two manuscripts: Cambridge, Gonville and Caius College Library, MS 175/96 (in which the beginning of the text is lost), produced around 1400 in Lincolnshire; and the mid-fifteenth-century London, British Library, Additional MS 31042 (also known as the London Thornton Manuscript); alongside two early printed editions by Wynkyn de Worde, likely publisher of the English prose *Mélusine*. It post-dates another version of *Richard* (*b*), which was composed before 1330 when it was integrated in Edinburgh, National Library of Scotland, Advocates MS 19.2.1 (the Auchinleck manuscript). *Richard b* omits the supernatural mother narrative, as well as other lurid elements of *Richard a*, including Richard's much-commented-upon anthropophagy.[41] *Richard b* has generally been understood to be closer to a chronicle, while *Richard a* has been commonly regarded as romance. This binary designation, however, blunts the discursive uncertainties of the *a*-text. *Richard a* shares a number of affinities with the *Mélusine* tradition, not least its relationship to common Latin historical *mirabilia*, re-imagined in line with the discursive conventions of romance.

*Richard a* is in some respects typical of those romances that position themselves as historically engaged in that – like *Mélusine* – it follows a hero from his conception to his death. This is a model lifted from saints' lives (the text is even entitled *Vita* and accompanies saints' lives in Additional MS 31042), but is also a feature of Arthurian romance, with which *Richard a* aligns itself in terms that are notably similar to Couldrette's prologue. In the prologue, the poem is situated in relation to 'romaunses' read in both England and France:

> Ffele romaunses men maken newe,
> Off goode kny3tes, stronge and trewe;
> Off here dedys men rede romaunce,
> Boþe in Engeland and in Ffraunce:
> Off Rowelond, and off Olyuer,
> And off euery Doseper;
> Off Alisaundre, and Charlemayn;
> Off Kyng Arthour, and off Gawayn,
> How þey were knyghtes goode and curteys;
> Off Turpyn, and of Oger Daneys;
> Off Troye men rede in ryme,
> What werre þer was in olde tyme;
> Off Ector, and off Achylles,
> What folk þey slowe in þat pres.
>
> (lines 7–20)[42]

This type of list is a relatively common feature of Middle English romance. Beyond the author's association of Richard with the Nine Worthies, as Yin Liu has observed, the prologue might be understood as evidence of the various uses of the category term 'romance' in Middle English, which at this stage still appears to function historically, or at least expansively, combining histories of Troy with *chanson de geste* and Arthuriana (the same contexts with which, we have seen, Couldrette's *Mélusine* was associated).[43] We might note the presence of Alexander – a hero who like the Richard of the romance is of remarkable parentage, and the subject of uncertain, wide-ranging geographical marvels. A similar contextual geographical awareness is, I suggest, fundamental to the shape of the community which the *Richard a*-author constructs.[44]

## Romance paradoxography in *Richard a*

The fairy mother in the Mélusinian tradition is, as I have argued in previous chapters, something of a paradox, the understanding of which involves a suspension of disbelief, and faith in the possibility of improbable occurrences. In *Richard a*, however, this is explicitly associated with the mixed discursive tradition of writing geographically distant marvels, which, as Karnes has noted, customarily combines 'observation' with more properly literary 'invention'.[45] This is a combining which other critics have understood to be a form of romance – proposing that we might write of 'medieval travel romance' – and certainly, this is a meaningful classification of *Richard a*, if approached as a mixed genre.[46] The discursive hybridity, and tenuous facticity, of the writing of geographical wonders finds a precedent as early as Augustine. In *De civitate Dei* Augustine writes of the Plinian peoples known to him from pagan histories, remediated in contemporary visual culture although never witnessed directly:

> hominum vel quasi hominum genera, quae in maritima platea Carthaginis musivo picta sunt, ex libris deprompta velut curiosioris historiae.
>
> (men and quasi-men such as are pictured in mosaic on the esplanade at Carthage, taken from books as samples of the curiosities of natural history.)[47]

Such persons are located, if they exist at all, beyond the sea, on the edge of the world; they are mediated through narrative and visual media rather than direct witness (notably, it is through a similar mediation that Couldrette's Geoffroy learns of his family's fairy origins – and certainly, this is something of a distancing mechanism). The uncertain marvels associated with the peoples on the margins, as Debra Higgs Strickland and John Block Friedman have noted, were extended to later medieval western European Christian imaginings of Jews and Muslims in both text and image, applications which existed in tension with lived and historical proximity but were not necessarily understood as purely fictive – although, as discussed in Chapter 2, such stereotypes are indicative of a process of pejorative fictionalisation.[48] As early as Isidore of Seville's description of Asia in his *Etymologies*, 'Saracenni' and 'Judaeus' are discussed in the same section of the text as the white-haired Albanians and the one-breasted Amazons.[49] Perceptions of proximity, and the collapsing of geographical distance – an inevitable consequence of a whistle-stop tour through a verbal *mappa mundi* – appear to have facilitated a transference of a type which is, I suggest, a feature of *Richard a*.

The re-imagined figure of Richard himself, whose giant stature, eastern origins, and uncertain morality have attracted considerable critical attention, possesses obvious paradoxographical affinities.[50] His impressive physical qualities are understood to be the product of his remarkable parentage and the seemingly impossible conditions of his birth, in which context the text introduces Cassodorien, Richard's fictionalised mother. The episode functions in relation to the anti-Angevin legend as recorded by Gerald of Wales and later Philippe Mousket. The fairy is here, as there, identified with the heretic or host abuser, although the paradigm is distinctively modified.[51] A marvellous woman from the east and a substitution for the historical Eleanor of Aquitaine, Cassodorien is encountered on a lavishly provisioned ship westbound from Antioch to England, propelled by the dream of her father, Corbaryng, of her marriage to Henry II. Although, as Wade notes, Cassodorien is never explicitly called a fairy, the construction of the episode suggests precisely such an identification, whether read through the lens of history or romance.[52] Cassodorien is married to Henry and the couple have children. One day, like her earlier counterparts, when presented with the mass Cassodorien flees from the chapel via aerial ascent through the roof and vanishes from the narrative entirely. Although, as we shall see, Cassodorien is the first supernatural mother to exhibit a familiar affective response to the eucharist (although unlike Mélusine, she is not a Christian), her demonic, or at least outsider, status is made clear. Association with the ex-communicant is a source of pointed comedy in her final departure: she attempts to take with her the future king John (excommunicated between 1209 and 1213), although, in a further joke, she drops him from the roof. In what follows, Richard establishes his stalwart, violently realised, Christian faith and his claim on the eastern lands adjacent to the kingdom from which his mother hails.

*Richard a* explores the same questions of parentage and belief characteristic of Augustine's account of the marvellous monsters of the Plinian tradition. Augustine asks whether such peoples are the descendants of Adam, and affirms that if they do exist, they share their humanity with the rest of mankind:

> Sed omnia genera hominum, quae dicuntur esse, credere non est necesse. Verum quisquis uspiam nascitur homo, id est animal rationale mortale, quamlibet nostris inusitatam sensibus gerat corporis formam ...
>
> (To be sure, we do not have to believe in all the types of men that are reported to exist. Yet whoever is born anywhere as a human being, that is, as a rational mortal creature, however strange he may appear to our senses in bodily form ...)[53]

Augustine concludes that, this being so, the monster contains the spiritual potential for Christian belief. The fairy mother narrative of *Richard a* asks precisely what, and how, such remarkable figures (if they exist) might believe, and in turn, what they might signify for the Christian belief of the reader. I suggest that as Augustine does with the Plinian peoples, the *Richard a*-author invites contemplation of the possible sanctity of such figures, and their place in a wider global history (or projection) of Christian expansionism. Richard's fictionalised mother is mediated by a narrative approached much as Augustine does the Plinian history encountered in tall tales and fabulous mosaics: her utility is on the level of the thought experiment.

*Richard a* is not the only medieval romance to entertain marvels of a type with the Plinian peoples. We might note, for example, the Alexander romances, which contain some of the most prolific vernacular applications of paradoxography in the classical vein in medieval Europe, and, as Venetia Bridges has suggested, might be understood in relation to a distinctive act of *translatio*, the balancing of opposites in the fashion of the scholastic paradox as a strategy carried over from Latin to vernacular composition.[54] We might also note the wonders of seemingly related works of western European travel writing, most famously *Mandeville's Travels*.[55] Like the English translation of the *Travels*, *Richard a* is customarily counted among those 'popular' texts accessible to an emerging class of middle-stratum readers, texts often characterised by sex, violence, and xenophobia,[56] although the class contexts of its first readers remain uncertain and aristocratic patrons have been suggested.[57] However we understand its early readership, it is a text which demonstrates a defensive reflection on the boundaries of the Christian community, which might be understood first and foremost in relation to assertions of cultural and religious difference.[58] This is a position which, I suggest, turns on the status of the marvel, its interpretive codes, and the communities, both in-text and of readers, in which it is received. It details the fortunes of not simply a single aristocratic or royal line but a wider community of English and Christian readers, with a marked interest in the goods, riches, and territories of the Middle East. Exemplifying this appropriative drive, the text participates in recognisable constructions of stereotyped perceptions of non-Christian misbelief, misperception, and credulity, in which the figure of the fairy plays an important part.

## Eucharistic wonder

Although it is a familiar episode participating in a wider set of conventions that go back to Gervase's account of the lady of L'Epervier, Cassodorien's complex comprehension of the eucharist contains some unfamiliar details. Upon the elevation of the host, she faints:

> A preest on morwe þe messe song;
> Befforn þe eleuacyoun
> Þe qwene fel in swowne adon;
> Þe folk wondryd and were adrad.
>
> (lines 188–91)

Cassodorien's response might be read as a sudden perception of the host's invisible matter (the blood and body of Christ), visible to the literally minded Jewish character of Christian conversion narratives – one of the triad of figures associated with eucharistic rejection, alongside the heretic and the witch. The Christian accepts as a matter of faith what must necessarily be made visible for the Jew, who lacks the spiritual and cognitive ability to conceive of invisible truths. Importantly, although associated with a different type of perception, the converting Jew shares the common affective response of the Christian: devotion, awe, and grief at the suffering of Christ. As Bale suggests, medieval antisemitic motifs, in their specific aesthetic and affective registers, may form the basis of cross-cultural affective identification, however complexly realised and pejoratively employed.[59] The fairy narrative of *Richard a* is engaged with wonder on all sides, of the fairy, the congregation, and the reader. Just as the congregation are filled with 'drede' and 'wonder' at the fairy's behaviour (as is the reader with them), so, it seems, is the fairy full of a 'drede' and 'wonder' of her own as she swoons before the mass.

The swoon preceding the flight is absent from the fairy mother narrative as we find it in Latin *mirabilia* but is a feature of the French *Mélusines*, where, unlike her Latin counterparts, the fairy possesses a fuller range of somatic emotional expression. Indeed, like the fairy's complex maternity, the swoon suggests a distinctly human embodied status as much as it does participation in recognisable emotional cues. As Corinne Saunders notes of the swooning heroes and heroines of medieval romance, in terms of medieval physiology the swoon is caused by the movement of vital spirits into the heart occasioned by an extreme emotional response – whether lovesickness or religious revelation.[60] The swooning fairies have a heart, both metaphorically and literally. Following Raymondin's public admonishment of her, immediately prior to her own flight, Mélusine swoons for grief. The swoon there takes the place of the familiar eucharistic denouement of the Gervasian tale type, which *Richard a* restores. In this combining, *Richard a* presents a wonder response of double significance, both secular and divine. Michael D. Barbezat has argued that the figure of the (initially) uncomprehending heretic or Jew is associated with the 'pure eroticism' of misdirected love for the earthly rather than the divine.[61]

This suggests an instinctive point of intersection with the eroticism of the fairy. Indeed, as in earlier Latin accounts (a common romance component) the wonder response to the fairy is overtly associated with lovesickness. The final allusion to Henry II introduces a similar conceptual association. Following his fairy wife's departure, the king vows never to love again:

> The kynge wondred of that thynge,
> That she made suche an endynge,
> For loue that he was serued so;
> Wolde he neuer after come there ne go.
>
> (lines 235–38)

The Cassodorien episode is a product, whether direct or indirect, of the substitutory and conflictual relationship between *fin'amor* and divine longing which underlies the fairy mistress tradition from the twelfth century onwards, as a sceptical, if not indeed parodic, presentation of courtly love. Yet this association is also here dependent on a level of affective recognition.

While this has much in common with the Latin *mirabilia* tradition, the *Richard a*-author's accounts of the wonder response are notable for their lack of interest in causation (demonic or otherwise), and courtly love principles are invoked as a form of narrative naturalisation. The king's wonder operates as a synonym for grief, a misadventure in love rather than contemplation of the mysterious mechanics behind a marvel. Although surely the reader is invited to contemplate the meaning of the fairy, the text does not do it with them. Further, the acknowledgement of wonder as we find it in the king's grief following his wife's departure appears to foreclose questions of the fairy's ontology. As Karnes notes, one of the distinctive qualities of the Middle English marvel is a lack of enquiry into 'the inner workings' of the marvel on the part of both the author and the characters. The marvel is 'typically presented without fanfare. Authors and characters scarcely inquire into their inner workings or acknowledge the wonder the reader can only assume they create'.[62] For Karnes, this type of romance marvel operates as a point of imaginative rather than mimetic representation. There is simply no causation to probe, for it stands outside any extra-textual frame of reference.

This is not to say, however, that the romance marvel does not demand a certain sophistication on the part of the reader. As a number of recent scholars, including Karnes, have noted, the function of the romance marvel is often explicitly metaphorical, and might even be understood in relation to traditions such as riddling.[63] The fairy marvel of *Richard a* reads as an abstraction of the exegetical applications of the fairy that we find in twelfth- and thirteenth-century historiography; and like the host aversion of the continental fairies of Gervase, Gerald, and Mousket, Cassodorien's revulsion at the sight of the host is testament to the host's apotropaic power, and the exposure of the fairy's true nature is again framed as an analogue to the host's revelatory (metamorphic) function. The swooning and flight of the fairy and the miracle of transubstantiation are held analogous to one another in the words of the earl, who suggests to Henry that the mass will expose his fairy bride:

> On a day, before þe rode
> Þe kyng at hys masse stode;
> Þer com an erl off gret pouste,
> Sere, he sayde, hou may þis be
> Þat my lady, ȝoure wyffe, þe qwene,
> Þe sacrement ne dar nouȝt sene?
> Geue vs leue to don here dwelle,
> Ffro þat begynnes þe gospelle
> Tyll þe messe be sungge and sayd,
> And þou schalt se *a queynte brayd*.
>
> (lines 207–16; my italics)

Truly, one will see a 'queynte brayd' at the mass – if we translate this as a remarkable occurrence, rather than (as is presumably the duke's intended primary meaning, if not the text's), a devious stratagem. The former applies not simply to the revelation of the fairy, but to transubstantiation, which is beyond direct comprehension and rationalisation. The fairy paradox functions as an analogy, a vehicle for understanding the irreducible reality of the eucharist. This is a familiar historiographical application, yet I suggest that the fairy is here not simply a paradox but paradoxography – a status which might be read in relation to her cultural and geographical position.

## A princess of Antioch

Cassodorien is not only aligned with the figure of the heretic or Jew but is the object of a supernaturally ciphered cultural over-signification. *Richard a* represents a new association with the figure of the mass-evading demon: the eastern princess. Cassodorien is identified by her father Corbaryng as a princess of Antioch, presented to Henry in response to her father's dream of their union, a positive re-imagining of the ominous dreams and prophecies of Angevin decline found in Gerald of Wales's writings. The significance of the author's geographical and nominative choices is relatively clear in terms of both the geopolitics of the romance and historical cues, which are here distorted: the crusading kingdom of Antioch presented a historical relationship to Eleanor, via her uncle, Raymond of Antioch, with whom hostile chroniclers alleged that Eleanor committed incestuous infidelities.[64] The fictionalised King of Antioch, however, is something of a split signifier. Although historically a bastion of regional Christian power, by the period of the composition of the *a*-text, Antioch was under the control of the Mamluk sultanate. Geraldine Heng has convincingly suggested that Corbaryng's name is a scrambled Arabic loan, recalling the Latin names for Karbuqa, the atabeg of Mosul, who defended Antioch immediately prior to the first Latin conquest of the city during the First Crusade. He is named in Latin chronicles 'Corbaras' and 'Curbarum'.[65]

The possible meaning of Cassodorien's name is less clear, although Heng proposes an association with the antique author Cassidorius, whose writings contain an early antisemitic eucharistic miracle story, of a type with what in later texts is termed the 'blood libel'; and certainly this would seem an appropriate point of recollection given the eucharistic resonance of the fuller episode.[66] Although Muslims were not associated with an explicit antipathy towards the eucharist, heresy was a familiar pejorative ascription to Islam, and we might also read Cassodorien in relation to the Arabic, Muslim significance of her father (the association of Islam with false fantasies, and its role in western European fiction-making, is a matter to which I return below).[67] Certainly, although the identification (as with Corbaryng) is never made explicit, her representation is aligned with that of the eastern princess of crusading romance, a component of an erotic economy promising to the western prince or knight all the riches of the east. In part, this is founded in certain geographical and commercial realities: Cassodorien and Corbaryng's ship contains luxury goods, such as ivory and silk, that were brought from the Levant to England via trade routes crossing the Mediterranean.[68] The literary construction of the eastern princess embodies the economic and sexualised longings of what Suzanne Conklin Akbari has termed 'medieval orientalism'.[69] This offers an obvious point of intersection with the figure of the fairy mistress, itself perhaps one of the most famous examples of sexual and economic wish fulfilment in western literature. This has a pre-existing tendency to look eastwards: as early as Marie de France's *Lanval*, the beauty and riches of the fairy are compared to those of the ancient Assyrian queen Semiramis.[70] Cassodorien is a culmination of this long-held association, representative of a collision between the wish fulfilment offered by fairy romance and orientalist fantasy.

Romance narratives of the eastern princess, always-already characterised by some level of Christian normativity, conventionally depict her conversion to Christianity, accompanied by her marriage to a Christian prince, the birth of heirs, and the expansion of a Christian empire.[71] Richard's crusading exploits are endorsed by an abstract notion of matrilineal inheritance in Antioch, although this is never quite made concrete in the text. The association of Richard with a Muslim mother, while pure fiction, may have a precedent in a rumour associated with Eleanor, which appears to have first emerged in a thirteenth-century continental context: Eleanor as the lover of Saladin (Yusuf ibn Ayyub ibn Shadi).[72] Cassodorien would appear to take this perception of Eleanor's sexual, and cultural, difference one step further: she herself is (pseudo-)Islamicised. Yet her cultural context and positioning remain ambiguous. Indeed, in Cassodorien we might detect something of the disruptive potential of the marvel of Middle English romance, as Nicola McDonald has understood it, destabilising authorised systems of knowledge.[73] Cassodorien is at no point overtly identified as Muslim, and so is never a convert. She

'*En rime l'istoire*'

remains forever outside the internal textual community of wonder, even as she wonders at the mass. Yet despite her alterity, her emotional cues are familiar, and indeed, the very operation of the narrative's wonder depends on their familiarity and so a moment of reader alignment – a shared recognition of the wonderful qualities of the eucharist. This is very similar to the emotional correspondence that Marcel Elias has noted in the late Middle English translations of the French *chansons de geste*, a genre with which we might align *Richard a*, where Muslim characters are represented as expressing Christian-centric emotional cues and interact with shared systems of value.[74] In *Richard a*, however, this affinity is especially complex. The reader wonders through Cassodorien, whose awe is at once the same as, and different from, their own, while her difference simultaneously intensifies wonder.

### Pejorative wonder

The type of cross-cultural affective response invited by Cassodorien recurs throughout representations of wonder in *Richard a*, through affinities constructed with increasing complexity. This is most apparent in the author's description of Richard's entry into Acre, identified as a 'mervayle' (line 2683), which terrifies the city's Muslim inhabitants. Richard makes use of Greek fire seized earlier in the narrative from one of Saladin's ships:

> Kyng Richard out off hys galye
> Caste wylde ffyr into þe skye,
> And ffyr Gregeys into þe see,
> As al on fyr weren hee.
> Trumpes ȝede in hys galeye,
> Men myȝten it here into þe skye,
> Taboures and hornes Sarezyneys;
> Þe see brente al off ffyr Gregeys.
>
> (lines 2643–50)

This highly dramatic episode recalls an often-repeated Augustinian marvel. Among the various flammable projectiles available in medieval naval warfare was lime, one of the likely ingredients of Greek fire.[75] The burning of lime was Augustine's much-used example of the perspectival relativism of wonder: wondrous only to those unaccustomed to it, and potentially remarkable to a witness in India in a way that it is not to one in Greece or Rome.[76] It is then, a fitting centre to an account treating perspectival wonder and cultural difference. A similar episode occurs in Jean d'Arras's *Mélusine* (this episode is truncated in Couldrette's version). Equipped by their fairy mother, Urien and Eudo arrive at Cyprus, much to the incomprehension of the 'Sarrasins', who see a great Christian fleet gathered as if from nowhere, trumping, as in *Richard a*, their 'cors sarrazinois' (war horns, a familiar feature of descriptions of Christian armies in crusading narratives, even serving as an indicator of a crusading context):

> Canons et arbalestres et sonner trompes et cors sarrazinois, et partir ces galees a force de gens d'avirons! C'estoit grant beauté a veoir. Quant les Sarrasins apperceurent si grant navire venir vers eulx, si ne sçorent que penser car jamais n'eussent cuidié que telle puissance de crestiens feussent si prez de la.
>
> (Cannons and crossbows were readied, trumpets and war horns [lit. 'Saracen horns'] were sounded. The galleys hastened towards battle in rhythm with the oars. It was a beautiful sight to behold! The Saracens didn't know what to think of the approach of vessels such as these, for they had never imagined that such a powerful Christian force was so near.)[77]

The alarmed 'Sarrasins' set fire to a ship intended to be recognised by the crusaders as one of their own, only to have the wind blow it back to the destruction of their own fleet. The stratagem of Richard is a variation on the luck of Eudo and Urien. The episode in *Richard a*, however, goes further. The sea of fire is accompanied by a devil automaton in the middle of the ship, which grinds red stones and gives the impression of blood:

> Beffore þe trouȝ þer stood on,
> Al in blood he was begon,
> And hornes grete vpon hys hede,
> The Sarezynes of hym hadde gret drede
> For it was within the nyght

They were agrysed of that syght,
And sayd he was the deuell of hell
That was come them to quell:
Ffor þe rubbyng off þe stones,
Þey wende it hadde ben mennes bones.
A lytyl beffore þe lyȝt off day,
Clenly þey were don away.

(lines 2671–82)

There is an interesting choice of wonder vocabulary here: 'drede' translates as fear but also awe (the same term appears in the context of Cassodorien's encounter with the eucharist), and the marvel appears to have been intended to be read in this double sense: what inspires awe in the reader, inspires (uncomprehending) terror in the Muslim witness. This terror is accompanied by a failed attempt at rationalisation: the people of Acre believe the mill to be a devil. This is, at least in part, its intended effect. It is an automaton, a fabricated marvel that appeared in European courts and public pageantry of the later Middle Ages, although, as E. R. Truitt notes, the automata of romance are often more sophisticated than those of historical western engineering.[78] The audacity of Richard's mill owes its fullest debt to western imaginings of technologies perfected in the practices of Greek and Arabic inventors. Medieval French and English authors long recalled the remarkable automata of the Abbasid court in in the eighth and ninth centuries – of mechanical birds and gardens evocative of the 'imaginary and mythic', testing 'the limits of credulity'.[79] We might expect to encounter automata to the east in a medieval travel romance such as *Richard a*, and the automaton as devil may recall a perceived association of automata with Arabic (coded as Muslim) invention, but here such cultural ownership is rejected even as it is invoked.[80] The fearful Muslim response is a failure to recognise the constructed, the fictive; to distinguish between a devil and a feat of engineering. The community of appropriate wonder rests on the ability to discern the meaning of the marvel, an activity rooted in a clear set of cultural cues, points of recognition, and, either implicitly or explicitly, intellectual competencies.

The *Richard a* episode is intended to inspire wonder in its Christian reader, as it does in the 'Sarassins', and the latter is invoked as an aid to the former. Like Cassodorien's experience of the eucharist, it demands a measure of cross-cultural empathy on behalf of the reader, an ability to occupy a different subject position. Yet the reader's wonder is of a different order from that of the inhabitants of Acre, for unlike the latter the reader possesses narrative context. The negotiations of 'Sarassin' wonder here might be understood in line with the rejection of wonder that we find in the Baconian position, where wonder is not the beginning of wisdom, but rather is indicative of ignorance.[81] Islam was for the *Richard a*-author a faith constructed (or rather, faith misplaced) in the service of the devil, and so Muslim 'drede', a term which we have seen contains a secondary meaning of divine awe, would appear to be a particularly appropriate group response.

## Islam and misperception

There is a long western Christian association of Islam with misperception. We might note the pseudo-etymology of the word 'Saracen' itself, a term that St Jerome understood to be adopted by the sons of Hagar who sought to pass as the sons of Sara, simultaneously disguising and exposing their illegitimate genealogy.[82] Jerome's etymology was repeated by Isidore, but here the reason behind the adoption of the name is presented less as an act of deliberate subterfuge than as misrecognition:

> Saraceni dicti, vel quia ex Sarra genitos se praedicent, vel sicut gentiles aiunt, quod ex origine Syrorum sint, quasi Syriginae. Hi peramplam habitant solitudinem. Ipsi sunt et Ismaelitae, ut liber Geneseos docet, quod sint ex Ismaele. Ipsi Cedar a filio Ismaelis. Ipsi Agareni ab Agar; qui, ut diximus, perverso nomine Saraceni vocantur, quia ex Sarra se genitos gloriantur.
> 
> (The Saracens are so called either because they claim to be descendants of Sarah or, as the pagans say, because they are of Syrian origin, as if the word were *Syriginae*. They live in a very large deserted region. They are also Ishmaelites, as the Book of Genesis teaches us, because they sprang from Ishmael. They are also named Kedar, from

the son of Ishmael, and Agarines, from the name Agar (i.e. Hagar). As we have said, they are called Saracens from an alteration of their name, because they are proud to be descendants of Sarah.)[83]

In time, 'Saracenni', and its French derivative 'Sarazins', came to be, without any clear logical articulation of this extension, re-applied from Ishmaelite Arabs to Muslims more generally, carrying something of this weight. Like the credulous associations of the Welsh – although a distinct cultural construction – western interest in Ishmaelite, and later Muslim, self-delusion was itself a longstanding fantasy.

*Richard a* is explicitly concerned with 'Saracen' misrepresentation. The first Christian–Muslim encounter of the text (whereby the English forces come into possession of Greek fire) is between Richard's fleet and a Muslim ship bound for Acre, which poses as a French supply ship launched from Apulia. Tellingly, the latimer of the 'Saracen' ship swears his false Christianity in the name of the eastern 'Seynt Thomas off Ynde' (line 2495), the first doubter of Christ's resurrection. The very formulation of his profession of faith conveys his faithlessness. The legacy of the pseudo-etymology of the 'Saracenni' as a locus of misrepresentation may even find a direct recollection in *Richard a*, in an episode explicitly concerned with fabricated maternities. In a scheme to take the king in battle, Richard's antagonist Saladin commands a 'maystyr nigromacien' (line 5532):

> Þat coniuryd, as j ȝow telle,
> Þorwȝ þe ffeendes crafft off helle
> Twoo stronge ffeendes off þe eyr
> In lyknesse off twoo stedes ffeyr,
> Lyke boþe of hewe and here;
> As þay seyde þat were þere,
> Neuere was þer sen non slyke.
> Þat on was a mere lyke,
> Þat oþer a colt, a noble stede.
>
> (lines 5533–41)

The colt will bring the English king to Saladin on the field as it will be drawn back to its mother to feed. The mare conceit recalls the same association constructed between Islam and demonic magic activated in the Muslim terror that meets Richard's devil, but it is also a variation on a motif in European writings on magic, and in international romance: the spectral horse as a form of supernatural transportation.[84] While the marvellous horse, as we find it elsewhere in Middle English romance of this period, has been understood as a space of pure fantasy and poetic innovation, this particular incarnation of it is explicitly interested in the historical, or at least quasi-historical, matter of genealogy.[85] The relationship between the mare and the foal re-imagines the relationship between Richard and his mother. Like the fairy, the spectral mare is material, or at least quasi-material, in her behaviours and effects, first and foremost on the level of her maternity (like Mélusine, in her final spectral form as she visits her children in the nursery, the mare is a phantom capable of producing milk). The mare is the familiar subject of a genealogical marvel in the Augustinian tradition, in a narrative which goes back at least as early as Homer. In his account of the inexplicable – but nonetheless true – marvels of nature, presented as analogues to the fires of purgatory, Augustine includes an account of the mares of Cappadocia (in modern-day Turkey) impregnated by the west wind, whose foals live only a short time, the marvellous mechanics of which, like the Dusii of Gaul, remain necessarily unexplained.[86] Into the later Middle Ages the marvellous impregnation of the mare appears to have been understood as an analogous rationalisation of demonic conception.[87] The brief life of the aery mare and foal of *Richard a* is a variation on a theme intimately connected to supernatural or preternatural maternities and the mysteries of demonic pro-generation.

This episode, concerned as it is with unusual, phantasmatic eastern and Islamic pro-generation, might be read in relation to a wider concern about the pro-generative Muslim marvel, or rather the pseudo-marvel, as a point of erroneous belief. An explicitly genealogical concern recurs throughout hostile Christian accounts of Islam, conflated with discourses of antisemitism and associated with faith in false marvels. This is a feature of hostile Latin lives of the Prophet Mohammed circulating from the early twelfth century onwards, falsely representing the Hadith and/or Qur'anic law as sexually permissive. These represent the Prophet as a trickster and author of false miracles, sometimes aided by a figure named 'Magus', presumably a recollection of the biblical Simon (and we might here remember the false wonders of the heretics discussed in Chapter 2), who may also find a re-imagining in the figure of Saladin's clerk.[88] Guibert of Nogent records the most famous false miracle associated with the Prophet in his *Dei gesta per Francos* (*c.* 1108), an influential account of the First Crusade containing a calumnious presentation of the origins of Islam.[89] Guibert writes that Mohammed wrote his laws and tied them between the horns of a trained cow that he hid in a cave on a mountaintop, as a fabricated *miraculum* authorising a new, obscene faith. A conflation between two incoherent conceptions of Islam as both Christian heresy and idol worship, the bull presents a transplanted re-imagining of the Israelites' golden calf and Moses's revelation of the laws on Mount Sinai (the mountain or volcano is, we have seen, invariably a site of medieval marvels, true, false, or uncertainly phantasmatic: a formulation which may well owe its debt to Christian anxieties about the Old Law as much as the purgatorial associations of the volcano). The episode is a characteristic combining of medieval Islamophobia and antisemitism:

> Quo facto infinitae multitudinis vulgus aggregat et, ut magis vaga corda premissa religione deciperet, triduo eis ieiunare imperat et ut deum attente postulent pro legis acceptione sollicitat. Hoc etiam eis signum dat quia, si deo sibi legem dare placuerit, more eis insolito et per manum de qua non speratur dabit. Interim vaccam habebat, quam ita manui suae assuefecerat, ut quotienscumque aut eius vocem audiret vel videret presentiam vix eam vis ulla teneret quin ad eum intolerabili quadam aviditate concurreret. Factum igitur labellum cornibus animalis circumligat et in tentorio quo verasabutur illud occultat. Tercio denique die super omnem qui convenerat populum eminens tribunal ascendit et declamare productis vocibus ad populum cepit. Quae cum, ut ita dixerim, summa aure verborum sonitum attigisset, e tentorio subteriancenti confestim egreditur et per medias coadunatarum gentium turmas, volumine cornibus imposito, ad pedes loquentis quasi congratulatura vacca contendit. Mirantur omnes, raptim volumen evolvitur, anhelanti turbae exponitur, petulantia turpi lege permissa gaudenter excipitur. Quid plura? Oblati libri miraculum centuplicatis favoribus celebratur.

(By doing this he gathered a huge mob of people, and the better to deceive their uncertain minds with the pretext of religion, he ordered them to fast for three days, and to offer earnest prayers for God to grant a law. He also gives them a sign, because, should it please God to give them law, he will grant it in an unusual manner, from an unexpected hand. Meanwhile, he had a cow, whom he himself had trained to follow him, so that whenever she heard his voice or saw him, almost no force could prevent her from rushing to him with unbearable eagerness. He tied the book he had written to the horns of the animal, and hid her in the tent in which he himself lived. On the third day he climbed a high platform above all the people he had called together, and began to declaim to the people in a booming voice. When, as I just said, the sound of his words reached the cow's ears, she immediately ran from the tent, which was nearby, and, with the book fastened on her horns, made her way eagerly through the middle of the assembled people to the feet of the speaker, as though to congratulate him. Everyone was amazed, and the book was quickly removed and read to the breathless people, who happily accepted the licence permitted by its foul law. What more? The miracle of the offered book was greeted with applause over and over again.)[90]

The book is understood by Guibert, as we find elsewhere in pejorative accounts of Islam from this period, as sexually permissive, presented in overt and knowing opposition to the laws and corresponding normative values of Christianity. The episode is suggestive of a perceived relationship between the growth of Islam and the book's (i.e. Muslim law's) function as 'indifferenter coeundi nova licentia' ('a new license for random copulation'), a concern not simply with sexual morality but pro-generation. The book's rationale would appear to be a prejudicial re-imagining of God's command in Genesis 1.28, 'Crescite et multiplicamini', applied to a people whose multiplication is met with horror, and who function simultaneously as a cipher and substitution for its original (Jewish) referent as a similarly abject site of pro-generation.

The motif exemplifies the paranoid Bhabhian discovery of the book, but here the undiscerning crowd do not misinterpret the book but rather read the wrong book entirely. They reject the laws of the Old Testament, without acceptance of the New Law of Christianity ('non Moysi antiquitas, non catholica novitas reputatur, quicquid ante legem').[91] Guibert triangulates improper belief or bad reading, the pseudo-miracle, and communal error. For Guibert, this taste for wonders is characteristic of the regions east of Rome, where the thinness of the air impedes critical discernment. He writes of Arianism and other heresies (Islam is for Guibert the most recent of a succession of eastern heresies), noting the seductive power of 'novarum' (novelty), a synonym for marvel: 'Orientalium ... fides cum semper nutabunda constiterit et rerum molitione novarum mutabilis et vagabunda fuerit, semper a regula verae credulitatis exorbitans' ('the faith of Easterners, which has never been stable, but has always been variable and unsteady, searching for novelty, always exceeding the bounds of true belief').[92]

Guibert's account of Mohammed was not necessarily understood as strictly historical so much as comically appropriate. The register of Guibert's treatment of the Prophet, as Robert Levine notes, mines a vein of racist humour rooted in the representation of Islam as a parodic re-imagining of Christianity; a racist humour that has similarly been understood to be fundamental to the operations of *Richard a*.[93] Not simply false but parodic marvels are a recurrent feature of western Christian writings on Islam into the later Middle Ages, concerned with Muslim gullibility and the cunning by which such hoaxes were perpetrated. A similar interest in simultaneous Muslim trickery and gullibility appears in widely disseminated western European accounts of the Assassins, the Ishmaeli Nizaris, understood in the context of medieval Islam as a heretical sect, but deployed by writers such as the *Mandeville*-author as a cipher for the indulgences and fantasies of a pejoratively constructed version of Islam. In the insular French version of the *Travels*, we read of the false paradise of the Assassins constructed by the Old Man of the Mountain (Hassan i Sabbah), a site of fantastical mechanical wonders and a coded reminiscence of the engineering feats of the Abbasid court, re-imagined, to use Heng's term with all its connotations of fictionalisation, as a 'fabulation'.[94] With man-made waterways filled with honey and milk, the garden is a variation on the Prophet Mohammed's falsified miracles on the mountain:

'Et avoit fait faire conduit par dessouz terre, si qe ces III fontaynes quant il volait il fesoi l'un courre de lait, l'autre de vin, et l'autre de meel, et cel lieu appelloit il Paradis' ('He had fashioned beautiful waterways through the garden, with three fountains – the one flowing with milk, the other with wine, and the other with honey, and he called this place Paradise').[95] The immediate source of the episode, in Marco Polo's text, makes this connection explicit, emphasising the credulity of the Assassins:

> Et pour ce l'avoit il fait de telle maniere que Mahommet dist que leur paradis sera beaulx jardins et plains de conduiz de vin et de lait et de miel et d'yaue et plain de belles fames au delit de chascun en telle maniere comme cellui du Viel. Et pour ce croient il que c'estoit paradis

> (He had had it made in the same way that Mohammed said that their Paradise will be beautiful gardens full of rivers of wine and milk and honey and water, and full of beautiful women, of whom each will take his enjoyment, like the Old Man. And because of this they believed it was Paradise)[96]

With the precedent of the mountain marvels of Mohammed clearly in mind, the Old Man is similarly understood to be something of a false prophet: he promises the Assassins the post-mortem reward of seventy virgins, a reward which never materialises. This episode is strikingly indicative of the broader cultural context, and set of Islamophobic assumptions, to which *Richard a* belongs. Looking beyond the mechanical devil to Corbaryng and Cassodorien, we see two familiar features of the western representation of Muslim falsehood and fantasy: a false prophet (the dreaming Corbaryng) bearing a false erotic promise, Cassodorien, who, like the seventy virgins, vanishes.

The accounts here surveyed were intended not simply to represent false wonder but to offer up that false wonder for the consumption, and wonder in turn, of western Christian readers. This material embodies, as Mary Baine Campbell has written of the pleasure effect of early modern travel literature, 'delight, wonder, frisson, satisfaction, existing as objects of a demand in a suddenly expanded marketplace', commodities as much as aesthetic principles.[97] Just as Campbell notes of the sixteenth century and the ethnographic writings of the New World, similarly we see a late medieval sensationalist engagement with Islam and with Muslim historical figures, associated not least with fantasies of opulent wealth and plentiful resources (the land of milk and honey). The possibility of wonder must necessarily be recognised for the narrative of pseudo-wonder to be effective (and indeed affective). The western reader marvels at the false wonders of those who marvel falsely and dispenses with Islam as another heresy represented in line with the long-familiar precedent of heretical marvels, yet in consuming this content the reader is similarly seduced by (or at least derives pleasure from) the pseudo-marvel. This subject position is replete with contradictions, and these texts construct an emotional cross-cultural alignment even as they disavow any such correspondence.

In *Richard a*, we encounter the familiar distinction between those who wonder truly and those who wonder falsely, associated with subjects imbued with a half-familiar strangeness – familiar in the sense that the *Richard a*-author tells of living (albeit erroneously and offensively fictionalised) communities who exist in historical relationships to western Christendom, made strange through the text's exclusionary practices (paradoxography included). Yet the distinction that is drawn is unstable, for the Christian reader is taught to wonder not simply at, but with and through, non-Christian alterity. Not despite but because of their credulity, the Muslims of Acre guide the reader's wonder response and, in doing so, make Richard, commissioner of the mill, himself marvellous – inspiring awe ('drede'). The function of the populace of Acre is very similar to that of Cassodorien, whose swooning reminds the reader to wonder at the eucharist. Indeed, we might orient the mill in relation to the earlier historiographical tradition of the eucharistic miracle. After all, the mill, which substitutes flour for flesh, enacts the transformation from bread to body, and, blood-soaked, recalls the transformation from wine to blood, which – like the antisemitic miracle story – makes visible the central mystery of the eucharist to literally minded non-communicants. Although manufactured, it is aligned with the eucharistic register of the metamorphic marvel. It is even a signifier of transformation that we might read in relation to Richard's subsequent (and much-discussed) anthropophagy, a piece, as McDonald has termed it, of 'blatantly literal eucharistic theory'.[98] As the eucharist does in Cassodorien, Richard's mill similarly inspires 'drede' in observers located outside the community of the mass. We here see imperfect religious understanding combined with a lack of technological comprehension: competencies associated with the power to discern truth. This resonates strikingly with (although it is an example drawn from a very different history) Bhabha's nineteenth-century Bible readers, and their anxious witnesses, under the tree in Delhi: 'never having heard of a printed book before ... its very appearance was to them miraculous'.[99]

We might understand the management, and the contingency, of wonder in *Richard a* through a return to Bhabha's writings on the ambivalence of postcolonial 'signs taken for wonders', a thesis productively applied by previous scholars of medieval religious prejudice. Bhabha writes: 'the field of the "true" emerges as a visible effect of knowledge/power only after the regulatory and displacing division of the true and the false'.[100] Truth is ambivalent, utilitarian, and contingent, and there is no distinction between false and true on the level of the marvellous occurrence itself (apparent transfiguration of an inanimate object to blood and flesh might indeed prompt 'drede'). Rather the deciding factor is the marvel or pseudo-marvel's significance for a given population, or a representative of an (antagonistically re-imagined) population who are stereotyped – and, indeed, whose lack of comprehension or discretion emerges as key feature of that stereotype. The wonder, and its categorisation, thus operate as a symbol of inclusion or exclusion. There is, however, also a point of identification and cross-cultural transference at work here. The reader necessarily wonders at the devil automaton, and is invited to contemplate its metaphorical function, via the text's unknowing internal audience. Once again, Muslim credulity is a tool for Christian wonder-creation, even (once again) for the appreciation of the eucharistic miracle. Yet the Muslim inability to read the cultural cues invoked by the apparent marvel is rooted not only in its eucharistic connotations, but in a specific set of narrative conventions derived from earlier traditions of paradoxography with an uncertain historical status.

*Richard a* presents an entirely imaginary paradox, rooted not in its marvellous historicity but in the uncertain moral meaning of the marvel: at once sacred and profane. This presents a notable departure from marvels that appear elsewhere in Middle English literature (the fairy included), which invoke wonder as a tool for an explicitly moral response.[101] Although it certainly shares the allegorical framework of medieval romance, morality here remains uncertain. Rather, the author's interest appears to be first and foremost in a culturally exclusionary mode of thought. The Muslim viewer is continually placed outside understanding of the marvel, and it is by their incomprehension, their inability to reconcile its apparently contradictory propositions, that the reader is made cognisant of it.

## Conclusion

The medieval process of reading those fairy marvels that in their discursive cues come closer to romance than history is no less sophisticated, and no less exclusionary in its logic, than the historiographical tradition discussed in the previous chapters, to which it owes some of its associations and strategies. Yet the fairy marvels of Couldrette and *Richard a* function in explicit contrast to earlier Latin historical *mirabilia* and their subsequent vernacular invocation in Jean d'Arras's *Mélusine*. In these earlier texts, the marvel is testament to the complexity of the natural world and an invitation to investigative scrutiny, however obscure aspects of it must necessarily remain. While Couldrette and the *Richard a*-author do treat matters of comprehension, they explore narrative moments of perception or misperception over and above attempts at causal deliberation. The *telos* or organising principle here is the marvellous *aventure* of romance. However, the marvel is not entirely lacking in extra-textual referentiality: both romances present active sites of political intervention, and in reshaping history – however knowingly fictive – both seek to reshape the world beyond the text.

## Notes

1 Finlayson, 'The Marvellous in Middle English Romance', p. 382. Finlayson suggests that we might compare such works to the modern spy thriller, set in the context of real-world referentiality (familiar settings, politics), while the events recounted are largely improbable. Modern historical fiction, especially modern historical romance, presents a closer comparison in the sense that the world-building at work here both draws on recognisable reference points and is largely non-referential (a space of fantasy), and is enjoyed as such.

2 Quotations are taken from Francisque Michel, ed., *Mellusine: poème relatif á cette fée poitevine, composé dans le XIVe siècle par Couldrette* (Niort: Robin et L. Favre, 1855), with modified translations based on Morris, ed. and trans., *A Bilingual Edition of Couldrette's Mélusine*. This is with the exception of lines 6857–66, which are omitted from the earlier edition and are quoted from Morris. My primary use of Michel was governed by the availability of this text during the Covid-19 lockdowns when this chapter was written.

3 For an understanding of Couldrette's Latin sources as an authorising fiction, see similarly, Zeldenrust, *The Mélusine Romance in Medieval Europe*, p. 18.

4 For the identification of Maubergon see Morris, ed. and trans., *A Bilingual Edition of Couldrette's Mélusine*, p. 542.

5 Spiegel, *Romancing the Past*, esp. pp. 2–7.

6 Spiegel, *Romancing the Past*, p. 62.

7 Walter W. Skeat, ed., *The Romans of Partenay, or of Lusignen: Otherwise Known as the Tale of Melusine* (London: Trübner & Co., 1866).

8 Tania M. Colwell, 'Patronage of the Poetic Mélusine Romance: Guillaume l'Archevêque's Confrontation with Dynastic Crisis', *Journal of Medieval History* 37.2 (2011): 215–29.

9 In Paris, Bibliothèque nationale de France, Français MS 18623 the *Romance of Parthenay* follows an anonymous chronicle of the deeds of the Breton knight Bertrand du Guesclin, which includes an account of the events of the early stage of the Hundred Years War. In Paris, Bibliothèque nationale de France, Français MS 19167 it follows the history of *La Belle Hélène* (Helena of Constantinople) and *Pierre de Provence*. In Paris, Bibliothèque nationale de France, Français MS 24383 it is followed by a short French prose chronicle. In Paris,

Bibliothèque nationale de France, Français MS 1631 it follows Benoît's *History of Troy*.
10 Zeldenrust, *The Mélusine Romance in Medieval Europe*, p. 36.
11 Zeldenrust, *The Mélusine Romance in Medieval Europe*, pp. 33–37.
12 Translation from Morris, ed. and trans., *A Bilingual Edition of Couldrette's Mélusine*, with modification to line 8 from my own translation. Apprehension implies more than 'to learn and understand': it is about perception and knowledge, significant concepts in our understanding of the ontological interests of historiographical, or quasi-historiographical, fairy narratives.
13 Alastair J. Minnis, *Medieval Theory of Authorship: Scholastic Literary Attitudes in the Later Middle Ages* (London: Scolar Press, 1984), p. 5.
14 Colwell, 'Patronage of the Poetic Mélusine Romance'.
15 Cooper, *English Romance in Time*, pp. 85–86.
16 Hume, *Fantasy and Mimesis*, p. 31.
17 Bruckner, *Shaping Romance*, p. 10; Douglas Kelly, '*Matiere* and *genera dicendi* in Medieval Romance', *Yale French Studies* 51 (1974): 147–59 (p. 155).
18 Bruckner, *Shaping Romance*, p. 10.
19 Bruckner, *Shaping Romance*, p. 115.
20 Kelly, '*Matiere* and *genera dicendi* in Medieval Romance', pp. 151–52.
21 Delogu, 'Jean d'Arras Makes History', p. 17.
22 Auerbach, *Mimesis*, p. 131.
23 See above, Introduction, pp. 21–26.
24 Jean d'Arras, *Mélusine*, ed. Vincensini, p. 130; *Mélusine*, ed. and trans. Maddox and Sturm-Maddox, p. 24.
25 Norris J. Lacy, ed. and trans., *Lancelot-Grail: Lancelot Parts III and IV* (Cambridge: D. S. Brewer, 2010), p. 400.
26 For discussion of the relationship between 'aventures merveilleuses' and place, in relation to which the grail is understood as a narrative *telos*, in the *Lancelot-Grail* cycle, see Kelly, *Art of Medieval French Romance*, pp. 155–56.
27 For discussion of the clearly presented distinction between Mélusine's serpentine forms and the serpents of this episode, see Zeldenrust, *The Mélusine Romance in Medieval Europe*, p. 27.
28 Gervase of Tilbury, *Otia*, pp. 684–89.
29 Skeat, ed., *The Romans of Partenay*, p. 205.
30 Colwell, 'Patronage of the Poetic Mélusine Romance', p. 217.
31 Colwell, 'Patronage of the Poetic Mélusine Romance', p. 226.
32 Colwell, 'Patronage of the Poetic Mélusine Romance', p. 228.

33 For an overview of the dissemination of the romance across western Europe, from manuscript to print, see Zeldenrust, *The Mélusine Romance in Medieval Europe*. For a discussion of the intersection of various international strands in a single version of the text, see Tania M. Colwell, 'Fragments of the *Roman de Melusine* in the Upton House Bearsted Collection', *The Library* 13.3 (2012): 279–315.

34 While there is no Welsh translation of *Mélusine*, the romance appears to have been familiar to the Welsh gentry readers of humanist works by the late sixteenth century. In the Welsh translation of the Spanish humanist Juan Luis Vives's treatise against romance, the title appears alongside other French, English, and Latin works, grouped with the French: 'Ac ar y llyfrau anrasol megis y mae yn vyngwlad vy hun yn Spaen Amadis / ffflorisand / tyrant / tristann / a celestina / mam yr holl ddrygioni / yn ffraingk launslod du lak / paris / vienna / ponthus / sidonia / a melucyne / yn lloegr parthenope / genarides / hyppomadon / Wiliam / meliour / libius / arthur / gei / a beuis / a llawer eraill a rrai a dreiglant or lladyg I iaith mameu / megis y llyfreu divlas o waith y pogius / eneas Syluis / eurialus / a Lucretia' ('And of the impious books from the land of Spain there are Amadas, Floris, Tristan and Celestina, origin of all wickedness; in France Lancelot of the Lake, Paris, Vienna, Ponthus, Sidonia, and Melusine. In England Partenope, Generides, Ipomedon, William, Melior, Libeaus [Desconus], Arthur, Kay and Bevis, and many other wicked things; from the Latin language comes the loathsome books of the deeds of Pogius, Aeneas, Sylvius, Eurialus, and Lucretia'). Aberystwyth, National Library of Wales, Peniarth MS 403, p. 34 (my translation). With thanks to Prof. Elena Parina for informing me of this example, encountered in the context of her DFG-funded project 'Early Modern Cultures of Translation in Wales', and for providing this transcription.

35 Anne F. Sutton and Livia Visser-Fuchs, *Richard III's Books: Ideals and Reality in the Life and Library of a Medieval Prince* (Stroud: Sutton, 1997), p. 223, n. 37.

36 Zeldenrust, *The Mélusine Romance in Medieval Europe*, p. 186. The English translation as found in this manuscript has been edited by A. K. Donald in *Melusine*, Early English Text Society, Extra Series 68 (London: Kegan and Paul, Trench, Trübner, 1895).

37 Zeldenrust, *The Mélusine Romance in Medieval Europe*, pp. 185–87.

38 Zeldenrust, *The Mélusine Romance in Medieval Europe*, pp. 187–92.

39 Zeldenrust, *The Mélusine Romance in Medieval Europe*, pp. 192–93; edited in Skeat, ed., *The Romans of Partenay*.
40 Zeldenrust, *The Mélusine Romance in Medieval Europe*, p. 194.
41 For a discussion of *Richard* in its manuscript contexts and early print, as well as the relationship between the *a* and *b* versions, see Karl Brunner, ed., *Der mittelenglische Versroman über Richard Löwenherz: kritische Ausgabe nach allen Handschriften mit Einleitung, Anmerkungen und deutscher Übersetzung* (Vienna and Leipzig: W. Braumüller, 1913), pp. 1–23. For discussion of Richard's anthropophagy, see below, n. 50.
42 Quotations are taken from Brunner, ed., *Der mittelenglische Versroman über Richard Löwenherz*, pp. 77–452.
43 Yin Liu, 'Middle English Romance as Prototype Genre', *Chaucer Review* 40.4 (2006): 335–53.
44 While the text has been positioned as a work of multiple authors, representative of a wider cumulative tradition of writing about Richard, for the sake of clarity I here refer to a singular author of the *a*-text, with an appropriate awareness of the multiplicity of medieval collaborative literary and manuscript production. Heng, *Empire of Magic*, p. 67.
45 Karnes, 'The Possibilities of Medieval Fiction', p. 215.
46 Heng, *Empire of Magic*, pp. 240–41.
47 Augustine, *City of God*, V, pp. 42–43.
48 Block Friedman, *Monstrous Races*, p. 67; Debra Higgs Strickland, *Saracens, Demons, and Jews: Making Monsters in Medieval Art* (Princeton, NJ: Princeton University Press, 2003). The extent of this perception of bodily alterity, as we find it across medieval genres, is one of the fundamental principles suggested by Geraldine Heng's in-depth survey of medieval race-making in *The Invention of Race in the European Middle Ages* (Cambridge: Cambridge University Press, 2018).
49 Isidore of Seville, *Etymologies*, pp. 194–95.
50 Jeffrey Jerome Cohen, 'On Saracen Enjoyment: Some Fantasies of Race in Late Medieval France and England', *Journal of Medieval and Early Modern Studies* 31.1 (2001): 113–46 (p. 128); Nicola McDonald, 'Eating People and the Alimentary Logic of *Richard Coeur de Lion*', in *Pulp Fictions of Medieval England: Essays in Popular Romance*, ed. Nicola McDonald (Manchester: Manchester University Press, 2004), pp. 124–50; Heng, *Empire of Magic*, pp. 63–114.
51 For a brief notice of Cassodorien's affinity with host-abusers, see McDonald, 'Eating People and the Alimentary Logic of *Richard Coeur de Lion*', p. 141.

52 Wade, *Fairies in Medieval Romance*, pp. 36–37. We might remember that Couldrette's Mélusine is not termed a fairy until Geoffroy reads the writing on Helmas's tomb; prior to this, the reader is dependent entirely on the recognisable cultural cues of fairy content.
53 Augustine, *City of God*, V, pp. 42–43.
54 For notice of the early romancing of scholastic methods in the twelfth-century Alexander romance *Roman de tout chevalerie* see Venetia Bridges, *Medieval Narratives of Alexander the Great: Transnational Texts in England and France* (Cambridge: D. S. Brewer, 2018), p. 159.
55 Daston and Park, *Wonders and the Order of Nature*, p. 26.
56 Nicola McDonald, ed., *Pulp Fictions of Medieval England: Essays in Popular Romance* (Manchester: Manchester University Press, 2004).
57 For a discussion of possible early patrons, see John Finlayson, '"Richard Coer de Lion": Romance, History, or Something in Between?', *Studies in Philology* 87 (1990): 156–80 (p. 166). Finlayson suggests the patronage of two Lincolnshire families with long historical antipathies to King John, the D'Oillys and Multons, given the inclusion of two knights of these names in *Richard a*.
58 McDonald, 'Eating People and the Alimentary Logic of *Richard Coer de Lion*'; Heng, *Empire of Magic*, pp. 63–114.
59 Anthony Bale, *Feeling Persecuted: Christians, Jews, and Images of Violence in the Middle Ages* (London: Reaktion Books, 2010), p. 188.
60 Saunders, 'Mind, Body and Affect in Medieval English Arthurian Romance', pp. 40, 45; Corinne Saunders, 'From Romance to Vision: The Life of Breath in Medieval Literary Texts', in *The Life of Breath in Literature, Culture and Medicine: Classical to Contemporary*, ed. David Fuller, Corinne Saunders, and Jane McNaughton (New York: Palgrave Macmillan, 2021), pp. 87–110 (pp. 87–88).
61 Michael D. Barbezat, 'The Corporeal Orientation: Understanding Deviance through the Object(s) of Love', in *The Routledge History of Emotions in Europe, 1100–1700*, ed. Andrew Lynch and Susan Broomhall (London: Routledge, 2020), pp. 119–32 (p. 121).
62 Karnes, 'Wonders, Marvels, and Metaphor in the "Squire's Tale"', p. 461. This builds on Finlayson, 'The Marvellous in Middle English Romance', although Karnes credits the audience of romance, as I do, with a much greater level of sophistication.
63 For the metaphorical function of the marvel, see Karnes, 'Wonders, Marvels, and Metaphor in the "Squire's Tale"'. For an important association of Middle English wonder with insular riddling traditions, see Jessica J. Lockhart, '"Something remains which is not open

to my understanding": Enigmatic Marvels in Welsh Otherworld Narratives and Latin Arthurian Romance', in *Cultural Translations in Medieval Romance*, ed. Victoria Flood and Megan G. Leitch (Cambridge: D. S. Brewer, 2022), pp. 45–64. Lockhart's perspective in part builds on McDonald's association of the marvel with unanswered questions. Nicola McDonald, 'The Wonder of Middle English Romance', in *Thinking Medieval Romance*, ed. Katherine C. Little and Nicola McDonald (Oxford: Oxford University Press, 2018), pp. 13–34 (p. 19).
64 See above, p. 143, n. 116
65 Heng, *Empire of Magic*, p. 343, n. 29.
66 Heng, *Empire of Magic*, p. 343, n. 29.
67 For an in-depth discussion of this perception, and its construction, see John Tolan, *Saracens: Islam in the Medieval European Imagination* (New York: Columbia University Press, 2002), esp. pp. 135–69. See further Suzanne Conklin Akbari, *Idols in the East: European Representations of Islam and the Orient, 1100–1450* (Ithaca, NY: Cornell University Press, 2009), p. 227; Heng, *The Invention of Race in the European Middle Ages*, p. 116; Kruger, *The Spectral Jew*, p. 30.
68 For discussion of the relationship between trading networks and cultural perceptions, see John Tolan, 'Forging New Paradigms: Towards a History of Islamo-Christian Civilization', in *A Sea of Languages: Rethinking the Arabic Role in Medieval Literary History*, ed. Suzanne Conklin Akbari and Karla Mallette (Toronto: University of Toronto Press, 2013), pp. 62–70 (p. 65); Heng, *The Invention of Race in the European Middle Ages*, p. 150.
69 For a discussion of the distinction between medieval and modern orientalism, shaped by historically distinct understandings of the world's geography, see Conklin Akbari, *Idols in the East*, pp. 20–66.
70 Kinoshita and McCracken, *Marie de France*, p. 55.
71 Heng, *The Invention of Race in the European Middle Ages*, p. 141 (which notes the limited historical basis for such marriages; although throughout the Middle Ages Muslim rulers did take Christian wives and had inter-faith marriages). For significant work on the Muslim princess or queen in western medieval literature, see Conklin Akbari, *Idols in the East*, pp. 173–89; Kinoshita, *Medieval Boundaries*, pp. 15–73.
72 This appears to have been the invention of an anonymous minstrel of Reims who included this in a collection of historical anecdotes. This is pure invention: Saladin was a child when Eleanor was in Palestine,

and he appears to function as a substitute for Raymond of Antioch. Turner, 'Eleanor of Aquitaine, Twelfth-Century Troubadours, and her Black Legend', p. 41.

73 See McDonald, 'The Wonder of Middle English Romance', p. 24, which discusses this in relation to the uneasy moral categorisation of Richard.
74 Marcel Elias, 'Interfaith Empathy and the Formation of Romance', in *Emotion and Medieval Textual Media*, ed. Mary Flannery (Turnhout: Brepols, 2018), pp. 99–124.
75 William Sayers, 'The Use of Quicklime in Medieval Naval Warfare', *The Mariner's Mirror* 92.3 (2006): 262–69. 'Pottes ful of lyme' appear in the sea battle of Chaucer's 'Legend of Cleopatra' in his *Legend of Good Women*, line 70. Larry D. Benson, ed., *The Riverside Chaucer* (Boston: Houghton Mifflin, 1987), p. 605.
76 See above, Introduction, p. 10. For discussion of the history of Greek fire, rooted in a long historical appreciation of the wonderful properties of lime, see J. R. Partington, *A History of Greek Fire and Gunpowder* (Baltimore, MD: Johns Hopkins University Press, 1960; reprinted 1999).
77 Jean d'Arras, *Mélusine*, ed. Vincensini, p. 314; *Melusine*, ed. and trans. Maddox and Sturm-Maddox, p. 77.
78 For automata at European courts, in public pageantry, and in romance see Truitt, *Medieval Robots*, pp. 116–40; Tara Williams, *Middle English Marvels: Magic, Spectacle and Morality in the Fourteenth Century* (University Park, PA: Pennsylvania State University Press, 2018), pp. 63–96. For discussion of the integration of automata in romance, see Richard Kieckhefer, *Magic in the Middle Ages* (Cambridge: Cambridge University Press, 2000), p. 107; Saunders, *Magic and the Supernatural*, pp. 140–45; Corinne Saunders, 'Subtle Crafts: Magic and Exploitation in Medieval English Romance', in *The Exploitations of Medieval Romance*, ed. Laura Ashe, Ivana Djordjevic, and Judith Weiss (Cambridge: D. S. Brewer, 2010), pp. 108–24. There is also a wealth of material on the uses of automata, among other practices understood as 'natural magic', in Chaucer's writings; for an important statement in this field, in addition to Karnes, 'Wonders, Marvels, and Metaphor in the "Squire's Tale"', see Saunders, *Magic and the Supernatural*, pp. 145–51.
79 Truitt, *Medieval Robots*, pp. 19–21 (quotations from pp. 20, 21).
80 This association finds one of its most famous statements in legends of Gerbert of Aurillac (Pope Silvester), alternative to the fairy narrative recorded in *De nugis*, discussed in Chapter 2. William of Malmesbury

wrote of a demonic talking head that Gerbert engineered, with the aid of a demon summoned through a book of Arabic magic acquired by Gerbert during his studies in Toledo. This striking conflation of automata and demonism, and its later medieval reception history, are discussed by Truitt, *Medieval Robots*, pp. 71–82.

81 See above, p. 136 n 14.
82 Heng, *The Invention of Race in the European Middle Ages*, pp. 111–12. While generally applied by romance authors to a homogenously conceived Muslim enemy, as John Tolan notes, the use of the term by Latin writers in medieval Christendom pre-dates the Prophet Mohammed, and was used in relation to non-Christians, applied to the descendants of Ishmael. Tolan, *Saracens*, pp. 10–11.
83 W. M. Lindsay, ed., *Isidori Hispalensis Episcopi Etymologiarum sive originum libri XX*, 2 vols (Oxford: Oxford University Press, 1911), I, IX.ii.57; Isidore of Seville, *Etymologies*, p. 195.
84 Richard Kieckhefer, *Forbidden Rites: A Necromancer's Manual of the Fifteenth Century* (University Park, PA: Pennsylvania State University Press, 1998), pp. 42–43.
85 Karnes, 'Wonders, Marvels, and Metaphor in the "Squire's Tale"'.
86 Augustine, *City of God*, VII, pp. 28–29.
87 Elliott notes this in the writings of the thirteenth-century Bishop of Paris William of Auvergne. *Fallen Bodies*, p. 56. Elliott suggests that the horse was an apt figure for a woman, with whom, within this misogynistic schema, she was understood to possess lustful appetites in common.
88 Tolan, *Saracens*, pp. 140–44. Like the heretic, and Simon Magus, Mohammed was associated in erroneous biographies with false flight. In a garbled recollection of Mohammed's ascension to heaven, the *mi'rāj*, Guibert of Nogent gives a deeply offensive revisionist account of the Prophet's death: eaten by pigs who left only his feet, leaving his followers to wrongly assume that he had ascended bodily into heaven. Guibert of Nogent, *The Deeds of God through the Franks*, trans. Robert Levine (Woodbridge: Boydell Press, 1997), p. 70.
89 Tolan, *Saracens*, p. 141; Heng, *The Invention of Race in the European Middle Ages*, p. 117.
90 Guibert de Nogent, *'Dei gesta per Francos' et cinq autres textes*, ed. R. B. C. Huygens (Turnhout: Brepols, 1996), pp. 97–98; *The Deeds of God*, p. 69.
91 Guibert de Nogent, *Dei gesta per Francos*, p. 98.
92 Guibert de Nogent, *Dei gesta per Francos*, p. 89; *The Deeds of God*, p. 58. Discussed by Tolan, *Saracens*, pp. 144–45.

93 Robert Levine, 'Satiric Vulgarity in Guibert de Nogent's *Gesta Dei per Francos*', *Rhetorica: A Journal of the History of Rhetoric* 7.3 (1989): 261–73; Heng, *Empire of Magic*, p. 76.
94 Geraldine Heng, 'Sex, Lies, and Paradise: The Assassins, Prester John, and the Fabulation of Civilizational Identities', *Differences* 23 (2015): 1–31; Truitt, *Medieval Robots*, pp. 38–39.
95 Christiane Deluz, ed., *Le Livre des merveilles du monde* (Turnhout: Brepols, 2000), p. 441.
96 Marco Polo, *La Description du monde*, ed. Pierre-Yves Badel (Paris: Livre de Poche, 1998), pp. 118–19. The modern English translation here given is based on the volume's parallel modern French translation.
97 Campbell, *Wonder and Science*, p. 26.
98 McDonald, 'Eating People and the Alimentary Logic of *Richard Coeur de Lion*', p. 140.
99 Bhabha, 'Signs Taken for Wonders', p. 145.
100 Tomasch, 'Postcolonial Chaucer and the Virtual Jew', p. 253; citing Bhabha, 'Signs Taken for Wonders', p. 152. As with the discussion of medieval Jewish subjects, medieval Christian perceptions of Islam do not offer a precise point of correspondence with postmedieval configurations; in this case, of course, western European supremacy in Muslim lands is itself a western fiction.
101 Williams, *Middle English Marvels*, pp. 11–35.

# Conclusion: between history and romance

We cannot necessarily tell from the medieval texts surveyed in this volume alone – beyond the apparent demand exhibited in the longevity of dynastic medieval fairy narratives – the precise effect of fairy belief, and disbelief, on the wider social mentalities of late medieval readers and writers. Nonetheless, in their scope they do appear to be evidence of a wider pan-European vogue. Indeed, we find similar, later, uses of fairy narratives, positioned on a fault line between fact and fiction, elsewhere in western Europe, into the sixteenth century. In the first half of the sixteenth century, the German-Swiss physician Paracelsus wrote of Mélusine as a category of demonic apparition, terrorising French villages, whose fearsome existence was attested by common report. Paracelsus appears to have included among his evidence not only popular report but the romance itself – he writes of Mélusines (plural) as the daughters of kings, doomed to endure in a phantom body until the Last Judgement, unless they can marry a mortal and die a natural death.[1] This allusion to romance earned Paracelsus the ridicule of at least one near-contemporary sceptic, who took romance as a synonym for untruth. Mélusine makes a notable appearance in the 1591 *Tractatus de magis, veneficis et lamiis* by the German juror Georg Gödelmann. Gödelmann understood the more spectacular phenomena of early modern witch-theory, including the witches' flight, to be the dreams of poor, elderly women (the most unreliable of witnesses) offered under duress. Gödelmann likened such beliefs to fables of the fairy Mélusine:

> Melusina Gallicanuum fuit monstrum, in forma venutissimae mulieris, eius fabula extat in libello Germanico ex Gallica lingua

translato, quam Paracelsus non fabulam, sed verissimam historiam esse, nugatur.

(The French Melusine was a monster, in the shape of a most attractive woman, the fable is recorded in a German book translated from the French language, which Paracelsus trifles, is not fabulous but true history.)[2]

The reference here is to the German translation of the French romance – presumably Thüring von Ringoltingen's late fifteenth-century prose translation of Couldrette.[3] For Gödelmann, the distinction between what was true and what false was fundamental to the legal basis of witchcraft prosecutions. As it appears in the erroneous testimony of the witch and thus the groundless phenomenological understandings of the orthodox witch theorist, the status of true history is a vital point of comparison for Gödelmann. The absence of a historical basis for the fairy (her metamorphosis and her flight) is at one with the absence of evidence for the witch's night flight. In Gödelmann's deluded women we might think of the predominately female testimonies alleged to be associated with the night flight in the 'Canon episcopi', and certainly here we have come full circle. Yet for the scholar of romance, it is particularly noteworthy that Gödelmann seizes on an especially damning element from Paracelsus's account: its affinity with romance as fabulous history. We see here the marginalising application of romance, not as a point of knowing engagement with fiction (as we find, for example, in *Richard a*), but as a fabrication accepted as history by the unsophisticated reader. This is very similar to the late twelfth-century English rejection of the Avalon legend, understood to be accepted by the credulous Welsh: it is a late manifestation of the same impulse, in which the fairy is similarly a figure of fiction.

In the seventeenth century, European clerical authors were still trying to work out quite what to do with Mélusine and her sisters, approaching the distinction between true history and false as an uncertain, and by extension debatable, proposition, however conclusively the individual author might understand himself to settle this question. Yet there are contrasts between this and the earlier medieval tradition: we find in the medieval material examined in this book that fairy belief was held not to be ahistorical because

## Conclusion: between history and romance 251

the fairy was a signifier of fiction (romance); rather, the fairy might herself function as a marker of history, not least in her prophetic guise, but only where the narrative was understood to have been generated within a legitimate community of proper belief. In such cases, as we find in dynastic romance, the fairy presents one of the few moments in medieval romance where – however counterintuitive this may seem to the modern reader – history intrudes, and the fiction gives way to at least the possibility of extra-textual referentiality. For the fairy was not necessarily fiction but a point of ambiguity to be resolved, or at least entertained, by the discerning authors and readers of history.

The distinction between fact and fiction mattered intensely for historical authors of fairy narratives in the later Middle Ages, however unstably these categories were constructed and however selectively they were deployed. In my account of the presence of the supernatural in medieval history, I have not proposed a return to an understanding of the Middle Ages as exceptionally credulous, and I have not meant for my readers to take from this book an impression of pre-rational pre-modernity, a waiting room to the intellectual sophistication of the Renaissance and the Enlightenment. Rather, I have argued that supernatural source material might offer an insight into the ways in which medieval history was imagined, accepted, and rejected. I have contended that acceptance or rejection of the reality status of a reported supernatural occurrence was made with the credibility of its tellers in mind – not simply on the level of the individual, but on that of the community within which the account was understood to have been generated in the world beyond the text, and their real or imagined political investments and concerns.

The question I have asked of these texts is not whether the fairy narrative might be regarded consistently across the period as fact or fiction, but rather where, how, and why it was understood to be historically valid – by, for, and about whom. These uses read in relation to my authors' applications of familiar conventions pertaining to the credibility of supernatural historical narratives. These emerged in the late twelfth century and were utilised by subsequent authors, including continental and insular authors of dynastic romance, as a way of assessing the validity of phenomena that might be understood as otherwise ambiguous, situated beyond the ordinary course of experience and familiar reality principles. Across these texts we see the multi-generic application of a wider discourse of supernatural historiography – of which, not least given her position between history and romance, the fairy ancestor provides a striking case study. I have intended to make visible the profound debt of one of our most familiar romance motifs (the fairy mother) to conceptualisations of history which, while they might seem spectacular, were neither necessarily the stuff of unthinking credulity nor overt fictionalisation. Rather, early historical texts stand in a generative relationship to the later fictions of romance where these are, however unexpectedly, indicative of the remarkable historical real. Fairy *mirabilia* are not precursors of the fictions of romance but rather are the remarkable matter upon which romance is based, a re-use contingent on shared historiographical conventions which demand a complex series of meditations on the reality of the marvel, which, like the miracle, is something which ought not to be true and yet is.

Although there are some points of direct influence between the earlier and later texts I have discussed, and all might broadly be brought within the orbit of traditions associated with the fairy Mélusine, these works do not embody a uniform literary tradition so much as discrete entry points into the clerical uses of fairy narratives in both Latin and vernacular written contexts, often with some evidence of engagement with oral cultures also. All these texts – consistently across period and language – necessarily first ask, Whose marvel is this? This includes recitation of the manner of its original telling, ordinarily situated beyond the text in oral exchange (which might be elite as often as popular). The author of a historical fairy narrative conventionally invokes the testimonies of a reputable chain of witnesses not only of sufficient standing but drawn from a community of common belief understood to be capable of considered distinctions between false and true marvels. This is derived directly from the precedent of Augustine's early medieval formulation of wonder, where the object of wonder must be verifiable on a wider community level – for wonder in the Augustinian tradition is necessarily rooted in the real. Here we encounter another foundational precedent of medieval *mirabilia*:

## Conclusion: between history and romance

the role played by earlier written accounts. Augustine's account of the Dusii of Gaul is in the background of the earliest fairy narratives I have examined, as, it seems, is Geoffrey of Monmouth's account of the incubus father of Merlin, or the wonders of Morgan le Fay, although this legacy is in many respects a double one. Geoffrey appears also, in the writings of English authors such as William of Newburgh, as a suspect textual authority, indicative of the obscure and dangerous prophetic beliefs of the Welsh. His book became a byword for sedition dressed as pseudo-history, encapsulated for many of his critics in the figure of the fairy Morgan, a creation not of the *Historia* at all but of Geoffrey's comedic *Vita*.

In part as a legacy of Geoffrey, or at least the English reception of his works, the late twelfth century saw the emergence of a fully developed association of the true marvel with the English (often the immediately pre- or post-conquest) past, and the false marvel with the demonic beliefs of the Britons or Bretons, distinctions based not on supernatural content per se but on its assumed use among a given community. This must be understood in relation to the cross-border movement of materials which, a later counterpart to the circumstances of Geoffrey's *Historia*, saw the mediation of new materials from Wales to England by border clerics such as Walter Map and Gerald of Wales. These principles endured. Despite previous critical understandings of an apparent shift in the writing of marvels found in the early thirteenth-century work of Gervase of Tilbury – a new interest in empiricism which banished old superstitions – Gervase's fairy materials exhibit a remarkable continuity with the principles in place in the writings of Map and Gerald. For Gervase, fairy narratives emerged as plausible when they were witnessed by credible persons (himself apparently included on occasion); when they were authorised by relevant written authorities (most notably, Augustine); and when they were endorsed by the truth of language itself, including vernacular etymologies – a convention in common with his late twelfth-century counterparts, and an interest extended in the later Mélusine tradition to discussion of the fairy's very name.

Underlying these various principles is the exclusionary function not only of the acceptance or rejection of supernatural content but of the internal logic of the narratives, which are engaged with the construction of an in-text community with intended extra-textual referentiality. Gervase's engagements present an exposure of the wiles of heretics – a point of material demonic encounter which demonstrates the power of the cross, the gospel, and the eucharist. This interest is prefigured in the background antisemitism of Map's earlier treatment of the legend of Gerbert and his demonic patron Meridiana, spiritual (or rather, satanic) ancestor to the Pierleoni. We might also note Gerald's, and later Philippe Mousket's, application of fairy narratives to recognisable female political figures as a point of revisionist history, ancestors of the Angevin kings of England approached as demonic doubles of Eleanor of Aquitaine; a narrative later applied to Eleanor herself in *Richard a*. The principles of historical discernment, here exercised in relation to the proper enjoyment of fairy fiction, are extended across the text, and the reader is encouraged to directly compare their own sophistication with the staged credulity of the text's demon-worshipping 'Saracens'. A true wonder is entertained as a false wonder is dismantled.

The texts surveyed in this study relate more than the deeds of the fairy and her children: they communicate a shared conceptualisation of history. The fairy facilitated a productive indeterminacy within the historical record, allowing a type of dynastic fiction-making which might be regarded, however incongruously, as history. This appears less incongruous, however, when we consider the marked interest across nearly all the narratives surveyed in this study in the fairy as a prophetic agent. Alongside the twelfth-century concerns regarding Welsh prophecy – or rather, its Galfridian and/or English reconstruction – that shaped English and Marcher writings on fairies, from the Avalon legend to the narratives of Wastin and Meilerius, we also see an engagement with analogous English prophecies of loss, and accounts that might be understood as more broadly eschatological, such as William of Newburgh's green children, speaking to the fate not of the kingdom but of the soul after death, or the apocalyptic interests of the Gervasian tradition. Later, Galfridian prophecy found direct application in Jean d'Arras's *Mélusine*, and while a tempered presence – without the striking appearance of the Welsh prophesied hero Owain – Couldrette's text is similarly invested in the prophetic aspects of the legend, envisaged in relation to imaginings of a new crusade. Prophecy thus here expresses the same imperial ambitions of the roughly contemporary *Richard a* – a text in which we encounter an interest in false prophets not entirely dissimilar to earlier English anxieties about Merlin and the Welsh.

The texts I have examined are all to varying degrees invested, however cynically, in the reality of the fairy – even those which are most obviously categorised as romance. While romance in many respects dominates Jean d'Arras's multi-discursive text, its author nonetheless is continually engaged with the wider shape of dynastic history and the realisation of prophecy, in a manner which is necessarily real-world referential. In Couldrette, in contrast, while we see a distinctive response to the same set of high medieval *mirabilia*, the fairy mother occupies a less certain historical position, although the motif is nonetheless historically located and dynastic prophecy is again a familiar component of the text. Without direct, credible access to (or recourse to invention of) contemporary witness narratives at Lusignan, Couldrette necessarily emphasises the symbolic value of the fairy mother, and Mélusine functions as a symbolic ancestor rather than (as Jean d'Arras imagines to be the case) a contemporary presence in the life of the text's patron. The differences between these iterations of the same narrative are informed by distinctive framing content which conditions reader understanding. This is thus, then, also a case study in the discursive reshaping that might characterise adaption – here adaptations which are largely strategic but nonetheless have a direct impact on the fairy's assumed reality status.

The implications of this field of study go beyond motif hunting or unreflecting historicism. The central issue with which these texts are concerned is the right to make history, an activity that is a social or collective proposition, and thus is almost inevitably political. This is even and especially when that history is wonderful and is dependent on a broad level of community acceptance. These texts ask: what is the agreed-upon past at which we might wonder? Whose versions must we therefore reject? Wonder is a historiographical tool – it authorises – and demands that some stories be false so that others might be true. Wonder, after all, must be rare. This exclusionary medieval wonder practice presents a necessary caveat and counter to the wonder we ourselves might feel when working with narratives of the medieval past. As Kabir and Williams have noted, wonder is one of the most useful tools in the armoury of the medieval literary critic, yet once alert to operations of this type we face the challenge of recuperation.[4] I would suggest that we might use wonder critically, to explore the limitations and prejudices of the past that make visible a world of pre-modern marvels which, while captivating, must be read knowingly. This is to say, we must wonder discerningly.

## Notes

1 Summary given by Robert J. Nolan, 'The Origin of the Romance of Melusine: A New Interpretation', *Fabula* 15.3 (1974): 192–201 (pp. 192–93). My engagement with this source material should not be taken as endorsement of Nolan's wider argument regarding the legend's origin; Paracelsus tells us far more about reception.
2 Johann Georg Gödelmann, *Tractatus de magis, veneficis et lamiis deque his recte cognoscendis et puniendis* (Nuremberg, 1676; first printed Hanau and Frankfurt, 1591), Lib. II, Cap. IV, Section 19 (my translation). We might compare Gödelmann's strategy to that of his near-contemporary, the Englishman Reginald Scot, who likened witch-beliefs to tales of Robin Goodfellow and fairies (although Scot was far more absolute in his rejection of the existence of witchcraft than Gödelmann). Even James VI/I, in his *Daemonologie*, necessarily dispensed with tales of feasts in fairy hills as demonic illusions rather than material realities: fairy affinities appear to have been a barrier to witch-belief, which even the most orthodox author must address. James VI/I, *Daemonologie* (Edinburgh: Robert Waldgrave, 1597).
3 For discussion of the German translations of *Mélusine* see Zeldenrust, *The Mélusine Romance in Medieval Europe*, pp. 64–101.
4 Kabir and Williams, 'Introduction', p. 2; responding to Greenblatt, *Marvelous Possessions*, p. xiv.

# Bibliography

## Manuscripts

Aberystwyth, National Library of Wales, Peniarth MS 403.
Cambridge, Gonville and Caius College Library, MS 175/96.
Cambridge, Trinity College Library, MS R.3.17.
Chantilly, Bibliothèque du Château de Chantilly, MS 65.
Chantilly, Musée Condé, MS 654.
Edinburgh, National Library of Scotland, Advocates MS 19.2.1.
London, British Library, Additional MS 31042.
London, British Library, Cotton MS Cleopatra C.iv.
London, British Library, Cotton MS Otho D.ii.
London, British Library, Royal MS 18.B.ii.
Oxford, Bodleian Library, MS 851.
Paris, Bibliothèque nationale de France, Français MS 1631.
Paris, Bibliothèque nationale de France, Français MS 2806.
Paris, Bibliothèque nationale de France, Français MS 17177.
Paris, Bibliothèque nationale de France, Français MS 18623.
Paris, Bibliothèque nationale de France, Français MS 19167.
Paris, Bibliothèque nationale de France, Français MS 24383.
Paris, Bibliothèque nationale de France, Nouvelles acquisitions Françaises MS 4166.
Paris, Bibliothèque nationale de France, Rothschild MS 3085.

## Printed primary sources

Aristotle, *On the Soul, Parva naturalia, On Breath*, trans. W. S. Hett (Cambridge, MA: Harvard University Press, 1957).
Augustine, *City of God: Volume III*, trans. David S. Wiesen, Loeb Classical Library 413 (Cambridge, MA: Harvard University Press, 1968).
Augustine, *City of God: Volume IV*, trans. Philip Levine, Loeb Classical Library 414 (Cambridge, MA: Harvard University Press, 1966).

Augustine, *City of God: Volume V*, trans. Eva M. Sanford and William M. Green, Loeb Classical Library 415 (Cambridge, MA: Harvard University Press, 1965).

Augustine, *City of God: Volume VI*, trans. William Chase Greene, Loeb Classical Library 416 (Cambridge, MA: Harvard University Press, 1960).

Augustine, *City of God: Volume VII*, trans. William M. Green, Loeb Classical Library 417 (Cambridge, MA: Harvard University Press, 1972).

Augustine, *The Literal Meaning of Genesis II*, ed. and trans. Hammond Taylor (New York: Newman Press, 1982).

Augustine, *Works*, VI: *Letters*, trans. J. G. Cunningham (Edinburgh: T&T Clark, 1872).

Barrett, W. P., ed., *The Trial of Jeanne d'Arc Translated into French from the Original Latin and French Documents* (London: Routledge, 1931).

*Beati Alberti Magni Summa de creaturis diuisa in duas partes* (Lyon: Claude Prost, Claude Rigaud, Jean Antoine Huguetan, Jérôme de La Garde, Petrus Jammy, and Pierre Rigaud, 1651).

Benson, Larry D., ed., *The Riverside Chaucer* (Boston: Houghton Mifflin, 1987).

Blacker, Jean, ed. and trans., *Anglo-Norman Verse Prophecies of Merlin* (Dallas, TX: Scriptorium Press, 2005).

Brereton, Georgine E., ed., *Des Grantz Geanz: An Anglo-Norman Poem* (Oxford: Blackwell, 1937).

Brewer, J. S., James F. Dimock, and George F. Warner, eds, *Giraldi Cambrensis opera*, 8 vols (London: Longman, Green, Longman, & Roberts, 1861–91).

Brie, Friedrich, ed., *The Brut, or the Chronicles of England*, 2 vols (London: K. Paul, Trench, Trübner, 1906–08).

Bromwich, Rachel, ed. and trans., *Trioedd Ynys Prydein: The Triads of the Island of Britain* (Cardiff: University of Wales Press, 2014).

Brunner, Karl, ed., *Der mittelenglische Versroman über Richard Löwenherz: kritische Ausgabe nach allen Handschriften mit Einleitung, Anmerkungen und deutscher Übersetzung* (Vienna and Leipzig: W. Braumüller, 1913).

Bryant, Nigel, ed. and transl., *Merlin and the Grail: Joseph of Arimathea, Merlin, Perceval: The Trilogy of Arthurian Prose Romances Attributed to Robert de Boron* (Cambridge: D. S. Brewer, 2008).

Burgess, Glyn S., trans., and Elisabeth van Houts, ed., with Anthony J. Holden's text, *Wace: The 'Roman de Rou'* (St Helier: Société Jersiaise, 2002).

Burgess, Glyn S., and Keith Busby, eds and trans., *The Lais of Marie de France* (London: Penguin, 2003).

Caesarius of Heisterbach, *Dialogus miraculum*, ed. J. Strange, 2 vols (Cologne: J. M. Heberle, 1851).

# Bibliography 259

Carley, James P., and Julia Crick, eds and trans., 'Constructing Albion's Past: An Annotated Edition of *De origine gigantum*', *Arthurian Literature* 13 (1994): 41–144.

Christine de Pisan, *Ditié de Jehanne d'Arc*, ed. and trans. Angus J. Kennedy and Kenneth Varty (Oxford: Society for the Study of Medieval Languages and Literature, 1977).

Deluz, Christiane, ed., *Le Livre des merveilles du monde* (Turnhout: Brepols, 2000).

De Reiffenberg, Frédéric Auguste Ferdinand Thomas, ed., *Chronique rimée de Philippe Mouskes*, 2 vols (Brussels: M. Hayez, 1836–38).

Donald, A. K., ed., *Melusine*, Early English Text Society, Extra Series 68 (London: Kegan and Paul, Trench, Trübner, 1895).

Fulton, Helen, ed. and transl., *Dafydd ap Gwilym Apocrypha* (Llandysul: Gomer Press, 1999).

Geoffrey of Auxerre, *On the Apocalypse*, trans. Joseph Gibbons (Kalamazoo, MI: Cistercian Publications, 2000).

Geoffrey of Monmouth, *History of the Kings of Britain*, ed. Michael D. Reeve and trans. Neil Wright (Woodbridge: Boydell Press, 2005).

Geoffrey of Monmouth, *Vita Merlini*, ed. and trans. John Jay Parry (Urbana, IL: University of Illinois, 1925).

Gerald of Wales, *The History and Topography of Ireland*, trans. John O'Meara (Harmondsworth: Penguin, 1982).

Gerald of Wales, *Instruction for a Ruler: De principis instructione*, ed. and trans. Robert Bartlett (Oxford: Clarendon Press, 2018).

Gerald of Wales, *The Journey through Wales and Description of Wales*, ed. and trans. Lewis Thorpe (Harmondsworth: Penguin, 1978).

Gervase of Tilbury, *Otia imperialia: Entertainment for an Emperor*, ed. and trans. S. E. Banks and J. W. Binns (Oxford: Clarendon Press, 2002).

Gödelmann, Johann Georg, *Tractatus de magis, veneficis et lamiis deque his recte cognoscendis et puniendis* (Nuremberg, 1676; first printed Hanau and Frankfurt, 1591).

Guibert of Nogent, *The Deeds of God through the Franks*, trans. Robert Levine (Woodbridge: Boydell Press, 1997).

Guibert of Nogent, *'Dei gesta per Francos' et cinq autres textes*, ed. R. B. C. Huygens (Turnhout: Brepols, 1996).

Hardy, Thomas Duffus, ed., *Willelmi Malmesbiriensis Monachi Gesta regum Anglorum atque historia novella*, 2 vols (London: Sumptibus Societatis, 1840).

Isidore of Seville, *The Etymologies of Isidore of Seville*, ed. and trans. Stephen A. Barney, W. J. Lewis, J. A. Beach, and Oliver Berghof (Cambridge: Cambridge University Press, 2006).

James VI/I, *Daemonologie* (Edinburgh: Robert Waldgrave, 1597).

Jean d'Arras, *Mélusine ou la noble histoire du Lusignan*, ed. Jean-Jacques Vincensini (Paris: Librairie Générale Française, 2003).

Jean d'Arras, *Melusine; or the Noble History of Lusignan*, ed. and trans. Donald Maddox and Sara Sturm-Maddox (University Park, PA: Pennsylvania State University Press, 2012).

Jeay, Madeleine, and Kathleen Garay, eds and trans., *The Distaff Gospels: A First Modern English Edition of 'Les Évangiles des quenouilles'* (Peterborough, Ontario: Broadview Press, 2006).

John of Salisbury, *Frivolities of Courtiers and the Footprints of Philosophers: Being a Translation of the First, Second, and Third Books and Selections from the Seventh and Eighth Books of the 'Policraticus' of John of Salisbury*, ed. and trans. Joseph B. Pike (New York: Octagon Books, 1972).

Kieckhefer, Richard, *Forbidden Rites: A Necromancer's Manual of the Fifteenth Century* (University Park, PA: Pennsylvania State University Press, 1998).

Kors, Alan Charles, and Edward Peters, eds and trans., *Witchcraft in Europe 400–1700: A Documentary History* (Philadelphia: University of Pennsylvania Press, 2001).

Lacy, Norris J., ed. and trans., *Lancelot-Grail: Lancelot Parts III and IV* (Cambridge: D. S. Brewer, 2010).

Lindsay, W. M., ed., *Isidori Hispalensis Episcopi Etymologiarum sive originum libri XX*, 2 vols (Oxford: Oxford University Press, 1911).

Mackay, Christopher S., ed. and trans., *Malleus maleficarum*, 2 vols (Cambridge: Cambridge University Press, 2006).

McNeill, John T., and Helena M. Gamer, eds and trans., *Medieval Handbooks of Penance* (New York: Columbia University Press, 1938).

Michel, Francisque, ed., *Mellusine: poème relatif á cette fée poitevine, composé dans le XIVe siècle par Couldrette* (Niort: Robin et L. Favre, 1855).

Morris, Matthew W., ed. and trans., *A Bilingual Edition of Couldrette's Mélusine or le roman de Parthenay* (Lampeter: Edwin Mellen Press, 2003).

Osterley, Hermann, ed., *Gesta Romanorum* (Hildesheim: Georg Olms Verlagsbuchhandlung, 1963).

Pignatelli, Cinzia, and Dominique Gerner, eds, *Les Traductions françaises des Otia imperialia de Gervais de Tilbury par Jean d'Antioche et Jean de Vignay* (Geneva: Droz, 2006).

Polo, Marco, *La Description du monde*, ed. Pierre-Yves Badel (Paris: Livre de Poche, 1998).

Ralph of Coggeshall, *Chronicon Anglicanum*, ed. Joseph Stevenson (London: Longman, 1875).

Richter, Aemilius Ludwig, ed., *Corpus juris canonici*, 2 vols (Leipzig: Tauchnitz, 1879).

Rowland, Jenny, ed. and trans., *Early Welsh Saga Poetry: A Study and Edition of the Englynion* (Cambridge: D. S. Brewer, 1990).

Scott, A. B., and F. X. Martin, eds and trans., *Expugnatis Hibernica: The Conquest of Ireland by Giraldus Cambrensis* (Dublin: Royal Irish Academy, 1978).

Skeat, Walter W., ed., *The Romans of Partenay, or of Lusignen: Otherwise Known as the Tale of Melusine* (London: Trübner & Co., 1866).

Sylwan, Agneta, ed., *Petri Comestoris Scolastica historia: liber Genesis* (Turnhout: Brepols, 2005).

Tolkien, J. R. R., and E. V. Gordon, eds, *Sir Gawain and the Green Knight* (Oxford: Oxford University Press, 1967).

Veysseyre, Géraldine, ed., *L'Estoire de Brutus: la plus ancienne traduction en prose française de l'"Historia regum Britannie' de Geoffroy de Monmouth* (Paris: Classiques Garnier, 2015).

Wade-Evans, A. W., 'The Brychan Documents', *Y Cymmrodor* 19 (1906): 18–50.

Wade-Evans, A. W., *Vita sanctorum Britanniae et genealogiae* (Cardiff: University of Wales Press, 1944).

Walter Map, *De nugis curialium: Courtiers' Trifles*, ed. and trans. M. R. James, revised by C. N. L. Brooke and R. A. B. Mynors (Oxford: Clarendon Press, 1983).

William of Newburgh, *The History of English Affairs: Book 1*, ed. and trans. P. G. Walsh and M. J. Kennedy (Oxford: Aries and Philips, 1988).

## Secondary sources

Abed, Julien, 'La Traduction française de la *Prophetia Merlini* dans le Didot-*Perceval*', in *Moult obscures paroles: études sur la prophétie médiévale*, ed. Richard Trachsler, Julien Abed, and David Expert (Paris: Presses de l'Université Paris-Sorbonne, 2007), pp. 81–105.

Ahmed, Sara, *Strange Encounters: Embodied Others in Post-Coloniality* (London: Routledge, 2000).

Alberghini, Jennifer, 'Matriarchs and Mother Tongues: The Middle English *Romans of Partenay*', in *Melusine's Footprint: Tracing the Legacy of a Medieval Myth*, ed. Misty Urban, Deva Kemmis, and Melissa Ridley Elmes (Leiden: Brill, 2017), pp. 146–61.

Anderson, Benedict, *Imagined Communities: Reflections on the Origins and Spread of Nationalism* (London: Verso Books, 2006).

Archibald, Elizabeth, 'Arthurian Latin Romance', in *The Arthur of Medieval Latin Literature: The Development and Dissemination of the*

*Arthurian Legend in Medieval Latin*, ed. Siân Echard (Cardiff: University of Wales Press, 2011), pp. 132–45.

Arnold, John H., 'Persecution and Power in Medieval Europe: The Formation of a Persecuting Society, by R. I. Moore', *American Historical Review* 123.1 (2018): 165–74.

Ashe, Laura, *History and Fiction in England, 1066–1200* (Cambridge: Cambridge University Press, 2007).

Ashe, Laura, 'Killing the King: Romance and the Politicization of History', in *Thinking Medieval Romance*, ed. Katherine C. Little and Nicola McDonald (Oxford: Oxford University Press, 2018), pp. 55–67.

Auerbach, Erich, *Mimesis: The Representation of Reality in Western Literature*, trans. Willard R. Trask (Princeton, NJ: Princeton University Press, 2003).

Bailey, Michael, 'Medieval Concept of the Witches' Sabbath', *Exemplaria* 8.2 (1996): 419–39.

Bailey, Michael, 'Superstition and Sorcery', in *The Routledge History of Medieval Magic*, ed. Sophie Page and Catherine Rider (London: Routledge, 2019), pp. 487–501.

Bale, Anthony, *Feeling Persecuted: Christians, Jews, and Images of Violence in the Middle Ages* (London: Reaktion Books, 2010).

Bale, Anthony, *The Jew in the Medieval Book: English Antisemitisms 1350–1500* (Cambridge: Cambridge University Press, 2006).

Barbezat, Michael D., 'The Corporeal Orientation: Understanding Deviance through the Object(s) of Love', in *The Routledge History of Emotions in Europe, 1100–1700*, ed. Andrew Lynch and Susan Broomhall (London: Routledge, 2020), pp. 119–32.

Bartlett, Robert, *Gerald of Wales: A Voice of the Middle Ages* (Stroud: Tempus, 2006).

Bartlett, Robert, *The Natural and the Supernatural in the Middle Ages* (Oxford: Oxford University Press, 2008).

Bartrum, P. C., 'Fairy Mothers', *Bulletin of the Board of Celtic Studies* 19 (1962): 6–8.

Bate, A. K. 'Walter Map and Giraldus Cambrensis', *Latomus* 31 (1972): 860–75.

Baumgartner, Emmanuele, 'Fiction and History: The Cypriot Episode in Jean d'Arras's *Mélusine*', in *Mélusine of Lusignan: Founding Fiction in Late Medieval France*, ed. Donald Maddox and Sara Sturm-Maddox (Athens, GA: University of Georgia Press, 1996), pp. 185–200.

Bernau, Anke, 'Bodies and the Supernatural: Humans, Demons, and Angels', in *A Cultural History of the Human Body in the Medieval Age*, ed. Linda Kalof (Oxford: Berg Publishers, 2010), pp. 99–120, 239–44.

Berthelot, Anne, '*Dragon rouge / dragon blanc / dragons d'or / dragon d'airain*: les avatars du dragon dans le corpus merlinesque', in *Le Dragon dans la culture médiévale: colloque du Mont-Saint-Michel, 31 octobre – 1er novembre 1993*, ed. Danielle Buschinger (Greifswald: Reineke-Verlag, 1993), pp. 11–25.

Bhabha, Homi K., *The Location of Culture*, 2nd edn (London: Routledge, 2004).

Bhabha, Homi K., 'Signs Taken for Wonders: Questions of Ambivalence and Authority under a Tree outside Delhi, May 1817', *Critical Inquiry* 12.1 (1985): 144–65.

Blacker, Jean, 'Where Wace Feared to Tread: Latin Commentaries on Merlin's Prophecies in the Reign of Henry II', *Arthuriana* 6.1 (1996): 36–52.

Bloch, R. Howard, *Medieval Misogyny and the Invention of Western Romantic Love* (Chicago: University of Chicago Press, 1991).

Block Friedman, John, *The Monstrous Races in Medieval Thought and Art* (Syracuse, NY: Syracuse University Press, 2000).

Boivin, Jeanne-Marie, and Proinsias MacCana, eds, *Mélusines continentales et insulaires: actes du colloque international tenu les 27 et 28 mars à l'Université Paris XII et au Collège des Irlandais* (Paris: Honoré Champion, 1999).

Boquet, Damien, and Piroska Nagy, *Medieval Sensibilities: A History of Emotions in the Middle Ages*, trans. Robert Shaw (Cambridge: Polity Press, 2018).

Brewer, Keegan, *Wonder and Skepticism in the Middle Ages* (London: Routledge, 2016).

Bridges, Venetia, *Medieval Narratives of Alexander the Great: Transnational Texts in England and France* (Cambridge: D. S. Brewer, 2018).

Brownlee, Kevin, 'Melusine's Hybrid Body and the Poetics of Metamorphosis', in *Melusine of Lusignan: Founding Fiction in Late Medieval France*, ed. Donald Maddox and Sara Sturm-Maddox (Athens, GA: University of Georgia Press, 1996), pp. 76–99.

Bruckner, Matilda Tomaryn, *Shaping Romance: Interpretation, Truth, and Closure in Twelfth-Century French Fictions* (Philadelphia: University of Pennsylvania Press, 1993).

Burns, E. Jane, 'Magical Politics from Poitou to Armenia: Mélusine, Jean de Berry, and the Eastern Mediterranean', *Journal of Medieval and Early Modern Studies* 43.2 (2013): 275–301.

Burns, E. Jane, 'A Snake-Tailed Woman: Hybridity and Dynasty in the *Roman de Mélusine*', in *From Beasts to Souls: Gender and Embodiment in Medieval Europe*, ed. E. Jane Burns and Peggy McCracken (Notre Dame, IN: University of Notre Dame Press, 2013), pp. 185–220.

Byatt, A. S., *On Histories and Stories: Selected Essays* (London: Vintage, 2001).

Byrne, Aisling, 'Fairy Lovers: Sexuality, Order and Narrative in Medieval Romance', in *Sexual Culture in the Literature of Late Medieval Britain*, ed. Amanda Hopkins, Robert Allen Rouse, and Cory James Rushton (Cambridge: D. S. Brewer, 2014), pp. 99–110.

Byrne, Aisling, *Otherworlds: Fantasy and History in Medieval Literature* (Oxford: Oxford University Press, 2015).

Byron Smith, Joshua, 'Gerald of Wales, Walter Map, and the Anglo-Saxon Past of Ledbury North', in *New Perspectives on Gerald of Wales: Texts and Contexts*, ed. Georgia Henley and Joseph McMullen (Cardiff: University of Wales Press, 2018), pp. 63–77.

Byron Smith, Joshua, *Walter Map and the Matter of Britain* (Philadelphia: University of Pennsylvania Press, 2017).

Caciola, Nancy, *Discerning Spirits: Divine and Demonic Possession in the Middle Ages* (Ithaca, NY: Cornell University Press, 2006).

Campbell, Mary Baine, *Wonder and Science: Imagining Worlds in Early Modern Europe* (Ithaca, NY: Cornell University Press, 1999).

Carey, John, 'The Location of the Otherworld in Irish Tradition', in *The Otherworld Voyage in Early Irish Literature*, ed. Jonathan Wooding (Dublin: Four Courts Press, 2000), pp. 113–19; first published in *Éigse* 19 (1982–83): 36–43.

Carruthers, Mary, *The Book of Memory: A Study of Memory in Medieval Culture* (Cambridge: Cambridge University Press, 2008).

Cartlidge, Neil, 'The Fairies in the Fountain: Promiscuous Liaisons', in *The Exploitations of Medieval Romance*, ed. Laura Ashe, Ivana Djordjevic, and Judith Weiss (Cambridge: D. S. Brewer, 2010), pp. 15–27.

Cartlidge, Neil, 'Masters in the Art of Lying? The Literary Relationship between Hugh of Rhuddlan and Walter Map', *Modern Language Review* 106.1 (2011): 1–16.

Chanaud, Robert, 'Le Chevalier, la fée et l'hérétique. Une ancêtre valentinoise de Mélusine, la dame du château de l'Épervier', *Le Monde alpin et rhodanien: revue régionale d'ethnologie* 13 (1985): 31–54.

Chapman, Robert L., 'A Note on the Demon Queen Eleanor', *Modern Language Notes* 70.6 (1955): 393–96.

Clanchy, Michael, *From Memory to Written Record: England, 1066–1307* (Oxford: Wiley-Blackwell, 2012).

Clark, Stuart, *Thinking with Demons: The Idea of Witchcraft in Early Modern Europe* (Oxford: Oxford University Press, 1997).

Clarke, Catherine A. M., 'Signs and Wonders: Writing Trauma in Twelfth-Century England', *Reading Medieval Studies* 35 (2009): 55–77.

Cohen, Jeffrey Jerome, 'The Flow of Blood in Medieval Norwich', *Speculum* 79.1 (2004): 26–65.

Cohen, Jeffrey Jerome, 'Green Children from Another World, or the Archipelago in England', in *Cultural Diversity in the British Middle Ages: Archipelago, Island, England*, ed. Jeffrey Jerome Cohen (New York: Palgrave Macmillan, 2008), pp. 75–94.

Cohen, Jeffrey Jerome, *Hybridity, Identity, and Monstrosity in Medieval Britain* (New York: Palgrave Macmillan, 2006).

Cohen, Jeffrey Jerome, 'Monster Culture (Seven Theses)', in *Monster Theory: Reading Culture*, ed. Jeffrey Jerome Cohen (Minneapolis, MN: University of Minnesota Press, 1996), pp. 3–25.

Cohen, Jeffrey Jerome, 'On Saracen Enjoyment: Some Fantasies of Race in Late Medieval France and England', *Journal of Medieval and Early Modern Studies* 31.1 (2001): 113–46.

Cohen, Jeffrey Jerome, ed., *Cultural Diversity in the British Middle Ages: Archipelago, Island, England* (New York: Palgrave Macmillan, 2008).

Cohen, Jeffrey Jerome, ed., *Monster Theory: Reading Culture* (Minneapolis, MN: University of Minnesota Press, 1996).

Cohen, Jeffrey Jerome, ed., *The Postcolonial Middle Ages* (New York: Palgrave Macmillan, 2000).

Cohn, Norman, *Europe's Inner Demons: The Demonization of Christians in Medieval Christendom* (London: Pimlico, 2005).

Cohn, Norman, *Warrant for Genocide: The Myth of the Jewish World Conspiracy and the Protocols of the Elders of Zion* (London: Serif, 1996).

Cole, Chera A., 'Passing as a "Humayn Woman": Hybridity and Salvation in the Middle English *Mélusine*', in *Melusine's Footprint: Tracing the Legacy of a Medieval Myth*, ed. Misty Urban, Deva Kemmis, and Melissa Ridley Elmes (Leiden: Brill, 2017), pp. 240–58.

Coleman, Janet, *Ancient and Medieval Memories* (Cambridge: Cambridge University Press, 1991).

Colwell, Tania M., 'Fragments of the *Roman de Melusine* in the Upton House Bearsted Collection', *The Library* 13.3 (2012): 279–315.

Colwell, Tania M., 'Mélusine: Ideal Mother or Inimitable Monster?', in *Love, Marriage and Family Ties in the Later Middle Ages*, ed. Isabel Davis, Miriam Müller, and Sarah Rees Jones (Turnhout: Brepols, 2003), pp. 181–203.

Colwell, Tania M., 'Patronage of the Poetic Mélusine Romance: Guillaume l'Archevêque's Confrontation with Dynastic Crisis', *Journal of Medieval History* 37.2 (2011): 215–29.

Conklin Akbari, Suzanne, *Idols in the East: European Representations of Islam and the Orient, 1100–1450* (Ithaca, NY: Cornell University Press, 2009).

Cooper, Helen, *The English Romance in Time: Transforming Motifs from Geoffrey of Monmouth to the Death of Shakespeare* (Oxford: Oxford University Press, 2004).

Cooper, Helen, 'Thomas of Erceldoune: Romance as Prophecy', in *Cultural Encounters in the Romance of Medieval England*, ed. Corinne Saunders (Cambridge: D. S. Brewer, 2005), pp. 171–88.
Corfis, Ivy A., 'Empire and Romance: *Historia de la linda Melosina*', *Neophilologus* 82.4 (1998): 559–75.
Crick, Julia, 'The British Past and the Welsh Future: Gerald of Wales, Geoffrey of Monmouth, and Arthur of Britain', *Celtica* 23 (1999): 60–75.
*Crossing Borders in the Insular Middle Ages* (Newcastle University, 2018), https://digitalcultures.ncl.ac.uk/projects/crossingborders/#/db [last accessed 11 March 2021].
Curley, Michael J., *Geoffrey of Monmouth* (New York: Twayne Publishers, 1994).
Daston, Lorraine, and Katharine Park, *Wonders and the Order of Nature 1150–1750* (New York: Zone Books, 1998).
Davies, R. R., *The Age of Conquest: Wales, 1063–1415* (Oxford: Oxford University Press, 1991).
Davenport, Tony, 'Sex, Ghosts, and Dreams: Walter Map (1135?–1210?) and Gerald of Wales (1145–1223)', in *Writers of the Reign of Henry II: Twelve Essays*, ed. Ruth Kennedy and Simon Meecham-Jones (New York: Palgrave Macmillan, 2006), pp. 133–50.
Delogu, Daisy, 'Jean d'Arras Makes History: Political Legitimacy in the *Roman de Mélusine*', *Dalhousie French Studies* 80 (2007): 15–28.
Echard, Siân, *Arthurian Narrative in the Latin Tradition* (Cambridge: Cambridge University Press, 2001).
Echard, Siân, 'Geoffrey of Monmouth', in *The Arthur of Medieval Latin Literature: The Development and Dissemination of the Arthurian Legend in Medieval Latin*, ed. Siân Echard (Cardiff: University of Wales Press, 2011), pp. 45–66.
Echard, Siân, 'Map's Metafiction: Author, Narrator and Reader in *De nugis curialium*', *Exemplaria* 8.2 (1996): 287–314.
Elford, Dorothy, 'William of Conches', in *A History of Twelfth-Century Western Philosophy*, ed. Peter Dronke (Cambridge: Cambridge University Press, 1988), pp. 308–27.
Elias, Marcel, 'Interfaith Empathy and the Formation of Romance', in *Emotion and Medieval Textual Media*, ed. Mary Flannery (Turnhout: Brepols, 2018), pp. 99–124.
Elliott, Dyan, *Fallen Bodies: Pollution, Sexuality and Demonology in the Middle Ages* (Philadelphia: University of Pennsylvania Press, 1999).
Elliott, Dyan, 'Seeing Double: John Gerson, the Discernment of Spirits, and Joan of Arc', *American Historical Review* 107.1 (2002): 26–54.
Evans, Ruth, 'The Devil in Disguise: Perverse Female Origins of the Nation', in *Consuming Narratives: Gender and Monstrous Appetite*

*in the Middle Ages and the Renaissance*, ed. Liz Herbert McAvoy and Teresa Walters (Cardiff: University of Wales Press, 2002), pp. 183–95.

Evans, Ruth, 'Historicizing Postcolonial Criticism: Cultural Difference and the Vernacular', in *The Idea of the Vernacular: An Anthology of Middle English Vernacular Theory, 1280–1520*, ed. Jocelyn Wogan-Browne, Nicholas Watson, Andrew Taylor, and Ruth Evans (University Park, PA: Pennsylvania State University Press, 1999), pp. 366–70.

Fabry-Tehranchi, Irene, 'Merlin as a Prophet in the Manuscripts of the *Chroniques des Bretons* and Jean de Wavrin's *Chroniques d'Angleterre*', *Reading Medieval Studies* 44 (2018): 81–143.

Faletra, Michael A., *Wales and the Medieval Colonial Imagination: The Matters of Britain in the Twelfth Century* (New York: Palgrave Macmillan, 2014), pp. 99–133.

Finke, Laurie A., and Martin B. Shichtman, *King Arthur and the Myth of History* (Gainesville, FL: University of Florida Press, 2004).

Finlayson, John, 'The Marvellous in Middle English Romance', *Chaucer Review* 33.4 (1999): 363–408.

Finlayson, John, '"Richard Coer de Lion": Romance, History, or Something in Between?', *Studies in Philology* 87 (1990): 156–80.

Firth Green, Richard, *Elf Queens and Holy Friars: Fairy Beliefs and the Medieval Church* (Philadelphia: University of Pennsylvania Press, 2016).

Flood, Victoria, 'Arthur's Return from Avalon: Geoffrey of Monmouth and the Development of the Legend', *Arthuriana* 25.2 (2015): 84–110.

Flood, Victoria, 'Political Prodigies: Incubi and Succubi in Walter Map's *De nugis curialium* and Gerald of Wales's *Itinerarium Cambriae*', *Nottingham Medieval Studies* 57 (2013): 21–46.

Flood, Victoria, 'Prophecy as History: A New Study of the Prophecies of Merlin Silvester', *Neophilologus* 102.4 (2018): 543–59.

Flood, Victoria, 'Prophecy of the Six Kings: Translation and Transmission', in *Crossing Borders in the Insular Middle Ages* (Newcastle University, 2018), https://digitalcultures.ncl.ac.uk/projects/crossingborders [last accessed 11 March 2021].

Flood, Victoria, *Prophecy, Politics, and Place in Medieval England: From Geoffrey of Monmouth to Thomas of Erceldoune* (Cambridge: D. S. Brewer, 2016).

Flood, Victoria, 'The Supernatural Company in Cultural Translation: Dafydd ap Gwilym and the *Roman de la Rose* Tradition', in *Cultural Translations in Medieval Romance*, ed. Victoria Flood and Megan G. Leitch (Cambridge: D. S. Brewer, 2022), pp. 65–84.

Flores, Nona C., '"Effigies amicitiae … veritas inimicitiae": Anti-Feminism in the Iconography of the Woman-Headed Serpent in Medieval and

Renaissance Art and Literature', in *Animals in the Middle Ages: A Book of Essays*, ed. Nona C. Flores (New York: Garland, 1996), pp. 167–95.

Fradenburg, L. O. Aranye, 'Simply Marvelous', *Studies in the Age of Chaucer* 26 (2004): 1–27.

Fraioli, Deborah A., *Joan of Arc: The Early Debate* (Woodbridge: Boydell Press, 2000).

Fulton, Helen, 'Magic and the Supernatural in Early Welsh Narrative: *Culhwch ac Olwen* and *Breuddwyd Rhonabwy*', *Arthurian Literature* 30 (2013): 1–26.

Fulton, Helen, 'Matthew Arnold and the Canon of Medieval Welsh Literature', *Review of English Studies*, NS 63 (2011): 204–24.

Fulton, Helen, 'Romantic Wales: Imagining Wales in Medieval Insular Romance', in *Cultural Translations in Medieval Romance*, ed. Victoria Flood and Megan G. Leitch (Cambridge: D. S. Brewer, 2022), pp. 21–44.

Fulton, Helen, 'Space: Place, Non-Place, and Identity in the Medieval Fairy World', in *A Cultural History of Fairy Tales in the Middle Ages*, ed. Susan Aronstein (London: Bloomsbury, 2021), pp. 135–55.

Gallagher, Catherine, 'The Rise of Fictionality', in *The Novel*, I: *History, Geography, and Culture*, ed. Franco Moretti (Princeton, NJ: Princeton University Press, 2006), pp. 336–63.

Geary, Patrick J., *Women at the Beginning: Origin Myths from the Amazons to the Virgin Mary* (Princeton, NJ: Princeton University Press, 2006).

*Geiriadur Prifysgol Cymru* (University of Wales, 2020), https://geiriadur.ac.uk/gpc/gpc.html [last accessed 28 February 2021].

Ghosh, Amitav, *The Great Derangement: Climate Change and the Unthinkable* (Chicago: University of Chicago Press, 2016).

Ginzburg, Carlo, 'Deciphering the Sabbath', in *Early Modern European Witchcraft: Centres and Peripheries*, ed. Bengt Ankarloo and Gustav Henningsen (Oxford: Clarendon Press, 1993), pp. 121–38.

Green, D. H., *The Beginnings of Romance: Fact and Fiction, 1150–1220* (Cambridge: Cambridge University Press, 2002).

Greenblatt, Stephen, *Marvelous Possessions: The Wonder of the New World* (Chicago: University of Chicago Press, 1991).

Greenblatt, Stephen, 'Resonance and Wonder', *Bulletin of the American Academy of Arts and Sciences* 43.4 (1990): 11–34.

Griffin, Miranda, *Transforming Tales: Rewriting Metamorphosis in Medieval French Literature* (Oxford: Oxford University Press, 2015).

Harf-Lancner, Laurence, *Les Fées au Moyen Âge: Morgane et Mélusine – la naissance des fées* (Paris: Honoré Champion, 1984).

Harf-Lancner, Laurence, 'L'Illustration du Roman de Mélusine de Jean d'Arras dan les éditions du XVe et XVIe siècle', in *Le Livre et l'image en France au XVIe siècle*, ed. Nicole Cazauran (Paris: Presses de l'École Normale Supérieure, 1989), pp. 29–55.

Harf-Lancner, Laurence, 'Littérature et politique: Jean de Berry, Leon de Lusignan et le Roman de Mélusine', in *Histoire et littérature au Moyen Âge: actes du colloque du centre d'études médiévales de l'Université de Picardie 1985*, ed. Danielle Buschinger (Göppingen: Kümmerle, 1991), pp. 161–71.

Henderson, Lizanne, and Edward J. Cowan, *Scottish Fairy Belief: A History* (Edinburgh: John Donald, 2007).

Heng, Geraldine, *Empire of Magic: Medieval Romance and the Politics of Cultural Fantasy* (New York: Columbia University Press, 2004).

Heng, Geraldine, *The Invention of Race in the European Middle Ages* (Cambridge: Cambridge University Press, 2018).

Heng, Geraldine, 'Sex, Lies, and Paradise: The Assassins, Prester John, and the Fabulation of Civilizational Identities', *Differences* 23 (2015): 1–31.

Higgs Strickland, Debra, *Saracens, Demons, and Jews: Making Monsters in Medieval Art* (Princeton, NJ: Princeton University Press, 2003).

Himsworth, Katherine, 'Brut y brenhinedd', in *Arthur in the Celtic Languages: The Arthurian Legend in Celtic Literatures and Traditions*, ed. Ceridwen Lloyd-Morgan and Erich Poppe (Cardiff: University of Wales Press, 2019), pp. 95–109.

Hinton, James, 'Notes on Walter Map's *De nugis curialium*', *Studies in Philology* 20 (1923): 448–68.

Holsinger, Bruce W., 'Medieval Studies, Postcolonial Studies, and the Genealogies of Critique', *Speculum* 77.4 (2002): 1195–1227.

Howlett, D., and R. Ashdowne, eds, *Dictionary of Medieval Latin from British Sources*, 17 vols (Oxford: Oxford University Press, 1975–2013); online edition compiled by R. E. Latham, https://logeion.uchicago.edu/nenia [last accessed 31 March 2021].

Huizinga, Johan, *The Waning of the Middle Ages: A Study of the Forms of Life, Thought and Art in France and the Netherlands in the XIVth and XVth Centuries*, trans. Frederik J. Hopman (New York: St Martin's Press, 1924).

Hume, Kathryn, *Fantasy and Mimesis: Responses to Reality in Western Literature* (New York: Methuen, 1984).

Huot, Sylvia, 'Dangerous Embodiments: Froissart's Harton and Jean d'Arras's Melusine', *Speculum* 78.2 (2003): 400–20.

Ingham, Patricia Clare, *Sovereign Fantasies: Arthurian Literature and the Making of Britain* (Philadelphia: University of Pennsylvania Press, 2001).

Jameson, Fredric, 'Magical Narratives: Romance as Genre', *New Literary History* 7.1 (1975): 135–63.

Jameson, Fredric, *The Political Unconscious: Narrative as a Socially Symbolic Act* (London: Routledge, 1983).

John, Simon, 'Godfrey of Bouillon and the Swan Knight', in *Crusading and Warfare in the Middle Ages: Realities and Representations: Essays in Honour of John France*, ed. Simon John and Nicholas Morton (London: Routledge, 2016), pp. 129–42.

John, Simon, 'Historical Truth and the Miraculous Past: The Use of Oral Evidence in Twelfth-Century Latin Historical Writing on the First Crusade', *English Historical Review* 130.543 (2015): 263–301.

Jones, Aled Llion, *Darogan: Prophecy, Lament and Absent Heroes in Medieval Welsh History* (Cardiff: University of Wales Press, 2013).

Justice, Steven, 'Did the Middle Ages Believe in their Miracles?', *Representations* 103.1 (2008): 1–29.

Kabir, Ananya Jahanara, and Deanne Williams, 'Introduction: A Return to Wonder', in *Postcolonial Approaches to the European Middle Ages: Translating Cultures*, ed. Ananya Jahanara Kabir and Deanne Williams (Cambridge: Cambridge University Press, 2005), pp. 1–21.

Kabir, Ananya Jahanara, and Deanne Williams, eds, *Postcolonial Approaches to the European Middle Ages: Translating Cultures* (Cambridge: Cambridge University Press, 2005).

Karnes, Michelle, 'Marvels in the Medieval Imagination', *Speculum* 90.2 (2015): 327–65.

Karnes, Michelle, 'The Possibilities of Medieval Fiction', *New Literary History* 51.1 (2020): 209–28.

Karnes, Michelle, 'Wonder, Marvels, and Metaphor in the "Squire's Tale"', *English Literary History* 82.2 (2015): 461–90.

Kelly, Douglas, *The Art of Medieval French Romance* (Madison, WI: University of Wisconsin Press, 1992).

Kelly, Douglas, 'The Domestication of the Marvelous in the Melusine Romances', in *Melusine of Lusignan: Founding Fiction in Late Medieval France*, ed. Donald Maddox and Sara Sturm-Maddox (Athens, GA: University of Georgia Press, 1996), pp. 32–47.

Kelly, Douglas, '*Matiere* and *genera dicendi* in Medieval Romance', *Yale French Studies* 51 (1974): 147–59.

Kelly, Henry Angsar, 'The Metamorphosis of the Eden Serpent during the Middle Ages and Renaissance', *Viator* 2 (1971): 301–27.

Kieckhefer, Richard, *European Witch Trials: Their Foundation in Popular and Learned Culture, 1300–1500* (London: Routledge, 1976).

Kieckhefer, Richard, *Magic in the Middle Ages* (Cambridge: Cambridge University Press, 2000).

Kieckhefer, Richard, 'The Specific Rationality of Medieval Magic', *American Historical Review* 99.3 (1994): 813–36.

Kiessling, Nicholas, *The Incubus in English Literature: Provenance and Progeny* (Pullman, WA: Washington State University Press, 1977).
Kinoshita, Sharon, *Medieval Boundaries: Translating Difference in Old French Literature* (Philadelphia: University of Pennsylvania Press, 2006).
Kinoshita, Sharon, and Peggy McCracken, *Marie de France: A Critical Companion* (Cambridge: D. S. Brewer, 2012).
Knapp, James F., and Peggy A. Knapp, *Medieval Romance: The Aesthetics of Possibility* (Toronto: University of Toronto Press, 2017).
Knight, Stephen, *Arthurian Literature and Society* (New York: Palgrave Macmillan, 1983).
Kratz, Dennis M., 'Fictus Lupus: The Werewolf in Christian Thought', *Classical Folia* 30 (1976): 57–78.
Kruger, Steven F., *Dreaming in the Middle Ages* (Cambridge: Cambridge University Press, 1992).
Kruger, Steven F., *The Spectral Jew: Conversion and Embodiment in Medieval Europe* (Minneapolis, MN: University of Minnesota Press, 2006).
Laidlow, J. C., 'Christine de Pizan, the Earl of Salisbury and Henry IV', *French Studies* 36 (1982): 129–43.
Lampert-Weissig, Lisa, *Medieval Literature and Postcolonial Studies* (Edinburgh: Edinburgh University Press, 2010).
Larrington, Carolyne, 'The Psychology of Emotion and Study of the Medieval Period', *Early Medieval Europe* 10 (2001): 251–56.
Lavezzo, Kathy, *The Accommodated Jew: English Antisemitism from Bede to Milton* (Ithaca, NY: Cornell University Press, 2016).
Lecouteux, Claude, 'Zur Entstehung der Melusinensage', *Zeitschrift für deutsche Philologie* 98 (1979): 73–84.
Le Goff, Jacques, *The Birth of Purgatory*, trans. Arthur Goldhammer (Chicago: University of Chicago Press, 1984).
Le Goff, Jacques, *The Medieval Imagination*, trans. Arthur Goldhammer (Chicago: University of Chicago Press, 1992).
Le Goff, Jacques, *Time, Work, and Culture in the Middle Ages*, trans. Arthur Goldhammer (Chicago: University of Chicago Press, 1982).
Leitch, Megan G., *Romancing Treason: The Literature of the Wars of the Roses* (Oxford: Oxford University Press, 2015).
Levine, Robert, 'Satiric Vulgarity in Guibert de Nogent's *Gesta Dei per Francos*', *Rhetorica: A Journal of the History of Rhetoric* 7.3 (1989): 261–273.
Lewis, Charlton T., and Charles Short, eds, *A Latin Dictionary* (London: Harper Brothers, 1898), www.perseus.tufts.edu/hopper/text?doc=nenia&fromdoc=Perseus%3Atext%3A1999.04.00599.
Liu, Yin, 'Middle English Romance as Prototype Genre', *Chaucer Review* 40.4 (2006): 335–53.

Lockhart, Jessica J., '"Something remains which is not open to my understanding": Enigmatic Marvels in Welsh Otherworld Narratives and Latin Arthurian Romance', in *Cultural Translations in Medieval Romance*, ed. Victoria Flood and Megan G. Leitch (Cambridge: D. S. Brewer, 2022), pp. 45–64.

Lomperis, Linda, 'Medieval Travel Writing and the Question of Race', *Journal of Medieval and Early Modern Studies* 31.1 (2001): 147–64.

Longnon, Jean, Raymond Cazelles, and Millard Meiss, eds, *Les Très Riches Heures du duc de Berry* (London: Thames and Hudson, 1989).

Maddox, Donald, and Sara Sturm-Maddox, 'Introduction: Melusine at 600', in *Melusine of Lusignan: Founding Fiction in Late Medieval France*, ed. Donald Maddox and Sara Sturm-Maddox (Athens, GA: University of Georgia Press, 1996), pp. 1–11.

Maddox, Donald, and Sara Sturm-Maddox, eds, *Melusine of Lusignan: Founding Fiction in Late Medieval France* (Athens, GA: University of Georgia Press, 1996).

Margolis, Nadia, 'Myths in Progress: A Literary-Typological Comparison of Mélusine and Joan of Arc', in *Mélusine of Lusignan: Founding Fiction in Late Medieval France*, ed. Donald Maddox and Sara Sturm-Maddox (Athens, GA: University of Georgia Press, 1996), pp. 241–66.

Matheson, Lister M., *The Prose Brut: The Development of a Middle English Chronicle* (Tempe, AZ: ACMRS Press, 1998).

McCracken, Peggy, *In the Skin of a Beast: Sovereignty and Animality in Late Medieval France* (Chicago: University of Chicago Press, 2017).

McDonald, Nicola, 'Eating People and the Alimentary Logic of *Richard Coeur de Lion*', in *Pulp Fictions of Medieval England: Essays in Popular Romance*, ed. Nicola McDonald (Manchester: Manchester University Press, 2004), pp. 124–50.

McDonald, Nicola, 'The Wonder of Middle English Romance', in *Thinking Medieval Romance*, ed. Katherine C. Little and Nicola McDonald (Oxford: Oxford University Press, 2018), pp. 13–34.

McDonald, Nicola, ed., *Pulp Fictions of Medieval England: Essays in Popular Romance* (Manchester: Manchester University Press, 2004).

Minnis, Alastair, 'Medieval Imagination and Memory', in *The Cambridge History of Literary Criticism*, III: *The Middle Ages*, ed. Alastair Minnis and Ian Johnson (Cambridge: Cambridge University Press, 2005), pp. 237–74.

Minnis, Alastair, *Medieval Theory of Authorship: Scholastic Literary Attitudes in the Later Middle Ages* (London: Scolar Press, 1984).

Mittman, Asa, *Maps and Monsters in Medieval England* (London: Routledge, 2006).

Monson, Don A., *Andreas Capellanus, Scholasticism, and the Courtly Tradition* (Washington, DC: Catholic University of America Press, 2005).

Moore, R. I., *The Formation of a Persecuting Society: 950–1250* (Oxford: Basil Blackwell, 1990).
Moore, R.I., *The War on Heresy: Faith and Power in Medieval Europe* (London: Profile Books, 2014).
*The Narrative Sources from the Medieval Low Countries* (Royal Historical Commission, Brussels, 2009), https://www.narrative-sources.be/naso_link_en.php?link=1136 [last accessed 5 January 2022].
Nichols, Stephen G., 'Melusine between Myth and History: Profile of a Female Demon', in *Melusine of Lusignan: Founding Fiction in Late Medieval France*, ed. Donald Maddox and Sara Sturm-Maddox (Athens, GA: University of Georgia Press, 1996), pp. 137–64.
Nolan, Robert J., 'The Origin of the Romance of Melusine: A New Interpretation', *Fabula* 15.3 (1974): 192–201.
Orlemanski, Julie, 'Who Has Fiction? Modernity, Fictionality, and the Middle Ages', *New Literary History* 50.2 (2019): 145–70.
Otter, Monika, *Inventiones: Fiction and Referentiality in Twelfth-Century English Historical Writing* (Chapel Hill, NC: University of North Carolina Press, 1999).
Padel, O. J., 'The Nature of Arthur', *Cambrian Medieval Celtic Studies* 27 (1994): 1–31.
Painter, Sidney, 'The Lords of Lusignan in the Eleventh and Twelfth Centuries', *Speculum* 31.2 (1957): 27–47.
Pairet, Ana, 'Melusine's Double Binds: Foundation, Transgression, and the Genealogical Romance', in *Reassessing the Heroine in Medieval French Literature*, ed. Kathy M. Krause (Gainesville, FL: University Press of Florida, 2001), pp. 71–86.
Pairet, Ana, 'Polycorporality and Heteromorphia: Untangling Melusine's Mixed Bodies', in *Melusine's Footprint: Tracing the Legacy of a Medieval Myth*, ed. Misty Urban, Deva Kemmis, and Melissa Ridley Elmes (Leiden: Brill, 2017), pp. 36–51.
Pappano, M. A., 'Marie de France, Alienor d'Aquitaine, and the Alien Queen', in *Eleanor of Aquitaine: Lord and Lady*, ed. Bonnie Wheeler and John C. Parsons (New York: Palgrave, 2003), pp. 337–67.
Partington, J. R., *A History of Greek Fire and Gunpowder* (Baltimore, MD: Johns Hopkins University Press, 1960; reprinted 1999).
Partner, Nancy F., *Serious Entertainments: The Writing of History in Twelfth-century England* (Chicago: University of Chicago Press, 1977).
Péporté, Pit, 'Melusine and Luxembourg: A Double Memory', in *Melusine's Footprint: Tracing the Legacy of a Medieval Myth*, ed. Misty Urban, Deva Kemmis, and Melissa Ridley Elmes (Leiden: Brill, 2017), pp. 162–82.
Perret, Michèle, 'Attribution et utilisation du nom propre dans Mélusine', in *Mélusines continentales et insulaires: actes du colloque international tenu les 27 et 28 mars à l'Université Paris XII et au Collège*

*des Irlandais*, ed. Jeanne-Marie Boivin and Proinsias MacCana (Paris: Honoré Champion, 1999), pp. 169–79.

Perret, Michèle, 'Invraisemblable verité: témoignage fantastique dans deux romans du XIVe et XVe siècles', *Europe: revue littéraire mensuelle* 61 (1983): 25–34.

Perret, Michèle, 'Writing History/Writing Fiction', in *Melusine of Lusignan: Founding Fiction in Late Medieval France*, ed. Donald Maddox and Sara Sturm-Maddox (Athens, GA: University of Georgia Press, 1996), pp. 201–25.

Peters, Edward, 'The Lady Vanishes: Gervase of Tilbury on Heresy and Wonders', in *Mind Matters: Studies of Medieval and Early Modern Intellectual History in Honour of Marcia Colish*, ed. Cary J. Nederman, Nancy Van Deusen, and E. Ann Matter (Turnhout: Brepols, 2010), pp. 177–90.

Peters, Edward, *The Magician, the Witch and the Law* (Philadelphia: University of Pennsylvania Press, 1978).

Peters, Edward, 'The Medieval Church and State on Superstition, Magic and Witchcraft: From Augustine to the Sixteenth Century', in *Witchcraft and Magic in Europe: The Middle Ages*, ed. Bengt Ankarloo and Stuart Clark (London: Athlone Press, 2002) pp. 173–245.

Pickens, Rupert T., 'The Poetics of Paradox in the *Roman de Melusine*', in *Melusine of Lusignan: Founding Fiction in Late Medieval France*, ed. Donald Maddox and Sara Sturm-Maddox (Athens, GA: University of Georgia Press, 1996), pp. 48–75.

Poirion, Daniel, *Le Merveilleux dans la littérature française du Moyen Âge* (Paris: Presses Universitaires de France, 1982).

Power, Daniel, 'The Stripping of a Queen: Eleanor of Aquitaine in Thirteenth-Century Norman Tradition', in *The World of Eleanor of Aquitaine: Literature and Society in Southern France between the Eleventh and Thirteenth Centuries*, ed. Marcus Bull and Catherine Léglu (Woodbridge: Boydell Press, 2005), pp. 115–36.

Prendergast, Thomas A., and Stephanie Trigg, *Affective Medievalism: Love, Abjection and Discontent* (Manchester: Manchester University Press, 2018).

Purkiss, Diane, *Troublesome Things: A History of Fairies and Fairy Stories* (London: Penguin, 2001).

Putter, Ad, 'Latin Historiography after Geoffrey of Monmouth', in *The Arthur of Medieval Latin Literature: The Development and Dissemination of the Arthurian Legend in Medieval Latin*, ed. Siân Echard (Cardiff: University of Wales Press, 2011), pp. 85–108.

Putter, Ad, *Sir Gawain and the Green Knight and French Arthurian Romance* (Oxford: Clarendon Press, 1995).

Radulescu, Raluca, 'Performing Emotions in the Arthurian World', *Arthuriana* 29.4 (2010): 3–7.

Reddy, William M., *The Making of Romantic Love: Longing and Sexuality in Europe, South Asia, and Japan, 900–1200 CE* (Chicago: University of Chicago Press, 2012).

Reynolds, Susan, 'Eadric Silvaticus and the English Resistance', *Bulletin of the Institute of Historical Research* 54 (1991): 102–05.

Richter, Michael, 'Gerald of Wales: A Reassessment on the 750th Anniversary of his Death', *Traditio* 29 (1973): 379–90.

Richter, Michael, *Giraldus Cambrensis: The Growth of the Welsh Nation* (Aberystwyth: National Library of Wales, 1996).

Rikhardsdottir, Sif, *Emotion in Old Norse Literature: Translations, Voices, Contexts* (Cambridge: D. S. Brewer, 2017).

Roberts, Brynley F., 'Copïau Cymraeg o Prophetiae Merlini', *National Library of Wales Journal* 20.1 (1977): 14–39.

Roberts, Brynley F., 'Geoffrey of Monmouth and Welsh Historical Tradition', *Nottingham Medieval Studies* 20 (1976): 29–40.

Roberts, Brynley F., 'Geoffrey of Monmouth, *Historia regum Britanniae* and *Brut y Brenhinedd*', in *Arthur of the Welsh: The Arthurian Legend in Medieval Welsh Literature*, ed. Rachel Bromwich, A. O. H. Jarman, and Brynley F. Roberts (Cardiff: University of Wales Press, 1991), pp. 97–116.

Roberts, Brynley F., *Gerald of Wales* (Cardiff: University of Wales Press, 1982).

Roberts, Brynley F., 'Melusina: Medieval Welsh and English Analogues', in *Mélusines continentales et insulaires: actes du colloque international tenu les 27 et 28 mars à l'Université Paris XII et au Collège des Irlandais*, ed. Jeanne-Marie Boivin and Proinsias MacCana (Paris: Honoré Champion, 1999), pp. 281–95.

Roberts, Brynley F., 'Oral Tradition and Welsh Literature: A Description and Survey', *Oral Tradition* 3/1–2 (1988): 61–87.

Rosenwein, Barbara H., *Emotional Communities in the Early Middle Ages* (Ithaca, NY: Cornell University Press, 2006).

Rosenwein, Barbara H., *Generations of Feeling: A History of Emotions, 600–1700* (Cambridge: Cambridge University Press, 2015).

Rosenwein, Barbara H., 'Worrying about Emotions in History', *American Historical Review* 107 (2002): 821–45.

Rosenwein, Barbara H., and Riccardo Cristiani, *What is the History of Emotions?* (Cambridge: Polity Press, 2018).

Rubin, Miri, *Corpus Christi: The Eucharist in Late Medieval Culture* (Cambridge: Cambridge University Press, 1991).

Rubin, Miri, 'Desecration of the Host: The Birth of an Accusation', *Studies in Church History* 29 (1992): 169–85.

Saul, Nigel, *Richard II* (London: Yale University Press, 1997).

Saunders, Corinne, 'From Romance to Vision: The Life of Breath in Medieval Literary Texts', in *The Life of Breath in Literature, Culture and Medicine: Classical to Contemporary*, ed. David Fuller, Corinne Saunders, and Jane McNaughton (New York: Palgrave Macmillan, 2021), pp. 87–110.

Saunders, Corinne, *Magic and the Supernatural in Medieval English Romance* (Cambridge: D. S. Brewer, 2010).

Saunders, Corinne, 'Mind, Body and Affect in Medieval Arthurian Romance', in *Emotions in Medieval Arthurian Literature: Body, Mind, Voice*, ed. Frank Brandsma, Carolyne Larrington, and Corinne Saunders (Cambridge: D. S. Brewer, 2015), pp. 31–46.

Saunders, Corinne, *Rape and Ravishment in the Literature of Medieval England* (Cambridge: D. S. Brewer, 2001).

Saunders, Corinne, 'Subtle Crafts: Magic and Exploitation in Medieval English Romance', in *The Exploitations of Medieval Romance*, ed. Laura Ashe, Ivana Djordjevic, and Judith Weiss (Cambridge: D. S. Brewer, 2010), pp. 108–24.

Sayers, William, 'The Use of Quicklime in Medieval Naval Warfare', *The Mariner's Mirror* 92.3 (2006): 262–69.

Schaeffer, Denise, 'Wisdom and Wonder in *Metaphysics* A:1–2', *Review of Metaphysics* 52.3 (1999): 641–56.

Shaw, Jan, 'Geographies of Loss: Cicilian Armenia and the Prose Romance of Melusine', in *Cultural Translations in Medieval Romance*, ed. Victoria Flood and Megan G. Leitch (Cambridge: D. S. Brewer, 2022), pp. 209–26.

Shaw, Jan, *Space, Gender, and Memory in Middle English Romance: Architectures of Wonder in Melusine* (New York: Palgrave, 2016).

Shepherd, G. T., 'The Emancipation of the Story in the Twelfth Century', in *Medieval Narrative: A Symposium*, ed. Hans Bekker-Nielsen, Peter Foote, Andreas Haarder, and Preben Meulengracht Sorensen (Odense: University of Odense Press, 1979), pp. 44–57.

Shyovitz, David I., 'Christians and Jews in the Twelfth-Century Werewolf Renaissance', *Journal of the History of Ideas* 75.4 (2014): 521–43.

Shyovitz, David I., *A Remembrance of his Wonders: Nature and the Supernatural in the Medieval Ashkenaz* (Philadelphia: University of Pennsylvania Press, 2017).

Sims-Williams, Patrick, 'Did Itinerant Breton "Conteurs" Transmit the Matière de Bretagne?', *Romania* 116 (1998): 72–111.

Sims-Williams, Patrick, 'The Early Welsh Arthurian Poems', in *The Arthur of the Welsh: The Arthurian Legend in Medieval Welsh Literature*, ed. Rachel Bromwich, A. O. H. Jarman, and Brynley F. Roberts (Cardiff: University of Wales Press, 1991), pp. 33–72.

Sims-Williams, Patrick, *Irish Influence on Medieval Welsh Literature* (Oxford: Oxford University Press, 2010).

Sims-Williams, Patrick, 'Some Functions of Origin Stories in Medieval Wales', in *History and Heroic Tale: A Symposium*, ed. Tore Nyberg, P. M. Sorensen, and A. Trommer (Odense: Odense University Press, 1989), pp. 91–131.

Sims-Williams, Patrick, 'The Visionary Celt: The Construction of an Ethnic Preconception', *Cambrian Medieval Celtic Studies* 11 (1986): 71–96.

Spiegel, Gabrielle M., 'Genealogy: Form and Function in Medieval Historical Narrative', *History and Theory* 22.1 (1983): 43–53.

Spiegel, Gabrielle M., 'Maternity and Monstrosity: Reproductive Biology in the *Roman de Melusine*', in *Melusine of Lusignan: Founding Fiction in Late Medieval France*, ed. Donald Maddox and Sara Sturm-Maddox (Athens, GA: University of Georgia Press, 1996), pp. 100–24.

Spiegel, Gabrielle M., 'Political Utility in Medieval Historiography: A Sketch', *History and Theory* 14.3 (1975): 314–25.

Spiegel, Gabrielle M., *Romancing the Past: The Rise of Vernacular Prose Historiography in Thirteenth-Century France* (Berkeley, CA: University of California Press, 1995).

Stephens, Walter, *Demon Lovers: Witchcraft, Sex, and the Crisis of Belief* (Chicago: University of Chicago Press, 2003).

Stock, Brian, *The Implications of Literacy: Written Language and Models of Interpretation in the Eleventh and Twelfth Centuries* (Princeton, NJ: Princeton University Press, 1983).

Sturm-Maddox, Sara, 'Configuring Alterity: Rewriting the Fairy Other', in *The Medieval Opus: Imitation, Rewriting, and Transmission in the French Tradition: Proceedings of the Symposium Held at the Institute for Research in Humanities, October 5–7 1995, the University of Wisconsin-Madison*, ed. Douglas Kelly (Leiden: Brill, 1996), pp. 125–38.

Sullivan, Karen, 'On Recognizing the Limits of our Understanding: Medieval Debates about Merlin and Marvels', in *Uncertain Knowledge: Scepticism, Relativism, and Doubt in the Middle Ages*, ed. Dallas George Denery, Kantik Ghosh, and Nicolette Zeeman (Turnhout: Brepols, 2014), pp. 161–84.

Sutton, Anne F., and Livia Visser-Fuchs, 'The Dark Dragon of the Normans: A Creation of Geoffrey of Monmouth, Stephen of Rouen, and Merlin Silvester', *Quondam et futurus* 2.2 (1992): 1–19.

Sutton, Anne F., and Livia Visser-Fuchs, *Richard III's Books: Ideals and Reality in the Life and Library of a Medieval Prince* (Stroud: Sutton, 1997).

Sweeney, Michelle, *Magic in Medieval Romance from Chrétien de Troyes to Geoffrey Chaucer* (Dublin: Four Courts Press, 2000).

Tasioulas, Jacqueline, 'Dying of Imagination in the First Fragment of the *Canterbury Tales*', *Medium Ævum* 82.2 (2013): 213–35.

Taylor, Jane H. M., 'Melusine's Progeny: Patterns and Perplexities', in *Melusine of Lusignan: Founding Fiction in Late Medieval France*, ed. Donald Maddox and Sara Sturm-Maddox (Athens, GA: University of Georgia Press, 1996), pp. 165–84.

Tiliette, Jean-Yves, 'Invention du récit: la "Brutiade" de Geoffroy de Monmouth (*Historia regum Britanniae*, § 6–22)', *Cahiers de civilisation médiévale* 39 (1996): 217–33.

Tolan, John, 'Forging New Paradigms: Towards a History of Islamo-Christian Civilization', in *A Sea of Languages: Rethinking the Arabic Role in Medieval Literary History*, ed. Suzanne Conklin Akbari and Karla Mallette (Toronto: University of Toronto Press, 2013), pp. 62–70.

Tolan, John, *Saracens: Islam in the Medieval European Imagination* (New York: Columbia University Press, 2002).

Tomasch, Sylvia, 'Postcolonial Chaucer and the Virtual Jew', in *The Postcolonial Middle Ages*, ed. Jeffrey Jerome Cohen (New York: Palgrave Macmillan, 2000), pp. 243–60.

Trachsler, Richard, 'A Question of Time: Romance and History', in *A Companion to the Lancelot-Grail Cycle*, ed. Carol Dover (Cambridge: D. S. Brewer, 2003), pp. 23–32.

Trachsler, Richard, 'L'*Historia regum Britannie* au XVe siècle. Les manuscrits New York, Public Library, Spencer 41 et Paris, Bibliothèque de l'Arsenal, 5078', in *L'Historia regum Britanniae et les 'Bruts' en Europe*, I: *Traductions, adaptations, réappropriations (XIIe–XVIe siècle)*, ed. Hélène Tétrel and Géraldine Veysseyre (Paris: Classiques Garnier, 2015), pp. 193–205.

Truitt, E. R., *Medieval Robots: Mechanism, Magic, Nature, and Art* (Philadelphia: University of Pennsylvania Press, 2015).

Turner, Ralph V., *Eleanor of Aquitaine: Queen of France, Queen of England* (New Haven, CT: Yale University Press, 2009).

Turner, R. W. V., 'Eleanor of Aquitaine, Twelfth-Century Troubadours, and her Black Legend', *Nottingham Medieval Studies* 52 (2008): 17–42.

Urban, Misty, Deva Kemmis, and Melissa Ridley Elmes, eds, *Melusine's Footprint: Tracing the Legacy of a Medieval Myth* (Leiden: Brill, 2017).

Van Houts, Elisabeth, 'Introduction: Medieval Memories', in *Medieval Memories: Men, Women and the Past, 700–1300*, ed. Elisabeth van Houts (London: Longman, 2001), pp. 1–16.

Van Houts, Elisabeth, 'The Memory of 1066 in Written and Oral Traditions', *Anglo-Norman Studies* 19 (1996): 167–79.

Veysseyre, Géraldine, 'Metre en roman: *les prophéties de Merlin*: Voies et détours de l'interprétation dans trois traductions de l'*Historia regum*

Britannie', in *Moult obscures paroles: études sur la prophétie médiévale*, ed. Richard Trachsler, Julien Abed, and David Expert (Paris: Presses de l'Université Paris-Sorbonne, 2007), pp. 107–66.

Veysseyre, Géraldine, and Clara Wille, 'Les Commentaires latins et français aux prophetie Merlini de Geoffroy de Monmouth', *Médiévales* 55 (2008): 93–114.

Wade, James, *Fairies in Medieval Romance* (New York: Palgrave Macmillan, 2011).

Walker Bynum, Caroline, *Metamorphosis and Identity* (New York: Zone Books, 2005).

Walker Bynum, Caroline, *The Resurrection of the Body in Western Christianity, 200–1336* (New York: Columbia University Press, 2017).

Walker Bynum, Caroline, 'Wonder', *American Historical Review* 102.1 (1997): 1–26.

Ward, H. L. D., *Catalogue of Romances in the Department of Manuscripts in the British Museum*, 2 vols (London: British Museum, 1883).

Warren, Michelle R., *History on the Edge: Excalibur and the Borders of Britain* (Minneapolis, MN: University of Minnesota Press, 2000).

Watkins, C. S., '"Folklore" and "Popular Religion" in Britain during the Middle Ages', *Folklore* 115.2 (2004): 140–50.

Watkins, C. S., *History and the Supernatural in Medieval England* (Cambridge: Cambridge University Press, 2007).

Watkins, C. S., 'Memories of the Marvellous in the Anglo-Norman Realm', in *Medieval Memories: Men, Women and the Past, 700–1300*, ed. Elisabeth van Houts (London: Longman, 2001), pp. 92–112.

Weisl, Angela Jane, 'Half Lady, Half Serpent: Melusine's Monstrous Body and the Discourse of Romance', in *Melusine's Footprint: Tracing the Legacy of a Medieval Myth*, ed. Misty Urban, Deva Kemmis, and Melissa Ridley Elmes (Leiden: Brill, 2017), pp. 222–39.

Wheeler, Bonnie, and John C. Parsons, eds, *Eleanor of Aquitaine: Lord and Lady* (New York: Palgrave, 2003).

Wiebe, Gregory D., *Fallen Angels in the Theology of St Augustine* (Oxford: Oxford University Press, 2021).

Williams, Ann, 'Eadric the Wild', *Oxford Dictionary of National Biography* (Oxford, 2005) http://www.oxforddnb.com/index/101008512/Eadric-the-Wild [last accessed 31 May 2020].

Williams, Ann, *The English and the Norman Conquest* (Woodbridge: Boydell Press, 1992).

Williams, Tara, *Middle English Marvels: Magic, Spectacle and Morality in the Fourteenth Century* (University Park, PA: Pennsylvania State University Press, 2018).

Wingfield, Emily, *The Trojan Legend in Medieval Scottish Literature* (Cambridge: D. S. Brewer, 2014).

Wood, Juliette, '*Caerleon Restaurata:* The Narrative World of Early Medieval Gwent', in *The Gwent County History*, I: *Gwent in Prehistory and Early History*, ed. Miranda Green and Ray Howell (Cardiff: University of Wales Press, 2004), pp. 317–30.

Wood, Juliette, 'The Fairy Bride Legend in Wales', *Folklore* 103 (1992): 56–72.

Wood, Juliette, 'Walter Map: The Contents and Context of *De nugis curialium*', *Transactions of the Honourable Society of Cymmrodorion* (1985): 91–103.

Wyatt, David R., *Slaves and Warriors in Medieval Britain and Ireland, 800–1200* (Leiden: Brill, 2009).

Zeldenrust, Lydia, *The Mélusine Romance in Medieval Europe: Translation, Circulation, and Material Contexts* (Cambridge: D. S. Brewer, 2020).

Zumthor, Paul, *Towards a Medieval Poetics*, trans. Philip Bennett (Minneapolis, MN: University of Minnesota Press, 1992).

# Index

Note: 'n' after a page reference indicates the number of a note on that page

Aberystwyth, National Library of Wales, Peniarth MS 403 242n34
Albertus Magnus 55, 101, 136n14, 155–6, 187n63
Albina, legend 170
Anderson, Benedict ('imagined community') 10, 171
*annwfn* (Welsh Otherworld) 66, 91n78
antisemitism 24, 30, 112–6, 121–4, 196, 219, 222–4, 232–5, 237
see also Pierleoni
Apuleius
*De deo Socratis* 48–49
*Metamorphoses (The Golden Ass)* 107, 109, 123
Aquinas, Thomas 15, 55, 65, 100, 101, 136n14, 143n107
Aristotle
*De anima* 16, 55–6, 59, 106, 123, 157
*Metaphysica* 136n14, 151–2, 162, 200–1
Arthur (legendary king) 66, 70, 83n13, 172
debated historicity 19–25, 45–8, 51, 62, 65, 98–9
in romance 201–9, 217, 242n34
Ashe, Laura 109
Auerbach, Erich 204
Augustine
antisemitism 113
*De civitate Dei* 1, 8–16, 21, 49, 56–7, 73–5, 79–81, 96–103, 107–9, 117–8, 151–54, 162, 170, 218, 220, 227–8, 232, 252–3
*De Genesi ad litteram* 72
*De predestinatione sanctorum* 65
*Letter VII* 24, 61, 155
automata 11, 228–29, 238
Avalon
Arthurian return legend 19, 21–4, 29, 45–8, 52, 62, 68, 98–9, 112, 250, 254
in *Mélusine* 204–9
Avicenna (Ibn Sina) 55, 155–6

Bacon, Roger 101, 135n3, 230
Baldwin, Archbishop of Canterbury 68
Bale, Anthony 112, 222

# Index

Barbezat, Michael D. 222
Bartholemew Iscanus, Bishop of Exeter 58
Battle Abbey 79
Bede 21, 106
Bernard of Clairvaux 81, 90n66, 142n95, 156
Bersuire, Pierre 182n16
Bhabha, Homi K. 26–7, 197, 234, 238
Blacker, Jean 70
Block Friedman, John 219
Boccaccio, Giovanni (*Decameron*) xi, xii
Bridges, Venetia 221
Brocéliande, forest 24–5, 160
Bruckner, Matilda Tomaryn 202
Brutus, legendary king of Britain 51, 164–70
Brychan, legendary king of Brycheiniog 62, 66–7
Brycheiniog 62, 63, 66–7
Byatt, A. S. xi–xii
Byrne, Aisling 4, 7
Byron Smith, Joshua 50

Cadog, St 66
Caerleon 68–72
Caesarius of Heisterbach (*Dialogus miraculum*) 93n105, 126–7
Cambridge, Gonville and Caius College Library MS 175/96 216
Cambridge, Trinity College Library MS R.3.17 216
Campbell, Mary Baine 236
'Canon episcopi' 57–9, 97, 110, 111, 118–9, 250
Capellanus, Andreas (*De amore*) 104
Chantilly, Bibliothèque du Château de Chantilly, MS 65 see *Les Très Riches Heures*

Chantilly, Musée Condé, MS 654 see *Les Évangiles des quenouilles*
Charles VI (King of France) 215
Chaucer, Geoffrey
    *Canterbury Tales* xi, 40n63
    'Squire's Tale' 246n78
    *Legend of Good Women* 246n75
Chrétien de Troyes 25, 160, 179, 197, 203
Christine de Pisan 150, 193n128
Circe 22, 23, 109, 159
Clark, Stuart 6
Clarke, Catherine A. M. 54, 79
Cohen, Jeffrey Jerome 79
Colwell, Tania 202, 213–4
Comestor, Peter (*Historia scholastica*) 106, 108, 120
condemnations by University of Paris 152
Conklin Akbari, Suzanne 226
Cooper, Helen 4, 162–3
Couldrette
    *Mélusine* (or *Roman de Parthenay*) 31, 148–9, 156, 173, 195–219, 222, 228, 239, 250, 254–5
    English translation 31, 197–8, 208, 216
    German translation (Thüring von Ringoltingen) 250
Council of Trent 20
Cynog, St 66

Daston, Lorraine 75, 154
David, St 74, 94n113
David II, Bishop of St David's 74
De Boron, Robert (*Merlin*) 20, 134
Delogu, Daisy 203
*De situ Brechaniauc* 67
Diana, goddess
    in 'Canon episcopi' 57–8, 60

# Index

in classical mythology 57, 60
in Geoffrey of Monmouth 164, 166, 188n83
*Domesday Book* 53
Dusii 13–4, 102–3, 109, 170, 232, 253
*see also* Augustine

Echard, Siân 19, 23, 64
Edinburgh, National Library of Scotland, Advocates MS 19.2.1 216
Edmund, St 77, 79, 80
Edward I (King of England) 28, 189n87
Edward IV (King of England) 215
Eleanor of Aquitaine 30, 31, 96, 124, 127, 130, 131–4, 225–6, 254
Elias, Marcel 227
Elizabeth Woodville 215
Elliott, Dyan 106
Eluned, St 66
*Englynion y Beddau* 47, 83n13
*Estoire des Bretons* 165
Ethelbert, St 53, 54
eucharist
    eucharistic analogies 110, 113–4, 128–9, 134–35, 156, 224, 227
    eucharistic incomprehension 27, 220–3, 229–30, 237–8
    eucharistic rejection 112–5, 119, 225
    power to compel demons 97, 111–2, 254

Faletra, Michael 73
female-faced serpent 106–8, 155
Finke, Laura A. 69–70
Finlayson, John 127, 195
Firth Green, Richard 6, 174

Fradenburg, L. O. Aranye 4, 159, 176
Francis I (King of France) 190n88
Frederick II (Holy Roman Emperor) 115
Fulton, Helen 28, 48

Geoffrey of Auxerre (*Sermon on the Apocalypse*) 114
Geoffrey of Monmouth
    *Historia regum Britanniae* 19–21, 25, 27, 31, 45, 48–51, 55, 62, 68–71, 73, 76–7, 99, 163–71, 197, 253
    *Prophetiae Merlini* 20–1, 70–1, 92n98, 94n113, 165, 177–8
    *Vita Merlini* 19, 21–4, 49, 98–9, 206, 253
    *see also* Arthur; Merlin; Morgan le Fay
Geoffroy, Viscount of Châtellerault 147–8
Gerald of Wales
    cultural contexts 2, 45–6, 63, 89n59, 96–7, 101, 253
    *De principis instructione*
        countess of Anjou 30, 97, 124–7, 131, 219, 224, 254
        Eleanor of Aquitaine's children 130, 134
        Henry II's prophecy 128
        hermit's prophecy 127, 130
    *Descriptio Cambriae* 45, 51
    *Expugnatis Hibernica* 143n108
    *Itinerarium Cambriae*
        children of Brychan 66–7
        early account of Avalon 98
        *see also* Gerald of Wales, *Speculum ecclesiae*
    Elidorus 73–6
    Glasbury 67

Gerald of Wales (*cont.*)
  Llangorse Lake 67
  Meilerius 29, 68–72, 74, 125, 132, 254
  *Speculum ecclesiae* 23–4, 153
  *Topographia Hibernica* 110
  *Vita Sancti Ethelberti* 53
Gervase of Tilbury
  cultural contexts 2, 30, 96–7
  *Otia imperialia*
    Avalon 98–9, 205–6
    Brutus 166
    Canigou 173, 207
    demonic flight 117–9
    French translations 150
    incubi and *lares* 101–4, 105, 111, 135, 149–51, 153, 162, 200
    lady of Chateau-Rousset 104–7, 110, 133, 145, 176
    lady of L'Epervier 110–5, 116, 118, 119, 124, 126, 128, 129, 132, 150, 153, 161–2, 215, 221, 222, 224, 253–4
    marvels and miracles 97–101
    in Ralph of Coggeshall 116–7
*Gesta Herewardi* 54
*Gesta Romanorum* 150
Ghosh, Amitav xii
Gödelmann, Georg (*Tractatus de magis, veneficis et lamiis*) 249–50
Gratian (*Decretum*) 58
  see also 'Canon episcopi'
Green, D. H. 19
Gruffydd ap Rhys, Welsh prince 67
Guendolen, legendary British queen 45, 51
Guibert of Nogent (*Dei gesta per Francos*) 233–5, 247n88
Guillaume l'Archevêque, Lord of Parthenay 31, 148–9, 196–9, 202, 206, 211–4

Guy of Lusignan (King of Jerusalem) 147
Gwyn ap Nudd, Lord of Annwfn 66

Haimo Dentatus 121
Harf-Lancner, Laurence 6, 22, 149
Hastings, Battle of 79
Heng, Geraldine 225, 235
Henry I (King of England) 67, 76
Henry II (King of England) 1, 50, 56, 76, 96, 126, 128–30, 171, 219, 223–5
Henry IV (King of England) 173
Henry V (King of England) 178
Hereford Cathedral 53
heresy 11, 24, 112–17, 119–24, 131, 135, 225, 233, 237
Herodias, goddess 58
  see also 'Canon episcopi'
Higgs Strickland, Debra 219
*Historia Brittonum* 20
  see also *Omen of the Dragons*
Holsinger, Bruce W. 26
Huizinga, Johan 7
Hundred Years War 31, 173, 178–9, 202, 240n9
Hywel ap Iorwerth, Welsh prince 68, 69, 71, 72
Hywel ap Maredudd, Welsh prince 67

incubus 12–5, 19–20, 48–50, 55, 68–70, 89 n 61, 101, 118, 127, 170, 253
Innocent III (Pope) 115
Isidore of Seville (*Etymologies*) 13–4, 22, 49, 61, 69, 78, 155, 219, 230
Islamophobia 11, 31, 113, 196, 219, 225–39, 254

Jacquetta of Luxemburg 215
Jameson, Fredric 3–4

# Index

Jean d'Arras
  *Mélusine* 30–1, 135, 145–80, 196–9, 200–16, 222, 228, 232, 239, 254–5
  English translation 216
Jean de Berry 30, 148–50, 161, 174, 178–79, 197, 199, 212, 214
Jean de Parthenay 212–3
Jean de Vignay 183n20, 183n23
Jean II (King of France) 148
Jeanne d'Arc 177, 193n128
Jerome, St 230
John Duke of Bedford 215
John (King of England) 220, 244n57
John of Salisbury (*Policraticus*) 56, 58, 72
Justice, Steven 16–7, 65

Kabir, Ananya Jahanara 26, 256
Karnes, Michelle 5, 60, 218, 223–4
Kelly, Doulgas 25, 146, 153
Kelly, Henry Angsar 108
Kieckhefer, Richard 152

*Lancelot-Grail* cycle 20, 25, 153, 202, 207–8
Lawgoch, Owain 31, 179, 254
*Le Bel inconnu* 192n124
Le Goff, Jacques 4, 147, 178
Le Roy, Emmanuel 4
Leitch, Megan G. 166
Leon V (King of Armenia) 172, 210
*Les Croniques des Bretons* 165, 177–8
*Les Évangiles des quenouilles* 184n32
*Les Très Riches Heures* 178
Levine, Robert 235
Liu, Yin 217

Llewellyn ap Gruffydd, Welsh king (Gruffydd ap Llewellyn) 63
Llyn Syfaddon (Llangorse Lake) 61, 66, 67
London, British Library
  Additional MS 31042 216–17
  Cotton MS Cleopatra C.iv 188n83
  Cotton MS Otho D.ii 215–6
  Royal MS 18.B.ii 216
Louis VIII (King of France) 30, 125, 130
Lusignan
  dynasty 2, 30, 135, 145–80, 195–215
  fortress 2, 31, 145, 149, 160, 167–9, 174, 178–9, 198–99, 200, 210–2, 255
lycanthropy 108–10

*Mabinogi* 66
*Malleus maleficarum* 141n83
*Mandeville's Travels* 221, 235–6
Map, Walter
  cultural context 1, 29, 45–7, 76–77, 96–8, 100–1, 106, 108, 111, 124, 253
  *De nugis curialium*
    Breton knight 56–7, 59, 64–5, 105
    court of Henry II 50, 126
    Eadric Wild 1–3, 15–16, 52–61, 62, 64, 68, 71, 76, 79, 103–5, 107, 121, 158
    Eudo 85n27
    Gerbert 121–4, 254
    Henno 120–1, 124, 128
    Herla 50–2, 59, 64, 73
    *historia* and *fabula* 17–8, 233
    Meilerius 92n89
    Paterine illusions 119–20

Map, Walter (*cont.*)
  *De nugis curialium* (*cont.*)
    Wastin Wastiniac 61–8, 73, 254
    reputed author of *Lancelot-Grail* cycle 153
Marco Polo 236
Marie de Bar 148
Marie de France 25, 89n61, 103, 133, 226
McDonald, Nicola 226, 238
Medea 24
Merlin
  association with Welsh prophecy 21, 47–8, 62, 99, 179, 255
  in Couldrette's *Mélusine* 207–9
  incubus father 19–20, 48–49, 69, 127, 134, 253
  Middle English prophecies 172–3
  Plantagenet prophecies 143n108
  *see also Omen of the Dragons*
Middle English *Brut* 172–3
Mohammed, Prophet (calumnious representations) 232–6, 247n88
Montagu, John, Earl of Salisbury 149–50, 197, 215
Moore, R. I. 115
Morgan le Fay
  in Avalon 19, 22–3, 99, 112, 206, 253
  a goddess 23, 25, 153
Mount Etna 57, 99
  *see also* Sicily
Mousket, Philippe (*Chronique rimée*)
  duchess of Aquitaine 30, 97, 130–5, 219, 224, 254
  Eleanor of Aquitaine's disrobing 133

Nichols, Stephen G. 170–1

*Omen of the Dragons* 19–20, 48, 176–9
*One Thousand and One Nights* xi–xii
Orderic Vitalis 58
Orlemanski, Julie 24
Otter, Monika 6, 46, 63, 69
Otto IV (Holy Roman Emperor) 30, 96, 114–5
Oxford, Bodleian Library, MS 851 91n85

Pairet, Ana 28, 155
Paracelsus 249–50
Paris, Bibliothèque nationale de France
  Français MS 1631 240n9
  Français MS 2806 165, 177–78
  Français MS 17177 165
  Français MS 18623 240n9
  Français MS 19167 240n9
  Français MS 243883 240n9
  Nouvelles acquisitions Françaises MS 4166 189n87
  Rothschild MS 3085 183n23
Park, Katharine 75, 154
Parthenay (line of) 148–9, 196–215
Partner, Nancy 14, 78
*Partonopeus de Blois* 89n61, 154, 216
Peters, Edward 101, 116
Pickens, Rupert T. 160
Pierleoni 123–4, 254
Pliny the Elder (*Historia naturalis*)
  lamps of Venus 12, 21, 57
  Plinian peoples 9, 74–5, 218, 220
Poitiers, Battle of 165
Power, Daniel 133
*Prophecy of the Six Kings* 172–3
*Prose Lancelot* 153
  *see also Lancelot-Grail* cycle
*Pseudo-Turpin Chronicle* 130

# Index

Purgatory 9–10, 12, 99, 117, 232
Putter, Ad 58–59

Ralph of Coggeshall (*Chronicon Anglicanum*)
    green children of Woolpit 94n128
    heretics of Rheims 116–7, 119, 120, 121, 132
Regino of Prüm (*Libri de synodalibus causis*) 57–8
    see also 'Canon episcopi'
Rhiannon 66
    see also Mabinogi
Rhys ap Gruffydd, Welsh prince 67
*Richard Coer de Lyon* 31–2, 196, 216–39, 250, 254, 255
Richard I (King of England) 125–6
    see also *Richard Coer de Lyon*
Richard II (King of England) 150
Richard III (King of England) 215
Roberts, Brynley F. 66
Rosenwein, Barbara H. 10–1
Rowland, Jenny 47
Rubin, Miri 113

Saladin (Yusuf ibn Ayyub ibn Shadi) 226, 227, 231–3
Saunders, Corinne 222
Schaeffer, Denise 151
Scota, legendary princess 191n104
Shaw, Jan 158
Shepherd, G. T. 45, 46
Shichtman, Martin B. 69–70
Sicily 9–10, 100, 64n140, 205
Simon Magus 116, 233
*Sir Gawain and the Green Knight* 187n61
Skeat, Walter 216
*South English Legendary* 85n27
Spiegel, Gabriel M. 8, 78, 128–9

St John's Gospel 69, 97, 119, 125, 132, 135, 254
St Martin's Land 77, 79, 80
    see also William of Newburgh
Stephen (King of England) 77, 78, 79
Stephens, Walter 121
Sullivan, Karen 20

Taliesin, prophet 22, 49
Triads, Welsh (*Trioedd Ynys Prydein*) 66
Troy, legend 73, 164, 166, 199, 217, 240n9
Truitt, E. R. 229
Turner, R. W. V. 132
*tylwyth teg* (fair company) 23

Van Houts, Elisabeth 54
Veysseyre, Géraldine 165, 177
Vincent of Beauvais 106
*Vita Sancti Gundleii* 66

Wace
    *Roman de Brut* 25, 165, 197
    *Roman de Rou* 24–5, 160
Wade, James 76, 160, 219
Walker Bynum, Caroline 9, 11, 110, 156
Watkins, C. S. 14, 58, 79, 119
Wauquelin, Jehan (*Roman de Brut*) 165
William of Auvergne 106, 142n107, 247n87
William of Conches 56
William of Malmesbury (*Gesta regum Anglorum*) 46–47, 52, 246n80
William of Newburgh (*Historia rerum Anglicarum*)
    fairy cup 76, 89n59
    green children of Woolpit 45, 54, 77–81, 109, 169, 254

William of Newburgh (*Historia rerum Anglicarum*) (*cont.*)
  on Welsh history and prophecy 20–1, 23, 29, 47, 52, 62–3, 70, 72, 98–9, 106, 253
William I (King of England) 53–4, 59, 121
William IX (Duke of Aquitaine) 127, 132

Williams, Deanne 26, 256
witch beliefs 6, 116, 119, 121, 152, 249–50
  *see also Malleus maleficarum*
Wood, Juliette 70
Wynkyn de Worde 216

Zeldenrust, Lydia 156, 207, 216
Zumthor, Paul 131

EU authorised representative for GPSR:
Easy Access System Europe, Mustamäe tee 50,
10621 Tallinn, Estonia
gpsr.requests@easproject.com

www.ingramcontent.com/pod-product-compliance
Lightning Source LLC
Chambersburg PA
CBHW051603230426
43668CB00013B/1958